J. R[illegible]CHILD ASSURANCE TAX GUIDE SUPPLEMENT

1997 – 98

JULY 1997 BUDGET SUPPLEMENT

by WALTER SINCLAIR

26 TH ANNUAL EDITION

INTRODUCTION

The first Budget of the new Labour Government took place on 2 July 1997 and included details of the expected 'Windfall Tax'. This is outside the scope of the book, but other measures relate to a variety of matters which are dealt with by the Tax Guide. Some of these take affect at once and others at a later stage.

The main taxation changes are dealt with in this supplement and include:

Tax credit relief on dividends (8.1)
Individual savings accounts and other investments
Corporation tax rates (13.2) and loss relief (13.11)
Capital allowances (11.9.1)
Home owners (24.4 & 4.6)
Films (11.21)
Private medical insurance (10.6.11)
VAT (23.5 & 23.11.11)
Anti-avoidance measures (15.10).

References are provided to the 1997-98 J. Rothschild Assurance Tax Guide giving the chapter and paragraph numbers. These identify the comparatively few changes to the current rules and those to be affected in the future. However, it must be emphasised that these notes have been based on the July Budget and prepared shortly afterwards. No account has been taken of any subsequent modifications.

One vital factor to consider, is that the next Budget has now been announced for Spring 1998. This allows time for planning, particularly regarding those matters such as capital gains tax and inheritance tax, not touched by this Budget. Such planning is considered at the end of this supplement.

TAX CREDITS ON DIVIDENDS (8.1)

The most radical reform in the Budget concerns the repayment of tax credits on dividends. This has been stopped from 2 July 1997 regarding dividends on shares held by pension funds, including occupational (14.3) and personal pension (14.6) schemes.

From 2 July 1997, tax credit repayment has been stopped for UK companies, apart from charitable ones. However, the Advanced Corporation Tax system (13.6) continues as before.

Note that the rules regarding Foreign Income Dividends (13.6.7) will not apply after 5 April 1999. An exception is regarding international holding companies.

Charities (15.2.1) will continue to obtain tax credit repayments in full until 5 April 1999. After this the repayments will be phased out over the next 5 years.

Regarding individuals (8.1), nothing changes until 5 April 1999. After that date, if you have no tax liability, you will no longer be able to reclaim tax credits on dividends.

If you pay income tax, the intention is that the change will result in your paying no more tax. After 5 April 1999, the tax credit will be halved to 10%. If you are a lower or basic rate payer, your tax on the dividend plus tax credit will be at 10%, leaving nothing to pay after setting off the 10% tax credit. As a higher rate payer, you will be taxed at 32.5% on your gross dividends, leaving 22.5% to pay net of the tax credit.

From 6 April 1999, a special tax rate of 25% will apply to the dividend income of those trusts which are at present liable to the 34% rate (21.2.1). This particularly applies to discretionary and accumulation and maintenance trusts.

INDIVIDUAL INVESTMENT ACCOUNTS AND OTHER INVESTMENTS

As well as the changes regarding tax credits mentioned above, the Budget includes several measures relating to investment. In particular, a new individual savings account (ISA) is planned to be in place for 1999. This is to provide tax reliefs and is intended to encourage those on lower incomes to save.

PEP schemes (8.10) will lose tax credit advantages in 1999 and investors will be able to transfer to ISAs. One feature of ISAs is expected to be a 5 year holding requirement, but in general, there is to be a full consultation period, before the final details are established.

Any VCT (8.11) and EIS (11.26) investments which you make from 2 July 1997 are subject to certain new rules. The details will be included in the 1998 Finance Act. The broad intention is to exclude arrangements which guarantee a substantial return or are backed by property, hence carrying reduced risk.

A measure is intended to make it more attractive to invest in Gilts. From 6 April 1998, you will be able to elect that interest on your gilts (8.2) is payable to you gross.

CORPORATION TAX RATES (13.2) AND LOSS RELIEF (13.11)

The corporation tax rates for the year to 31 March 1998 had previously been set at 33% (13.2) and (for smaller Companies) 23% (13.7). The July Budget has unexpectedly reduced each by 2%. Thus the full corporation tax rate has become 31%, with a 21% small companies rate.

Company trading losses (13.11) arising from 2 July 1997 can only be carried back against profits for the preceding year. This compares with a previous three year carry back facility. This change also applies to losses on loan arrangements, financial instruments and foreign exchange transactions. However, the carry back period remains three years for trading losses in the year before a trade ends (13.14).

CAPITAL ALLOWANCES (11.9.1)

First-year allowance (11.9.1) has been reintroduced at 50% for plant and machinery acquired in the year to 1 July 1998. This applies to small and medium sized businesses, broadly satisfying two of the following conditions:

- turnover not over £11.2m
- assets not over £5.6m
- no more than 250 employees.

In the case of "long life assets" (11.9.8), a special first year allowance of 12%, applies for expenditure during the year to 1 July 1998. Exclusions from the new rates include machinery and plant leasing, cars and sea-going ships.

HOME OWNERS

Two detrimental measures have been announced. Broadly, for contracts made after 7 July 1997, increased rates of stamp duty

(24.4) apply on transfers of property apart from shares. The new scale is:

Price	
£60,000 and under	Nil
£60,000-£250,000	£1 per £100 or part of £100
£250,000-£500,000	£1.50 per £100 or part of £100
Above £500,000	£2 per £100 or part of £100

The existing £30,000 limit on loans qualifying for mortgage interest relief (4.6) remains unchanged for 1998-99. However, from 6 April 1998, the rate of relief is being reduced from 15% to 10%.

FILMS (11.21)

Relief is improved for British qualifying films costing no more than £15m to make. There is to be 100% write off for production expenditure incurred after 2 July and for certain acquisition expenditure on films completed and acquired after that date.

PRIVATE MEDICAL INSURANCE (10.6.11)

Tax relief is abolished on private medical insurance for those over sixty. Premium payments on policies taken out or renewed after 1 July generally will not qualify for relief. If you have an existing annual contract, you will continue to obtain relief until it falls due for renewal.

VAT

The VAT rate on fuel and power (23.11.11) is being reduced from 8% to 5%. This takes effect from 1 September 1997.

The registration threshold (23.5) is going up to £49,000 from 1 December 1997. At the same time, the deregistration level becomes £47,000. Regarding acquisitions from other EU countries, the registration and deregistration limits will be £49,000 as from 1 January 1998.

ANTI-AVOIDANCE MEASURES (15.10)

Several measures take effect from 2 July 1997, although in some cases, the legislation will be in the 1998 Finance Act. These include:

- stopping finance lessors accelerating capital allowances and transferring unused allowances
- taxing as trading income the dividends on shares which are trading assets
- ensuring that PAYE applies to schemes involving trade debts and
- stopping schemes designed to get round the rules on company purchase and abandonment, allowing the Revenue to collect tax from the previous owners of a transferred company, etc,

TAX PLANNING

Apart from a few specific anti-avoidance measures mentioned above, the July Budget has little affected basic tax planning strategy (1.1). However, for how long this situation will remain is another matter. So the message is take advantage of the existing opportunities whilst they are still available.

Nothing was mentioned in the Budget about Inheritance Tax, whilst consultations on Capital Gains tax are to be completed in time for the next one. This indicates a window of opportunity for capital tax planning. The following is a selection of points to consider:

CAPITAL GAINS TAX

* Use your annual exemption for 1997-98, "bed and breakfasting" if necessary (1.3.1).

* Realise large gains in 1997-98, profiting from indexation relief and reinvestment relief; also reinvesting in VCTs and EIS investments (1.3.6).

* Fully utilise the reliefs available to your spouse and yourself (1.3.4).

* If you have reached age 50, take advantage of any retirement relief to which you may be entitled (1.3.5).

* Gifts holdover relief is available regarding family company shares, business assets and gifts to certain settlements. Plan to use this relief during 1997-98 (1.3.3).

INHERITANCE TAX

* Lifetime gifts which are potentially exempt transfers are free of inheritance tax. However, this exemption may go and so use this facility as appropriate (1.4.1 & 1.4.2).

* Leave up to the nil rate band (£215,000) to others than your spouse in your will. Do not rely on your heirs rewriting your will to this effect by way of a deed of variation (1.4.5), since new rules could render such deeds ineffective for inheritance tax purposes.

* Set up one or more settlements, since these receive favourable inheritance tax treatment. In particular, consider accumulation and maintenance and discretionary settlements (1.4.2).

* 100% relief is at present available regarding certain business property and agricultural property. If appropriate, avail yourself of this relief by gifts and settlements (1.4.7).

The exact details of the projected capital tax reforms are not yet known, nor which of the exsting reliefs will go. However, provided you act wisely and in good time, you and your heirs are likely to benefit.

COMPUTATION

1997

To Mark

Hope this will
be of some
value

Regards

Tony [illegible]

J. ROTHSCHILD
ASSURANCE

TAX GUIDE

1997–98

Orion Books Ltd
A Division of the Orion Publishing Group Ltd
Orion House
5 Upper St Martin's Lane
London WC2H 9EA

ISBN 0 75280 528 2

A CIP catalogue record for this book is available from the British Library.

Photoset in Helvetica and Times by
Interactive Sciences, Gloucester
Printed and bound in Great Britain by
Butler & Tanner Ltd,
Frome and London.

J. ROTHSCHILD
ASSURANCE

TAX GUIDE

1997–98

WALTER SINCLAIR, FCA

ORION BUSINESS
BOOKS

Abbreviations

ACT	advance corporation tax
AEI	average earnings index
AVC	additional voluntary contribution
BES	business expansion scheme
CAA	Capital Allowances Act 1990
CGT	capital gains tax
CGTA	Capital Gains Tax Act 1979
CIC	close investment holding company
COMP	contracted out money purchase
DLTA	Development Land Tax Act 1976
EEIG	European economic interest grouping
EIS	enterprise investment scheme
ESOP	employee share option plan
FA	Finance Act
F2A	Finance (No 2) Act
FIFO	first in, first out
FPCS	fixed profit car scheme
FSAVC	free standing additional voluntary contribution
HMSO	Her Majesty's Stationery Office
ITA	Inheritance Tax Act 1984
LAPR	life assurance premium relief
LEL	lower earnings limit
MIRAS	mortgage interest relief at source
NRE	net relevant earnings

PAYE	pay as you earn
PEP	personal equity plan
PET	potentially exempt transfer
PHI	permanent health insurance
PIBS	permanent interest bearing share
PPP (PRO)	personal pension plan (protected rights only)
PRAS	pension relief at source
PRP	profit related pay
PSO	Pension Schemes Office
QCB	Qualifying corporate bond
RPI	retail prices index
S (Ss)	section (sections) of an Act
SAYE	save as you earn
Sch (Schs)	Schedule (schedules) of an Act
SERPS	state earnings related pension scheme
SFO	Superannuation Funds Office
TA	Income and Corporation Taxes Act
TCGA	Taxation of Chargeable Gains Act 1992
TESSA	tax exempt special savings account
TMA	Taxes Management Act 1970
UEL	upper earnings limit
USM	Unlisted Securities Market
VAT	value added tax
VATA	Value Added Tax Act 1994

About this book

Originally establishing itself as the *Hambro Tax Guide* twenty-five years ago, this book has appeared annually ever since. The book has been designed to be used both by the professional and non-professional. Solicitors, accountants and company secretaries will find it especially useful as a concise ready reference. Many others, company directors and executives, partners and sole-traders, employers and employees, will find in it much helpful information and advice when dealing with problems of personal and company taxation.

It illustrates the working of income tax, capital gains tax, corporation tax, inheritance tax and VAT in the UK. It is intended to continue revising the book annually in order to keep it up to date in accordance with the annual changes to the law. This is the twenty-sixth edition and is based on the law as at 1 April 1997, including the 1997 Finance Act.

I am most grateful to all those who have written to me with kind and helpful comments concerning the previous editions, some of which have been taken into account in the preparation of this volume.

Because the book concisely covers a very wide field, it has been necessary to omit some of the exemptions and qualifications with which tax law abounds: to adopt a familiar saying, 'When I say never, I mean hardly ever and when I say always, I mean almost always'. The book is intended to be only a general tax guide. If it cannot solve a problem, the time has come to look at one of the multi-volume tax textbooks or to consult a tax specialist.

I gratefully acknowledge the help given to me on this edition by E B Lipkin, LLB, FCA, ATII, TEP of Kidsons Impey, Malcolm Cooper-Smith and Rob Gaines LLB of J. Rothschild Assurance and P D Silke, BPhil, MSocSc, Solicitor.

Walter Sinclair

Preface

When I worked with Walter Sinclair in launching the first edition of his *Tax Guide* back in 1972, I little imagined that I would find myself writing the preface for its 26th edition a quarter of a century later.

Over the intervening years, the *Tax Guide* has amply achieved its original objective, to distil the complexities of the UK tax system into a single volume which would prove readable and reliable for taxpayers and professional advisers alike.

Along the way, it must have helped hundreds of thousands of people to get to grips with their tax affairs and, in many cases, to identify opportunities to make significant savings. As the country's tax system has become increasingly complicated and opaque, the book's ability to clarify and to illuminate has become all the more important — and admirable.

26 years on, Walter Sinclair's clear, concise work is firmly established as one of the most authoritative and widely-read guides of this country's tax regime.

At J. Rothschild Assurance, our own commitment is to provide high quality advice to our clients, and to propose financial solutions which take full account of their particular circumstances. Plainly, taxation is one of the most important issues for us to understand and consider. For this reason, I am once again delighted to link our name to a new edition of Walter Sinclair's admirable book.

Sir Mark Weinberg. Chairman, J. Rothschild Assurance

Introduction

This, the twenty-sixth edition, deals with the tax system at the time of writing for the 1997–98 fiscal year. Every chapter has been amended to reflect the many tax changes which have been made since the previous edition, including those relating to income tax and personal reliefs, investments, National Insurance, capital gains tax, corporation tax, inheritance tax, VAT and many, many others. To help keep track of the changes, this edition includes, at the end of the Contents section, a summary of the 1997 Finance Act with references to the relevant paragraphs in the Guide.

Particular changes in this edition include:

- Further rules related to self-assessment.
- Increased income tax rate bands and allowances.
- Inheritance tax threshold — increase.
- Reduction in small companies corporation tax rate.
- Capital allowances on long life assets.
- Self-assessment tax return details.
- Profit-related pay — phasing out of tax relief.
- Rent a room scheme improvement.
- Changes to various VAT rules.

The revolutionary move to self-assessment and a current year basis for Schedule D assessment has continued and is now fully operative. This is fully reflected in the book, which has been substantially changed in accordance with the new system.

Because of the volume of changes, it is not possible to retain in each new edition *full* information for previous years. Thus for the tax rules for previous years, reference to past editions is occasionally necessary.

Ideas on tax saving appear throughout the book. However, the *Tax Savings Hints* chapter comes first with many references to the later chapters for easy location of topics. Furthermore, this chapter contains particular reference to future tax planning in a section entitled 'The way ahead — planning beyond the election.' (1.8). This is a vital topic to consider at present.

A particular feature to note is that all indexing and cross-referencing uses chapter and topic numbers. Thus **7.6** means the sixth-numbered topic in Chapter 7. Similarly **7.6.3** would mean the third subsidiary topic within that main heading. Also, a glossary to help with the meanings of certain terms appears at the end of this book.

The 1997–98 *J. Rothschild Assurance Tax Guide* brings together in a single volume all of the main taxes which are operating at present, enabling their total effect to be borne in mind. In planning for the future, however, account should be taken of the various avenues for short-term reform, as well as the longer-term possibilities for capital gains tax, inheritance tax, income tax, etc. As new developments are crystallised, they will be covered in the future annual editions of this book.

Contents

13 Companies 205

14 Pensions 233

Finance Act 1997 — Checklist

FINANCE ACT 1997

Main Subject	*Sections*	*Schedules*	*References*
Customs and Excise—			
Customs duties, gaming duty, vehicle excise duty	1–20	1–3	—
Insurance Premium Tax	21–30	4	—
Value Added Tax—			
Aggregation of businesses	31		—
Voluntary registration	32		—
Zero rating—charities	33–34		—
Buildings and land	35–37		—
Exempt insurance supplies	38		—
Bad debt relief	39		23.11.9
Groups containing different bodies	40		23.7
Group supplies using overseas members	41		23.7
Services subject to the reverse charge	42		—
Payments on account: appeals	43		—
Payments and Overpayments— Indirect Taxes—			
Value added tax	44–49	5	23.2
Excise duties, etc	50	6	—
Enforcement of payment	51–53		—
Income Tax Charge, Rates and Reliefs—			
Income tax rates for 1997–98	54		5.0.1 & 15.5

Main Subject	*Sections*	*Schedules*	*References*
Modification of indexed allowances	55		3.2
Blind person's allowance	56		3.2.9
Limit on interest relief	57		4.6
Corporation Tax Charge and Rates—			
Rate for 1997	58		13.2
Small companies rate	59		13.7
Payments for Wayleaves	60		7.2
Schedule E—			
Phasing out of relief for profit related pay	61		10.15
Travelling expenses	62		10.6.4
Work-related training	63		10.6.3
Relieved Expenditure—			
Postponed company donations	64		—
National Insurance contributions	65		11.3.1
Production wells expenditure	66		—
Annuity business of insurance companies	67		—
Consortium group relief	68		13.13
Distributions—			
Special treatment of some types	69	7	13.24
Distributions of exempt funds	70		—
Set-off against franked investment income	71		13.6
FIDs paid to unauthorised unit trusts	72		13.6
Tax advantages to include tax credits	73		15.10.1
Investments—			
Enterprise investment scheme	74	8	11.26
Venture capital trusts	75	9	8.12
Stock lending and manufactured payments	76	10	—
Bond washing and repos	77		—
National Savings Bank interest	78		—
Payments under life policies	79		9.5

Main Subject	*Sections*	*Schedules*	*References*
Futures and options— guaranteed returns	80	11	—
Transfer of Assets Abroad	81		15.10.2
Leasing and Loan Arrangements—			
Finance leases and loans	82	12	15.10.6
Loan relationships: transitions	83	13	13.27
Capital Allowances—			
Writing down allowances on long-life assets	84	14	11.9.8
Schedule A cases, etc	85	15	7.1
Capital allowances on fixtures	86	16	11.10
Chargeable gains—			
Reinvestment relief	87	17	20.25.2
Conversion of securities: QCBs and debentures	88		20.18.6 & 20.19
Earn-out rights	89		20.18.6
Double Taxation Relief—			
Underlying tax relief restriction	90		—
Disposals of loan relationships	91		—
Time from which repayment supplement runs	92		—
Inheritance tax—			
Rate bands	93		22.5
Agricultural property relief	94		22.21
Stamp duty and stamp duty reserve tax	95–106		24.2 & 24.6
Miscellaneous and supplemental—			
Petroleum revenue tax	107		—
Dividends on government stock	108		—
Miscellaneous	109–111		—
Interpretation, repeals, etc	112–114	18	—

Key Rates and Allowances — 1997–98

(*Companies year to 31 March 1998*)

Reference

INCOME TAX 5.01

Taxable income £	*Slice* £	*Rate* %	*Total tax* £
4,100		20	820
26,100	22,000	23	5,880
Over 26,100		40	

Income tax allowances 3.0.1

Personal allowance—single	£4,045	
Additional personal relief for children*	£1,830	
Age allowance—single	£5,220	
Age 75 or over—single	£5,400	
income limit	£15,600	
Married couple's allowance*		
Age—under 65	£1,830	
—65–74	£3,185	
—75 and over	£3,225	
Widow's bereavement allowance*	£1,830	
Life assurance premium relief—only on pre-14 March 1984 policies	$12\frac{1}{2}$%	

*relief restricted to 15%

Companies

Full corporation tax rate	33%	13.2
Small companies rate	23%	13.7
Advance corporation tax rate	1/4th	13.6

CAPITAL GAINS TAX

Rate (individuals)	20%/23%/40%	20.1

Annual exemption (individuals etc) (available separately for husband and wife)	£6,500	20.6

INHERITANCE TAX

Band £	*Death rate %*	22.5
0–215,000	Nil	
215,000 upwards	40	
Annual exemption	£3,000	22.17

VAT

Rate	$17\frac{1}{2}$%	23.1
Registration threshold from 27 November 1996	£48,000	23.5

1 Tax saving hints

1.1 Tax planning

The following pages deal with various ways in which you can arrange your affairs to reduce your tax bill. This should not be done by tax evasion which is completely illegal (15.10) and may result in your tax bill being increased by the addition of interest and penalties (16.9.2). You should always fully disclose your taxable income to the Revenue in your income tax return (16.2).

You are fully entitled, however, to arrange your affairs legally in such a way that your tax liability is reduced. This is known as tax avoidance (15.9). There are various anti-avoidance rules (15.9) but providing you are able to steer clear of these provisions you can make substantial tax savings by sensible planning. This chapter covers numerous tax saving hints with references to fuller explanations later in the book.

Tax planning is a very complex subject and many complicated schemes have been evolved. Such schemes are outside the scope of this book and in any event should be treated with great caution, following certain court decisions (*Ramsay, Furniss v Dawson*, etc). If you have substantial income and/or assets you should obtain professional advice on tax planning if you have not already done so.

1.1.1 Tax planning don'ts

(1) DON'T save tax at the expense of commercial benefits. (It is no good losing money in your business just to pay no tax.)

(2) DON'T cause unhappiness to yourself and your family in order to save tax. (Don't emigrate if you know you will not like your new country.)

(3) DON'T enter into tax-saving schemes which run on for a long time. These may be effective when you set them up but could be the target of future anti-avoidance legislation before they are completed.

(4) DON'T jeopardise your future financial security. (Do not give away all of your money just to reduce inheritance tax.)
(5) DON'T make inflexible arrangements. It is always necessary to review your tax planning in the light of changes in your financial position and family. You must also take full account of changes in the tax system, such as the drastic cuts in tax rates.
(6) DON'T forget that the law may change. Particularly remember that with inheritance tax on death it will be the law at your death and not necessarily the law now that will govern the liability.
(7) DON'T rigidly segregate capital and income. Good tax planning sometimes involves saving income and sometimes spending capital. Each has its own taxes and you should aim to maximise both after tax.

1.1.2 A basic plan

Before examining in detail ways of saving income tax, capital gains tax and inheritance tax, the following general guidelines are given, which are applicable to the tax and financial planning of many people:

(1) Buy your own house when you marry, or as soon afterwards as you can afford. If you remain single, house purchase is also desirable in appropriate circumstances. Tax is saved on *mortgage interest payments* (4.7) as explained. Also, your home may prove a good long-term tax-free investment.
(2) Divide your assets and income with your spouse so that the best use is made of the independent taxation rules (6.1). Savings of both income tax and capital gains tax can be made in this way.
(3) Arrange to have the maximum pension cover possible in your particular circumstances. If you are self-employed, etc you should pay *personal pension contributions* (14.6).
(4) Arrange adequate *life cover* (9.2) to protect your family.
(5) If you have spare funds when your children marry, make outright gifts to them. Provided you survive for seven years no inheritance tax (22.3) will be payable, even if the marriage and other exemptions are exceeded.
(6) When your children have married, if your house is larger than you need, consider selling it and investing part of the proceeds for your retirement.
(7) If you have spare funds over and above your retirement needs you and your wife should each make outright gifts to and settlements on your children and others. In order to cover inheritance tax, which might be payable if you die within seven years (22.3), appropriate term life assurance is advisable.

(8) Subject to there being sufficient funds for your spouse, leave at least £215,000 in your will to others (1.4.5), otherwise the £215,000 *nil rate inheritance tax band* (22.5) may be wasted.

1.2 Income tax saving

1.2.1 Personal reliefs and allowances

Always claim all of the *personal reliefs and allowances* (3.0.1) to which you are entitled. Notify the Revenue as soon as you qualify for an additional allowance such as married couple's allowance (3.2.1) when you marry. If possible, make sure your spouse and yourself have sufficient income to cover your respective personal reliefs.

1.2.2 Businesses

Make sure that you claim all *business expenses* (11.3) to which you are entitled. If you are able to use your *car in your business* (11.9.11) you can claim a reasonable proportion of the running costs (it is sometimes better if your business, etc actually owns the car).

1.2.3 Capital allowances

Do not overlook *capital allowances on plant and machinery* (11.9) and *industrial buildings* (11.11). Bear in mind that 100 per cent initial allowance is still available on buildings in enterprise zones (11.12).

1.2.4 Incorporation

Once your business profits bring your top income tax rate above 23 per cent, consider incorporation. Operating as a limited company will involve the 23 per cent *small companies corporation tax rate* (13.7), until the limit is passed. (An exception would be if your company is a close investment holding company (13.18) when 33 per cent may be payable.) You will probably become a director and thus be employed by your company; the National Insurance burden will change, but on balance, tax savings are likely. Also, you can normally improve your pension cover.

1.2.5 Employments

Make sure you claim all *allowable expenses* (11.3). Try to obtain part of your wages or salary in tax-free ways such as profit related pay (10.15) or luncheon vouchers. Tax savings may result if for example you have a company car or are given an interest-free loan or join your firm's pension scheme. However, watch changing tax rules such as the higher car benefit scales (10.6.5). If you are not covered by an *occupational scheme* (10.11) you should consider effecting a *personal pension scheme* (14.6).

1.2.6 Saving tax for your employees

If you are an employer you can enhance the after-tax income of your employees by various means including the following:

(1) Have a *canteen* for your staff or supply *luncheon vouchers* (10.6.3).
(2) Provide *business cars* (10.6.5) for employees (including wives who are employees) where appropriate and tax effective. However, the new system based on car list prices for 1994–95 may lessen the tax advantages.
(3) Grant *interest-free loans* to staff (but see 10.6.9 for restrictions).
(4) Provide *housing accommodation* (10.6.13) if the employees have to live close to their work.
(5) Operate *pension schemes* for staff (10.11). Remember that employers can contribute to personal pension schemes.
(6) Provide workplace *sports and recreation facilities* for your staff — the cost is normally a business expense and the employees will not be taxed on the benefit (10.6.17).
(7) In appropriate circumstances, introduce a *profit related pay* scheme (10.15) for your employees. Up to certain limits (10.15) profit related pay is free of income tax.
(8) If appropriate, operate a *share option* scheme (10.9.2).
(9) If you wish to make leaving payments to any employees make the payments in such forms as to qualify for relief from tax under the '*golden handshake*' *provisions* (10.12 and 10.12.1).
(10) Provide *childcare facilities* (10.6.15).

Note that (2), (3) and (4) above are subject to the fringe benefit rules for *directors and employees earning over £8,500 annually* (10.6.2). It is still of considerable value to provide such benefits in most cases, however. For example, normally a *car* will involve the appropriate *scale charge* (10.6.5) and employer's National Insurance contributions (25.2) but the employee may obtain a larger benefit from having the use of the car. This includes its capital value, insurance, car tax, repairs and, subject to an additional scale charge (10.6.5), any petrol bought for him.

1.2.7 Repayment claims

If you are entitled to make any income tax *repayment claim* (16.7), make sure that you do so at your earliest opportunity. In any event you should not allow the relevant time limit to expire. (This is normally six years after the end of the tax year concerned but is sometimes earlier.)

1.2.8 New businesses and fresh sources of Schedule D income, etc

By planning your starting and accounting dates it was possible to minimise your total *assessments for the opening years* (11.7.1 & 11.7.4). You should still make the appropriate claims for assessment on an 'actual' basis in the second and third years if still available and beneficial. Similarly employ the *cessation rules* (11.7.2) and *partnership changes provisions* (12.5), to your best advantage. However, bear in mind that for businesses starting after 5 April 1994, the new current year basis applies at once (11.7.4).

By 1996–97, with the introduction of self assessment, the previous year basis has been phased out (11.7.4). This removes the commencement and cessation opportunities under the previous rules but sometimes created transitional benefits.

For example, 1996–97 was on a special transitional basis. The assessment was on half the profits for the accounts ending in that year and half for the previous accounts. So normally tax savings could be made from moving profits into those years from the adjacent ones where legally feasible. Subject to the anti-avoidance rules, only half of the transfers were then taxed.

If you make a *loss in a new business* (11.23), make the best use of it, not forgetting the option of relieving general income going back up to three years before you started to trade. This is particularly useful where income tax rates fall, since your new business losses might be offset against more highly taxed income for previous years.

1.2.9 Using your home as an office

If you use your home as an office, make sure that you obtain tax relief as appropriate. If you are an employee, you will need to show that your business use is wholly, exclusively and necessarily required for the purposes of your job. If, on the other hand you have your own business, the 'necessity' test is dropped.

You should be able to claim a proportion of such items as council tax, light and heat, cleaning, insurance and repairs. The proportion is normally calculated on the basis of the main rooms (excluding kitchens and bathrooms) used for your work. A different fraction would be appropriate for claiming your telephone bills. Of course, any expenses reimbursed to you by your employer cannot be claimed.

One word of warning. By claiming that a fixed part of your home is used for business, you might lose your capital gains tax main residence exemption (20.23). However, if you use no rooms exclusively for business purposes, this is understood not to apply.

1.2.10 Wife's earnings

If you have a business, pay your husband or wife properly for any work that he or she does for it. In view of independent taxation, it is important that both spouses have adequate income, so as to use their allowances and lower rate (20 per cent) and basic rate income tax bands. Also, appropriate pension arrangements can be made.

You must be careful that your business does not pay your spouse more than the job is worth, or else the Revenue might seek to disallow part of the spouse's wages and so you will be taxed on the amount as a disallowed business expense. Also note that if the spouse's wage is £62 per week or more, National Insurance contributions must be paid.

Note that from 6 April 1990, the separate taxation of husband and wife is automatic and, as a result, the wife's earnings election (6.4) is no more. However, it is even more advantageous than before for each spouse to have income, because the wife is now taxed on her investment as well as earned income.

A satisfactory arrangement is to form a business partnership with your wife which will give her an entitlement to a share in the profits, normally treated as earned income, and to a personal pension plan. However, note that if your wife's share of the annual profits is over £7,010 the excess is charged at 6 per cent (maximum £1,030.20) under the *Class 4 National Insurance Contribution Scheme* (25.5).

1.2.11 Independent taxation — investments

Ensure that you and your spouse split your investments between you so that you each have investment income and capital gains. In this way, the one with the lower income will be better placed to use his or her allowances, lower rate and basic rate bands.

Since 6 April 1993, an opportunity arises with dividend income, where say you are a higher rate payer and your spouse pays tax at no more than the basic rate. In that situation, you pay an extra 20 per cent on each grossed up dividend. However, your spouse pays no more tax, being liable for only 20 per cent on each gross dividend, which is covered by the tax credit (8.1.1). Hence you can make worthwhile tax savings by transferring shares to your spouse.

From 6 April 1996, the above extends to most other investment income apart from where it arises from property. The maximum rate on this savings income in the hands of a basic rate (23 per cent) tax payer is 20 per cent. Thus where you pay 40 per cent and your spouse no more than 20 per cent, transfer investments such as gilts, and building society and bank deposits to him or her.

1.2.12 Independent taxation—elections

Make sure that you use the elections under the independent taxation scheme to the best effect (6.1). If you and your spouse jointly own assets, you can elect for the income to be split between you in the ratios that you own them, otherwise the income is split equally for tax purposes.

Joint mortgage interest is divided equally between spouses unless you elect for a different split. These elections enable taxable income to be diverted to the spouse with unused allowances or a lower income tax rate, thus saving tax.

1.2.13 House purchase

By purchasing your house or flat instead of renting it you will normally save income tax. This is because unless you make some business use of your home you obtain no tax relief in respect of rent paid. However, up to the limits (generally £30,000 loan), *mortgage interest* (4.6) (on your main residence) is normally allowable for tax purposes, although this relief is restricted to 15 per cent (4.6).

If your mortgage is linked with some form of pre-14 March 1984 life assurance your tax bill is effectively reduced by 12.5 per cent of the premiums paid subject to the relevant rules (3.2.6). You must carefully consider the most favourable way to finance your house purchase, particularly since no life assurance relief is due on post-13 March 1984 policies.

As a basic method, you could select the conventional mortgage repayments system. Under this you will normally make monthly payments to the building society etc, partly consisting of the capital advanced to you and partly of interest. Subject to the limits (4.6) you obtain full tax relief for the interest as well as life assurance relief on any mortgage protection life policy which you effected prior to 14 March 1984. Even if you are not liable for tax, you still obtain the benefit of paying the interest net of the basic rate of tax.

If you have a comfortable income you might consider tying your mortgage to a life assurance endowment policy. Under this system you borrow a fixed sum from a building society or insurance company for a given term (20 years, etc).

You effect a life assurance endowment policy for the sum borrowed, the policy being held by the lender as security. Every year you pay the mortgage interest and policy premiums. At the end of the term your life endowment policy matures and the capital sum is paid to the lender in settlement of the mortgage.

Your policy can be with or without profits. The latter is cheaper but the former will generally prove a better investment. Indeed, most building societies will allow an endowment policy for a sum assured that is initially less than the loan, but the maturity proceeds of which will grow to equal or exceed the debt on conservative bonus assumptions. Extra decreasing life assurance covers any shortfall if you die before repayment. This type of endowment has the advantage of being cheaper than one for the full amount of the loan. In some cases, unit-linked endowment policies may be used.

The advantages of this system are that your life is covered automatically so, if you should die, the mortgage is automatically discharged. Also, for 1995–96 and subsequently you get income tax relief at 15 per cent on your interest payments on up to £30,000 of your mortgage. You also obtain income tax relief in respect of the life assurance policy if taken out before 14 March 1984.

Note, however, that under the endowment system you pay rather more in the earlier years than under a repayment mortgage. Inflation exaggerates this effect because the earlier payments are made in 'dearer' money. Therefore if you are able to invest the difference more profitably, there is a case for choosing a repayment mortgage. A particular instance would be if otherwise you could not afford your total permitted *personal pension* contributions (14.6).

Since life assurance relief is not available for post-13 March 1984 policies, the balance has moved away from the endowment system and towards the repayment method or more beneficial personal pension basis (below). However, every case must be considered on its merits.

If you make regular *personal pension* payments you may be able to have an interest only mortgage. The capital sum will then be repaid out of the *cash sum on retirement* (14.6.4) which you can receive. This method is attractive for tax purposes since the *personal pension* contributions (14.6) which you pay qualify for tax relief at your highest earned income rates, subject to the rules.

A more recent development is the use of personal equity plans (PEPs) to repay the capital element in a mortgage. With the annual amount allowed to be invested in PEPs now £6,000 plus £3,000 in single company PEPs (8.10), there is ample scope for ongoing schemes to be set up to repay quite substantial mortgages.

1.2.14 Tax-free investments

Various forms of tax-free income are given in a table in Chapter 2 (2.6.1). Avail yourself of the opportunities open to invest in tax-free situations. However, weigh up the interest you might receive tax-free with the after-tax interest on other investments.

Particular investments on which the income is tax-free are PEPs (8.10) and TESSAs (8.11). PEPs (personal equity plans) provide an attractive way to invest in equities, unit trusts, etc and also carry capital gains tax exemption. TESSAs (tax exempt special savings accounts) took effect from 1 January 1991. Their freedom from income tax on the interest, subject to the rules (8.11), makes TESSAs very competitive. You should certainly consider investing all or part of the £9,000 five-year maximum.

1.2.15 Enterprise Investment Scheme (EIS)

EIS investment normally saves you tax at 20 per cent (11.26). Thus, if you invest say £1,000, the net cost is £800. Provided you are able to select sound investments, the tax advantages are most attractive. These include capital gains tax exemption, tax relief for any losses and the option to carry back part of the relief to the previous tax year (11.26). Even more advantageous, is the facility for rolling over capital gains into the purchase of EIS shares (1.3.6). For 1997–98, your EIS investment is limited to £100,000.

1.2.16 Venture Capital Trusts (VCTs)

As with EIS investment, VCTs save you tax at 20 per cent (8.12). But if you are able to hold over gains by investing in either (1.3.6), up to 60 per cent relief can be obtained. (Heldover gains are taxable on sale unless reinvested again.) VCTs have the advantage of being dealt with on the Stock Exchange. This means that once you have held them for the required five year period, disposal should be straight-forward.

1.2.17 Life assurance (9.2)

As well as in connection with house purchase, life assurance provides a valuable method of coupling profitable investment with life cover. Subject to the rules (3.2.6) you obtain 12.5 per cent tax relief on qualifying premiums for policies effected before 14 March 1984. Normally, the 12.5 per cent would be deducted from your premiums on payment. Since relief is not available for policies effected subsequently, any existing at that date should be continued so that relief is obtained on the premiums. (Of course this does not apply to policies no longer appropriate to your needs.)

There are many schemes in which life assurance is linked to property bonds, unit trusts, shares and combinations of these, under which you obtain life cover. Despite the withdrawal of tax relief on premiums, life assurance policies remain attractive as investments (quite apart from the life cover they provide) because of their ability to provide tax-free proceeds and a wide spread of investments for a small outlay, etc.

1.2.18 Personal pensions (14.6)

If you have earned income in any year, regarding which you are not in an occupational pension scheme, and on which you pay income tax, you obtain full relief from such tax in respect of any personal pension contributions paid, up to the permitted maximum. The full rules are set out later in this book (14.6), subject to which you obtain relief from income tax in respect of the entire contributions paid. Thus you can obtain relief of up to 40 per cent of your contributions if your income is sufficiently high. This is a most valuable form of relief and so if you are eligible, personal pensions should feature prominently in your planning.

You obtain relief at the highest tax rates attributable to your income. Thus suppose on the top £1,000 of your income you pay income tax of £400; if you pay an allowable contribution of £1,000 under a personal pension scheme, you will obtain £400 tax relief and so your net cost is effectively only £600 (£1,000–£400). This will secure for you a pension at retirement when your top tax rate may well be lower. Personal pension annuity contracts provide a very cheap way of obtaining life cover. This is because part of the available limit each year can be applied in *temporary* (term) *life assurance cover* (14.6). Again, full tax relief at your top rate is obtained on the contributions paid.

New 1995 rules enable you to defer taking your annuity. For the deferral period, you can take taxable income from the pension providers. This is a valuable new feature which you can use to good advantage where annuity rates are currently low. Subject to the withdrawals, your fund will be available to buy your annuity when rates improve.

Over the years, the personal pension contributions limits have, in general, been increased, particularly at higher income levels (14.6). You should take full advantage of the increased facility particularly bearing in mind that with current trends you will probably need to provide for a higher pension to compensate for inflation. Particularly valuable is the facility of paying contributions in respect of unused relief for the previous six years. This can enable a large contribution to be paid in a year of exceptionally high income.

At least as valuable is the rule allowing contributions paid in one tax year to be treated as paid in the previous one. This is particularly useful if you can elect for contributions to be taken back to a year when your top tax rate was higher than for the year when the contributions are paid.

From 1 July 1988, the personal pensions relief provisions absorbed the old rules for retirement annuities (14.6). Also, some improvements have taken place, such as in permitted contribution levels for those in their fifties (as from 6 April 1987). In addition there is the facility for *employees* to pay *personal pension* contributions net of basic rate income tax.

The 1989 changes to the personal pension rules have important planning implications. The more beneficial contribution limits ranging up to 40 per cent of earnings at age 61 (14.6.3), should enable all but very high earners to increase their contributions. However, the limit on earnings qualifying for cover may mean that if you come within this category, you would do better to pay increased contributions on existing retirement annuity contracts. You will then only be able to pay up to the old limits ranging up to 27.5 per cent of earnings at age 61 (14.6.3), but you will not be subject to the £84,000 earnings limit (£82,200 for 1996–97).

1.2.19 Pension schemes for controlling directors

If you are a controlling director of a family company, it can implement a *pension scheme* (14.3.5) for you. Contributions paid by the company will enjoy tax relief as a deductible business expense and you can be provided with similar benefits to those of any employee under an occupational pension scheme, such as a pension of up to two-thirds of final salary, or a tax-free cash lump sum and a reduced pension, a pension for your widow in the event of death either before or after retirement and substantial life assurance cover for your family in the event of death in service.

1.2.20 Deeds of covenant (6.5)

Deeds of covenant still in force, which were effected prior to 15 March 1988 to others than your minor unmarried children produce tax savings. Such covenants needed to be capable of exceeding six years.

However, subject to the rules (6.5) deeds of covenant effected after 14 March 1988 in favour of individuals produce no tax savings. This makes it all the more important to keep existing ones in force. (New deeds in favour of charities carry full relief.)

The covenantor who makes the payments under a pre-15 March 1988 deed deducts basic rate income tax and pays the net amount to the beneficiary. If the latter is not liable for income tax because his income is less than his tax allowances, he reclaims the income tax deducted by the covenantor (6.5). With the level of *personal relief* (3.2.1) at £4,045 and 23 per cent basic rate this advantage is worth up to £930.35. Also, the 20 per cent lower rate band would enable a further £123 (£4,100 × 3 per cent) to be reclaimed in larger cases.

Payments under *deeds of covenant to charities* (15.2.1) are of benefit to them since they reclaim the basic rate income tax which you deduct on payment. Furthermore, charitable covenants qualify if they are capable of exceeding three years; and you obtain higher rate tax relief for any such payments (15.2.1).

1.2.21 Gifts and settlements

If you are a higher rate taxpayer and have more income and capital than you need, you can divest yourself of the surplus altogether and thereby save yourself the income tax on the income concerned. You can probably arrange that the income ends up in the hands of individuals with lower tax rates than yourself. Alternatively the income may be *accumulated* in a *trust* (21.1) where no more than 34 per cent income tax is payable. If trusts are created you should take care that the *settlor* is not *taxed on the income* (21.3). Note that inheritance tax may apply in some circumstances (22.30). Similarly watch the effect of *inheritance tax on gifts* (22.1).

This facility for moving income to lower rate taxpayers, such as grandchildren, became more important with the withdrawal of tax relief on new deeds of covenant (1.2.18). For example, accumulation and maintenance settlements can be used to produce worthwhile income tax savings by making payments for the education and maintenance of beneficiaries. Income tax repayment claims are then likely covering the 11 per cent additional rate; also the 23 per cent basic rate on up to the

£4,045 personal relief and an extra 3 per cent on the £4,100 lower rate band.

Gifts to charities which are at least £250 (net) each carry full tax relief. You deduct basic rate tax and the charity reclaims this. At the same time the gross gift carries higher rate tax relief (15.2.1).

1.2.22 Lower rate band

The introduction of the 20 per cent lower rate band from 1992–93 has modestly increased the scope for income tax saving. You should see that your spouse and, where practicable, children have sufficient income to cover their respective £4,100 lower rate bands. If this means transferring your own income to them and you are a 40 per cent tax payer, a maximum of £820 (£4,100 at 20 per cent) could be saved in each case. This depends upon each child being at least 18 years old or married if younger (6.6).

1.2.23 The use of overseas income, taxable on the remittance basis

Generally speaking the *remittance basis* (18.1.1) only applies in certain limited cases. If, however, you obtain any *income overseas* which is taxable here under *Schedule D Case IV or V* (18.1), or under *Schedule E Case III* (18.5.1), and such income is taxed on the remittance basis, do not bring the income into the country unless you need it to cover your living expenses. Note, however, that any *bank deposit interest* (8.7) or other income derived from any investment made with the funds is normally liable to UK tax on an arising basis, if you are *resident and domiciled* in the UK, subject to the detailed rules.

You can use your overseas deposits for spending on holidays abroad, etc (18.1). Furthermore, once your overseas source of income has come to an end you can bring your funds into this country in a subsequent tax year without any charge to income tax.

(If your work takes you overseas, remember that if your period of absence extends to a year, you obtain 100 per cent relief (18.5.1).)

1.3 Capital gains tax saving

A number of simple ways are open to you for saving capital gains tax. Some of these are described on the following page.

1.3.1 £6,500 net gains exemption

Make the best use of this relief. If your sales of chargeable assets produce net gains which are not normally far in excess of £6,500 in any tax year, try to spread your realisations so that your net gains are no more than £6,500 each year — you will then pay no capital gains tax.

Remember that your spouse and each of your minor children can also realise up to £6,500 of net gains each year and pay no capital gains tax. It is thus a good idea to spread any share dealings, etc throughout your family. This is made easier by *capital gains tax gifts relief* (20.28) which now applies in certain circumstances, subject to the necessary election. However, gift elections are no longer normally of use regarding quoted shares, etc (1.3.3).

Under the system for taxing husband and wife, you each have a capital gains tax exemption now of £6,500. In order to make full use of both reliefs, split your investments between you.

If your net gains are less than £6,500 in any tax year, realise further profits by means of '*bed and breakfast*' *transactions* involving the sale of shares followed by their subsequent repurchase. In this way, you will be able to make better use of the exempt band. At the same time you will be increasing the base costs of your holdings. In order for 'bed and breakfasting' to be effective for shares, in general you merely need to wait until the next day before you buy them back.

1.3.2 Loss relief

Make sure that you keep a proper record of all your capital losses. These are relievable against any capital gains in the same tax year and any balance is carried forward to be used in future years.

If you make a loss in your non-incorporated trade or profession in 1991–92 or future years, do not overlook claiming to set this against your capital gains. Trading losses can now be offset against capital losses for the same and next tax years (11.22).

1.3.3 Capital gains tax gifts election

Since the scope for capital gains tax gifts elections is restricted (20.28), it is important to structure your gifts to avoid a capital gains tax charge, if possible. For example, make gifts of cash or quoted securities on which you have little or no capital gains, as well as gilts and loan stocks. Also, chattels worth no more than £6,000 each and gifts within your £6,500 annual exemption.

Furthermore, make gifts still within the scope of the election. These include certain unquoted and family company shares and other business assets (20.28); also gifts which involve immediate inheritance tax. This last category includes discretionary settlements and applies even if no tax arises because the nil rate band has not been exceeded.

1.3.4 Husband and wife

Sales and gifts of assets between yourself and your spouse are not normally liable to capital gains tax (20.9). This enables you to redistribute your assets for inheritance tax purposes without paying any capital gains tax.

1.3.5 Retirement relief

If you have a family business or company and are at least 50 years of age, use the *capital gains tax retirement relief* (maximum £250,000 exemption, together with £750,000 at 50 per cent relief) to its best advantage. This will mean waiting until you reach the age of 50 before selling your business and also continuing to work in it until that time. Since the entire relief is available at age 50 and there is no longer any tapering relief, it is vital to wait until that age before disposing of your business. If you have not owned it for ten years, more relief will be available if you wait until you have completed ten years of ownership. Remember that, subject to the rules, your wife can also get the relief if she works in the business and owns part of it.

From 6 April 1993, the scope of retirement relief was extended to cover full-time employees as well as directors (20.29). Also, the shareholding requirement is now 5 per cent. Thus you may find that you are eligible for relief if you sell your shares, in view of the rule changes.

Should you wish to pass your business to your children, a combination of gifts election and retirement relief may be useful. However, because retirement relief takes precedence, make gifts subject to the election before you reach 50.

1.3.6 Roll-over relief

Another important capital gains tax relief related to businesses is roll-over relief (20.25). If you sell a business or business assets, consider replacing them within one year before and three years after the disposal. Subject to the rules, you will then pay no capital gains tax until you dispose of the replacements.

Up to 15 March 1993, company shares did not qualify. However, after that date, roll-over relief is available where shares in one qualifying unquoted trading company are sold and shares in another are acquired, subject to the rules (20.25.2). You originally needed to have held at least 5 per cent of the shares for at least a year and be a full-time working director or employee.

From 30 November 1993, this relief was extended. Gains on any assets realised from that date can be rolled-over into the purchase of shares in qualifying unquoted trading companies (20.25.2). There are no requirements as to working in the companies or as to the number of shares to be held. However, you should take care that investing into any particular company makes commercial sense.

Furthermore, from 1 January 1994, purchases of EIS shares (1.2.15) afford re-investment relief for post-28 November 1994 gains. Similarly, from 6 April 1995, Venture Capital Trust shares (1.2.16) also provide such relief.

1.3.7 Timing

Timing your sales of shares or other chargeable assets can have an important bearing on your capital gains tax. If you postpone a sale until after 5 April it means that you delay the payment of your tax for one year. Also if you know that you will be incurring a capital loss during the next tax year you should defer making any potential capital profits until that year because, although capital losses can be carried forward, they cannot be set off against capital profits in earlier tax years.

Similarly if you have already made a lot of capital profits during the current tax year you should consider incurring *capital losses* during the same year which can then be offset. You should not normally sell investments unless it is sound to do so from a commercial point of view. A loss may be established on a shareholding, however, even if you buy it back the next day. Such transactions may be taxable, however, if done by companies (13.15).

1.3.8 Indexation

Pay careful attention to the effects of the *indexation rules* (20.12) on your capital gains tax position. In choosing which investments to sell, have regard to the indexation relief available due to the level of base cost and time held. If you wish to retain an investment it may still be of value to sell it and buy back the next day so as to obtain an enhanced base cost on which future indexation is calculated.

Subject to the transitional rules, indexation relief can no longer be used to create or increase a loss on disposal (20.13). Thus consider holding shares which are likely to improve. If you are able to sell these at a profit, your indexation relief will no longer be lost.

1.3.9 Charities

Gifts made to charities are completely free of capital gains tax. Thus if you wish to make a generous gift to a charity of a capital amount (rather than recurring annual amounts under deed of covenant) you will save yourself future capital gains tax if you gift a chargeable asset on which you have a large potential profit. For example if you wish to give £20,000 to a charity and own shares in A Ltd which cost £4,000 in 1983 and are now worth £20,000 you should gift those shares. (If you sold the shares and donated cash they would only produce £13,600 net of 40 per cent capital gains tax — assuming you are a 40 per cent taxpayer and ignoring indexation and any annual exemption.)

1.3.10 Main private residence

Ensure that you gain the maximum benefit from this exemption (20.23). If you have two residences (even if one is rented), claim within two years of the date of purchase of your second abode which should be treated as your main private residence to be free of capital gains tax. You have a free choice in this matter and so should select the house or flat likely to increase in value the most.

1.4 Inheritance tax planning

The essence of inheritance tax planning is the conservation of wealth. Remember that most lifetime gifts are now free of inheritance tax provided you survive for seven years (22.3). Thus timely action is advisable. Also, bear in mind that a future government could radically change the system and make it much harsher.

In broad terms you should aim to spread assets amongst your family to minimise the effects of these two taxes. Do not make gifts which you cannot afford, however, nor give too much money outright to young or irresponsible children.

1.4.1 Reducing your assets by gifts

Take advantage of the various *exempt transfers* (22.17). By this means you can gift to your children, and others, considerable amounts over a period of years, free of any inheritance tax charge, even if you die within seven years. Gifts to your wife are normally free of inheritance tax in any event (22.17.1).

If you have funds surplus to your requirements, you can make gifts totalling £3,000 in any year (22.17.2). In addition, you can make outright gifts of up to £250 each year to any number of other individuals and, furthermore, if you have surplus after-tax income you can make *normal expenditure gifts out of income* (22.17.2). Do not overlook the reliefs applied to *marriage gifts* (22.17.2) for your children and grandchildren, etc.

By means of all the above transfers you can reduce your estate without risking any inheritance tax liability on your premature death. Furthermore, by making the required election any capital gains tax on the gift (20.28) of certain assets will be held over until the recipient's disposal. The scope of capital gains tax gifts relief now mainly applies to gifts of business assets including shares in family companies, etc (20.28). Another important category of gifts qualifying for the relief is those on which inheritance tax may be immediately payable.

Remember that the above exemptions apply to both your wife and yourself. Also, do not forget that unused portions of the £3,000 limit can be carried forward for one year only. Thus your wife should also make gifts, and if her resources are insufficient you should put her in funds. But watch the associated operations rules (22.29.3).

1.4.2 Larger gifts and settlements

If you have a large estate, you should consider making more substantial gifts which will entail the payment of inheritance tax, should you die within seven years. The rate would be nil for the first £215,000 of chargeable transfers, however (22.5). Your relief would effectively be more if *business property relief* (22.18) or *agricultural property relief* (22.21) applies. Subject to the inheritance tax charge if you die within seven years, large gifts are now the most tax-efficient method of passing on wealth in many cases. Provided the recipients are sufficiently mature to look after the money, etc large outright gifts are to be strongly recommended. Unless you are in poor health or of advanced years, the contingent inheritance tax liability can be covered by temporary life assurance (1.4.10) at moderate cost.

For elderly people with smaller estates it is not necessarily advisable, however, to gift the £215,000 tax-free band since this is equally tax-free on death and it could be better to retain this sum for contingencies.

It may be desirable to make larger gifts in the form of settlements, but if these are discretionary the *periodic charge* (22.30.2) would normally apply at some future time, as well as the tax which you pay when you make the settlement and further tax when benefits are paid to the beneficiaries. Also, you are liable for inheritance tax at half the death rates when you set up the trust.

However, *settlements* (22.30) set up within your £215,000 nil rate band are not likely to give rise to significant inheritance tax liability, subject to the detailed rules. *Small* discretionary settlements of this kind are thus useful for passing funds to your dependants whilst maintaining a degree of flexibility. (Note that you should not be a beneficiary under a new settlement.) A further advantage regarding discretionary settlements is that they qualify for capital gains tax gifts relief (1.3.3). This is true whether or not any inheritance is paid on the capital introduced.

Accumulation and maintenance settlements (22.30.1) are useful for the benefit of your minor children and grandchildren. Provided you survive for seven years after establishing the settlement, you pay no inheritance tax. Furthermore, if the beneficiaries obtain fixed interests (eg, in the income) which they become entitled to when they are no more than 25 years old, then no subsequent inheritance tax is payable (22.30.1), even if the payment of the ultimate capital is deferred to an older age. (An exception is where a beneficiary with a life interest dies.)

Fixed trusts are also of use if you wish your grown-up children to have income but no capital until a stipulated time. Thus, if you settle money on your 26-year-old son giving him an entitlement to the annual income until he is 35 and then the capital, you are immediately divested of the capital. The amount which you settle is treated as a potentially exempt transfer, so that inheritance tax applies if you die within seven years. Your son eventually gets the capital at age 35 and no more inheritance tax is payable. Your son is fully taxed on the income, however, and if his other income becomes high as he matures, his income tax burden could be heavy.

In establishing settlements unless they are discretionary remember that capital gains tax gifts relief will be limited. Thus either settle cash or assets which will give rise to no capital gains tax, unless you are able to settle assets still qualifying for gifts relief (20.28).

1.4.3 Gifts to charities, etc

Gifts to charities and political parties are completely free from inheritance tax. Thus you should consider making such gifts during your lifetime and bequests in your will. Both will reduce the value of your estate for inheritance tax purposes, and capital gains tax relief applies concerning charitable dispositions (20.29.1).

1.4.4 Equalisation of assets of husband and wife

Provided the recipient is UK domiciled (or deemed domiciled) no inheritance tax is payable on transfers which you make to your wife or she makes to you, either during your lives or on death (22.17.1). But do not keep all of your assets until you die and then leave them to your wife because this may ultimately result in high inheritance tax on her death which is more than the combined tax if your estates were equal and you each left your assets to your children.

Thus, suppose you have £430,000 and your wife has nothing. If you die first, leaving it all to her, no tax is then payable. But if she still has £430,000 when she dies and has made no previous chargeable transfers, the inheritance tax at the present rate will be £86,000 (22.5.1). If you had given or bequeathed your wife £215,000, however, and left your remaining £215,000 to your children, on your death no inheritance tax would be paid. Similarly, on your wife's death nothing would be paid so that altogether £86,000 of inheritance tax would be saved compared with the position where your wife inherits all of your wealth. (Of course the position can be further improved if you both make lifetime gifts to your children.)

If your wife otherwise has insufficient funds, giving her assets will also enable her to make gifts to your children. These will not attract inheritance tax unless she dies within seven years (22.3) and her estate is sufficiently high. This strategy is particularly desirable if your wife is younger and in better health than you are. Note, however, the *associated operations rules* (22.29.3). As mentioned earlier (1.1.2) equalising your assets is likely to produce income tax and capital gains tax savings.

A further point in favour of equalising your estate with your wife's is that wealth tax, if it is ever introduced, would be expected to apply separately to husband and wife at progressive annual rates. Thus less tax is payable on two smaller estates rather than a larger one. Of course, these tax planning considerations must be tempered by practical points, such as making sure your wife has sufficient to maintain her, should you die first. Also, a certain mutual trust is necessary. Your planning should also take account of your respective ages and states of health by arranging for a larger share to be in the hands of the one likely to live longer.

If you are buying a new home, you should ensure that this is put into the joint names of your wife and yourself. Since the matrimonial home often comprises the major part of the assets of a married couple, this is a very useful step towards equalising their respective estates.

1.4.5 Wills

You should think carefully about the preparation of your will and, of course, obtain good legal advice. Substantial inheritance tax savings can result from a well drawn will. For example, you should ensure that both your wife and yourself by your separate wills leave at least £215,000 to other people so that you each get the benefit of the £215,000 nil rate band. (This presupposes the free band has not been exhausted by lifetime gifts and also that the survivor will have adequate funds for his or her old age.)

To take full advantage of indexation, instead of £215,000 you could stipulate the amount of your unused nil rate band at death. Also, avoid leaving too much directly to your children if they are already wealthy; it is more beneficial for tax planning purposes to leave money in trust for your grandchildren. Such will trusts, however, should probably not be discretionary, but rather of the accumulation and maintenance variety (22.30.1).

1.4.6 Annuities

If you need to increase your income, annuities provide a means of doing this which at the same time immediately reduces the value of your estate. For example, if you buy an annuity for £10,000 which produces, say, £1,200 yearly until your death, no part of your original capital outlay is charged to inheritance tax on your death. You have thus saved potential tax on your death. Do not overlook the effects of inflation, however; an unindexed annuity which is sufficient for your present needs soon may be worth too little to maintain you.

1.4.7 Using business and agricultural relief

If you have a business, farm or shareholding in an Unlisted Securities Market (USM) company, the further improved relief rates (22.18) offer great potential inheritance tax savings. Subject to the rules, 100 per cent or 50 per cent relief will normally be obtained. You should therefore take advantage of the opportunity to create settlements and make gifts with less, or no, inheritance tax, even if you die within seven years. If any capital gains arise, it will normally be possible to obtain holdover relief. However, in cases where death is imminent, it may be better to hold the assets so as to obtain the tax free uplift in base value for capital gains tax purposes.

1.4.8 Protecting family companies

The *'related property' valuation rules* (22.12) may apply if you transfer valuable holdings in your family company to your children, etc. Thus, if you die within seven years, inheritance tax might be payable on the transfers. However, up to 100 per cent *business property relief* (22.18) may be available. The charge (if any) on the shares on your death could be even higher, however, particularly if the rules change and so you should plan to transfer shares to your children before they become too valuable, and your wife should do the same. The best time would be on the formation of a new company or early in its development.

If you are planning a new business venture, then do not put it into your main family company. Form a new company whose shares are owned by your children (or others whom you wish to succeed to your business). The new company should be encouraged to expand as much as possible and you may even let your old company run down. In this way the next generation of your family eventually will be left controlling the major company.

In the case of a partnership, the interest of each partner is valued on the appropriate share of the underlying assets. If, however, the partnership is incorporated into a company, the value of each partner's interest is normally reduced appreciably.

1.4.9 Deeds of family arrangement

Variations or disclaimers made within two years of any death not only effectively change the destination of property left by will (22.29.6), they are effective in changing the inheritance tax position. Property might be diverted from the surviving spouse to other beneficiaries, so as to use fully the nil rate band. Alternatively, substantial legacies may go to others than the surviving spouse, resulting in high inheritance tax. Assets can then be diverted to the surviving spouse, who might in turn pass the assets to others at a later stage, with a good chance of saving tax.

However, if you disclaim your legacy, it will revert to the estate and be re-allocated according to the will (or rules on intestacy if there is no will). Thus whether or not inheritance tax can be saved will depend on the facts in each case. Deeds of variation are effective in changing wills after death, provided that those involved take the necessary steps. However, it is better to ensure that your will is effectively drawn up so as to minimise inheritance tax. In this way, you will be more certain that your estate is passed on in accordance with your wishes. Then regular review is essential.

1.4.10 Providing the funds to pay inheritance tax on death

You may not be able, or indeed wish, to avoid leaving a large estate when you die. In this case you should ensure that sufficient funds are available for paying the inheritance tax. This avoids forced realisations of assets and, for example, the sale of shares in a family company which it might be desirable to keep.

Life assurance provides one of the best means of providing money to pay inheritance tax arising on your death, as well as being a very suitable vehicle for exempt gifts. Ensure, however, that the policy proceeds themselves are not subject to the tax, which could happen if the policy were taken out (with no trust provisions) by you on your own life. Consider taking out policies in trust for your children where you leave assets to them; this will put cash into their hands to pay the tax. They should be 'whole of life' policies, under which capital sums, with or without profits, or unit-linked to combat inflation, are payable when you die.

If both you and your wife have large estates then you should each insure your respective lives in trust for your children, assuming that you each leave your estates to them. If, however, you each leave your estate to the other by your will, then a joint life last survivor policy could be useful, under which a payment is made only on the second death. If the policy is correctly drawn (in trust for the eventual heirs on the second death) it will not attract inheritance tax. Further, the premium rate for such a policy is usually substantially lower than for two individual policies.

The policy can be written in trust for your heirs, under the Married Women's Property Acts or otherwise. Take care that there is at least one trustee other than you so that the proceeds may be claimed without delay on your death.

Temporary life assurance may be used to cover the five-year period following a gift or settlement on which you have paid tax at the lifetime rate. The amount covered should be the additional tax payable on that transfer should you die within five years (22.6). Temporary life assurance written in trust is also most useful for covering any inheritance tax payable on a gift (potentially exempt transfer (PET)) if you die within seven years.

1.5 Change of residence and domicile

Reference to the table at the beginning of Chapter 17 will illustrate the importance of residence and domicile in ascertaining whether or not an individual is liable to income tax, capital gains tax and inheritance tax. If you are able to become non-resident for tax purposes you will avoid liability to UK income tax on many classes of income and if you are also not ordinarily resident here you will not be liable for any UK capital gains tax on sales of assets here or abroad.

If you become neither domiciled (17.2) nor *deemed domiciled* (22.4) in this country you will only be liable for UK inheritance tax on assets situated here.

A very effective way of avoiding liability from UK taxes is to emigrate and take all of your assets out of this country. Once you have ceased to be resident and are no longer domiciled nor deemed domiciled here you will be outside the UK tax net regarding all income arising and assets situated abroad. (You should note that if you have shares in a UK company with its registered office here, the shares are treated for inheritance tax purposes as located in this country unless they are bearer securities kept abroad.)

If you have a large potential capital gain you should defer taking this until you have ceased to be resident and ordinarily resident here; in this way you will avoid capital gains tax. (If you wish you may then return to this country in a future tax year.)

As a pure tax-saving exercise, you should only consider emigrating if you are a very wealthy person; and even then you should only go to a country where you feel that you will be happy. If, however, you wish to retire to a 'place in the sun', then in choosing to which country you should go, you should take into account the tax which you would have to pay there. Once you have established your foreign residence and domicile, in order to preserve this situation, you must avoid paying regular substantial visits to the UK (19.4).

1.6 Year-end planning

Towards the end of the tax year (5 April), you should consider various tax-saving opportunities.

The following is a list of reliefs to use up and other things to be done on or before 5 April. Further details are given elsewhere in this book.

(1) Capital gains tax annual exemption (20.6).
(2) 'Bed and breakfasting' (1.3.1).
(3) Inheritance tax annual exemption (22.17.2).
(4) Inheritance tax relief of £250 per gift to one person (22.17.2).
(5) Normal expenditure gifts for inheritance tax (22.17.2).
(6) Nil rate band for inheritance tax (22.5.1).

(7) Take extra dividends and salary for yourself and your spouse from your family company to maximise the benefits of independent taxation (6.1).
(8) Effect charitable deeds of covenant (6.5) or single 'gift aid' donations of at least £250 net (15.2.1), thus getting relief for the current tax year.
(9) Pay personal pension contributions (14.6).
(10) Elect to carry back personal pension (and retirement annuity) premiums to the previous tax year (14.6.2).
(11) Make investments qualifying for relief under the Enterprise Investment Scheme (11.26).
(12) Buy plant and machinery to obtain 25 per cent writing down allowance.
(13) Buy industrial and commercial buildings in enterprise zones obtaining 100 per cent initial allowance on the building content (11.12).
(14) Increase your contributions to your company pension scheme (10.11). (Your employer's contributions are geared to the company accounting date.)
(15) Do extra business mileage in your company car, so as to clear the 2,500 or 18,000 mile requirements for lower scale charges (10.6.5).
(16) Ensure you make any necessary tax elections to do with your business and private affairs within the required time limits. A particular instance is trading loss relief (11.22).
(17) Make investments and re-investments in a Personal Equity Plan by 5 April each year (8.10).

1.7 The seven ages of tax planning

Although tax planning is important at all stages of one's life, different features may be relevant at particular times. There follows a summary of particular tax planning points to remember at seven selected 'ages':

(1) Childhood.
(2) Student days.
(3) Early working life.
(4) Newly married.
(5) Parenthood.
(6) Middle age.
(7) Retirement.

Much of the advice given earlier in this chapter applies at most times in your life and thus is not highlighted in what follows; for example, tax planning for businesses (1.2.2), employments (1.2.5), companies (13.1) and capital gains tax (1.3). The points now classified under different 'ages' have particular relevance to certain times in your life. References are given to earlier paragraphs in this chapter, which will in turn refer you to further detail in the text.

1.7.1 Childhood

Tax planning for children normally involves other people such as their parents and grandparents. A chief objective is to provide for education and maintenance in the most tax-efficient way. Educational schemes may have become less attractive in view of, for example, the withdrawal of life assurance relief. However, lump sum school fee payments in advance by grandparents may prove of value in saving higher rate income tax and inheritance tax.

Older children may work in the family business at weekends and during the holidays, in which case a reasonable salary should be paid. This will be tax free to the extent of the unused personal allowance (£4,045). To avoid any National Insurance contributions the salary should be kept below £62 per week. Also, older children might occasionally buy and sell shares and thus make use of their annual capital gains exemption (£6,500).

Other tax planning points to note include:

(1) Changing wills to include new children (1.4.5).
(2) Settlements by grandparents (1.4.2).
(3) Repayment claims for children (1.2.7).
(4) Gifts to children to save inheritance tax (1.4.1).
(5) Accumulation and maintenance settlements (1.4.2).
(6) Discretionary settlements (1.4.2).
(7) Paying income from settlements for maintenance and education with possible tax repayments (1.2.7).

1.7.2 Student days

If you are a student (post-school), you will normally have attained your majority and this facilitates tax planning. In particular, none of your income will be assessed on your parents even though it arises from gifts which they make to you.

Your single personal allowance (£4,045) will normally cover income from jobs, investments, etc before you pay any tax. Also, income distributions from certain settlements are likely to entitle you to reclaim at least part of if not the entire 34 per cent tax already suffered.

Your parents and grandparents might save inheritance tax by making gifts to you or in trust (1.4.2). If you invest the money given to you directly in stocks and shares you will have the annual exemption (£6,500) to cover any capital gains (1.3.1).

1.7.3 Early working life

In your early working days you may well be able to benefit from some of the tax planning points regarding employments (1.2.5) and businesses (1.2.2), noting particularly new businesses (1.2.8). If you work overseas in a business or employment, some tax benefits may result (1.2.23).

Make sure that you claim all the expenses to which you may be entitled in your employment (1.2.5) or business (1.2.2) including a proportion of your home expenses if relevant.

Whether you are employed or self-employed, you should consider pensions (1.2.19) or personal pension arrangements (1.2.18) as soon as practicable. These provide a very tax-effective way of providing for your security.

1.7.4 Newly married

When you marry, the opportunity arises for the parents and grandparents on both sides to make gifts and settlements (1.4.1 and 1.4.2), using the special inheritance tax marriage exemptions or otherwise. Also they should re-examine their wills.

Particular tax planning matters for you both to consider include:

(1) Wife's salary (1.2.10).
(2) Independent taxation of husband and wife (6.1)—separate rates and allowances for income and capital gains.
(3) House purchase (1.2.13).
(4) Life assurance (1.2.17).
(5) The making of new wills (1.4.5).

1.7.5 Parenthood

This is the time when you are likely to have a growing income but also to incur the largest expenses. Gifts (1.4.1) and accumulation and maintenance settlements (1.4.2) made in favour of your children by their grandparents are tax-efficient ways in which the gap can be bridged.

As you progress in your employment (1.2.5), business (1.2.2) or profession, the relevant tax planning points become even more important. Particular matters to note include new businesses (1.2.8) and incorporation (1.2.4). Also, you will be well advised to improve your life assurance (1.2.17) and pension (1.2.19) or personal pension (1.2.18) cover as appropriate. You may work overseas (1.2.23) or even completely change your domicile and residence (1.5) if, for example, you become extremely well-to-do.

As you become more wealthy, *capital tax planning* will grow in importance, including capital gains tax (1.3). Inheritance tax planning should include an examination of gifts and settlements (1.4.2), charitable gifts (1.4.3) and equalisation (1.4.4); attention to your will (1.4.5); the protection of family companies (1.4.8) and the provision of funds to pay the tax (1.4.10). Furthermore, assets producing income and capital gains should be split between you, so as to maximise the benefits of independent taxation.

1.7.6 Middle age

You will still need to consider the relevant business (1.2.2) or employment (1.2.5) tax planning points as well as life assurance (1.2.17), pensions (1.2.19) and personal pensions (1.2.18). Even if your earlier pension cover was inadequate, there is scope for compensating for this in later life.

As your children come of age, consider passing them income producing assets. When they marry, make use of the appropriate inheritance tax exemptions (1.4.1), thus guarding against tax payable if you die within seven years. Cover larger gifts by life assurance (1.2.17). When they in turn have children, consider accumulation and maintenance settlements in favour of your grandchildren (1.2.21).

Capital tax planning is vital during this period and if you can afford it, you should make gifts and settlements (1.3.3) to pass on your wealth during your lifetime. Also, provide for the payment of any inheritance tax (1.4). If you have a family company try to guard against future heavy inheritance tax on its shares and help succession by passing on shares to the next generation (1.4.8). Should your house be larger than you need, consider selling and re-investing or gifting the proceeds.

1.7.7 Retirement

Take advantage of the tax planning opportunities arising when your pension (1.2.18) becomes due, such as taking your full tax-free lump sum entitlement or deferring your benefits.

If you have a family company or business, maximise your capital gains tax retirement relief (1.3.5) on sale or gift. At the same time, use the limited capital gains tax gifts election (20.28) if appropriate. Also, do not overlook the valuable inheritance tax business relief (22.18) and agricultural relief (22.21). These will eliminate or substantially reduce the inheritance tax payable if you die within seven years of a gift.

Since more of your income is likely to arise from investments, you may be able to claim repayment of the income tax deducted at source (1.2.7). If your respective incomes are sufficiently small, you may both be entitled to age relief (3.2.10), together with a higher married couple's allowance.

With the sale of your business and perhaps house (1.2.13), you will have the chance of reviewing your will (1.4.5) and making gifts (1.4.1), including settlements (1.4.2). If you have surplus funds, then gifts to charity should be considered, being free of inheritance tax and capital gains tax; whilst the purchase of an annuity will increase your income but reduce your estate.

1.8 The way ahead — planning beyond the election

The political factor is always important in tax planning. This is particularly true in a General Election year, with the first budget of the new Parliament awaited.

Whichever government was in power, drastic tax reforms seemed likely. The Conservatives had stated their intention to abolish both inheritance tax and capital gains tax. They also aim for a 20 per cent basic rate. Labour are not expected to abolish capital taxes and whilst possibly reducing tax rates on lower incomes, may increase higher rates.

But when will the changes take place? In theory, changes can be announced in Parliament with immediate effect. However, the most likely time seems to be the November 1997 Budget. Hence, there may still be time to benefit from the existing rules, but you should act promptly particularly since there could be an earlier Budget date.

Inheritance tax is an area where early action can prove most fruitful. In particular, you should maximise the benefits of the £215,000 nil rate band and business property (22.18) and agricultural reliefs. These could well be reduced in the next Budget. So act now, making gifts and settlements, if appropriate.

However, most gifts are potentially exempt transfers, which are taxed if you die within 7 years. The rates applying are those at death. So even if you were within the £215,000 nil rate band when you made the gifts, this band could be reduced by the time you die.

So far as your will is concerned, it is advisable to leave up to the full £215,000 to others than your spouse, so that the nil rate band is not wasted. Should the nil rate band be reduced, it will be a simple matter for you to vary your will.

Make good use of your annual and other exemptions. These include the £3,000 annual exemption, small gifts up to £250 per person, relief for normal expenditure out of income and certain marriage gifts. These reliefs normally take effect at once and so should be safe from future changes.

A more elaborate way of safeguarding your £215,000 nil rate band is by means of a *discretionary trust*. Funds settled on such trusts are immediately liable to inheritance tax at 20 per cent (22.30.2) unless you are within the nil rate band, when none is due. However, should the inheritance tax regime become harsher, extra tax may become due within the trust. So make sure that it can be quickly wound up, if necessary.

If you feel that capital gains tax will become harsher, there is a case for taking gains now. This is particularly true if they are covered by reliefs, such as for example retirement relief (now available at 50).

Turning now to *income tax*, to guard against higher tax rates, consider taking extra remuneration (and dividends) from family companies. However, you should take account of the extra National Insurance contributions likely. Furthermore, increased pension contributions could well make sense, particularly if you feel that future relief may be restricted.

Those are just a few pointers to tax planning in the General Election year. In essence, it is a question of acting promptly and retaining flexibility, in order to cope with change.

2 The basis of your tax liability

2.1 Who is taxable?

Individuals, partnerships, estates, trusts, companies, and certain other organisations that are resident in the UK are taxable on their income arising here. They are also liable on income arising abroad subject to the rules outlined later in this book. The taxation of the income of individuals is covered first; partnerships, estates, trusts and companies being dealt with in later chapters.

The UK income of non-resident individuals, companies and other entities may also be subject to tax here (19.1).

Similarly capital gains tax is payable on certain capital profits made by UK residents anywhere in the world (20.3). Non-residents, however, are not normally liable to UK capital gains tax.

2.2 The taxes payable
(TA 1988 S1 & FA 1997 Ss54, 58 & 59)

A unified system of personal taxation operates under which there is, for 1997–98, a lower rate of 20 per cent, a basic rate of 23 (previously 24) per cent and a higher rate of 40 per cent (5.0.1). Your investment income falling within your basic rate band generally attracts 20 per cent tax (8.1–7). Certain different rates apply for previous years (26.2).

The capital gains tax rates for individuals are 20, 23 and 40 per cent. However, the first £6,500 of your net capital gains is not taxed (20.1).

Special rules apply to companies which are taxed on both income and capital gains at corporation tax rates (13.2).

Inheritance tax applies to wealth passing on death and in some other circumstances (Chapter 22).

2.3 What income is taxable?
(TA 1988 Ss1 & 15–20 & FA 1994 Ss189–197)

The table below summarises the classes of income that are subject to income tax, or corporation tax for companies. The table also shows the 'Schedules' and 'Cases' under which the income is classified and taxed under the law.

2.3.1 Table: Classes of income

Schedule A Income from land and buildings including rents and certain premiums from leases (7.1).

Schedule C Prior to 6 April 1996 income from 'gilt-edged securities', payable in the United Kingdom as well as certain overseas public revenue dividends that are paid through a banker or other person here (8.2). Has been abolished from 1996-97 (accounting periods ending after 31 March 1996 for companies), whereupon Schedule D Cases III, IV or V apply as appropriate.

Schedule D This is divided into the following separate 'Cases':

Case I	Trades (11.1).
Case II	Professions or vocations (11.1).
Case III	Interest received, annuities and other annual payments (8.4).
Cases IV and V	Overseas income from certain investments, possessions and businesses (18.1).
Case VI	Miscellaneous profits not falling within any of the other Cases of Schedule D (15.1).

Schedule E Wages and salaries from employments (including directorships). There are the following 'Cases':

Case I	This normally applies where the employee is resident in the UK and the work is done here (10.1).
Case II	Work done here by a non-resident, etc (10.2).
Case III	Work done wholly abroad by a UK resident whose salary is sent here during the course of the overseas employment excluding, however, income taxed under Case I or Case II (10.3).

Schedule F Dividends paid by companies and certain other distributions that they make (8.1).

2.4 Deduction of tax at source and tax credits

Under Schedule D Case III (and previously Schedule C) tax at now 20 per cent is frequently deducted at source by the payers and the recipients get the net amount. The former pay the tax over to the Revenue. Company dividend payments, however, are made without any tax deductions although the recipients are 'imputed' with a credit of 20/80ths of the dividend. (The company pays tax of 1/4th of its dividend payments by way of advance corporation tax (13.6).)

Thus suppose you receive a dividend of £80: you will get a tax credit of £20 (£80 × 20/80ths) which you may be able to reclaim if your income is sufficiently low (16.7). If your income is high enough, however, you may be taxed at higher rates (5.0.1) on £100 (80 + 20); but you deduct the £20 tax credit from your total bill. Prior to 6 April 1993, the tax credit was at the basic income tax rate (25 per cent).

Tax is also deducted at source in the case of certain annual payments (4.1) and income from wages and salaries under Schedule E (see 2.3.1). In the former case the payer of the income is entitled in certain circumstances to retain the tax deducted and need not pay it over to the Revenue.

2.5 The distinction between capital and revenue profits

Most of your income is subjected to income tax at the basic and perhaps higher rate, whereas normally, capital profits are liable to capital gains tax or are tax free. The tax rates borne by income and capital gains are now broadly similar. However, the rules and reliefs are very different. The question is then: What is a capital profit?

Generally speaking, a capital profit is a profit which you realise on the sale of an asset where it is clear that you are not making it your business to buy and sell assets of that type. On the other hand, if you conduct a business in such assets your profits will be income.

2.5.1 Examples of capital transactions

The sale of the house in which you live (also normally free of capital gains tax unless used for business) (20.23).
The sale of your private motor car (also free of capital gains tax).
The sale of shares you held as investments.
The sale of a plot of land you inherited.
The sale of the goodwill of your business.
The receipt of an inheritance (also free of capital gains tax).
The sale of a property which you had bought for investment purposes.
The sale of a picture unless you are the artist or a picture dealer.

The receipt of the proceeds of a 'qualifying' life assurance policy (9.3). (This is also normally free of capital gains tax.)

2.5.2 Examples of revenue transactions

The sale of houses and land if you are a property dealer.
The sale of motor cars if you are a car dealer.
The sale of shares if you are a share dealer.
The sale of pictures if you created them or are a picture dealer.
The receipt of salaries, commissions, interest, dividends, rent, royalties, etc.

2.6 Revenue and capital expenses

In the same way that income and capital profits must be distinguished, you must separate revenue and capital expenses for tax purposes. The latter can only be charged against capital profits and the former against income. For example, the commission on the sale of shares acquired for investment is deducted in calculating your capital gains but if you are a share dealer then it is a revenue expense.

Also, in determining the assessable profits of a business, only revenue expenses may be deducted and capital expenses are prohibited as a deduction (11.3.2).

2.6.1 Table: Tax-free income

Certain items in your income may be entirely free of tax. These are listed below.

(1) Casual gambling profits (eg pools, horse racing, etc).
(2) Premium Bond winnings.
(3) Lottery prizes.
(4) Interest on authorised holdings of National Savings Certificates (TA 1988 S46).
(5) Bonuses paid at the end of 'save as you earn' contracts.
(6) Maturity bonuses payable on Defence Bonds, British Savings Bonds and National Development Bonds.
(7) Interest on Post-war Credits.
(8) Wedding and certain other presents from your employer that are in truth not given in return for your services as an employee.
(9) Certain retirement gratuities and redundancy monies paid by your employer (10.12).

(10) Any scholarship or other educational grant that you receive if you are a full-time student at school, college, etc.

(11) War widows' pensions; also comparable payments overseas (TA 1988 S318).

(12) Certain social security benefits (25.3.1) including:
 (*a*) earnings-related supplement of unemployment benefit (but not unemployment benefit itself)
 (*b*) sickness benefit (but not statutory sick pay)
 (*c*) maternity allowance and grant (but not maternity pay)
 (*d*) attendance allowance
 (*e*) child benefit
 (*f*) family income supplement (but retirement pensions under the National Insurance Scheme and family allowances are assessable)
 (*g*) mobility allowance
 (*h*) certain payments of income support, family credit or housing benefit; but taxable up to given limits if related to trade disputes or conditional upon availability for employment (TA 1988 S617)
 (*i*) short-term incapacity benefit paid during the first 28 weeks of incapacity (FA 1995 S141).

(13) Housing grants paid by local authorities, etc.

(14) German compensation payments to victims of National-Socialist persecution. Also Austrian and German state pensions paid to such victims from 6 April 1986 (previously 50 per cent taxable).

(15) Wound and disability pensions.

(16) Allowances, bounties and gratuities paid for additional service in the armed forces.

(17) The capital part of a purchased life annuity (but not the interest portion).

(18) Your first £70 of interest each year from National Savings Bank Ordinary Deposits. This exemption from tax applies separately to husband and wife (TA 1988 S325).

(19) Certain allowances paid under job release schemes, as described in the Job Release Act 1977, within a year of pensionable age.

(20) Additional pensions and annuities paid to the holders of certain gallantry awards by virtue of those awards (TA 1988 S317).

(21) Part of your Profit Related Pay under an approved scheme (10.15).

(22) Income from 1 January 1991 on a TESSA (8.11).

(23) Compensation for mis-sold personal pensions (FA 1996 s.148).

(24) Jobfinder's grant (FA 1996 S152)

2.7 Bank and building society interest

Any bank or building society interest which you receive normally has 20 per cent income tax deducted from it at source (8.6). If your income is sufficiently high, however, you will be charged to additional tax on the grossed up equivalent of the interest as if you had suffered tax on it at 20 per cent. The additional tax payable consists of higher rate income tax on the grossed up equivalent of the income, less tax on it at 20 per cent. Thus if you receive building society interest of £80 in the year then

£100 (the grossed up equivalent) will be included in your total taxable income. The grossed up equivalent is determined by the formula:

Interest received $\times \frac{100}{80}$ (ie, 100 less 20 per cent).

Prior to 6 April 1996, the rate of tax deducted from building society and bank interest was 25 per cent.

2.8 Year of assessment

Income tax is an annual tax; thus it is your total income over each 12-month period that is assessed to tax. The year of assessment runs from 6 April to the following 5 April and so the tax year 1997–98 means the year ending 5 April 1998.

The income chargeable to tax for each year of assessment is computed according to the rules relevant to the various Schedules (see 2.3.1) as described later in this book. In general, an 'actual' basis is now required in which the income received during a particular year is assessable for that year.

For tax years prior to 1997–98, it was sometimes the income of the preceding year of assessment or of the accounting year ending in the preceding year of assessment, that was assessed. This 'preceding year basis' was normally used for the profits from trades and vocations, as well as interest assessed under Schedule D. For details please see later chapters (11.7 etc).

The year to 5 April also forms the year of assessment for capital gains tax.

2.9 Period of assessment less than full year

It is possible for a taxpayer to have a period of assessment of less than 12 months. For example, a baby born during any year has a period of assessment running from the date of its birth until the next 5 April. If a taxpayer dies, his period of assessment runs from 6 April to the date of his death.

Notwithstanding that the period of assessment may be less than a year, the taxpayer receives the personal reliefs applicable to a whole year of assessment. But see 3.2.1 for the restriction of the married couple's allowance in the year of marriage.

3 Personal reliefs

According to your circumstances you can claim certain personal tax reliefs which are deducted from your total income in arriving at the amount on which you pay income tax.

The rules applying for 1990–91 onwards differ from those for earlier years. This is due to the introduction of independent taxation for husbands and wives as from 6 April 1990. The married personal relief was abolished, as were the married age allowances. At the same time, a married couple's allowance was introduced.

3.0.1 Table: Personal reliefs at a glance — 1997–98

Type	*Circumstances*	*Relief*
Personal allowance	Single	£4,045*
Life assurance relief (3.2.5)	Policy effected before 14 March 1984 on your own or wife's life — deduction from premium	$12\frac{1}{2}$% of premiums
†Additional personal allowance for children (3.2.8)		£1,830*
Blind person's allowance (3.2.9)		£1,280*
Age allowance (3.2.10)	Age 65–74 — Single Age 75 or over — Single	£5,220* £5,400*
	Reduced by £1 for every £2 of excess income over £15,600 down to personal reliefs level	
†Married couple's allowance (3.2.1)	Age under 65 Age 65–74 Age 75 and over	£1,830* £3,185* £3,225*
†Widow's bereavement allowance (3.2.11)		£1,830*

* These allowances will be increased for future years in line with the retail price index (unless the Treasury otherwise orders).
† These allowances are restricted to 15%.

3.1 Earned and unearned income

For tax purposes income is classified as being either 'earned' or 'unearned'. Earned income includes the following:

(1) The salary or wages from your job including any taxable benefits.
(2) Certain pensions or retirement annuities paid to you, including those under a Revenue approved scheme (10.11.1).
(3) Any income from a trade or profession in which you engage.
(4) Any income from a partnership provided that you work in it and are not merely a sleeping partner.
(5) Old age pensions and widow's pensions received under the National Insurance Act.
(6) Income from a patent or copyright if you actually created the subject matter.
(7) After leaving your employment, trade or profession, any taxable amounts that you receive from that source.
(8) Income from holiday lettings as defined (7.7).

The rest of your income is 'unearned' and includes:

(1) Dividends.
(2) Bank deposit interest.
(3) Building society interest received.
(4) Rents from property investments.
(5) Income from trusts.
(6) Interest from government or local authority stock.

3.2 Personal allowances
(TA 1988 S257, FA 1989 Ss31 & 33 & FA 1997 S55)

For 1997–98 there is a personal allowance of £4,045 (previously £3,765). This is available to individuals generally. However, a higher allowance may apply to those who have attained their 65th birthdays (3.2.10).

3.2.1 Married couple's allowance
(TA 1988 S257A)

From 6 April 1990, each married couple normally obtains a married couple's allowance, according to their ages attained during the tax year. The following apply from 1994–95 to 1997–98:

	1994–95	1995–96	1996–97	1997–98
husband and wife both aged under 65	£1,720	£1,720	£1,790	£1,830
husband or wife aged 65–74	£2,665	£2,995	£3,115	£3,185
husband or wife aged 75 and over	£2,705	£3,035	£3,155	£3,225

For 1994–95 relief for married couple's allowance was restricted to the lower rate (20 per cent) and to 15 per cent subsequently.

The higher allowances for older people are reduced if the husband's annual income exceeds £15,600 (£15,200 for 1996–97, £14,600 for 1995–96 and £14,200 for 1994–95). For every £2 of income received in excess of £15,600, the higher allowances are reduced by £1 until the basic allowance (£1,830) is reached.

Married couple's allowance automatically goes to the husband. However, any unused balance may be transferred to the wife. To do this, an election must be made to your inspector of taxes within six years of the end of the tax year. For example, for 1997–98 Mr A has an income of £5,045. His personal allowance of £4,045 reduces this to £1,000 and this leaves £830, unused, from the married couple's allowance. Provided an election is made by 5 April 2004, £830 will be transferred to Mrs A, to set against her income for 1997–98.

From 6 April 1993, you can elect for the married couple's allowance to be split equally between you or go entirely to the wife. Otherwise, it goes to the husband. The election is needed before the start of the first tax year to which it applies. The wife may elect for the equal split but both must elect for her to receive it all.

In the year of marriage, the allowance is reduced by one-twelfth for each complete month from 6 April until your marriage date.

Transitional relief applies for 1990–91 and subsequent years where the husband's income is not sufficient to cover his personal allowance. Prior to 6 April 1990, the unused allowance would be used against any income of the wife. The transitional relief is designed to ensure that the position is no worse than previously.

3.2.2 Personal allowances before 6 April 1990

Before the introduction of independent taxation (6.1) there was a separate personal allowance for single people (£2,785 for 1989–90). For married men, the allowance was higher, being £4,375 for 1989–90 (reduced proportionately if marriage took place during the year). In addition, unless an election had been made for the separate taxation of her earnings (6.4), a working wife obtained relief of up to £2,785 for 1989–90 against her earnings.

3.2.3 Child relief
(TA 1970 S10 & FA 1979 S1)

Income tax child relief no longer operates but prior to 1979–80 was generally available at different rates depending on the age of the child. Child relief was replaced by child benefit (see below).

3.2.4 Child benefit
(FA 1977 S23)

Tax-free child benefit has applied since 4 April 1977. It applies in respect of your children under age 16 and those under 19 receiving full-time education, satisfying the necessary rules. From 10 April 1997, the weekly rate is £11.05 for the first child and £9.00 for each other child.

3.2.5 Life assurance relief
(TA 1988 Ss266–274 & FA 1988 S29)

Tax relief in respect of pre-14 March 1984 life assurance policies is given based on the premiums paid in the tax year. You now normally deduct the relief from your premium payments (see table below). The relief only applies to policies taken out *prior to 14 March 1984*. Premiums in respect of policies effected after that date attract no relief. Similarly, relief is not due on existing policies for which the benefits are enhanced after that date, for example, by exercising an option to increase the policy term.

3.2.6 Table: Rules for life assurance relief — pre-14 March 1984 policies

(1) The policy benefits must include a sum payable on death or in certain circumstances provide for a deferred annuity.
(2) The policy must be effected with a UK, Dominion or Irish insurance company or one carrying on business here; or a Lloyd's Underwriter; or a registered friendly society.

(3) The policy must be on your own or your wife's life and either of you may pay the premiums.

(4) Special relief is given for sums paid under an Act of Parliament or under the rules of your employment to secure a deferred annuity for your widow or children after your death. The relief is given according to your income level by deducting the following percentages of the premiums from your tax bill:

Total income	*% Relief*
Not over £1,000	half of basic rate of income tax.
£1,001–£2,000	three-quarters of basic rate.
over £2,000	basic rate of income tax.

(5) Policies taken out after 19 March 1968 or changed after that date have to be 'qualifying policies' (9.3).

(6) A fixed percentage of each premium is deducted by you on payment and you keep this relief. The premium limit is the larger of 1/6th of your total income (after charges) and £1,500. Any over-deduction by you will be adjusted in your assessment at the end of the tax year or you may be directed by the Revenue to pay premiums without the deduction of tax relief.

(7) From 6 April 1981 to 5 April 1989 the relief percentage was 15% and from 6 April 1989 the relief is $12\frac{1}{2}$%.

3.2.7 Example: Life assurance relief restrictions for 1997–98

			Date effected	*1997–98 premium*
Policy A	— Sum assured	£10,000	1.1.80	£1,000
Policy B	— "	£20,000	5.4.82	£1,500
Policy C	— "	£25,000	1.5.84*	£2,000

*Policy C was effected after 13 March 1984 and thus does not qualify for relief. If total income for year = £12,000

Premiums eligible for relief restricted to
1/6th × £12,000 = £2,000

Life assurance relief for year = £250 ($12\frac{1}{2}$% × £2,000)

3.2.8 Additional personal relief for children

(TA 1988 S259, FA 1988 S30 & FA 1994 S77 & Sch 8)

(1) This relief of £1,830 applies to widows, widowers and others, such as single parents, not entitled to married couple's allowance. You also get it if you are married but your wife is totally incapacitated for the year.

(2) Legally adopted and legitimated children are included, as are stepchildren. To qualify for relief for 1997–98, the child must be under 16 on 6 April 1997; or a full-time student at school or university, etc; or studying full-time for not less than two years for a profession or trade.

(3) If the child is not your own, he or she must be under 18 on 6 April 1997 in any event and maintained by you at your own expense.
(4) You only get one £1,830 relief no matter how many children reside with you. (This includes any children of your common law husband or wife.)
(5) From 1993–94, the relief applies for the year of separation if you have a qualifying child living with you (TA 1988 S261A).
(6) For 1993–94 and earlier years, the relief was given at your full tax rates. However, for 1994–95 the relief was restricted to 20 per cent and to 15 per cent for subsequent tax years.

3.2.9 Blind person's relief
(TA 1988 S265 & FA 1997 S56)

(1) The relief is given to registered blind persons.
(2) For 1997–98, the relief is £1,280.
(3) For 1996–97, the relief was 1,250.
(4) From 6 April 1990, if a spouse cannot use all his or her allowance, it can be transferred to the other spouse even if he or she is not blind.
(5) Anyone who also qualified for son's or daughter's services relief prior to 6 April 1988 (£55) needed to disclaim it or else he was not allowed blind person's relief.

3.2.10 Age allowance
(TA 1988 Ss257 & 257E & FA 1997 S55)

(1) This applies for 1997–98 if you are over 65 by 5 April 1998.
(2) The personal allowance is increased to £5,220 if your age on 5 April 1998 is between 65 and 74 and to £5,400 if you have reached your 75th birthday.
(3) For 1989–90 and previous years, higher age allowance was available for married couples where at least one partner was 65 years of age.
(4) The above allowance figures are restricted if your income exceeds £15,600. The restriction is one-half of the excess of your income over £15,600. Thus if your income is £16,600 your allowance is restricted to £5,220 – £500 = £4,720. Note that the £15,600 restriction is based on your 'total income' (5.2), which is before tax but after certain deductions, such as mortgage interest. If you have any life policy gains, these must be included without top slicing relief (9.7).
(5) If your income is sufficiently high your personal relief is restricted to the normal rate (£4,045); but not below this.

(6) Previously, if your wife had earned income, she still obtained wife's earned income allowance, even though you got age allowance. This allowance was lost if an election for separate taxation was made (6.4). This no longer applies due to the introduction of independent taxation from 6 April 1990.

(7) After 5 April 1987, a higher level of age allowance applied to those aged 80 and over. From 6 April 1989 the higher allowance applies from age 75. For 1997–98 the rate is £5,400. You qualify for this allowance if you have reached 75 by 5 April 1998. For the extra age allowance for married people, only one of you needs to be 75 by that time.

(8) Transitional relief is available from 1990–91 where a man married to an older wife might have his allowances reduced due to the change to the new system. If the transitional relief is claimed, the husband's personal allowance is replaced by the single age allowance frozen at the 1989–90 level of £3,400, etc. He also obtains the higher married couple's allowance appropriate to his wife's age.

3.2.11 Widow's bereavement allowance
(TA 1988 S262 & FA 1994 S77)

(1) This allowance applies to certain widows whose husbands die after 5 April 1980.

(2) The relief for 1997–98 is £1,830 (previously £1,790) which is given if the husband died in the two years to 5 April 1998.

(3) The relief is equal to the married couple's allowance (for those under 65). Like that allowance, it was restricted to 20 per cent for 1994–95 and 15 per cent subsequently.

(4) Originally, the relief only applied if the husband was entitled to married personal allowance when he died, ignoring the effect of the wife's earnings election (6.4). If the death is after 5 April 1990, the couple must have been living together.

(5) The allowance applies to the tax year of death, and to the following year also, unless the widow remarries before it begins. It is given in addition to any other available reliefs.

(6) For the year of death, the widow may be entitled both to married couple's allowance and widow's bereavement allowance. From 1993–94, the former is first to be deducted from the late husband's income, in spite of any election to the contrary (6.1).

3.2.12 Vocational training
(FA 1991 Ss32–33, FA 1994 S84 & FA 1996 S144)

If you pay for your own vocational training, tax relief is available from 6 April 1992, subject to the rules. Relief will be given for training leading to National Vocational Qualifications and Scottish Vocational Qualifications at any level including (from 1 January 1994 only) level 5.

From 6 May 1996, wider relief extends to individuals over 30 who pay fees for full time vocational courses lasting between 4 weeks and a year. Such courses need not lead towards a National Vocational Qualification or its Scottish equivalent.

Under Inland Revenue regulations basic rate tax relief is given by deduction at source, even if you pay no income tax. Otherwise, a claim is needed. (The recipient is normally able to reclaim your tax deduction.) Higher rate tax relief is also available where appropriate.

The relief only applies if you are UK resident or a Crown servant serving overseas and you obtain no other tax relief for it, nor public financial assistance. From 1 January 1994 children under 16 are excluded, as are those between 16 and 18 in full time education at school. Training for leisure or recreation purposes is also excluded.

3.3 Indexation of personal reliefs

(TA 1988 S257C & FA 1997 Ss55 & 56)

For 1981–82 and subsequent years, certain personal reliefs were to be increased from their previous levels by not less than the proportionate increase in the retail prices index for the last calendar year. Starting with 1993, the year for comparison runs to September. With parliamentary approval, however, a lower increase (or none at all as for 1993–94 and 1994–95) may be ordered by the Treasury.

The reliefs concerned are personal allowance, married couple's allowance (3.2.1), additional personal allowance for children (3.2.8), age allowance (3.2.10) and widow's bereavement allowance (3.2.11). Also, blind person's allowance (3.2.9) is to be indexed for 1998–99 and subsequently.

3.3.1 Example: Personal reliefs — General illustration

Mr A lives with his family at 1 Bridge Street. Their income consists of:

	Income assessable for 1997–98	
Name	*Earned*	*Unearned*
Mr A	£13,400	£4,105
Mrs A	4,000	695

Mr A pays £1,100 interest during 1997–98 on a mortgage of 1 Bridge Street. The mortgage was arranged to purchase the house and so the interest is wholly allowable. Mrs A pays an annual premium of £200 on a qualifying life assurance policy on Mr A's life taken out before 14 March 1984. How much income tax is payable by Mr A and Mrs A for 1997–98?

1997–98	*Mr A*	*Mrs A*
Earned income	£13,400.00	£4,000.00
Unearned income	4,105.00	695.00
Total Income	17,505.00	4,695.00
Less:		
Personal allowance	4,045.00	4,045.00
	£13,460.00	£650.00
Income tax payable: at 20% (on £4,100)	820.00	£130.00
on investment income (£4,105) at 20%	821.00	
at 23% (on £5,255)	1,208.65	
	£2,849.65	
Less: Married couple's allowance £1,830 at 15%	274.50	
Mortgage interest £1,100 at 15%	165.00	
	439.50	
	£2,410.15	

Notes

(*a*) On the levels of income shown above Mr A is not liable to higher rate (5.0.1).

(*b*) Life assurance relief of $12\frac{1}{2}\% \times £200 = £25$ will be obtained by deduction from the premium payments.

(*c*) Relief for the mortgage interest would normally be obtained by Mr A deducting income tax at 15% of £165 on payment. He would thus pay £935 net mortgage interest. However, his final income tax payments would be increased by £165 to £2,575.15.

(*d*) Under the independent taxation rules, the married couple's allowance will be allocated to Mr A (unless a contrary election is made).

(*e*) Mr A only pays 20% income tax on his investment income, since it lies within his basic rate band.

4 Annual payments and interest

4.1 Annual payments apart from interest
(TA 1988 Ss348–350 & FA 1988 Ss36–40)

If you make an annual payment it is normally considered for tax purposes as being the income of the recipient and is usually subject to income tax at the basic rate (23 per cent) by deduction at source. You should therefore deduct this tax in making each payment. You will be allowed to retain all of the tax deducted provided that your income taxed at the basic or higher rate is sufficient to cover the amount of the payment.

For example, if you have suffered basic rate income tax of £200 in the tax year and you made an annual payment of £100 you deduct tax from the latter amounting to £23. You thus pay only £77 when making your annual payment. Your effective income tax bill is £200 – £23 = £177. If, however, your taxed income is less than your annual payments you will have to pay to the Revenue income tax at 23 per cent on the difference. So if your taxed income is nil in any tax year, you will have to account to the Revenue for basic rate income tax on your entire annual payments for that year.

The result of this procedure is to give you basic rate income tax relief on your annual payments provided your income taxable at the basic rate exceeds those payments. From 15 March 1988, new deeds of covenant and maintenance payments are covered by different rules. Broadly, no tax relief applies to the payer and the recipient is not taxed on the payments.

Under certain circumstances relief is available against tax at the higher rates as well as the basic rate.

Examples are as follows:

(1) Annual payments under court orders entered into before 15 March 1988 for maintenance or alimony (6.8.3). (Relief also applies if

the court order was applied for on or before 15 March 1988 and made by 30 June 1988.)

(2) Annual payments under deeds of covenant to individuals that were entered into before 7 April 1965.

(3) Certain annual payments under partnership agreements to retiring partners or their widows.

(4) Certain annual payments which you make in connection with the purchase of a business where the payments are made to the former owner of the business or his widow or dependants.

(5) Unlimited donations under deeds of covenant to charities (15.2.1).

4.2 What are annual payments?

(1) Examples of annual payments are annuities, alimony payments, maintenance payments to your divorced or separated wife, payments under *deeds of covenant* (6.5) and certain interest payments which are subject to special tax rules (4.3).

(2) They are normally paid under a binding legal obligation such as a contract or deed of covenant.

(3) The payments must be recurrent although repeated gifts (unless under covenant) are not annual payments.

(4) In the hands of the recipient an annual payment must neither form part of his trading profits nor consist of a payment for services rendered.

(5) Payments consisting of instalments of capital are not annual payments for tax purposes. In the case of life annuities, however, each payment is split between an income element (which is treated as an annual payment) and a capital element which is tax free.

4.3 Interest payments
(TA 1988 Ss353–379)

Subject to the following, you must not deduct income tax from any payments of interest that you make. This means that most types of interest payments made by you personally will be gross without any tax deduction. An important exception concerns mortgage interest (4.7).

If you pay 'annual interest' to anyone who lives outside the UK (unless you get permission to pay gross under a double tax agreement) you must deduct income tax at the basic rate (23 per cent) in making the payment.

If, however, you pay 'annual interest' in this country on an advance from an overseas bank carrying on business in the UK, you should not deduct income tax.

'Annual interest' is interest paid on a loan which is capable of continuing for a period exceeding one year. If, at the start of a loan, you agree that it should last for a stated period of less than one year then any interest arising will not be 'annual interest'.

Companies and local authorities must normally deduct income tax in making 'annual interest' payments and this applies to a partnership of which a company is a member. Interest paid by a bank in the normal course of its business is normally paid subject to the deduction of income tax (8.7).

Subject to the rules which are outlined in the following pages, certain interest payments are allowed as deductions in computing your total income for income tax at basic and higher rate.

4.4 Interest paid for business purposes

Note that interest paid for business purposes is allowable against your taxable business profits provided the loan is used wholly and exclusively for the purposes of your business, profession or vocation. This basic rule includes interest on bank overdrafts as well as that on other loans.

4.5 Tax relief for interest payments
(TA 1988 Ss353–379 & FA 1989 Ss47–48)

In order to obtain relief for interest paid you must show that it is 'eligible for relief'. This term specifically excludes bank overdraft or credit card interest.

4.5.1 Table: Tax relief for interest payments

Your interest is 'eligible for relief' if it is paid on loans raised for the following purposes:

(1) Subject to various restrictions, the purchase and improvement of buildings and land in the UK or Eire (4.6).

(2) Buying plant and machinery for use in a partnership which gets capital allowances on it where you are one of the partners.

(3) Buying plant and machinery (eg, a motor car) which is used in connection with an office or employment that you hold and for which you personally get capital allowances.

(4) Acquiring ordinary shares in a close company (13.17) or lending it money for use in its business. (This does not apply to a close investment company, nor for shares bought after 13 March 1989 on which BES or EIS relief is claimed — 11.25 and 11.26.) To qualify for relief you must either own more than 5% of its shares, or own some shares and work for the greater part of your time for the company. Shares owned by 'associates' (13.17) are included in the 5% but not, after July 1989, if owned by an employee trust of which you are a beneficiary.

(5) Purchases by employees of shares in their company as part of an employee buy-out. (Employees and their spouses must together own more than 50% of the company, ignoring excesses over 10% holdings.)

(6) Purchasing a share in a partnership, or lending it money for use in its business if you are a partner. This applies whether or not you work in the partnership and also extends to investing in a co-operative.

(7) Paying inheritance tax arising on death. The personal representatives of the deceased obtain relief for interest paid within a year of raising the loan. If the interest cannot be relieved wholly in the year of payment it can be spread forward or backwards.

Note: Relief for interest on loans to purchase plant and machinery (see (2) and (3) above) is given for three years after the year of assessment in which the loan is taken out.

4.6 Loans for purchase and improvement of buildings and land

(TA 1988 Ss354–358, FA 1988 Ss42–44, FA 1993 Ss56–57, FA 1994 Ss80–81 & Sch 9 & FA 1997 S57)

Within the limits mentioned below, any interest which you pay on a loan raised to buy land or buildings, or to improve them, is 'eligible for relief'. This does not include overdraft interest but covers fixed bank loans and building society mortgages, etc. (Improvement loans only qualify for relief if applied for this purpose before 6 April 1988.) When you pay the interest you must normally own the property. However, from 16 March 1993, you continue to obtain relief when you buy a new home which becomes the security for a loan taken to buy and originally secured on the previous one.

The interest on any loan that you raise to pay off another loan previously obtained to buy property is also 'eligible for relief'. However, no relief is available on a loan obtained after 5 April 1988 to replace money borrowed to improve property. Land and buildings include caravans, previously of restricted categories before 6 April 1991, but now unrestricted.

'Property improvements' include:

Central heating installations.
Garages and garden sheds.
Garden construction and landscaping.
Double glazing installations.
Plumbing improvements (excluding maintenance).
Conversions of houses into flats.
Construction of swimming pools, tennis courts, etc.

If, however, you merely carry out repairs to existing property without improving it then any loan interest incurred will not normally be treated as 'eligible for relief'.

The Revenue gives sympathetic consideration to cases where, for example, the husband buys the property and the wife pays the interest — the couple would usually get tax relief.

From April 1983 mortgage interest up to certain limits is normally paid net of tax at the basic rate or less (see below).

Concerning a new property loan raised after 26 March 1974, you only obtain tax relief if either (*a*) it is to purchase or improve your only or main residence or (*b*) you let the property at a commercial rent for at least 26 weeks in the year and it is available for letting at other times. However, from 6 April 1995, interest is treated as a deduction from Schedule A income in the same way as other expenses are allowed. At the same time, the old rules cease to have effect. (The old rules continue to apply for corporation tax purposes.)

Under (*a*) your interest is restricted to that on a loan of £30,000 and if your borrowing exceeds this figure your interest relief is proportionately restricted. (In considering the £30,000 limit, no account is taken of interest which has been added to capital up to £1,000.) Before 6 April 1991, relief was available at the basic and higher rates of income tax. However, from that date, higher rate relief was withdrawn and relief was only granted at the basic rate.

From 6 April 1994, relief was restricted to 20 per cent on existing and new loans. An exception is for people over 65 who take loans on their homes to buy life annuities and will continue to obtain relief at the basic rate. From 6 April 1995, relief is further restricted to 15 per cent.

Under (*b*) (see previous page) you are only allowed interest relief against your income from letting property. You continue to obtain higher rate relief under this category after 5 April 1991.

You also get relief for interest on a loan which you obtained before 6 April 1988 (but not subsequently) to buy a house for a former or separated spouse, or a dependent relative of your wife or yourself. A dependent relative is broadly defined as an elderly or infirm relative; also your widowed, divorced or separated mother. This interest counts, however, towards the £30,000 limit. Loans obtained for these purposes after 5 April 1988 do not qualify for relief.

Your interest relief is not restricted because you do not reside in your property, if you live in job-related accommodation (10.6.13) and intend to make your property your main residence in due course (TA 1988 S356). A similar rule applies to interest paid on a loan to buy job-related accommodation where you are self-employed.

Up to 31 July 1988, unmarried people purchasing their own main residence together each obtained relief for the interest on a loan of up to £30,000. However, from 1 August 1988, relief on *new* loans is limited to £30,000 per residence, regardless of the number of people sharing. Normally, relief would be allocated equally to the borrowers. However, certain transfers of unused relief are allowed.

4.6.1 Temporary relief

You obtain relief for interest on a bridging loan of up to £30,000 for normally up to one year (or longer at the discretion of the Revenue) when you change houses. Higher rate relief continued after 5 April 1991 on your existing but not your new bridging loan, if both were in place by that date. This includes where there has been a formal offer and binding contract. This higher rate relief would normally only continue for up to one year, but could be extended at the discretion of the Revenue.

The position is improved from 16 March 1993, provided your old property is up for sale. It is no longer necessary to take a mortgage to buy a new home in order to obtain relief on your existing loan. This continues for 12 months from when the old property ceases to be your main residence (FA 1993 S57).

Similar rules apply if you are over 65 and have a life annuity 'home income plan'. You may now leave your home without losing relief on the loan to buy your annuity. Again, you need to have the property up for sale and relief continues for 12 months from when you move out. In both cases, the Revenue have a discretion to extend this period.

4.7 Deduction of tax from mortgage interest payments
(TA 1988 Ss369–370 & FA 1994 S81 & Sch 9)

The current rules relating to mortgage interest payments apply from April 1983. These operate from 1 April 1983 for payments to building societies, other authorised lenders such as certain banks, insurance companies and local authorities; otherwise in general from 6 April 1983. However, if your mortgage is from a private lender, the previous system applies (and so you must pay the interest gross).

Broadly, under the present system, you are able to deduct tax from mortgage interest payments, provided the loan qualifies for relief. Income tax was deducted at the basic rate (25 per cent) from interest paid up to 5 April 1994. Subsequently, lower deduction rates apply. From 6 April 1994, the MIRAS (mortgage interest relief at source) rules applied using the 20 per cent lower rate instead of the basic rate of tax. Similarly, from 6 April 1995, the deduction rate is 15 per cent.

If your loan exceeds £30,000, you may deduct income tax from the interest on the £30,000 fraction, provided that you notify the building society, etc and they agree and contact the Revenue. New loans above £30,000 after 5 April 1987 come into the deduction system automatically.

Under the present scheme the lenders will normally arrange for you to deduct the appropriate tax on paying the interest. You may even deduct tax and keep it if your income is less than your personal allowances or you have none at all.

5 Computing your income tax bill

Your 'total income' (see below) less your allowances for the tax year (3.0.1) will be subjected to income tax at the lower, basic and higher rates according to the following table:

5.0.1 Table: Income tax rates for 1997–98

Slice of income	*Rate*	*Total income (after allowances)*	*Total tax*
4,100 (£0–4,100)	20%	4,100	820
22,000 (£4,100–26,100)	23%	26,100	5,880
Remainder	40%		

5.1 Indexation of income tax bands *(TA 1988 S1 & FA 1997 S54)*

Prior to 6 April 1988 there was a basic rate band followed by five higher rate bands. Each of those bands was to be increased in line with the retail price index. The index comparison was made for the previous December each year and the figures rounded up to the next £100. However, from 1993 onwards, September is used.

As with the indexation of personal reliefs (3.3), Parliament has the power to modify the effects of indexing the income tax bands. In fact no indexation increases were made at all for some years, whilst increases above the index were made for others. Starting with 1988–89, one higher rate of 40 per cent replaced the previous five. From 6 April 1992 the 20 per cent lower rate band applies. The starting levels for the income bands continue to be indexed, although no indexation increases were made for 1993–94 and 1994–95.

5.2 What is total income? *(TA 1988 S835)*

Your total income comprises your income for the tax year less specified deductions (5.3). The following classes of income will be included for each tax year:

(1) Income as assessed for the tax year under the following schedules:

Schedule		*Details*	*Para*
A		Land and buildings	7.1
B		Woodlands (up to 5 April 1988)	7.9
D	Cases I & II	Trades and professions	11.1
	Case III	Interest, etc	8.4
	Cases IV & V	Overseas securities and possessions	18.2
	Case VI	Miscellaneous	15.1
E		Earnings from employment (see also below)	10.1
F		Dividends	8.1

(2) *The gross income actually paid to you in the tax year under the deduction of income tax at the source.* This will include income taxed at source under Schedule C (prior to 1996–97) and Schedule D Case III. You will receive the net amount after suffering income tax but you will pay the higher rate of tax if appropriate on the gross amount. You will obtain a tax credit for the income tax suffered at source which will be deducted from your tax bill. The following would come within this category:

The income portion of annuities.
Interest on certain investments.
Any annual payments which you receive (4.2).

Prior to 1996–97, tax was deducted at the basic rate, but a special 20 per cent rate now applies regarding deductions from savings income. However, annual payments are likely to have tax deducted at the basic rate (23 per cent).

(3) *Income distributions from discretionary and accumulation settlements* (21.4). Net payments made to you must be grossed up at 34 per cent and carry with them a tax credit of this amount which represents income tax (20 or 23 per cent) and additional rate tax (14 or 11 per cent) effectively suffered by the settlement. Thus if you receive £66 this is included in your total income together with a tax credit of £34. If you have an interest in possession (22.30), then your income only carries 23 per cent tax in the settlement. To the extent that the income from 6 April 1993 consists of dividends, your tax credit is 20 per cent. (Prior to 6 April 1996, discretionary and accumulation settlements carried an aggregate rate of 35 per cent.)

(4) *Dividends received together with the relevant tax credits.* After 5 April 1993, your dividends from UK companies carry with them tax credits of 20/80ths of the actual payments. This is equivalent to 20 per cent of the gross. Thus a dividend of £80 is included in your total income together with a tax credit of £20 (£80 × 20/80). If your dividends, taken to be the top slice of your income, fall within your basic rate (23 per cent) band, although the tax credit is only 20 per cent, you pay no more tax. (Before 6 April 1993, the tax credit was 25 per cent of the gross.)

(5) *Your gross income taxed at source under PAYE* (10.14). This consists of your salary, etc derived from your employment; it is subjected to lower, basic and higher rate income tax at source. The tax suffered at source is naturally deducted from the tax bill on your total income.

(6) *The grossed up equivalent of any building society interest received.* This income is subject to 20 per cent income tax deducted at source but must be included in your total income gross. You gross it up by multiplying the income received by $\frac{100}{100-20}$ (ie, $\frac{100}{80}$). You obtain a credit for the tax. For example, if you receive £80 building society interest, your total income will include £80 $\times \frac{100}{80}$ = £100 and you obtain a tax credit of £20. For 1995–96 and earlier years, basic rate tax (25 per cent) was deducted. Prior to 1991–92, the credit was not repayable (8.6) but effectively exempted you from the first 25 per cent of tax on the grossed interest.

(7) *The grossed up equivalent of any bank interest, etc paid to you* (8.7).

5.3 Total income — deductions

As well as normal business expenses, etc, which are deducted in arriving at the various income tax assessments, the following are deductible:

(1) Loan interest subject to the relevant rules (4.3). Regarding mortgage interest paid after 6 April 1991 in connection with your home, no deduction is allowable for relieving the excess of your higher rate over your basic rate liability (FA 1991 S27). For 1994–95, mortgage interest relief was restricted to 20 per cent with only 15 per cent relief applying from 1995–96.

(2) Business losses and capital allowances.
(3) Annual payments under court orders for maintenance or alimony provided they are made before 16 March 1988 or applied for before that date and made by 30 June 1988. (For 1994–95, the relief was restricted to 20 per cent and to 15 per cent from 1995–96.) Payments under new arrangements must be gross and are not deductible (6.8.3).
(4) Annual payments under deeds of covenant to individuals (excluding your infant children) that you entered into before 7 April 1965.
(5) Certain annual payments under partnership agreements to retiring partners or their widows.
(6) Annual payments to individuals under deeds of covenant entered into after 6 April 1965 and before 15 March 1988. In general these are not deductible from your income for higher rate income tax purposes. However, they reduce your total income for the purposes of the life assurance relief one-sixth rule (3.2.6).
(7) Certain annual payments which you make in connection with the purchase of a business where the payments are made to the former owner of the business or his widow or dependants.
(8) Covenanted donations to charities without limit. Also charitable donations of at least £250 net under the 'Gift Aid' scheme (15.2.1).
(9) Allowable personal pension contributions, retirement annuity premiums (14.6) and additional voluntary contributions (AVCs) (14.4).
(10) A proportion of certain transfers to reserves made by underwriters at Lloyd's or other approved underwriters.
(11) Personal reliefs and allowances (see Chapter 3). (These are, strictly speaking, deductions which are made from your total income rather than in its computation.)
(12) Half of your Class 4 National Insurance Contributions (11.29) from 6 April 1985. However, this rule does not apply for 1996–97 and subsequently.

5.4 Charges on income
(TA 1988 S276)

The annual payments mentioned above (3)–(8) as well as various other charges on income (4.1) are paid under the deduction of basic rate income tax (23 per cent) (as was your allowable mortgage interest for 1993–94 (4.7)). From 1995–96, mortgage interest is generally payable under the deduction of tax at 15 per cent (20 per cent for 1994–95). To the extent that your income less allowances is not sufficient to cover your annual charges payments, your personal allowances, etc must be restricted. (This restriction does not apply regarding mortgage interest.)

Thus, if your income for 1997–98 is £4,500 and your personal allowances and reliefs total £3,500, you can pay up to £1,000 annual charges without restriction. The £1,000 is paid by you under deduction of basic rate income tax (15 per cent if mortgage interest). Thus you actually pay only £1,000 – 23 per cent × £1,000 = £770. You also pay to the Revenue tax at 23 per cent on £1,000 = £230. If your annual charges were £1,500, your total reliefs would be reduced to £3,000 so that your taxable income after allowances (£1,500) would be sufficient to cover your charges.

The income tax which you deduct from your annual payments must effectively be paid over to the Revenue. This is done by paying tax on that part of your income which is equal to such annual payments. Where, however, the payments in question are allowed as deductions in computing your total income (eg, (3)–(8) in 5.3) you get relief for the excess of your higher rate tax over basic rate tax or tax credit on income covered by those charges.

5.5 Deductions from tax payable

When your total tax liability is computed certain deductions from the tax payable must be made, either because you have already paid part of it or because of special reliefs. These deductions include the following:

(1) Life assurance relief on policies effected before 14 March 1984 only (3.2.5). Normally $12\frac{1}{2}$ per cent of your qualifying premiums (9.3) (subject to the various rules) is deductible from your tax payable. You normally obtain this relief by deducting it from each premium payment.
(2) 20/80ths of your building society interest received; similarly 20/80ths of bank deposit interest, etc (8.7). (This fraction was 25/75ths for 1995–96 and earlier.) From 6 April 1991 (but not previously), this tax is capable of being repaid.
(3) Tax credits on dividends received (8.1). The tax credit is 20/80ths of each dividend received (25/75ths prior to 6 April 1993).
(4) Tax paid under PAYE (10.14).
(5) Income tax deducted at the source at 20 per cent (25 per cent for 1995–96) on certain investment interest paid to you (such as on company debentures).

(6) Basic rate tax deducted from annual payments made to you during the year which are included in your total income.

(7) Tax at 34 per cent (35 per cent for 1995–96) on income distributions made to you during the tax year by discretionary settlements (21.5). The tax is computed on the gross equivalent of the distributions.

5.6 Investment income surcharge (additional rate)

(TA 1988 S686)

For 1983–84 you were liable to an additional rate of 15 per cent on so much of your investment income as exceeded £7,100. Subsequently, the additional rate no longer applies to individuals.

Certain discretionary and accumulation settlements (21.5) are subjected to the additional rate (now generally 11 per cent, but 14 per cent on dividends and other savings income). In this case, the charge is made on all the income including both that from investments and otherwise. The effect is that a combined 34 per cent rate is paid. Although the additional rate no longer applies to individuals, it still applies to these settlements. Higher rate tax is not normally charged on the trust income, however, unless it is distributed to beneficiaries who are themselves liable to the higher rate of tax. (See Chapter 21, 21.5, for fuller details.)

Effectively, as a higher rate tax payer, you suffer extra tax on your dividend income from 6 April 1993, because of the reduction in the tax credit from 25 to 20 per cent. However, if you are a basic rate payer you are not adversely affected since your tax on such investment income is limited to 20 per cent.

5.7 The assessment and payment of your income tax

(TA 1988 Ss2–5 & FA 1994 S193)

This matter is considered in detail in Chapter 16. A uniform set of dates for the payment of income tax and capital gains tax has been introduced as a part of the new self-assessment system. These apply for 1996–97 and subsequent years of assessment. The earliest payments under the new rules were due on 31 January 1997. Further payments on account of your 1996–97 liability may be due on 31 July 1997, the final balance being payable on 31 January 1998, based on your income tax return.

Long standing rules normally apply for assessments raised for years upto and including 1995–96. In general, you needed to pay income tax at the lower, basic and higher rate by 1 January in the year for which the income was assessed, if the income had not already been taxed. If, however, your assessment is not agreed in time, then the tax is normally payable 30 days after the assessment is issued. Special rules apply where you appeal (16.4).

An exception to the above rule concerns your tax on business profits (11.1) which was payable in two equal instalments on 1 January in the year of assessment and the following 1 July. (For 1996–97 you make equal payments on account on 31 January 1997 and 31 July 1997, with the balance on 31 January 1998 and similarly for future years.)

Income tax at higher rates was due for payment by 1 December (31 January from 1996–97) following the year of assessment on any income from which basic rate tax has been deducted at source. This includes income like building society and bank deposit interest as well as dividends, etc. If the assessment was not issued by 1 November following the year of assessment, the tax is normally payable no earlier than 30 days after the date of issue, special rules applying if you appeal (16.4).

5.7.1 Example: Income tax computation

Mr B has his own business from which his assessable profit for 1997–98 is £30,000. His other income for 1997–98 consists of £1,200 building society interest and £8,000 dividends received (tax credits £2,000). He pays £1,200 gross interest on a mortgage for the purchase of his house to which MIRAS does not apply. (Mr B is married, and for 1997–98 his wife's income will be taxed separately.) From the above, compute Mr B's income tax liability.

Mr B – Income tax computation for 1997–98

Earned income – business assessment		£30,000.00
Investment income – building society interest:	£1,200.00	
Add: 20% income tax		
£1,200 × 20/80ths	300.00	
	£1,500.00	
Dividends	8,000.00	
Add: Tax credit	2,000.00	
		11,500.00

Total income before personal reliefs and allowances		£41,500.00
Less: Personal allowance		4,045.00
Taxable balance		£37,455.00
Tax payable:		
£4,100 at 20%		£820.00
22,000 at 23%		5,060.00
11,355 at 40%		4,542.00
£37,455		
Total tax		10,422.00
Less: Married couple's allowance £1,830 at 15%	£274.50	
Tax credit on dividends	2,000.00	
Tax credit on building society interest	300.00	
Tax relief on mortgage interest 15% × £1,200	180.00	
		2,754.50
Net further tax payable		£7,667.50

5.8 Interest on overdue tax
(TMA S86, etc)

If you are late in paying your income tax you may be charged interest at $8\frac{1}{2}$ per cent from 6 February 1997. Previous recent rates have been:

From	*Rate* %
6 January 1994	$5\frac{1}{2}$
6 October 1994	$6\frac{1}{4}$
6 March 1995	7
6 February 1996	$6\frac{1}{4}$

This interest is not deductible for income tax purposes. The exact rules are given later (16.8.2).

5.9 Fluctuating income

Because of the graduated nature of income tax rates, if your income fluctuates greatly from year to year you may find that your tax liability is high in some years and low in others. The result is that your total income tax over the years is more than it would have been had your income been spread evenly over those years. Certain special rules exist which have the effect of spreading lump sums of income over the period during which they have been earned. For example, lump sum payments received for the copyright, etc of artistic works may be taxed as if spread over up to three years, depending on the time taken to produce the work (15.4).

So-called 'top slicing' relief is obtained when you receive certain large taxable sums in one year. You may effectively spread these sums over a stated period and recompute your tax liability on the basis that the income had been paid in this way. (The tax is payable for the year when you receive the income but the rate is normally lower.) What you do is to divide the lump sum (L) by the stated period (P) and calculate the tax payable (T) for the year on your other income plus (L/P). You then calculate the tax payable on your other income by itself and deduct it from (T). This gives the total tax payable on (L/P) and this tax is multiplied by P to give the total tax payable on (L).

A particular example where 'top slicing' applies is regarding the profit element in the proceeds of non-qualifying life assurance policies (9.7). Such policy proceeds are taxed at the excess of higher rate income tax over income tax at the basic rate, subject to the relief outlined above.

With effect from 1988–89, two forms of 'top slicing' relief were removed. These related to premiums for certain leases and relief previously given on the merger of professional firms, resulting in a change in accounting basis.

6 Husband, wife and children

This Chapter deals, in particular, with the taxation of husband and wife. The independent taxation system operating from 6 April 1990 is covered. Also, the previous rules are considered, which apply for 1989–90 and earlier years. These are important for open assessments and returns for those years. (Some of the rules for independent taxation have been mentioned in Chapter 3.)

6.1 Independent taxation of husband and wife
(FA 1988 Ss33–35 & Sch 3)

From 6 April 1990, you and your spouse are each taxed separately on all of your income and capital gains. Each has a single person's relief and income tax rates (for 1997–98 the first £4,100 at 20 per cent, the next £22,000 at 23 per cent and the remainder at 40 per cent). Similarly you each have a full capital gains tax annual exemption (£6,500).

There is an allowance known as the married couple's allowance amounting to £1,830 each year. Normally, this goes to the husband. However, if his income is insufficient to use it, part or all can be transferred to the wife. In the year of marriage, the married couple's allowance is reduced by one-twelfth for each month between 6 April and the marriage date. A higher married couple's allowance is given to those entitled to age allowance. For 1994–95, relief was restricted to 20 per cent (3.2.1). The relief is further restricted to 15 per cent for 1995–96 and subsequently.

A new rule applies from 6 April 1993. You are able to elect for the married couple's allowance to be split equally between you or go entirely to the spouse (3.2.1). Otherwise it will be used as before.

Income from jointly owned property is taken as split equally between husband and wife, subject to the right to make a joint declaration to the contrary. The effect of the election is to split the income in the ratio of the respective shares of husband and wife in the asset. Interest on mortgages in your joint names is split equally between you. However, you can elect for any different split to apply, which could well save tax.

For example, if you and your spouse have a joint mortgage and he or she has no income you should elect to receive all of the mortgage interest relief.

The old-established wife's earnings election (6.4) has no validity for 1990–91 and subsequent tax years. However, as mentioned above, all income is taxed separately, as are capital gains. As a result, your spouse and yourself will each have the annual capital gains tax exemption (20.6) for 1990–91 and subsequently. Thus each has £6,500 exemption for 1997–98.

An election for transitional relief (3.2.1) is available where a couple might have been worse off in 1990–91, because most of the income belongs to the wife and the husband's personal allowance exceeds his own income. The relief is limited for 1990–91 and future years to the husband's excess personal allowance.

6.2 When you marry

If you marry after 5 April 1990, various new rules will apply to both of you (6.1). Essentially you will be taxed separately on your income and capital gains, remaining responsible for your own tax returns.

As a married man, prior to 6 April 1990 you were taxed not only on your own income but also normally on that of your wife. You were not taxed, however, on your wife's income for the tax year during which you married. You obtained personal relief at a higher rate than a single person (3.0.1). If your wife was working then against her earnings was set her (wife's) earned income relief (maximum £2,785).

At the end of the year in which you married both you and your wife had to complete income tax returns. Naturally, this continues under the present system since now you each need to submit your own returns.

In the year of your marriage your wife obtained her own personal relief but no wife's earned income relief.

6.2.1 Tax returns

Under the old system, your own return, for the year of marriage, covered the full tax year and needed to include all of your own income for that year but none of your wife's.

Even though you were single for part of the year you were taxed as a married person for the whole of that year. But your personal allowance was restricted by £132.50 (for 1989–90) for every completed month during that tax year prior to your date of marriage, provided your marriage was after 5 April 1989. A similar rule applies for married couple's allowance (3.2.1) and the monthly restriction is £152.50 for 1997–98 (previously £149.17).

6.3 Separate assessment
(TA 1988 Ss283–285)

Prior to 6 April 1990, despite the fact that it was the husband who was taxed on both his own and his wife's income, it was nevertheless possible for a married couple to be assessed separately and to pay their respective shares of tax separately. However, from 6 April 1990, husband and wife are both taxed and assessed on their own income (6.2). Separate assessment was not the same as the separate taxation of your wife's earned income (6.4). Full details are given in earlier editions of this book.

6.4 Separate taxation of wife's earnings
(TA 1988 Ss287 & 288)

Before the introduction of independent taxation from 6 April 1990, it was still possible to elect for the wife to be separately taxed on her earnings up to 5 April 1990 as if she were a single person. The husband was then taxed on the balance of their joint incomes (including the wife's unearned income) as if he also were single. Fuller details appear in previous editions of this book.

6.5 Deeds of covenant
(FA 1988 S36)

Payments under deeds of covenant to charities (15.2.1) provide a most tax-efficient means of passing money regularly to them. Such payments are a class of annual payments (4.1). The deed must be properly drawn up (most charities have prepared forms for covenanted donations) otherwise seek professional advice.

Beneficial treatment also applies to payments under deeds of covenant to individuals, provided the deeds were entered into before 15 March 1988. A further condition is that an Inspector of Taxes must have received the deed by 30 June 1988, otherwise, payments under such deeds are disregarded for tax purposes. The previous beneficial tax treatment which made deeds of covenant so popular for student children and also grandchildren was withdrawn for new covenants.

The deed needs to provide for payments at annual or more frequent intervals for a period capable of exceeding six years or until your death if earlier. (Note that this also applies to any supplementary deeds.) However, deeds of covenant in favour of charities (15.2.1) need only be capable of exceeding three years.

You are required to deduct income tax at the basic rate (23 per cent) from each payment according to the rules for annual payments (4.1). This does not apply to payments made by you under deed of covenant to any of your children who are less than 18 years of age and unmarried. These payments are disregarded for tax purposes as are payments under a reciprocal arrangement.

Payments to individuals under deeds of covenant entered into before 7 April 1965 are allowable deductions for additional and higher rate tax. Deed of covenant payments to charities (15.2.1) are normally deductible from your total income for higher tax rate purposes without limit (FA 1986 S30).

Subject to the above, recipients of payments under deeds of covenant with low incomes can reclaim basic rate tax on them up to the amount of their unused income tax personal relief (£4,045). Thus suppose your grandson has no other income and you pay him £1,540 net under deed of covenant each year, tax of £460 will be reclaimable for him for 1997–98. (This assumes that you entered into the deed of covenant before 15 March 1988.)

6.6 The income of your children

No matter how young they are, there is nothing to prevent your children earning income in their own right and being taxed on that earned income. This also applies to investment income unless the investments were given by your wife or yourself and the child is neither married nor over the age of 18 at the time that the income is paid.

Settlements and arrangements made by you through which your child gets investment income normally result in your being taxed on that income if the child is neither married nor over 18. If the child's investment income which would otherwise be treated as your own is less than £100, however, you will not pay tax on that income (TA 1988 S660B). (This limit applies for each parent.)

You should obtain a tax return each year for each of your minor children who has any income (including trust income). Completing a return will often prove beneficial since if the child has suffered tax at source on any income this may be reclaimable in whole or part depending on its nature and on how much other income there is to set against the child's tax allowances. In such circumstances a repayment claim form can be submitted instead of a normal tax return (16.7).

If the child had little or no other income, then it was of benefit for it to be paid an annual amount under deed of covenant (6.5) by a friend or relative (not its parents, unless the child is over 18 or married). From 15 March 1988 the rules were changed (6.5) but existing deeds of covenant attract relief as before. The covenant payments are made under the deduction of income tax at the basic rate (24 per cent). If the child's income is small enough then the tax can be reclaimed on its behalf because he or she has the benefit of the full personal allowance (£4,045) and lower rate (20 per cent) tax band.

6.6.1 Example: Income of child

Mr A has one child, B, aged ten years, whose income for 1997–98 is as follows:

		Gross
(1)	Dividends, including tax credits, on shares given to B by Mr A	£200
(2)	Dividends, including tax credits (20% of gross), on shares given to B by his grandfather	£800
(3)	Annual payment under deed of covenant from B's uncle effected before 15 March 1988	£2,000
(4)	Interest on bank deposit (capital gifted by grandmother)	£2,000

How much income tax is reclaimable on behalf of B for 1997–98?

Item (1) is not treated as B's income for tax purposes because it is regarded as the income of Mr A who gifted the shares to his child B.

The income tax payable by B for 1997–98 is calculated as follows:

		Gross	Income tax deducted or tax credits
(2)	Dividends including tax credits on shares from grandfather	£800	£160
(3)	Annual payment from B's uncle	2,000	460
(4)	Deposit interest	2,000	400
Total income		£4,800	£1,020
Less: Personal allowance of		4,045	
Taxable amount		£755	
Income tax due £755 at 20%			£151
Less:	Income tax suffered by deduction at source and tax credits		1,020
Net income tax reclaimable			£869

6.7 Death of husband or wife

If you are a widower or widow you are regarded as a single person for tax purposes. This means that the personal reliefs for single persons will apply to your income. You may, however, qualify for the £1,830 additional personal relief for children (3.2.8).

6.7.1 If husband dies

If a husband dies during the tax year his income for the period from 6 April to the date of his death will be subject to tax. A return of this income must be made by his executors who must arrange for payment of tax out of the estate funds. If the death was before 6 April 1990, the wife's income must be included.

Even though his period of assessment will be less than a full year, where a husband died during 1989–90 he obtained the full married man's personal allowance (£4,375), and various other reliefs in full including the £2,785 (maximum) earned income allowance for his wife against her earned income.

Where the husband dies after 5 April 1990, he will have the full personal allowance (£4,045 for 1997–98) and married couple's allowance (£1,830). However if his income is not sufficiently large to absorb the full married couple's allowance, the balance will go to his widow.

Where the husband died before 6 April 1990, his widow became a taxpayer in her own right and was taxed on the income derived by her during the period from the date of death to the next 5 April. She completed a separate tax return and received the full personal allowance as a single person for that period. After 5 April 1990, husbands and wives are independently taxed in any event. However, widow's bereavement allowance (£1,830) is available as before (3.2.11).

6.7.2 If wife dies

Where a wife dies after 5 April 1990, she is entitled to the entire personal relief (£4,045 for 1997–98). (Age allowance would alternatively be available in full if she is so entitled.)

If a wife died during the tax year 1989–90 this did not normally affect her husband's tax return. He included with his own income for the full year the income of his wife up to the date of her death. He got personal allowance as a married man for the full year and also wife's earned income allowance if appropriate.

6.8 Divorce or separation

If you are divorced or permanently separated you are regarded as a single person for tax purposes. This means that the personal reliefs for single persons will apply to your income. If, however, you were separated but maintained your wife by voluntary maintenance payments for which you got no tax relief, prior to 6 April 1990, you obtained the married man's personal allowance. Subsequent to that date, married couple's allowance (£1,830) applies in the tax year of separation only, subject to transitional relief (6.8.3).

You are treated as being permanently separated from your wife if you are separated under a court order or deed of separation; also if you are separated in such circumstances that the separation is likely to be permanent.

6.8.1 Divorce or separation during the tax year

On her divorce or permanent separation prior to 6 April 1990, a woman became a taxpayer in her own right and needed to submit a return from the date of divorce or separation to 5 April. She was then taxed as a single person getting the full 1989–90 personal allowance. Naturally, the independent taxation rules mean that after 5 April 1990, a woman is a taxpayer in her own right in any event.

Where a man is divorced or permanently separated during 1990–91 or later, he obtains the full personal relief (£4,045 for 1997–98) and married couple's allowance for the year.

A man who was divorced or permanently separated during the year 1989–90 still needed to submit a return for the full year in the usual way. He included with his own income for the year that of his wife up to the date of the divorce or separation but not the income derived by her after that date. He got the full married man's personal allowance for that year as well as the wife's earned income relief.

6.8.2 Who may claim the additional personal relief?
(TA 1988 S260)

For any tax year only one payment of additional personal relief (£1,830) is normally allowable for your children. If you are separated or divorced from your wife you must agree jointly who should claim the tax relief for your mutual children or you should agree a basis of apportioning the relief between you. If you do not agree a basis, then the relief will be split in proportion to the respective contributions made by you and your ex-wife (or separated wife) towards the children's maintenance and education for the tax year.

As an exception to the general rule, if each parent looks after one or more children of a broken marriage, each can claim additional personal relief of £1,830. However, in the year of separation, only the wife (or ex-wife) is able to claim the relief.

6.8.3 Alimony and maintenance payments
(FA 1988 Ss36–39 & FA 1994 S79)

The rules regarding alimony and maintenance payments were changed in 1988. Where payments are made under agreements dated after 14 March 1988, they are to be made without the deduction of tax. At the same time, the recipients are not taxed on the payments. The payer obtains a limited amount of relief, equal to the annual amount paid or, if less, £1,830 (the married couple's allowance). This applies where one divorced or separated spouse makes payments to the other. For 1994–95, the relief is restricted to 20 per cent and to 15 per cent subsequently.

If you are separated or divorced and you make any payments under a court order or a binding agreement entered into before 15 March 1988, for the maintenance of your children or your separated or ex-wife, then you should not deduct income tax at the basic rate from the gross payments. (Such deduction was normally required before 6 April 1989.)

This extended to court orders applied for before 16 March 1988 and made by 30 June 1988; also maintenance agreements made before 15 March 1988 and variations of such orders or agreements.

After 5 April 1989, special rules apply to payments under these agreements. The payer gets tax relief on payments up to the level for which he obtained relief for 1988–89 and the recipient is taxable on no more than was taxable in 1988–89 (taking account of the exemption for a divorced or separated spouse of £1,720, etc). All payments of maintenance due after 5 April 1989 should be made gross. Relief on up to £1,830 of the payments is limited to 15 per cent for 1997–98 (20 per cent for 1994–95 and 15 per cent for 1995–96). However, payments to the adult children from 1996–97 are no longer to be treated as charges on the income of the payer nor as taxable income of the recipient (FA 1996 S149).

Purely voluntary payments of maintenance should be paid without any tax deductions and these are not allowable as annual charges against your income; nor are they taxed on the recipient. As indicated, however (6.8), if you maintained your separated wife by voluntary payments only, then prior to 6 April 1990, you obtained the married man's personal allowance. Married couple's allowance normally applies in the tax year of separation only. However, if you separated before 6 April 1990 and the foregoing circumstances apply, you will normally continue to obtain this relief. This does not apply if you are divorced.

Under the previous rules, if maintenance payments under a court order were made direct to the children, then these were treated as their own income. If, however, the payments were made to the mother for the maintenance of the children then the income was treated for tax purposes as her income. This no longer applies under the current provisions.

6.8.4 Foreign divorces

If the divorce is effected by a foreign court then different rules relate to the receipt or payment of alimony by residents of this country. Normally no tax will be deductible from the payments by a United Kingdom resident and a recipient resident in this country will be assessed to tax on the amount arising.

However, for 1992–93 and subsequent years, tax relief extends to payments under court orders of countries which are members of the EC;

also written agreements enforceable under the law of those countries. Payments must be to a divorced or separated wife or husband for their maintenance, or for the maintenance of a child of the marriage. The relief is limited to £1,830 for 1997–98 (F2A 1992 S62).

7 Income from land and property

The amount of income that you derive during the tax year from letting property such as a house, flat, factory or shop, less the deductions you may claim represent your net income from letting property and must be shown separately on your tax return. You must return your gross property income including certain lease premiums and also give full particulars of your expenses. If up to 5 April 1995 the income was derived from furnished lettings then the assessment was under Schedule D Case VI (15.1); otherwise it was generally under Schedule A. From that date, Case VI on furnished lettings only continues for corporation tax purposes.

From 6 April 1995, new rules apply under which all property income is pooled and assessed under Schedule A (7.1). This includes income from furnished lettings. (The rules only relate to income tax and not corporation tax.)

7.1 New property income tax system
(FA 1995 Ss39–42 & Sch 6 & FA 1997 S85 & Sch 15)

New, simplified rules apply to the taxation of the property income of individuals, partnerships, trusts and non-resident companies from 6 April 1995. However, the old rules continue to apply for companies. Thus, if you have appropriate property income, your assessments for 1995–96 and subsequent years will be covered by the new system. Points to note include the following:

(1) All of your property income normally is put into a "pool" and taxed together under Schedule A, but on trading principles. Thus expenses are deducted on this basis (11.3), although the net is treated as investment rather than trading income.
(2) Your furnished lettings income is no longer taxed under Schedule D Case VI, but pooled with the other Schedule A income.

(3) Any property losses which you are carrying forward from 1994–95 are offsetable against the combined profits of your property business for 1995–96. Similarly, any unused losses are carried forward to set off against future property business profits.
(4) The capital allowance rules (11.9) broadly continue for Schedule A purposes. However, from 6 April 1997 (1 April for companies), a 'pooling' basis applies (11.9.2). So far as furnished lettings are concerned, you are still be able to make the 10 per cent wear and tear claim based on rents (7.5).
(5) Relief for interest payable in respect of a Schedule A business is obtained by deducting it like any other expense. Thus any excess of interest over your other net property income produces a loss. Furthermore, the old requirement is removed under which the property must be let or available for letting for at least 26 weeks in a year (4.6).
(6) Remember that under normal trading principles, any proportion of expenses attributable to personal use is not deductible but accrued expenses often would be.
(7) Overseas property income remains taxable under Schedule D Case V. However, the rules have been aligned more closely with the system for UK property income. For example, interest payable on a loan to purchase the property is deductible.

7.2 Income falling within Schedule A
(TA 1988 S15)

Annual profits or gains (ie, after deducting expenses) in respect of:

(1) Rents under leases of land (and buildings) in the UK.
(2) Income after 5 April 1995 from furnished lettings.
(3) Rentcharges, ground annual and feu duties, and any other annual payments arising out of land in the UK. This includes some wayleaves and easements such as for cables and telephone lines (FA 1997 S60), etc.
(4) Other receipts arising to a person from the ownership of land in the UK or from rights or interests in such land.

7.2.1 Exceptions

(1) Yearly interest.
(2) Income including royalties from mines, quarries, etc which are charged under Schedule D.
(3) Income from various other sources charged under Schedule D such as ironworks, gasworks, canals, docks, fishing rights, railways, bridges, etc.

(4) Income up to 5 April 1995 (and subsequently for corporation tax) from furnished lettings (ie, tenant entitled to use of furniture). This is assessed under Schedule D Case VI unless you elect within two years of the end of the relevant tax year that it should be taxed under Schedule A.

7.2.2 Expenses allowed against Schedule A income
(TA 1988 Ss25–33)

(1) Repairs and maintenance including redecorating the premises during the lease.
(2) Insurance premiums against fire and water damage, etc to the building.
(3) Management costs including costs of rent collection, salaries, advertising for new tenants, legal and accountancy charges, etc. If your wife takes part in the management, consider paying her a salary (1.2.9).
(4) Services that you are obliged to provide for the tenants but for which you get no specific payment.
(5) Any payments that you make for general, business and water rates, and council tax, but not in general community charge.
(6) Any payments that you make for any rent, rentcharge, ground annual, feu duty or other periodical payment in respect of the land.
(7) The cost of lighting any common parts of office blocks or flats and otherwise maintaining them.
(8) The upkeep of gardens of flats, etc where the lease requires you to be responsible for this expense.
(9) Architects' and surveyors' fees in connection with maintenance but not improvements.
(10) Capital allowances (11.9) on any plant or machinery that you might use in the upkeep of your property (unless a dwelling-house).
(11) The upkeep of any private roads, drains and ditches, etc on your land if part or all of the property is let and the expenditure is for the benefit of your tenants.
(12) In the case of an industrial building which is used by the tenant for industrial purposes (eg, manufacturing) you may get capital allowances on the building (11.11). This also applies to some hotels (11.15).
(13) When you live in a part of the premises you let to others you may not deduct the full amount of your expenditure from your income. Instead you must subtract from your expenditure some reasonable proportion because the premises were not wholly used to produce

the income. You may calculate this proportion as being, for example:

$$\frac{\text{Area (or rooms) used by you}}{\text{Total area (or rooms)}} \times \text{Expenses}$$

7.2.3 Special rules concerning expenses — old rules

Your expenditure in respect of maintenance and repairs is deductible if incurred by reason of dilapidation attributable to a period falling within the duration of the lease. All other expenditure must be incurred in respect of that period. If, however, you bought the premises subject to a lease, you normally get no relief for your expenses relating to the period prior to the purchase.

Special rules relate to a 'lease at full rent' which is one that produces sufficient income for you to pay for the maintenance, repairs, insurance and management of the premises in accordance with the undertakings in the lease. In that case you can charge expenses relating to a period after your purchase when the premises were empty immediately before they were let at full rent. You can also deduct expenses relating to a previous full rent letting that you made of the premises or a void period between lettings.

If you have a number of 'leases at full rent' that are not 'tenant's repairing leases', then you can set off expenses attributable to one such lease against the rents derived from another (a tenant's repairing lease is one where the lessee (tenant) is under an obligation to maintain the premises). The above rules relate to 1994–95 and earlier years for income tax, but continue for corporation tax (7.1).

7.3 Losses

If in any tax year before 1995–96 your expenses for any property exceeded the rent and you did not get relief as above then the resultant loss was carried forward to be set off against future Schedule A income from the same property, or against income from other properties (provided let on 'leases at full rent' that were not 'tenant's repairing leases' (see above)). A loss from a property cannot be set off against income derived from a trade or business carried on.

From 6 April 1995 (7.1), any property losses carried forward are offsetable against your combined property business profits for 1995–96.

Unused losses are available to carry forward to be relieved against future property business profits.

7.4 Assessment under Schedule A

(TA 1988 S22 & TMA S59A)

Tax under this Schedule is charged by reference to the income to which you become entitled in the tax year. This applies whether or not you actually receive the rents, etc unless:

(1) You did not receive an amount to which you were entitled because of the default of the person who owed you the money and you took reasonable steps to enforce payment; or
(2) you actually waived payment of the rent, etc (without receiving any other benefit) for the purpose of avoiding hardship.

Thus your 1996–97 assessment is based on the rents, etc to which you are entitled in the year to 5 April 1997 less your allowable Schedule A deductions for that year.

Prior to 1996–97, Schedule A income tax was payable on 1 January in the tax year. Thus your 1994–95 demand was payable on 1 January 1995. Since your income less expenses for that year would not have been known until after 5 April 1995 you were first assessed on the basis of the previous year (ie, 1993–94). When your rents, etc and expenses were computed for the year 1994–95 and agreed with the Revenue, the assessment was adjusted and the required payment or refund made.

For 1996–97 and subsequent years of assessment, the new self-assessment rules apply. Payments on account are required on 31 January in the year of assessment and the following 31 July, with any balance being due on the next 31 January. However, for 1996–97 itself, only one payment on account was normally required, on 31 January 1997. Each payment on account is generally based on half of the assessment for the previous year.

Income assessable under Schedule A is normally treated as investment income and prior to 6 April 1984 was subjected to the 15 per cent additional rate (5.6), if your investment income was sufficiently high. This still applies for certain trusts and the 1997–98 rate is 11 per cent (5.6).

7.4.1 Example: Assessment under Schedule A

Mr A bought an old house some years ago and divided it into three flats each of which he lets unfurnished. Taking the rents and expenses shown in the example, assuming that Mr A has already used his personal reliefs and lower rate tax band and that he is not liable for the higher rate of tax, his assessments are as follows:

Year ended 5 April:	*1997*		*1998*	
Rents receivable		£6,000		£6,500
Less:				
Expenses				
Business rates	£900		£1,000	
Water rates	120		130	
Garden upkeep	520		520	
Maintenance, light and heat of hall and stairs	330		350	
Exterior repairs and decorating	400		200	
Fire insurance of structure of building	220		220	
Accountancy	200		220	
Agents' rent collection charges	450		450	
		3,140		3,090
Net Schedule A assessments		£2,860		£3,410
Income tax payable		*1996–97*		*1997–98*
	(24%)	£686.40	(23%)	£784.30

Note: Income tax will be payable for 1996–97 as follows:

Provisionally on 1996–97 basis		
31 January 1998 $\frac{1}{2}$ × £686.40	£343.20	
31 July 1998 $\frac{1}{2}$ × £686.40	343.20	
		686.40
Balance on 31 January 1999		97.90
Total income tax liability for 1997–98		£784.30

7.5 Furnished lettings

Under the old rules, unless you elected for Schedule A to apply (7.2), your income from furnished lettings was normally taxed under Schedule D Case VI on the actual income less expenditure for the tax year.

However, from 6 April 1995, furnished lettings income is automatically assessed under Schedule A (7.1) except for corporation tax.

As well as expenses normally allowable for Schedule A purposes (7.2.2), you are also entitled to a deduction to cover depreciation on furniture and furnishings. This may be given to you as a deduction of the entire replacement cost from year to year.

More likely you will obtain a yearly deduction of 10 per cent of your rents less any rates, etc and service costs which you pay. Thus, if your annual rents are £1,000 and you pay £200 in council tax, you can deduct £80 yearly to cover the depreciation and replacement of furniture and furnishings.

If, under the terms of a letting, you provide services such as laundry, meals, domestic help, etc then you can charge the cost of these items against your taxable profit. If you provide such services, then your lettings income might possibly be treated as earned income. However, case law has made this less likely. Otherwise it would be unearned income, subject to special rules for holiday lettings (7.7).

As from 6 April 1992, the existing practice of including within the furnished lettings rules payments under licences was confirmed (F2A 1992 S58).

7.6 'Rent a room'
(F2A 1992 Sch 10)

If you let a room in your house, valuable new relief may be available to you for 1992–93 and subsequent years. The relief applies if you are an owner occupier, or a tenant and let furnished accommodation in your only or main home.

The relief covers gross rents of up to £4,250 for 1997–98 and subsequently (previously £3,250). If the gross rent is higher, you have the option of paying tax on the excess over £4,250, without any relief for expenses, or according to the normal furnished lettings rules (7.5). (Where any others share the rents, your exemption is limited to £2,125.)

For example, suppose that you let a room in your house and your gross rent for 1997–98 is £5,250, with allowable expenses of £1,250. If you are a basic rate tax payer, on the conventional basis, your income tax (ignoring any other allowances) is £920 (£5,250–£1,250 × 23%). However, if you elect for the 'alternative basis', you only pay (£5,250–£4,250) × 23 per cent = £230.

You will need to elect for the 'alternative' basis to apply within one year of the end of the tax year to which it applies. After that, it remains in force until you withdraw it. Note that whilst the election is in force, no capital allowances are available, losses from previous years are carried forward to subsequent ones and balancing charges are added to your gross rental income.

7.7 Holiday lettings

(TA 1988 Ss503–504 & FA 1995 Sch 6)

Furnished holiday letting businesses which satisfy certain requirements qualify for reliefs only normally available where the activity is a trade for tax purposes. The accommodation must be available for holiday letting for at least 140 days during the year and actually let for at least 70 days (no let to normally exceed 31 days). The income is treated as earned income; also capital gains tax roll-over relief (20.25) and retirement relief (20.29) apply. In general, although the income is normally assessed under Schedule D Case VI the letting activity is treated as a trade for the purposes of many tax provisions. These include payments by instalments, loss relief (11.22), capital allowances (11.8), personal pension contracts, etc.

The rules have been changed from 6 April 1995. Subject to the above, the holiday lettings income is taxable under Schedule A, except for corporation tax.

7.8 The taxation of lease premiums

(TA 1988 Ss34–39 & Sch 2; FA 1988 S75 & FA 1995 Sch 6)

If you obtain a premium in connection with the granting of a lease of not more than 50 years' duration on any property that you own, then you will be assessed to tax (under Schedule A) on part of such premium. The amount to be included in your Schedule A assessment is the premium, reduced by 1/50th of its amount for each complete period of 12 months (other than the first) comprised in the duration of the lease. The balance of the premium which is not charged under Schedule A normally attracts capital gains tax (20.1).

If you sell a lease rather than grant one you will normally be assessed to capital gains tax on any profit unless you are a dealer (7.10) or it is an 'artificial transaction' (7.11).

The following are also included with your taxable premiums:

(1) The value of any work that the tenant agreed to do to your premises to the extent that the present value of your property is enhanced.
(2) Any premiums paid to you in instalments. You include the aggregate of the instalments in the year that you grant the lease; but you can claim on grounds of hardship to pay the tax by instalments over a period not exceeding eight years, or ending with your last premium instalment if earlier.
(3) If you are granted a lease at a premium (£P) that is less than its market value (£M) and you then assign the lease at a profit, the amount of your profit is taxed under Schedule D Case VI to the extent that it does not exceed (£M – £P). From 6 April 1995, the charge is under Schedule A, unless corporation tax applies.

7.9 Woodlands

(TA 1988 S16 & FA 1988 S65 & Sch 6)

Prior to 6 April 1988, you were assessed to income tax under Schedule B in respect of woodlands if you occupied them with a view to obtaining a profit and managed them on a commercial basis. Subject to certain transitional provisions, income from woodlands has now been removed from the tax regime. Special treatment for inheritance tax (22.22) and capital gains tax (20.8.1) still applies.

7.10 Dealing in property

Normally when you sell a property which you acquired as an investment you will be liable to capital gains tax on any profit that you make (20.1). The maximum tax rate would then be 40 per cent.

If, however, you carry out a number of purchases and sales of land and/or buildings you are likely to be treated as dealing in property and you will be taxed accordingly. This means that your profits must be computed as if you were conducting a trade (11.1) and you will be taxed on your adjusted profits under Schedule D Case I. This income will be treated as being earned and you will be charged to income tax at the lower, basic and higher rate where applicable.

7.11 Artificial transactions in land

This is the heading of Section 776 of the 1988 Taxes Act. It may operate wherever you make a capital profit from selling land (or buildings) that you had purchased with a view to selling later at a profit. The Section also applies to sales of land indirectly held as trading stock and the sale of land (and buildings) that had been developed with the intention of selling them at a profit. However, it does not apply to trading profits from land already taxed as income.

Any capital profit arising in the above circumstances can be treated by the Revenue as being income falling under Schedule D Case VI on which you will be liable to pay income tax instead of capital gains tax. However, this has become less significant now that the top income tax and capital gains tax rates are both 40 per cent.

This Section does not apply to any purchase or sale by you of the house or flat in which you reside provided that it is your principal private residence (20.23).

If you believe that Section 776 might apply to any property sale that you have made or are planning, then you can apply for a clearance to the Inspector of Taxes to whom you submit your annual tax return. You should give the Inspector full written particulars of how the gain has arisen or how it will arise. He must then let you know within 30 days whether or not he is satisfied that your gain is outside the ambit of Section 776. If the Inspector does give you a clearance then provided your transaction proceeds exactly as you have described it to him, you will not be taxed under Section 776 in respect of your gain.

7.12 Agricultural land, etc
(TA 1988 S33)

Basically farmers are chargeable to income tax in the same way as persons who carry on a trade or business (11.1). Certain special rules apply, however (15.6).

If you own any sand or gravel quarries, any rents and royalties to which you are entitled will be payable to you under the deduction at the source of basic rate income tax at 23 per cent.

7.13 Land sold and leased back
(TA 1988 S780)

Special provisions may apply when you sell a lease with less than 50 years to run and take a fresh lease on the same premises. If you had been obtaining tax relief for your rent payments under the old lease and your new lease is for a term of less than 15 years, you will be charged to income tax on a proportion of the capital sum that you receive for your old lease.

The proportion is given by the formula $\frac{16-n}{15}$ where n is the term in years of your new lease. Thus if you have, say, a 40-year lease, which you sell for £15,000 and take back a ten-year lease you will be charged to income tax on $£15{,}000 \times \frac{16-10}{15} = £6{,}000$.

The balance of £15,000 – £6,000 = £9,000 will be treated as capital on which you may be liable to pay capital gains tax.

The income tax charge is raised under Schedule D Case VI unless the premises are used in your business, in which case your taxable trading profits are correspondingly increased.

The above rules are applicable to trusts and partnerships. They also apply to companies in which case the corporation tax charge (13.2, 13.2.1) may be adjusted.

There are certain rules for treating leases for longer periods than 15 years as being periods shorter than that time. This applies if you sell a lease and take a new one under which the rent for the earlier years of the lease is greater than that for the later years. For example, suppose you sell a 45-year lease for £30,000 and take back one for 20 years at £3,000 annual rent for the first ten years and £1,000 per annum for the remainder. Your new lease will then be treated as being for ten years and you will be charged to income tax on

$$£30{,}000 \times \frac{16-10}{15} = £12{,}000.$$

7.14 Landfill tax

(FA 1996 Ss39–71 & Sch 4)

A tax on waste disposals in and on landfill sites in the UK was introduced on 1 October 1996. Details are included in the 1996 Finance Act and these are supplemented by legislation in the summer of 1996.

There are to be two rates of tax. Inactive waste (which does not decay, pollute groundwater or contaminate land) will be taxed at £2 per tonne, with £7 per tonne applying otherwise. HM Customs & Excise administer landfill tax and the operators of relevant sites should have notified their liability to be registered by 31 August 1996.

8 Income from dividends and interest

8.1 How dividends are taxed

(TA 1988 S20 & FA 1993 S77)

Any dividend paid to you by a United Kingdom company does not have tax deducted. The amount paid to you carries with it a tax credit of currently 20/80ths (13.6). Prior to 6 April 1993, the tax credit was 25/75ths. These amounts respectively correspond to 20 and 25 per cent of the grossed up dividends. Special rules may apply to any shareholders who live abroad (19.1.5).

United Kingdom companies in turn pay to the Revenue advance corporation tax (ACT) of normally 1/4th of the dividends paid (13.6). Prior to 6 April 1994 the ACT rate was 9/31sts and before 6 April 1993 it was 25/75ths. The following are examples of payments by companies to their shareholders (distributions) that are treated in this way:

(1) Dividends on ordinary shares.
(2) Dividends on shares with special rights such as preference and deferred shares.
(3) Capital distributions made in cash, such as dividends, paid out of the capital profits of a company.
(4) Scrip dividend options (8.9).

The gross amounts of your dividends including tax credits (and taxed interest) receivable in the tax year are included with your investment income for total income purposes (5.2).

8.1.1 Special rules after 5 April 1993

(FA 1993 S77)

With the reduction of the tax credit on dividends from 25 to 20 per cent, if you are not liable to tax, your repayment is reduced. Thus if you receive a dividend of £60, instead of reclaiming £20 (£60 × 25/75) before 6 April 1993, you can only reclaim £15 (£60 × 20/80).

If your top rate is 20 per cent, then so far as your dividends fall within this, there is no more tax to pay or be reclaimed. Previously your 25 per cent tax credit would have exceeded the 20 per cent lower rate and a repayment was available.

Where your dividends, taken to be the top slice of your income, fall within your basic rate (23 per cent) band, although the tax credit is only 20 per cent, you pay no more tax. To achieve this effect, the income tax rate on your dividends is taken to be 20 per cent. Any dividends in the higher rate band (40 per cent) are fully taxed, subject to a 20 per cent tax credit, compared with the basic rate previously.

The reduction in the tax credit adversely affects charities (15.2.1), for which transitional relief applies for four years. The rate falls by 1 per cent each year. The tax credits reclaimable by pension funds will be less and the position of trusts is also affected (21.5).

8.1.2 Example: Income tax on dividends

Mr A has a taxable income for 1997–98 of £27,500 after allowances. This comprises dividends of £4,000 together with tax credits of £1,000 and £22,500 salary.

Mr A will be liable to tax as follows for 1997–98:

Salary	£4,100	at 20%	£820
	18,400*	at 23%	4,232
Dividends	3,600*	at 20%	720
	1,400	at 40%	560
			6,332
Less: Tax credits			1,000
Net tax payable			£5,332

* Basic rate band £22,000

8.1.3 Dividends, etc and your return

You must enter the amounts of your dividends in your income tax return (16.2). You show, in the separate section provided, details of your dividends from each of your shareholdings with a full description of each holding, as well as the actual payments and relevant tax credits. If there is no room on the form, you should prepare a separate list and submit it with your return.

As well as dividends, etc from companies, you must include in your return the gross amounts of any payments due to you for taxed interest on government securities, trust income, and the income proportion of annuities, etc. All of these will have been taxed by deduction at the source before you receive them. Also include in this section any loan interest that has been taxed before you receive it and all unit trust dividends including those converted into new units instead of being paid direct to you.

8.1.4 Income tax deduction vouchers

Dividend vouchers show the actual dividend payment made to you together with the tax credit. The vouchers certify that advance corporation tax of an amount equal to the tax credit will be accounted for to the Collector of Taxes. They may be sent to you even though the dividends are credited to your bank account (F2A 1992 S32).

Different certificates are provided for interest payments under deduction of income tax. These show the gross interest and the tax which is certified to have been deducted on the payment of the net interest to you. In the case of income distributions from trusts, tax deduction certificates are provided by the trustees (form R185E). All of these tax deduction certificates are accepted by the Revenue in connection with income tax repayment claims (16.7).

8.1.5 Dividends from overseas companies

Any dividends that you receive from overseas companies are normally net of both overseas tax deducted at source and United Kingdom income tax at 20 per cent. Prior to 6 April 1993, UK income tax was deducted at the basic rate (25 per cent).

The United Kingdom income tax is sometimes at a lower rate than 20 per cent. This is because you have been given some measure of relief from double taxation by the paying agents and collecting agents who are concerned with transmitting to you your overseas dividends. (For a fuller treatment of double tax relief see 18.6.)

You should enter on your tax return the gross amounts of your overseas dividends and also show the amounts of foreign and UK tax deducted at source.

The gross amounts of your overseas dividends are included in your total income (5.2) but you may get some double tax relief in respect of the overseas taxes against your tax liability.

8.1.6 Authorised unit trusts
(FA 1994 Ss111 & 113 & FA 1996 Sch 5)

Dividends which you receive from an authorised unit trust carry a tax credit of currently 1/4th. As with other dividends, if you are a basic rate tax payer you pay no further tax. (Previously the trust paid a special corporation tax rate of 25 per cent, but from 1 April 1996, this has become 20 per cent.)

For distribution periods beginning after 31 March 1994, special interest distributions may be made. These were originally net of income tax at the basic rate (25 per cent) for which you obtained a tax credit. The tax deduction and credit from 6 April 1996 is 20 per cent. The trust obtains relief for the interest payments against its corporation tax on its interest income.

The tax treatment of foreign investors in authorised unit trusts has improved. Payments to them from certain underlying income, such as from Eurobonds, is now free of UK tax. Otherwise relief is often available under the interest article of the relevant UK tax treaty.

8.2 Interest paid on government securities, etc
(TA 1988 Ss17 & 44–52 & FA 1996 Ss73 & 79 & Schs 6 & 7)

Prior to 1996–97, the normal basis of charge to income tax was by deduction at source under Schedule C. This applied to interest payable on certain ‘gilt edged securities’ of the United Kingdom and overseas governments where the interest was paid here. However, from 1996–97, Schedule C has been abolished. (For companies, this applies for accounting periods ending after 31 March 1996.) Instead, Schedule D Case III applies (8.4). From 6 April 1996 normally income tax is deducted at the lower rate (20 per cent). Previously, basic rate income tax was deducted.

The tax is assessed on the Bank of England or other paying authority concerned who deduct it from the interest paid to you resulting in your receiving only the net amount. The gross amounts, however, must be entered in your income tax return. No tax deduction is required where paying agents pay foreign dividends into recognised clearing systems.

Certain UK government securities may be held for you on the National Savings Stock Register or Trustee Savings Bank Register in which case the interest will be paid to you gross without any tax deduction. Interest is also paid gross on 3½ per cent War Loan and on holdings of UK government securities which produce less than £2.50 gross interest for you half-yearly. Income tax will then be assessed under Case III of Schedule D (8.4).

Provided that a claim is made to the Revenue on behalf of the individual concerned, the interest on certain specified United Kingdom government securities will be paid gross to any owner who is not ordinarily resident in this country (17.3.1).

8.2.1 Table: UK securities on which interest may be paid gross to non-residents

2½%	Treasury Loan, 2024*	8%	Treasury Loan, 2003
3½%	War Stock 1952 or after	8%	Treasury Loan, 2013
4⅛%	Treasury Loan, 2030*	8%	Treasury Loan, 2015
4⅜%	Treasury Loan, 2004*	8%	Treasury Loan, 2021
4⅝%	Treasury Loan, 1998*	8½%	Treasury Loan, 2000
5½%	Treasury Stock, 2008–12	8½%	Treasury Stock, 2005
6%	Treasury Loan, 1999	8½%	Treasury Loan, 2007
6¼%	Treasury Stock, 2010	8¾%	Treasury Loan, 1997
6¾%	Treasury Loan, 2004	8¾%	Treasury Loan, 2017
6¾%	Treasury Loan, 1995–98	9%	Conversion Stock, 2000
7%	Treasury Loan, 1997	9%	Treasury Loan, 2008
7%	Treasury Loan, 2001	9%	Conversion Stock, 2011
7¼%	Treasury Loan, 1998	9%	Treasury Loan, 2012
7½%	Treasury Loan, 2006	9½%	Treasury Loan, 1999
7¾%	Treasury Loan, 2006	9½%	Conversion Stock, 2001
7¾%	Treasury Loan, 2012–15	9¾%	Conversion Stock, 2003
8%	Treasury Stock, 2000	15½%	Treasury Loan, 1998
8%	Treasury Loan, 2002–06	Floating Rate	Treasury Stock 1999
*	Index Linked		

8.3 Bond washing — accrued income
(TA 1988 Ss710–728, FA 1991 Sch 12 & FA 1995 S77)

(1) Rules were introduced to prevent tax saving by selling *securities* with accrued interest and thereby receiving extra capital instead of

income. Previously, this would have at most only borne capital gains tax.

(2) The accrued income scheme covers transfers after 27 February 1986. In addition, anti-avoidance rules cover the previous year. A special new regime regarding companies is included in the 1996 Finance Act, mainly affecting corporation tax for accounting periods ending after 31 March 1996 (13.27).

(3) *Securities* excludes shares in a company but covers loan stocks, etc whether issued by the UK or other governments or companies. Thus 'Gilts' are included and 'Corporate Bonds' (20.19). National Savings Certificates and War Savings Certificates are excluded, as are certain securities redeemable at a premium. Certificates of Deposit are also excluded but profits on disposal are assessable under Case VI (15.1).

(4) If you transfer *securities* with accrued interest, so that the purchaser receives the next interest payment, you are taxed under Schedule D, Case VI (15.1) on a portion of that interest. The proportion is A/B. 'B' is the total days in the period for which the interest is paid and 'A' is the part of the period during which you held the *securities*. When the purchaser receives his first interest payment, his taxable amount is reduced by the proportion A/B.

(5) If you transfer *securities* but receive the next interest payment, your taxable amount is reduced by the proportion (B – A)/B. The purchaser is taxed on the same proportion, which actually corresponds to his ownership.

(6) The above rules do not apply if you trade in securities, nor if you are neither UK resident nor ordinarily resident (17.3.1). You are also excluded if the nominal value of your *securities* does not exceed £5,000 at any time in the year of assessment or previous year. A similar rule applies to the estates of deceased persons and trusts for the disabled.

(7) If you sell foreign securities but are not permitted to have the proceeds remitted to you, your tax charge is delayed until they can be sent.

(8) Transactions taxed under these rules are normally excluded from other anti-avoidance provisions.

(9) Special rules apply to the issue of securities in tranches after 18 March 1991. Accrued interest included in the issue price qualifies for relief and tax relief for the interest deemed to be paid by the issuer is restricted to the amount taxable in the hands of the subscriber.

(10) The accrued income scheme no longer normally applies to transfers under sale and repurchase agreements (FA 1995 S77 & FA 1997 S76).

(11) For deaths after 5 April 1996, the accrued income scheme no longer applies to the transfer of a person's securities to his or her personal representatives, nor normally to legatees.

8.4 Interest not taxed at source (Schedule D Case III)

(TA 1988 S18 & FA 1996 S79 & Sch 7)

Subject to the deduction of tax at source (8.6 and 8.7), tax is charged under Schedule D Case III on the following:

(1) Any interest whether receivable yearly or otherwise.
(2) Any annuity or other annual payment received without the deduction of tax.
(3) Discounts.
(4) Income from securities payable out of the public revenue unless already charged under Schedule C (8.2). From 1996–97 (accounting periods ending after 31 March 1996 for companies) all income previously assessed under Schedule C comes within Schedule D Case III.
(5) Small maintenance payments up to 5 April 1989 (6.8.4).
(6) Various kinds of investment income as specifically directed.
(7) The discount portion of the proceeds of 'deep discount securities' (8.8).

8.4.1 Table: Examples of Schedule D Case III income

Bank deposit interest generally up to 5 April 1985. (Composite rate rules then applied up to 5 April 1991 followed by tax deduction at source — 8.7.)
Discount on treasury bills.
Interest on $3\frac{1}{2}$% War Loan.
National or Trustee Savings Bank interest (FA 1997 S 77) apart from the £70 tax free portion from National Savings Bank Ordinary Deposits (2.6.1).

Income received gross on government securities (8.2):

(*a*) held on post office register.
(*b*) amount under £2.50 half-yearly.

Income from government securities in general following abolition of Schedule C (8.2).

Gross payment of share and loan interest by a registered industrial and provident society.

8.5 Basis of charge under Schedule D Case III

(TA 1988 S64 & FA 1994 S206 & Sch 20)

For years prior to 1996–97 you were normally assessed to income tax on your Case III income arising during the previous tax year. However, an actual basis of assessment applies from 1997–98, 1996–97 normally being based on half the income for the two years to 5 April 1997. Special rules must be followed for fresh income and sources that have come to an end (see below). No deductions are allowed in computing the assessable income.

A company is assessed to corporation tax on its actual Case III income for each of its accounting periods (13.6.2).

Your income is normally included when it is due to be paid to you whether or not it is actually paid. For example, if Case III interest is payable for each year ended 31 December in June and December, your assessment for 1996–97 would normally be based on the income for the year to 31 December 1996.

Your 1995–96 assessment would have been payable on 1 January 1996. However, under the new system, you pay on account on the basis of the previous year's assessment. This is normally in one sum on 31 January 1997 for 1996–97, and two instalments on 31 January and 31 July 1998 for 1997–98 and any balance is then payable on the next 31 January.

8.5.1 Special rules for fresh income

(TA 1988 S66)

If you acquire a new source of Case III income your assessments will be as follows:

(1) If your new source of income is acquired after 5 April 1994, you will be assessed on an actual basis for 1994–95 and all subsequent years.

(2) For the tax year when the income first arose, provided before 1994–95, you were assessed on the income actually arising in that year.

(3) Where the income first arose on 6 April in the preceding tax year your assessment for the second year was based on the income of the first tax year (subject to (5) below).

(4) Where the income first arose on any day other than 6 April in the preceding tax year your assessment for the second tax year is based on the income actually arising in that year.

(5) Your assessment for the third tax year is based on the income arising in the previous tax year (subject to (6) below).

(6) You have the right to elect that your first assessment to be made on the basis of the income for the previous tax year, should be adjusted to the actual income arising in the year of assessment. This would normally apply to the third year of assessment except in (2) above. The election should be made to your Inspector of Taxes within six years of the end of the year of assessment concerned.

(7) Where you elect for the year 1995–96 to be on actual (see above) the transitional basis for 1996–97 does not apply. Instead, 1996–97 is on actual.

8.5.2 Example: Fresh Schedule D Case III income (old system)

Mr A opened a National Savings Investment Account on 31 May 1990 when he deposited £1,000. He has varied the amounts in the account since that time but has not yet closed the account. He has obtained interest on his account as follows:

December	1990	£18
	1991	50
	1992	33
	1993	52
	1994	60

What are his Schedule D Case III assessments based on the above income?

Mr A – Assessments under Schedule D Case III

1990–91:	Actual income arising in year to 5 April 1991		£18
1991–92:	Actual income arising in year to 5 April 1992 (source not held at 6 April 1990)		£50
1992–93:	(*a*)	Normal basis – income arising in preceding tax year, ie year to 5 April 1992	£50
	(*b*)	Optional basis – Actual income in year to 5 April 1993	£33

(Mr A should elect for (*b*) and his 1992–93 assessment will be the lower amount of £33.)

1993–94:	Preceding year, ie, to 5 April 1993	£33
1994–95:	Preceding year	£52
1995–96:	Preceding year	£60

8.5.3 Special rules where source of income ceases
(TA 1988 S67 & FA 1994 Sch 20)

(1) Under the new system operating for new sources from 1994–95 and otherwise from 1998–99, cessation will not affect the assessment basis. Otherwise, the rules are as follows.

(2) Under the old system, if a source of Case III income ceases during a tax year you will be assessed for that year on the actual income arising from 6 April in that tax year until the closure or disposal of the source.

(3) Your assessment under Schedule D Case III for the tax year preceding that in which the source ceases will be adjusted if the actual income for that year is greater than the assessment already made.

(4) Any adjustment required for the preceding year (see (2)) will be separately assessed on you.

(5) Strictly speaking the cessation rules should be applied to each source but in practice the Revenue did not apply them to the closure of one bank deposit account if you had others that continue.

8.5.4 Example: Cessation of Schedule D Case III source (old system)

Mr C, who has held money in a National Savings Investment Account, closed this on 15 June 1997. He received interest as follows:

December 1994	£100
December 1995	£120
December 1996	£150
15 June 1997	£70

What were Mr C's Schedule D Case III assessments on his income?

Original Assessments

1995–96	Preceding year, ie, to 5 April 1995	£100
1996–97	Half of income for 2 years to 5 April 1997	£135
1997–98	Actual income from 6 April 1997 to 15 June 1997	£70

Note: For 1996–97 Mr C's assessment was first £135. However, on learning of the cessation, the Revenue would normally increase the total 1996–97 assessment to the actual interest received by raising an additional assessment of £150 – £135 = £15.

8.6 Building society interest
(TA 1988 Ss477A–482 & FA 1996 S73 & Sch 6)

Building society interest is normally paid to you less the deduction of 20 per cent income tax at source (25 per cent prior to 1996–97). The system is similar to that which applies for bank interest (8.7). If your income is sufficiently low (8.7) you can request that the interest is paid to you gross.

Any building society interest which you received prior to 6 April 1991 was free of basic rate tax (2.7). You were charged to higher rate tax on the grossed up equivalent as if you had suffered basic rate income tax at 25 per cent on your interest (5.2). This notional 25 per cent basic rate tax was, however, deducted from your tax bill. The reason that building societies were empowered to pay interest to you in this way was that they were assessed to a special composite tax rate on their own profits. By means of this arrangement the Revenue were able to make good the basic rate income tax not charged on the interest (15.7).

The composite rate arrangement for building societies and banks (8.7) was abolished as from 6 April 1991. Basic rate income tax is now deducted from the interest, subject to a self-certification arrangement, if you are not liable to tax (8.7).

As an exception, certain certificates of deposit for at least £50,000 issued by building societies after 5 April 1983 carry gross interest. Interest payable on 'qualifying time deposits' (broadly time deposits for at least £50,000 and for less than a year) is paid gross. Building societies are able to pay interest gross to non-resident individuals and quoted Eurobond holders; also to charities and registered Friendly Societies.

Certain changes were introduced in the 1991 Finance Act (15.7). These include provisions dealing with interest paid to investors during the transitional period up to 1986, tax being paid by the building societies at 1985–86 rates. Also, rules were introduced to deal with permanent interest bearing shares (PIBS). You are taxed as if they are 'debt' rather than 'equity'. Thus income tax is deducted from your interest. No capital gains tax arises but the bond washing and accrued income scheme (8.3) apply.

8.7 Bank interest

(TA 1988 Ss479–485 & FA 1996 S73 & Sch 6)

From 6 April 1991, bank deposit interest is normally paid subject to the deduction of income tax at source. From 6 April 1996, tax is deducted at 20 per cent (previously 25 per cent). In contrast to the previous composite rate scheme (next page), where appropriate, you are able to reclaim the tax. If your income is sufficiently large, higher rate tax will apply, any assessments being on an actual basis.

There are arrangements under which if you are not liable to tax you may receive the interest gross. You need to complete a certificate enabling each financial institution to pay you gross. You must certify that to the best of your knowledge, you do not expect to be liable to tax and the information which you have given in the form is correct. If you knowingly make a false declaration, you may be subject to penalties. This also applies where you deliberately fail to inform your bank or building society that you have become liable to tax.

Until 5 April 1991, the same composite rate as for building societies applied to interest paid by banks and certain other financial institutions. Foreign currency deposits and local authority deposits were also within the scheme. Individuals receiving interest were treated as having suffered basic rate tax, giving rise to a notional tax credit as with building society interest (above).

The institutions covered included recognised banks and licensed deposit takers, the National Giro Bank and Trustee Savings Bank but not National Savings Accounts. The scheme covered individual depositors if ordinarily resident (17.3.1) in the UK, but not companies, charities, pension funds, societies, clubs, associations, churches, etc.

If you are not ordinarily resident in the UK (17.3.1), you can be excluded from the tax deduction arrangements, so that deposit interest is paid to you gross. However, you need to supply the bank, etc with a declaration regarding your residence status and that you must tell them if this changed. Note also that under Extra Statutory Concession B13, if you are not resident in the UK and receive bank interest, etc without the deduction of income tax, in certain circumstances, the Inland Revenue will take no steps to pursue your liability to income tax.

Exclusions from the composite rate included debentures, loans by a deposit taker in the course of business, certain quoted loan stocks, also 'qualifying certificates of deposit' and 'qualifying time deposits', both of which needed to exceed £50,000 when issued and had a life of at least seven days. The income on such deposits is normally payable gross, even if now in 'paperless' form. Lloyd's premium trust funds and solicitors' and estate agents' undesignated client accounts were also excluded.

8.8 Deep discount and deep gain securities

(TA 1988 Sch 4, FA 1989 Sch 11, FA 1990 Sch 10 & FA 1996 S102 & Sch 13)

Special rules apply to deep discount securities issued after 13 March 1984. These are securities issued at a discount of more than half of one per cent for each year of their life or more than 15 per cent overall. Effectively the discount is treated as income accruing over the life of the security and when you dispose of your investment, you are normally taxed on the accruals under Schedule D Case III.

Exceptionally, you are taxed on the 'income element' arising on certain securities issued after 19 March 1985 from 'coupon stripping operations'. These are where a company acquires securities and issues its own related stocks — normally deep discounted with varying maturity dates.

The company issuing the security gets *annual* relief for the accruing discount. The rules do not apply to certain securities exchanged for others issued before that date, not of the deep discount type, provided the new redemption date and price do not exceed the original ones.

For disposals after 13 March 1989, the deep discount rules apply to a wider range of investments. Certain variable deep discount securities are now included, but not index-linked bonds satisfying various conditions. These conditions include a limit on capital profits on redemption equal to the rise in the retail price index. Also, the interest rate must be reasonable and commercial; payments being at least annual. The securities must be issued for a period of at least five years.

A security issued after 31 July 1990 is not a 'deep discount security' if under the terms of issue there is more than one date when the holder can require it to be redeemed. Where securities are issued in tranches after 18 March 1991, any accrued interest included in the issue price is excluded from the price used to compute the 'deep discount' or 'deep gain'.

'Deep gain securities' issued after 13 March 1989 are treated in a similar way to deep discount securities. A 'deep gain' means that the redemption price exceeds the issue price by more than 15 per cent or half of one per cent for each completed year.

A security is not to be classed as a 'deep gain security' solely because it may be redeemed early if the issuer fails to comply with the issue terms, is taken over or is unable to pay its debts. Also, 'qualifying convertible securities' are excluded. These are, in general, bonds issued from 9 June 1989 which are convertible into ordinary shares of the issuing company and give the investor an option to 'put' the bond back to the issuer. Bonds issued from 12 November 1991 are not caught simply through the potential operation of default or event risk clauses.

From 1996–97, one set of new rules broadly covers the above ground, relating to securities which have effectively been issued at a discount and are held by private investors. (Unstripped gilts are not covered.) In general, you are assessed under Schedule D Case III or IV (not capital gains tax) on any profits on the disposal or redemption of such securities.

8.9 Scrip dividend options

(TA 1988 Ss249–251)

Your taxable dividend income (8.1) includes any shares in UK resident companies (17.3.3) which you obtain by exercising an option to take a dividend in such a form. In this case, you are treated for tax purposes as if you had received the dividend in cash. If, however, the cash equivalent is substantially less than the market value of the shares, on the day when market dealings commence, the Revenue may substitute that market value for the cash value.

8.10 Personal Equity Plan

(TA 1988 S333, FA 1991 S70, FA 1993 S85 & FA 1995 S64)

A scheme to encourage the purchase of shares in UK incorporated companies commenced on 1 January 1987. It is called the Personal Equity Plan (PEP). Substantial changes apply from 6 April 1989, including changing the basis to the fiscal, rather than calendar year. From 6 April 1995, certain corporate bonds and preference shares are included.

(1) Provided you are aged over 18, resident and ordinarily resident in the UK (17.3.1) you are eligible.

(2) A maximum of £6,000 can be invested each year from 6 April 1990 (£500 each month if preferred). In addition, from 1 January 1992, you are able to invest £3,000 in a 'single-company PEP' each tax year starting with 1991–92. (Such a PEP is one which invests in the shares of only one company.)

(3) For tax relief, investments needed to be held for at least one complete calendar year from 1 January to 31 December. However, from 6 April 1989 there is no minimum holding period.
(4) The funds must be substantially invested in the ordinary shares of public companies quoted on a UK (or EC) stock exchange or dealt in on the Unlisted Securities Market. However, a unit trust and investment trust element is allowed. From 6 April 1992, the limit is £6,000 each tax year in qualifying unit and investment trusts (£3,000 previously). After 5 April 1993, this includes investment trusts investing exclusively in qualifying unit trusts.
(5) The unit or investment trusts themselves must invest at least 50 per cent in UK (or EC) equities, subject to certain relaxations. For example, unquoted shares and third market shares in UK companies may be included; also preference shares from 6 April 1995. (Before 6 April 1993, as an alternative, limited investment in non-qualifying investment trusts could be made.)
(6) From 1 January 1992, PEPs may invest in equities quoted on a recognised stock exchange of any EC member state. A similar extension applies to the 50 per cent rule for unit trusts. UK incorporated companies quoted in EC states and EC holding companies of trading groups are included after 5 April 1993.
(7) From 6 April 1995 the PEP scheme includes investment in specified corporate bonds and convertibles in UK non-financial quoted companies. Also included are preference shares in UK and EC quoted companies.
(8) A manager must look after your PEP investments but they will belong to you and you are able to choose which you buy.
(9) Re-investment of dividends and proceeds is allowed in excess of the limits.
(10) There is now no limit on the amount of cash that can be held in a PEP. However all interest on the cash was subject to tax up to 5 April 1991, but not thereafter, provided the cash is eventually invested in shares, etc.
(11) From 6 April 1989, you are allowed to buy shares through new issue offers and transfer all or part of your allocation into a PEP. This includes privatisation issues and also issues of shares in building societies converting to plc status. This must now be done within six weeks from the day the share allocation is announced and the value at the offer price goes towards your total PEP entitlement for the year.
(12) Subject to the above, re-invested dividends are free of income tax. (Also, tax can be recovered on dividends distributed.) Similarly re-invested capital profits are not subjected to capital gains tax.
(13) Subject to the overall £3,000 limit (see (2) above), employees are able to transfer shares acquired under employee share schemes

into 'single-company PEPs'. This applies to savings related share option schemes and profit sharing schemes (10.9.5). You must transfer the shares within six weeks of getting them from the scheme and no capital gains tax will be charged.

8.11 Tax exempt special savings accounts (TESSAs)

(FA 1990 S28 & FA 1995 Ss62–63)

(1) You are able to invest in one TESSA only and the accounts have been available from 1 January 1991.
(2) Only individuals aged at least 18 are eligible.
(3) Your TESSA may be with a bank or a building society.
(4) The account must run for a five year period and maximum total deposits of £9,000 are allowed. Of this, up to £3,000 may be invested in the first year and no more than £1,800 in subsequent years, up to the £9,000 maximum.
(5) No capital must be withdrawn before the five year period expires, otherwise all tax advantages are lost.
(6) Income may be withdrawn subject to a notional basic rate deduction (23 per cent). Thus if there is £400 of gross income in your TESSA for the year, you will be allowed to withdraw £308.
(7) When your TESSA matures, you can open a new one in accordance with the above rules. Alternatively, you have the following option.
(8) If you have held your TESSA for the full five year term, you can open up a new one within 6 months, with a maximum first-year deposit of the capital from your first TESSA. However, the accumulated income is not available for reinvestment in this way.

8.12 Venture Capital Trusts (VCTs)

(FA 1995 Ss70–73 & Schs 14–16, FA 1986 S161 & FA 1997 S75 & Sch 9)

A new form of highly tax efficient investment was introduced in 1995–96. The actual shares in VCTs must be quoted, but because they invest mainly in smaller non-quoted companies, there is a tangible degree of risk. However, the tax benefits are substantial.

(1) VCTs need Inland Revenue approval, which can be provisional for up to three years.
(2) The conditions for approval include the VCT's income being mainly from shares or securities, at least 70 per cent of its investment being in 'qualified holdings' of which at least 30 per cent is

in ordinary shares. The holding in any one company may not exceed 15 per cent of the VCT's investments, nor must it retain more than 15 per cent of its income from shares and securities. In general, VCTs may not provide majority funding for companies, ignoring all fixed rate preference shares and loans.

(3) 'Qualified holdings' are in unquoted companies which exist wholly for the purpose of carrying on one or more qualifying trades. This is broadly defined as for EIS purposes (11.26). From 27 November 1996, investment in the parent of a group may qualify where non-qualifying activities do not form a major part of the group's activities as a whole. Investments of no more than £1m in any one company count towards the 70 per cent requirement mentioned above, but not if its gross assets (or those of its group) broadly exceed £10m. If any of the companies become quoted after holdings are acquired by a VCT, their shares are treated as qualifying for a further five years.

(4) The following tax benefits are available to you provided you are at least 18 years of age, invest no more than £100,000 in VCTs each tax year (to 5 April) and hold your VCT shares for at least five years.

(5) You obtain 20 per cent relief on your investments in new VCT shares, which you deduct from your income tax liability.

(6) Any dividends which you receive from a VCT will be free of income tax.

(7) Your disposals of VCT shares will be free of capital gains tax.

(8) If you subscribe for new VCT shares, you will be able to defer paying tax on a corresponding amount of capital gains on any asset disposals after 5 April 1995. The gains must arise during the year before and the year after the VCT shares are issued. This reinvestment relief (maximum 40 per cent) is available in addition to the 20 per cent relief (5). However, the relief will in general be recalled if you dispose of your VCT shares without replacing them by others.

(9) If a VCT makes a further issue of shares, it will have up to three years in which to invest the money from each tranche in companies which qualify for the scheme.

9 Life assurance

9.1 Introduction

Earlier in this book, certain tax aspects of life assurance are touched on. This chapter deals with them in more detail, together with related subjects such as permanent health insurance and purchased life annuities.

Life assurance used to enjoy a highly favoured status for tax purposes. Since 1984, this has been reduced but some benefits still remain and these are examined below.

The Inland Revenue published a Consultative Document in November 1996 with proposals for changing some aspects of the way in which policy proceeds are taxed in the hands of the policyholder. These proposals are summarised later in the chapter. They are not law, and it is thought that if they do become law it will not be until 1999.

Remember, you should not enter into life assurance arrangements merely to save tax, but for the primary benefits they confer. However, the tax benefits certainly make them more attractive.

9.2 Types of life assurance

There are three main kinds of assurance policy which you can take out on your life:

(1) Term assurance: the sum assured is only payable if you die during the term of the policy.
(2) Whole of life: the sum assured is payable on your death at any time.
(3) Endowment: the amount assured is payable on your death within the term of the policy or otherwise at its end.

However, the tax treatment of your life assurance premiums and policy proceeds mainly depends upon whether the policies are 'qualifying' or 'non-qualifying'. (*Single premium bonds* are probably the most important type of non-qualifying policy.) But for both categories, whilst the policy is in force, the income and gains are the responsibility of the insurance company.

In recent years *critical illness policies* have become available. These pay the benefits when the life assured suffers from and survives a serious illness from a range which typically includes heart attack, cancer and stroke.

9.3 Qualifying policies
(TA 1988 Sch 15)

Qualifying policies have various tax advantages. For example, if you took out the policy before 14 March 1984, subject to the rules (3.2.6) tax relief would be available on the premiums.

If you realise any gains under your policy, you are not liable to basic rate tax. Furthermore, the proceeds are generally completely tax-free provided you have been paying the premiums for at least ten years (9.5). In the case of an endowment policy, this period is three-quarters of the policy term, if less.

The main rules which must be satisfied for a life policy to be treated as 'qualifying' are as follows:

(1) The premiums must be payable at annual or more frequent intervals. The total term must be at least ten years although term assurance policies may be shorter.
(2) The premiums payable in any 12 month period should not exceed twice those in any other 12 month period, nor for whole life policies one-eighth of the total premiums payable in the first ten years and in the case of an endowment policy the full term.
(3) For an endowment policy, the sum assured must represent at least 75 per cent of the total premiums for its term. However, this percentage becomes 2 per cent less for each year that your age at the start of the policy is more than 55.
(4) The sum assured under a whole of life policy must be at least 75 per cent of the total premiums assuming death occurs at 75. But for a term policy on your life, expiring before your 75th birthday, there are no restrictions on the sum assured.
(5) Benefits under a policy can include participating in profits and those arising through disability.

(6) Different rules may relate to certain categories of policy, such as industrial assurance, mortgage protection and family income.
(7) A policy may contain certain options. If so, they must all be considered together at the start of the policy to make sure that the policy remains a qualifying one no matter which options are exercised.
(8) Certain policies which are connected to each other are non-qualifying. This applies where one policy has to lapse if the other one does and both would be non-qualifying if taken together. Another instance is where either policy carries benefits which are beyond normal and reasonable expectations.

9.4 Life assurance relief
(TA 1988 Ss 266–274 & FA 1988 S29)

Tax relief is only available in respect of premiums which you pay on qualifying policies which were effected before 14 March 1984. The detailed rules are described earlier (3.2.6).

Subject to these rules, you deduct the relief from your premium payments. Since 6 April 1989, the relief rate has been 12.5 per cent of the eligible premiums, prior to which it was 15 per cent for eight years.

Where a qualifying policy was made paid-up or surrendered during its first four years, the life assurance premium relief could be clawed-back in whole or part. These rules are now outdated, but partial surrenders from policies effected after 26 March 1974 and before 14 March 1984 may give rise to a 'claw-back'.

The rules only apply if there is a surrender of part of the policy rights later than its fourth year and this has happened at least once previously. The claw-back is limited to relief on the premiums for the year of the surrender, etc and the insurance company will pay it over to the Revenue.

9.5 The taxation of life assurance policy proceeds
(TA 1988 Ss 539–552 & TCGA 1992 S210)

Whether your policy is qualifying or not, you will pay no basic rate income tax (23 per cent) on the proceeds. However, you may be liable to the excess of higher rate tax over the basic rate. This applies particularly for non-qualifying policies, as is described over the page.

The position with qualifying policies is that you will normally incur no income tax on the proceeds in any event, provided you pay premiums for a required period. This is at least ten years (or until death, if earlier). For an endowment policy, the required period is limited to three-quarters of the term of the policy.

In the normal course of events, you will have no capital gains tax liability on the proceeds of a life assurance policy (22.8.1). However, if you are not the original beneficial owner and purchased the policy for money or money's worth, the exemption does not apply.

Income tax on your policy proceeds may arise, if a *chargeable event* occurs. As mentioned earlier, no basic rate income tax is payable. However, if your income, together with the appropriate proportion of your policy gain is large enough, higher rate tax will arise (9.6) and the excess over the basic rate is payable.

Chargeable events in the case of a non-qualifying policy include its maturity or total surrender, where you assign it for money or money's worth and the death of the person whose life was assured. Also included are 'excesses' on partial surrenders. However, if you assign a policy to your husband or wife, this is not a chargeable event.

The above chargeable event rules are modified for qualifying policies. Maturity or death is only included where the policy had been made paid up within its first ten years (limited to three-quarters of its term for an endowment policy).

Similar modified rules apply for an assignment for money or money's worth, a surrender, making the policy paid up within the policy period, or an 'excess' on a partial surrender. These will only be chargeable events if they take place within that period (ten years, etc).

If you borrow money against a non-qualifying policy at an uncommercial rate of interest, this could be treated as a chargeable event if the policy dates from after 26 March 1974.

9.6 How the gains on chargeable events are computed and taxed

(TA 1988 S541)

(1) The gain on a chargeable event must be ascertained and in general the details will be supplied by the life assurance company. In any event, it is their duty to send a certificate to the Revenue giving

detailed information about your policy and the gain made (TA 1988 S552).

(2) In general, the gain is the investment profit on the policy, taking account of earlier capital benefits (other than any related to disability).

(3) Any benefit from death included in the proceeds is not treated as part of the taxable gain.

(4) No basic rate income tax, nor normally capital gains tax will be payable (9.5).

(5) 'Top slicing relief' is often available on your gain. This is described below (9.7) and effectively adjusts the tax taking account of the number of complete years for which you have held the policy.

(6) A gain is regarded as the top part of your income for tax purposes and higher rate income tax is calculated, taking account of any top slicing relief. However, since no basic rate income tax is payable, you only pay the excess.

(7) Normally it is the policyholder who will be liable for any tax on a gain. However, if a policy is held on trust, the settlor is charged, but can recover the tax from the trustees (TA 1988 Ss587 & 551).

(8) Since 1990–91, your spouse and yourself are taxed separately on your policy gains. Earlier all gains were assessed on the husband.

(9) The way in which gains are taxed is set to change from April 1996. The new rules have not yet been published but will be before then.

9.7 Top slicing relief
(TA 1988 S550)

This relief is available to individuals but not companies. The rules include the following:

(1) The tax on your gain is payable for the fiscal year when it arises, but you obtain spreading relief on the basis of the number of complete years (Y) for which you have held the policy.

(2) What you do is to divide your investment gain (G) by (Y). This gives the 'slice'.

(3) Next, calculate the tax (T) payable for the year on your other income plus the 'slice' (G ÷ Y).

(4) You then calculate the tax payable on your other income by itself and deduct it from (T). This gives the total tax on the 'slice' (G ÷ Y).

(5) The total tax on the 'slice' is then divided by the 'slice' to give the tax rate on it and the basic rate (23 per cent) is deducted, since this is not payable on your gain. The remaining percentage is applied to your gain (G) to give the tax payable.

(6) Certain categories of income and relief are ignored for the purposes of the above. Examples are lease premiums charged as rent (7.8.1), compensation for loss of office (10.12) and BES relief (11.25) (but apparently not EIS relief (11.26)).

9.8 Example: Top slicing

Mr A purchased a single premium bond for £15,000 in February 1992 and realises it in March 1998 for £27,000, his gain being £12,000. His other taxable income for 1997–98 is £25,100. The tax on the gain is as follows:

'Slice' = gain £12,000 ÷ 6 (complete years held)		£2,000
Other taxable income + 'slice'		£27,100
Tax rate on 'slice'		
£25,100–£26,100 at 23%	230	
£26,100–£27,100 at 40%	400	
Total tax on 'slice'	£630	
Average tax rate on 'slice' $\frac{630}{2000} \times 100\%$	31.5%	
Less: basic rate	23%	
Rate applicable to gain	8.5%	
The tax payable on the gain is thus 8.5% × £12,000 =		£1,020

9.9 Partial surrenders and excesses *(TA 1988 S546)*

If you make a partial surrender of a life policy (often by cashing in part of a single premium bond) it may give rise to tax, subject to the following rules:

(1) You have an allowance of 5 per cent for each 'policy year' (which starts with the day you took it out and each subsequent anniversary). This is calculated on the premium(s) (normally a single premium on a bond) and is set against your partial surrenders.
(2) Your total allowances are limited to 100 per cent of your premium(s).
(3) Unused allowances and partial surrenders are carried forward from previous years. When a partial surrender is made, you only pay tax on any excess.
(4) When your policy ends, you may have an overall gain on it which is less than the excesses on which you have previously paid tax. If so, you can obtain higher rate relief (the excess over basic rate) on the difference.
(5) When there is an excess in a policy year, you obtain top slicing relief (9.7). As usual, you pay tax for the fiscal year in which the policy year ends based on your highest rate, less the basic rate (23 per cent).
(6) For the first partial surrender or on final termination, the period which you use for the purposes of top slicing is the number of policy years since your policy started. Otherwise, you take the number of complete policy years since the last 'excess'.
(7) If any of your policies were issued before 14 March 1975, special rules apply. Broadly, withdrawals used to be fully taxed with no 5 per cent allowance each year. Such policies only obtain the benefit of this allowance for partial surrenders in policy years beginning after 13 March 1975.

9.10 Example: Partial surrenders — excesses

Mr A takes out a £20,000 single premium bond and withdraws £2,000 after each of policy years 3, 4, 5 and 7. He then surrenders the remainder for £20,000 after the end of policy year 8. His gains will be as follows:

Years	*Allowances Available*	*Cumulative Withdrawals*	*Gain*
	£	£	£
1	1,000 (5% × £20,000)	0	0
2	2,000	0	0
3	3,000	2,000	0
4	4,000	4,000	0
5	5,000	6,000	1,000
6	1,000	0	0
7	2,000	2,000	0
8		*surrender*	*see below*

When the bond is surrendered after eight policy years, Mr A will have a further gain of £7,000. This is the excess of the bond proceeds (£28,000) over the original cost (£20,000), less the earlier gain (£1,000).

The earlier gain of £1,000 will be top-sliced (9.7) over five years and the £7,000 gain over eight years. The excess of higher rate tax over the basic rate will then be charged as appropriate.

9.11 Inheritance tax

There are two aspects of inheritance tax in relation to life assurance. There is the incidence of the tax on life assurance policies, particularly the proceeds on death. There is also the important use that can be made of life policies in inheritance tax planning. These subjects are dealt with in Chapter 22 (22.27).

9.12 'Key man' policies

These are policies taken out by a company on the lives of its directors or executives. The following points should be noted:

(1) The normal purpose is to protect the company against the death of the 'key man', although in certain cases where the employee and company are unconnected the proceeds can be paid out free of inheritance tax to the next of kin.

(2) Provided the 'key man' is not 'connected' with the company and a term policy is used for not more than about five years, the premiums are allowable for tax but the company will be taxed on any proceeds.

(3) Where the 'key man' has a substantial holding of the company's shares so that he is 'connected' with it, the premiums will not be deductible. Any proceeds will normally only be taxable if there is a chargeable event (9.5).

(4) This treatment (in (3) above) is also likely where the policy has one or more of the following attributes: a term of more than about five years; is for a capital purpose; has a surrender value.

(5) The treatment of the proceeds of pre-14 March 1989 policies held by companies is broadly similar to those owned by individuals.

(6) Where a company-owned policy has been effected after 13 March 1989, it is treated as non-qualifying in any event, for the chargeable event provisions. Any chargeable gains are in general taxable on the company under Schedule D Case VI. The charge is limited where the policy is taken out to secure a company debt, and the

debt was incurred to buy land or construct property that is used in the trade.

9.13 Permanent health insurance

This is intended to provide you with an income, should illness or disability prevent you from working. Contracts frequently take the form of non-qualifying life assurance policies. For taxation purposes, disability benefit payments are not regarded as rights surrendered (9.5).

If your employers pay the premiums on your policy, they would normally obtain a tax allowance on the basis that it is part of your own taxable remuneration package. Where you pay the premiums, you will not usually obtain any tax relief.

Any permanent health benefits paid to you from personally owned policies will be tax free from 6 April 1996. This applies to policies already in force before that date. Previously only the first 12 months payments were tax free. The insurance company paying the benefit will not deduct any tax from the payments it makes to you.

9.14 Purchased life annuities
(TA 1988 Ss656–8)

When you buy an annuity from a life assurance company, the effect is the reverse of a life assurance policy. Instead of paying periodic premiums and getting back a lump sum, you pay a lump sum to receive an annuity periodically. This is based on your age when you purchase it. However, you may have a joint annuity together with your spouse and then the younger of your respective ages would be used.

Annuities are of great importance to pension arrangements (Chapter 14). When you retire, one or more annuities are often purchased for you by the pension fund(s) and special tax rules apply.

The normal tax rule for a purchased life annuity is that it is treated as comprising a non-taxable capital element and the rest is taxable income. The capital part is regarded as a return of the premium and is fixed from the start of the annuity. The life company will normally inform you of the split and deduct basic rate income tax from the income part of each payment.

For example, suppose you pay £10,000 for an annuity of £1,000 for the rest of your life. The company tell you that the capital part of each instalment is £400 and the income part is £600 from which they will deduct basic rate tax of £138. You will thus be paid £862. If you are a higher rate payer, you will pay further income tax of £600 × (40%–23%) = £102.

Because of the tax-free element, annuities are useful tax-planning tools. This is particularly true as you become older, since the rates improve. But remember that you will be parting permanently with the capital. Some annuities compensate for this by guaranteeing a minimum span, even if you should die meanwhile. One point to watch is that you will not be able to save tax through the independent taxation rules by assigning an annuity to your spouse (TA1988 S685 (4A)).

9.15 Guaranteed income bonds

Guaranteed income bonds normally provide you with a fixed income for a stated period. After that, your original investment is returned to you, or you might be able to take an annuity for life. These bonds resemble annuities but have various structures.

For example, there could be a combination of a temporary immediate annuity and a deferred lifetime one. Another common arrangement is to have a series of term or endowment life policies.

Considering an annuity combination, you would receive a temporary annuity for, say, ten years. The income element would be subject to income tax, but not the capital portion of each instalment. You would then either take an annuity for life under the deferred contract or receive your original outlay.

If you choose the money-back option, you will be charged basic rate income tax (and higher rate if your income is sufficiently high) on the excess of the proceeds over the original cost of your deferred contract. This applies for contracts effected from 26 March 1974. Profits on earlier contracts are not subject to the basic rate.

9.16 European insurance policies

If you take out a policy with a European insurance company, rules will ensure that you only pay the difference between the higher rate and the basic rate of tax (currently 16 per cent) provided tax of at least 20 per cent has been paid within the company's funds. This puts European policies on a broadly similar tax basis to UK policies.

9.17 Proposed policy proceeds taxation

In November 1996 the Inland Revenue published a Consultative Document outlining proposals to change the way in which life policies are taxed. At the time of writing it is not known if the proposals will become law, but if they do, it is thought it will be in 1998/99 at the very earliest, perhaps 1999/2000. The changes are intended to remove some anomalies in the way in which non-qualifying policies in particular are taxed, some of which currently operate in favour of the taxpayer and some of which operate in favour of the Revenue.

(1) *Changes to the qualifying rules*

For policies taken out after a Designated Day, yet to be announced, there will be new conditions which, if satisfied, will result in any gains being tax free. The proposed rules are less stringent than the current qualifying policy rules and could lead to more flexible policies being offered by insurance companies.

(2) *Policies that are non-qualifying or which do not meet the proposed new rules*

For policies issued by UK Life Companies, the proposal is that any gain will still only be liable to higher rate tax, not basic rate tax, and only then if the individual is a higher rate taxpayer after adding the gain to their income. It is proposed that top-slicing relief (which can help reduce any higher rate tax charge) will still be available, much as at present.

The major change is to the way in which partial withdrawals are to be taxed. The changes are intended to treat a withdrawal as part return of capital and part gain, the gain broadly reflecting the proportionate profit in the whole policy. For example, if the bond, with initial premium of £10,000, has grown in value to £15,000, and the owner takes a withdrawal of £1,500, one third of this – ie, £500 – will be treated as gain.

Depending on the amount taken and the investment performance of the bond, gains under the new rules could be greater or smaller than those calculated under the current system which permits 5% annual withdrawals.

(3) *Policies owned by trusts*

Under the current rules, where non-qualifying policies are held by trustees, any gain is normally added to the income of the settlor (the person who created the trust) in order to calculate whether there is any higher rate tax to pay. The proposals intend to change this rule for certain types of trust, such that the gain will be added to the income of the beneficiary of the trust, rather than the settlor.

In addition, under the current rules, there can be situations where the gain escapes tax altogether (typically, where the settlor is no longer alive). It is intended that this anomaly is removed.

(4) *Summary*

These proposed changes represent a significant shift from the current rules, some of which will result in less tax being paid by policyholders, some resulting in more tax. In view of the fact that it may be some years before these proposals are implemented, if at all, there is no need for existing owners of non-qualifying policies to take any particular action yet because of these proposals.

10 Income from employments and PAYE

Your income from employments or from any office that you hold is normally taxed under Schedule E. From 6 April 1989, a receipts basis broadly applies (10.13). Schedule E is divided into *three cases* as follows (TA 1988 S19):

10.1 Schedule E Case I

This applies if you are both resident and ordinarily resident (17.3.1) in the UK. Your income tax assessment under this case is usually based on the actual UK income during the tax year.

This case also applies to any work which you do wholly abroad (unless you work for a non-resident employer and are yourself not UK domiciled). If you are absent from this country for a continuous period of 365 days or more, you are not charged to UK tax on your overseas earnings during that period (18.5). (You are allowed to spend up to 1/6th of your time in the UK without losing this relief.) Tax is due on all earnings, even when the employment is not held at the time they are received. This also applies for Cases II and III (below).

10.2 Schedule E Case II

This applies if you are either not resident in the UK or are resident but not ordinarily resident here. Then you will normally be assessed to tax under this case on your earnings for duties performed here.

10.3 Schedule E Case III

This applies if you are UK resident and do work wholly abroad but remit salary here during the course of your overseas employment. The assessment is based on the actual amounts remitted to this country in the tax year (18.1) but if one of the other cases (see above) applies to the income, then Case III does not operate. This case now normally only applies to non-UK domiciled people.

10.4 The distinction between Schedule D Case I or II and Schedule E

This distinction is sometimes very fine—for instance in the case where you have a number of part-time employments and do some of the work at home. If you can show that you are in fact working on your own account and are self-employed (not an employee) then you will be assessed under Schedule D which normally results in your being able to deduct more of your expenses from your taxable income than if you were assessed under Schedule E. Divers and diving instructors are normally assessable under Schedule D (TA 1988 S314). The Inland Revenue are becoming increasingly insistent that entertainers and journalists should be assessed under Schedule E. When this happens, agents' fees will still be allowable as expenses (FA 1990 S77). These include fees to co-operative agencies (FA 1991 S69).

10.5 Employment outside the UK

If your UK employment involves you in work abroad this is normally treated as being derived from your employment in this country and is included in your taxable income. However, in respect of any work that you do abroad, special rules apply which may result in your paying less tax (18.3).

10.6 Amounts included in your income

Any amount that you derive from your office or employment is normally included in your taxable income. This applies to the value of any payments in kind as well as cash.

10.6.1 Typical items

Normal salary or wage.
Overtime pay.
Salary in lieu of notice (often tax free — see 10.12).
Holiday pay.
Sick pay from your employer, including statutory sick pay.

Sickness insurance benefits paid to you (all sickness benefits are taxable immediately except to the extent that you have paid for these yourself).
The value of luncheon vouchers in excess of 15 pence per day.
Cost-of-living allowance.
Christmas or other gifts in cash excluding personal gifts such as wedding presents.
Annual or occasional bonus.
Commission.
Director's fees.
Director's other remuneration.
Remuneration for any part-time employment.
Salary paid in advance.
Payment for entering into a contract of employment.
Tips from employer or from customers or clients of employer.
Settlement by employer of debts incurred by employee.
Payment by employer of employee's National Insurance contributions.
Value of goods supplied free of cost to employee by employer.
Value of shares or other assets received from employer for no charge, or amount by which their market value exceeds any payment made for them.
Fringe benefits (see below).
Unapproved pension scheme contributions.
Travelling allowances in excess of expenditure incurred for business use (10.6.4).
Share options (10.9.2).
Job release allowances capable of beginning earlier than a year before pensionable age.
Maternity pay.
Payments under *restrictive covenants* including (after 9 June 1988) where separate from the contract of employment (FA 1988 S73).

10.6.2 Fringe benefits

(TA 1988 Ss135–147, 153–168 & 191A & B, Schs 6–10 etc, FA 1995 Ss43–45 & 91–92, FA 1996 Ss106–110 & FA 1997 Ss62 & 63)

This is a wide term used to describe any tangible benefit which you obtain from your employment that is not actually included in your salary cheque. Fringe benefits are taxable according to the rules outlined below.

If you are an employee earning less than £8,500 each year, including the value of any benefits, then the taxation of your fringe benefits is on a comparatively favourable basis. If, however, you earn over £8,500 or are a director, then you are normally taxed more strictly on the actual value of the benefits obtained. If you fall into this latter class then your employers must submit to the Revenue a form P11D for you every year. This form covers your expenses and benefits (10.7).

You are not caught by the rules as being a *director*, if you own no more than 5 per cent of the company's shares and work full time for it. Any shares owned by relatives and associates count towards your 5 per cent. (In the case of charities, etc you do not need to work full time.) If you work for several companies which are connected, your earnings including benefits must be taken together for the purposes of the rules.

The taxation of certain fringe benefits is summarised in the following table according to whether or not you are a P11D employee (ie, a director or earning over £8,500).

10.6.3 Table: Fringe benefits — taxation 1997–98

	Details	*Non-P11D employee*	*P11D employee or director*
(1)	Free private use of motor car supplied by your employers. Car mileage allowance.	Tax free (provided some business use is made).	Taxable (10.6.5).
(2)	Provision of motor van.	Tax free (provided some business use).	Taxable (10.6.7).
(3)	Company house occupied rent free.	Taxed on annual value of benefit (ie, open market rental and expenses paid) unless you need to occupy house to do your job properly.	Taxed on annual value unless you must live there to perform your duties (10.6.13).
(4)	Board and lodging.	If you receive cash you are taxed on it. Otherwise tax free.	Taxed on cost to employer of board and lodging subject to a limit (10.6.13).
(5)	Working clothing, eg, overalls.	Tax free.	Tax free.
(6)	Suits and coats, etc.	Taxed on estimated second-hand value.	Taxed on full cost to employer.
(7)	Private sickness insurance cover.	Tax free.	Taxed on premiums paid by your employer (10.6.11).

(8)	Interest-free loan.	Tax free.	Taxable subject to certain exemptions (10.6.9) — to participator, etc of close company (13.17.3) — employee shareholdings (10.9.4).
(9)	Share options.	Taxable (10.9).	Taxable (10.9).
(10)	Employee's outings.	Tax free.	Normally tax free.
(11)	Luncheon vouchers.	Tax free up to 15p per day — excess taxable.	Tax free up to 15p per day — excess taxable.
(12)	Subsidised staff canteen.	Tax free.	Tax free provided facilities available to all staff.
(13)	Pension and death in service cover.	Normally tax-free (10.11).	Normally tax–free (10.11).
(14)	Cash vouchers.	Taxable (10.6.12).	Taxable (10.6.12).
(15)	Season tickets and credit cards.	Generally taxable (10.6.12).	Generally taxable (10.6.12).
(16)	Assets at employee's disposal.	Normally tax free.	Taxable (10.6.8).
(17)	Scholarships from employer for children of employee.	Normally tax free.	Taxable with some exceptions (10.6.14).
(18)	Long service awards of articles or employer company shares; after 20 years' service; maximum £20 for each year.	Tax free.	Tax free.
(19)	Security assets and services provided after 5 April 1989 (10.6.8).	Tax free.	Tax free.
(20)	Childcare.	Tax free.	Tax free subject to conditions (10.6.15).
(21)	Mobile telephones, if privately used.	Tax free.	Tax on £200 per year (10.6.16).
(22)	In-house sports and recreational facilities.	Tax free.	Tax free (10.6.17).

(23) Removal expenses and benefits.	Tax free up to limit (10.6.18).	Tax free up to limit (10.6.18).
(24) Employee liabilities and indemnity insurance.	Tax free (10.6.19).	Tax free (10.6.19).
(25) Work-related employer-funded training.	Tax free.	Tax free.

10.6.4 Travelling and entertainment allowances
(TA 1988 S198, FA 1988 Ss47–49 & 72, FA 1995 S93 & FA 1997 S62)

An allowance or advance that you derive from your employer to meet the costs of travelling, entertaining or other services you perform on his behalf is not taxable provided that you actually incur expenditure for these purposes. (Your employer is able to deduct the payments from his taxable profits. Entertaining expenses, however, are not normally deductible.) Should you incur expenditure of less than the full allowance or advance and are not required to pay back the unexpended portion to your employer, this excess must be included in your taxable income.

If you are a P11D employee (10.6.2) any allowance made to you by your employers for travelling, etc is normally included in your taxable income in full. If you incur travelling expenses, etc in the course of your employment you must make a claim to that effect and you will be allowed to deduct from your taxable income the amount of your expenses. If you are not a P11D employee (or director) any expense allowances or payments on your behalf are not normally included in your taxable income.

Payments made to you by your employer to cover your personal incidental expenses when you stay away from home overnight on business are now tax-free up to certain limits. The expenses covered include newspapers, personal telephone calls and laundry. The exemption runs from 6 April 1995 and the limits are £5 each night in the UK and £10 overseas.

You are not in general allowed any deduction for your travelling expenses between your home and your employer's place of business. Thus if your employer makes you any allowance for this expense it is wholly taxable in your hands. No tax is payable on travel facilities provided for *servicemen* and *servicewomen* going on and returning from *leave* (TA 1988 S197).

From 6 April 1998, site based employees will get relief for the cost of travelling to and from the site and for subsistence when staying there. Also, the basis of relief will be clarified from that date, regarding travel and subsistence between home and a temporary place of work. This involves relief for the business leg in triangular journeys (FA 1997 S62).

If you *travel abroad* in connection with your employer's business, the cost is allowable. If you also have a holiday abroad during the same trip you will be taxed on an appropriate proportion of the cost of your trip as a personal benefit. If your employers pay for your wife to accompany you (and she is not an employee herself) her own trip would normally be taxed as a personal benefit although some allowance could be obtained if, for example, she acted as your secretary during the trip or it was necessary for her to go for reasons of your health.

No benefit is assessed on you if your employer pays for the actual journeys of your family in visiting you, provided you *work abroad* for at least 60 continuous days. This applies to your wife (or husband) and any of your children who are under 18 on the outward journey. Also covered are journeys by your family in accompanying you at the beginning of your overseas period or by you back to the UK at the end. Two return trips for each person are covered by the rule, in any tax year (TA 1988 Ss193–5).

Any travel expenses paid by your employer covering journeys to and from the UK will be tax free where you are UK resident and working abroad.

Members of Parliament are allowed no deduction for expenditure incurred to cover staying away from home in London or the constituency. However, the Additional Costs Allowance paid to meet these expenses is not taxable (TA 1988 S200). From 1 January 1992, exemption extends to payments for travelling and related expenses when MPs visit EC institutions in Brussels, Luxembourg or Strasbourg on Parliamentary duties (FA 1993 S124).

Certain payments by employers to their employees for travel between work and home are tax free. Exemption is given by an Inland Revenue concession which covers working until at least 9 pm on no more than 60 occasions in a tax year. Furthermore, there must be no regular pattern. Subject to these points, the cost of a taxi or hired car will not give rise to tax on the employee.

Another concession concerns gifts from third parties (ie, not the employer). These are tax free in an employee's hands providing the cost is no more than £150 in the tax year from any one source. There is a similar exemption regarding entertainment provided by third parties. Credit tokens and non-cash vouchers are included. There is no limit but the person providing the benefit must not be the employer or anyone connected with him, nor must it be provided in recognition of particular services regarding the employment.

Employees are not taxed on annual staff parties such as for Christmas if the total expenditure per head is no more than £75.

10.6.5 Motor cars

(TA 1988 Ss157–159 & Sch 6 & FA 1995 Ss43 & 44)

The following rules apply to you if yours is a director's or *higher paid* employment (10.6.2):

(1) If your employment carries a car but your business use is 'insubstantial', you are assessed on 150 per cent of the scale benefit appropriate to your car (see (2) below). This similarly applies to second cars. 'Insubstantial' is defined as no more than 2,500 miles each year.

(2) If you make *more substantial* business use of your company car, you will be taxed on a benefit figure derived from a scale. The scale is to cover both the capital value and all running costs of your company car. If you are reimbursed for any money which you lay out, you are assessed on the amount and must make an expenses claim for business use. If your business mileage reaches 18,000 for a year your scale benefit is halved.

(3) Provided you do not have the use of a particular car but simply take one from a car pool and do not garage it at home overnight, you will not normally be assessed to any benefit; subject, however, to the further condition that any private use of the car is merely incidental to your business use thereof.

(4) The provision of petrol for a higher paid employee is taxed by applying an additional scale charge. This only applies if your employer bears any of the cost. If your scale benefit was halved because your business mileage reached 18,000 (see (2) above), your fuel benefit was also halved. However, this relief does not apply to the fuel benefit for 1993–94 and subsequent years. From 1994–95, the petrol scales are:

Engine size	*Scale charges*			
	1994–95	*1995–96*	*1996–97*	*1997–98*
0–1400cc	£640	£670	£710	£800
1401–2000cc	810	850	890	1,010
Over 2000cc	1,200	1,260	1,320	1,490

(5) For 1992–93 and 1993–94 the car scale and fuel benefits were as follows:

Cylinder capacity – original market value	*Scale benefits assessed* *Cars under 4 years old*		*Cars over 4 years old*		*Fuel Benefit (Petrol) (see (6) below)*	
	1992–93	*1993–94*	*1992–93*	*1993–94*	*1992–93*	*1993–94*
Up to £19,250						
1400cc or less	£2,140	£2,310	£1,460	£1,580	£500	£600
1401cc–2000cc	2,770	2,990	1,880	2,030	630	760
Over 2000cc	4,440	4,800	2,980	3,220	940	1,130
£19,251–£29,000	5,750	6,210	3,870	4,180	940*	1,130*
Over £29,000	9,300	10,040	6,170	6,660	940*	1,130*

* provided over 2,000cc

(6) From 6 April 1992, a more favourable car scale applies for diesel vehicles as follows:

	Scale charge					
Engine size	1992–93	1993–94	1994–95	1995–96	1996–97	1997–98
0–2000cc	£460	£550	£580	£605	£640	£740
2001cc +	590	710	750	780	820	940

(7) *Benefit basis from 6 April 1994*: From 6 April 1994, company car benefits are based on their list prices. A classic car over 15 years old is taxed on its market value provided this is over both £15,000 and list price. The price of your car is taken as its list price when first registered plus the price of any extras provided with the car. Also included is the cost of accessories added after 31 July 1993 if over £100 including delivery and fitting. However, from 1995–96 accessories designed solely for the disabled are not included.

You are taxed on 35 per cent of this, with discounts of one-third if you drive over 2,500 business miles in a year and two-thirds if more than 18,000. This adjusted figure is reduced by one-third, if the car is more than four years old at the end of the tax year. Where the list price plus accessories, etc exceeds £80,000, the benefit is calculated on this figure.

(8) From 6 April 1988, the provision of *car parking facilities* near to the place of work is not assessed on an employee as a benefit.

Furthermore, any open cases for earlier years are not being pursued by the Inland Revenue, although no repayment will be made of tax already paid.

(9) Special rules apply if you own your car but are paid a mileage allowance (10.6.6).

(10) From 6 April 1991, private use of car telephones is separately taxed based on a standard £200 annual assessable amount. However, this does not apply if you are required to make good to your employers the full cost of your private use, and do so. From 6 April 1993, this rule extends to vans and heavier commercial vehicles.

(11) From 5 July 1994, changes in motor vehicles provided for staff must be notified to the Revenue quarterly.

(12) If you would otherwise be within the car benefit scheme and you are offered an alternative to the car of say cash, the offer of an alternative will not, of itself, alter your tax. You will be taxed on what you actually get, car benefit or cash.

10.6.6 Car mileage allowances

(FA 1990 Ss23 & 87 & Sch 4)

(1) You are entitled to relief for travelling expenses concerning your employment. Mileage allowances paid to you where you use your own car for work are taxable to the extent that they exceed your allowable expenses, including capital allowances.

(2) To reduce the administrative work involved there is the *fixed profit car scheme* (FPCS). Under this, your taxable mileage 'profit' may be calculated using the excess of the mileage rate paid to you over the appropriate FPCS 'tax free' rate. These rates are as follows for 1995–96 and 1996–97:

	Cars up to 1000cc		*Cars 1001–1500cc*		*Cars 1501–2000cc*		*Cars over 2000cc*	
	97–98	*96–97*	*97–98*	*96–97*	*97–98*	*96–97*	*97–98*	*96–97*
Up to 4,000 miles	28p	27p	35p	34p	45p	43p	63p	61p
Over 4,000 miles	17p	16p	20p	19p	25p	23p	36p	33p

(3) Capital allowances are available to you if you use your car for work. The allowances are based on the proportion relating to business use. (However travelling to and from work is naturally excluded.) Wider relief is available from 1990–91 since, previously, it was necessary to show that you had no alternative but to use the car in performing your duties. Depreciation is included in the FPCS 'tax free' rates and so if that system applies, you receive no capital allowances.

(4) If you borrow money to buy a car to use for work, interest relief is available on a more general basis since 6 April 1990.
(5) Volunteer drivers receiving car mileage allowances are only taxed on a fraction of the full 'profit' element before 1995–96 (1992–93 one-quarter, 1993–94 one-half and 1994–95 three-quarters). However, this concession does not apply to taxi and mini-cab drivers who drive for the hospital car service, etc.

10.6.7 Vans, etc
(FA 1993 Ss73 & 74 & Sch 4)

From 6 April 1993, you will be taxed on any benefit that you obtain from having the use of a company van, using a standard amount of £500. This is reduced to £350 for vans which are at least four years old at the end of the tax year. The charge is apportioned if several employees share a van. However, you can elect to be taxed on £5 for each day that you have the use of a van.

No extra charge is made for any fuel provided by your employers. Furthermore, vans over 3.5 tonnes are usually outside the benefit charge, as in general are other commercial vehicles above that weight.

10.6.8 Use of assets
(TA 1988 S156 & FA 1989 Ss50–52)

If your employer places an asset at your disposal for your personal use (eg, a television set) your annual taxable benefit is 20 per cent of its market value when you first began to use it. (For assets placed at your disposal prior to 6 April 1980, the benefit is 10 per cent.) This rule does not apply to cars (see above) nor to land for which 'annual value' is used (S531) and only relates to those in director's or *higher paid* employment (10.6.2).

For assets provided after 5 April 1980 by your employer, a special rule applies if you subsequently become the owner. You will then have a taxable benefit of the excess over what you pay for the asset, of the original market value less the previous annual benefit assessments. This is increased to the excess of market value over price paid when you obtain the asset from your employers.

From 6 April 1989, employees (and self-employed people) who face a special threat to their *personal physical security* obtain special relief. However, the threat must arise directly out of their particular job or business. The relief extends to services and assets provided by the employer, such as alarm systems, security guards, bullet-resistant windows, etc. In appropriate circumstances, no benefit charge will be made.

10.6.9 Beneficial loan arrangements

(TA 1988 Ss160–161 & Sch 7, FA 1994 S88, FA 1995 S45 & FA 1996 S107)

(1) If you or a 'relative' have a loan by reason of your director's or *higher paid* employment at no interest or at a lower rate than the 'official' one then you will be taxed on the benefit of your interest saving compared with the official rate, subject to the following rules.

(2) The 'official rate' varies periodically. Recent rates are:

From 6 October 1991	$11\frac{1}{4}$%
From 6 March 1992	$10\frac{3}{4}$%
From 6 June 1992	$10\frac{1}{2}$%
From 6 November 1992	$9\frac{3}{4}$%
From 6 December 1992	9%
From 6 January 1993	$8\frac{1}{4}$%
From 6 March 1993	$7\frac{3}{4}$%
From 6 January 1994	$7\frac{1}{2}$%
From 6 November 1994	8%
From 6 October 1995	$7\frac{3}{4}$%
From 6 February 1996	$7\frac{1}{4}$%
From 6 June 1996	7%
From 6 November 1996	$6\frac{3}{4}$%

(3) 'Relative' means parent, grandparent, child, grandchild, etc, brother, sister or spouse of yourself or any of the relatives aforementioned.

(4) For 1994–95 and subsequent years, the benefits from loans totalling up to £5,000 are exempted. No charge to tax was made for 1991–92, 1992–93 or 1993–94 if the annual cash value of the benefit did not exceed £300.

(5) Before 6 April 1994, no charge to tax was made if tax relief would have been available for any interest paid on the loan. After 5 April 1991 if you were a higher rate tax payer, the difference between basic rate and higher rate tax was charged on a beneficial loan which you had connected with your house purchase.

(6) From 6 April 1994, you are taxed as if you had been given the equivalent in cash of a cheap or interest-free loan. Where appropriate you are then given tax relief as if you had paid interest on the loan at the 'official rate'.

(7) Up to 1994–95, any loan which replaced a beneficial loan was treated as the original one and was thus potentially taxable. From

1995–96, this no longer applies for arms-length replacement loans.

10.6.10 Director's PAYE
(TA 1988 S164)

Where a company accounts for PAYE (10.14) to the Inland Revenue from 6 April 1983 in respect of certain directors and this exceeds the amounts which they suffer, the excess is treated as their income. This does not apply to directors owning less than 5 per cent of the company's shares who work full time for it, nor to directors of charities, etc.

10.6.11 Medical insurance
(FA 1989 Ss54–57 & FA 1994 S83 & Sch 10)

From 1976–77 until 1981–82 all directors and employees were taxed on any medical insurance premiums borne by their employer. (This does not apply, however, to medical insurance covering overseas service.) However, from 1982–83 non-directors earning less than £8,500 annually are not taxed on such premiums.

For 1990–91 and subsequently, relief for private medical insurance is available for those aged 60 and over. The relief is given by deduction of basic rate tax at source. Higher rate relief was given by adjusting PAYE codings, etc.

From 6 April 1994, relief is limited to the basic rate (now 23 per cent). The relief no longer enters into the calculation of income for other tax purposes, such as age relief. Where a contract covers a married couple and one dies, the other can now claim relief for its remainder, even though the survivor is younger than 60.

10.6.12 Vouchers and credit tokens
(TA 1988 Ss141–144 & FA 1994 S89)

All employees (and directors) are normally taxed on the value of cash vouchers received as a result of their employment. That value is the money for which the vouchers are capable of being exchanged. The rules include cheque vouchers and credit tokens such as credit and charge cards. However, lower paid employees of transport undertakings are not taxed on transport vouchers provided under arrangements existing at 25 March 1982.

Rules in the 1994 Finance Act aim to ensure that vouchers and credit tokens are properly valued for tax purposes. This must be according to the expense to those paying for the vouchers, etc.

10.6.13 Living accommodation provided for employees

(TA 1988 Ss145 & 146 & FA 1996 S106)

In general, living accommodation provided to you because of your employment results in a taxable benefit. You are taxed on the open market rental value of the property, or the actual rent paid by your employer, if this is more. Amounts which you pay towards the cost are deducted.

You are exempted from the charge, however, if any of the following circumstances apply:

(1) You have to live in the accommodation in order to perform your duties properly.
(2) It is customary in your type of employment to have accommodation provided and it helps you to do your job better.
(3) Your employment involves you in a security risk and special accommodation is provided with a view to your safety.

The above exemption also covers rates paid for you, but does not apply in circumstances (1) and (2) if you are a director, unless you have broadly no more than a 5 per cent shareholding and work full time or work for a charity, etc.

If your employment is 'director's or *higher paid*' (10.6.2), you will still be assessed on payments by your employer for your heating, lighting, cleaning, repairs, maintenance and decoration, etc as well as on the value (20 per cent — 10.6.8) of domestic furniture and equipment provided. A limit applies, however, which is 10 per cent of your net emoluments from your job which is after deducting capital allowances, pension contributions and expenses claims, and excludes the expenditure for your benefit.

From 6 April 1984 an additional charge applies to houses costing the employer more than £75,000 or, if purchased more than six years previously, worth more than that figure when first occupied by the employee after 30 March 1983. The additional benefit is broadly based on the excess of the cost, etc over £75,000. This is subjected to the rate of interest in force in relation to beneficial loans (now $6\frac{3}{4}$ per cent) at the start of the year of assessment (10.6.9). (From 6 April 1996, the above special rules take precedence and only the balance is charged as basic Schedule E income, if that is in point.)

10.6.14 Scholarships
(TA 1988 S165)

You will be assessed on the value of any scholarships awarded by your employer to your children, provided you are a director or *higher paid* employee (10.6.2), subject to certain exceptions. However, the scholarships will remain tax free in the hands of your children.

The above did not normally apply to awards made before 15 March 1983, provided the first payment was before 6 April 1984. However, payments after 5 April 1989 were caught unless the student was still at the same full-time college, school, etc as at 15 March 1983 or when the first payment was made, if later. Another exception is where a scholarship comes from a fund or scheme from which at least 75 per cent by value goes to scholars otherwise than by reason of their parents' employment. From 6 April 1984, but not before, overseas employees who are the parents of scholars are not included in the 75 per cent.

10.6.15 Childcare
(TA 1988 S155A)

From 6 April 1990, subject to certain rules, childcare facilities provided by your employer will not give rise to any benefit charge on you. You must either be a parent or foster parent of the child and the care may not be provided on domestic premises. Other conditions include your employer running the nursery at your workplace or elsewhere; or jointly with other employers.

10.6.16 Mobile telephones
(FA 1991 S30)

You will be taxed on a standard amount of £200 yearly, from 6 April 1991, on each mobile phone provided by your employers. (This includes car phones — 10.6.5.) However, if you have no private use, or are required to make good the full cost of such use and do so, there is no tax charge.

There are rules for reducing the charge if the phone is only available to you for part of the year. This applies if you receive or part with the phone during the tax year, or cannot use it for at least 30 consecutive days.

10.6.17 Sporting and recreational facilities
(TA 1988 S197G)

From 6 April 1993, benefits in kind are not taxable in connection with workplace sports and recreational facilities provided by your employer for use by staff generally. The exemption covers in-house facilities and those provided by outside firms for the staff in general. However, the exemption does not extend to yachts, cars and aircraft, nor overnight stays.

10.6.18 Removal expenses and benefits
(TA 1988 Ss191A & B & Sch 11A)

If you start a new job or move with your present employer after 5 April 1993, statutory relief is available for relocation expenses and benefits. (Previously there was certain extra-statutory relief.) The relief covers such items as disposal and acquisition expenses, transporting belongings, travelling and subsistence and bridging loans. However, there is an overall limit of £8,000 and this also applies to freedom from benefit charge where your employer bears the costs. The £8,000 limit does not cover existing reliefs for expenses concerning work overseas (18.5.3).

If your employer provides you with a bridging loan, any unused part of your £8,000 expense allowance will result in reducing the beneficial loan charge (10.6.9). There is a formula that converts unused allowance into a number of days which reduces the period for which the charge is made.

10.6.19 Employee liabilities and indemnity insurance
(FA 1995 Ss91 & 92)

From 1995–96, if you incur expenditure on indemnity insurance or legal costs etc relating to your employment, you obtain tax relief. Similarly you are not taxed if your employer meets these costs. Relief extends six years after you leave the employment, for any years when you incur such expenses relating to your former employment.

10.6.20 PAYE Settlement Agreements
(FA 1996 S110)

Under 'annual voluntary settlements', employers may meet their employees' tax liabilities on a range of minor benefits in kind and expense payments. From 1996–97, these are known as 'PAYE settlement agreements' and new regulations apply.

10.6.21 Income from employment and your return

You must enter in your return your occupation and your employer's name and address. Show your total gross earnings before any deductions unless this is not required by the type of return that you are sent by the Revenue. If your duties are performed wholly abroad, this must be indicated.

Include separate details of any director's fees voted by each company before deductions. Also show any part-time or casual earnings. If your spouse has any income of this kind, it must be shown separately in his or her own return. (Prior to 6 April 1990, it was normally all included in the husband's return.)

You must give details of your benefits-in-kind including goods and vouchers received as well as living accommodation. Also show details of any share options granted by your employer (10.9), when these are exercised.

If you are a P11D employee (10.6.2) you must enter the total amount of any expenses payments made to you and the total cost to your employer of any benefits provided for you. If the Inspector has granted a dispensation to your employer, however, you may leave the relevant expenses payments out of your return. (A dispensation will be granted if the Inspector is satisfied that all of the expenses payments are covered by allowable expenses.)

Any leaving payments and compensation must be separately shown (10.12). A separate section in your return is provided for details of your expenses in employment (10.8) including fees or subscriptions to professional bodies and superannuation contributions.

10.7 Expense payments for directors and others (form P11D)

If you have a director's or higher paid employment (10.6.2), your employers must complete a form P11D for each tax year in respect of all benefits in kind and expense payments made to you or on your behalf.

For 1996–97, the following particulars must be entered by your employer on your form P11D regarding any expenses payments made and benefits, etc provided by him, unless covered by a dispensation. (Inland Revenue Pamphlet IR69 explains the procedure under which your employer can request a dispensation from the Inspector of Taxes regarding various business expenses such as scale rate payments for travelling and subsistence.) The amounts entered must include VAT even though this is recovered by the employer.

(1) Cars owned or hired by employer —

  (i) Make, model and date of registration.

(ii) Price of car and optional extras provided originally and those added later.
(iii) Period for which car available to you in year.
(iv) Payment by you towards running costs.
(v) Wages of any driver provided for you.
(vi) If car is used less than 2,500 miles or more than 18,000 miles in a year for business this must be indicated in boxes provided.
(vii) Appropriate car fuel scale and other related details.
(viii) Annual business mileage (for second car also).

(2) Cars owned by you —
(i) Allowances from employer towards your running expenses.
(ii) Contribution from employer towards purchase price, depreciation or hire.

(3) Entertainment — all payments made exclusively for entertaining including the amount of any round sum allowance, specific allowances, sums reimbursed and sums paid to third persons (entertaining disallowable to your employer must still be included).
(4) General round sum expense allowances not exclusively for entertaining.
(5) Travelling and subsistence — fares, hotels, meals, etc and payments from your employer for travel between your home and work from which no PAYE has been deducted — expenses regarding overseas employments.
(6) Subscriptions.
(7) Private medical and dental attention, treatment and insurance.
(8) Educational assistance for self or family including scholarships awarded to you or your family after 14 March 1983.
(9) Goods and services supplied free or below market value — equivalent cash benefit.
(10) Work done to your own home or other assets by your employer.
(11) Wages and upkeep of personal or domestic staff provided by your employer.
(12) Cost of vouchers and credit cards given to you by your employer.
(13) House, flat, etc provided by employer — address of property.
(14) The market value of any cars or other assets given to you by your employer (other than personal gifts outside the business).
(15) Home telephone — cost of rental — calls; also mobile telephone.
(16) Nursery places provided for your children.
(17) Other expenses and benefits including your own national insurance contributions (if paid by your employer), holidays, home telephone, etc payments towards cost of your own car.

(18) Beneficial loans — particulars of loans giving rise to benefit assessment including the maximum amount during the year (10.6.9).
(19) Should you have any share related benefits, a box is provided to be ticked.
(20) Vans available for private use (10.6.7) — enter the standard charge (£500 or £350 for older vans) and reduce this for shared vehicles etc.
(21) Tax paid on behalf of the employee.
(22) Qualifying and non-qualifying relocation expenses.

Optional working sheets are available regarding cars and fuel, vans and relocation expenses.

The above items are entered on your P11D and then your employer deducts the following:

(1) The amounts of any of the above expenses that you have repaid to your employer (unless already deducted from the items shown).
(2) Amounts included above from which tax has been deducted under PAYE.

Forms P11D must be sent to the Inland Revenue so as to arrive by 6 July 1997. Employees should receive copies by the same date.

It is also necessary for employers to complete a simple confirmation that all necessary forms P11D have been completed and returned to the Revenue.

10.8 Deductions you may claim
(TA 1988 Ss198–201 & 332)

You may claim any expenses which you have to incur wholly, exclusively and necessarily in performing the duties of your employment. These do not include:

(1) The cost of travel between home and work.
(2) The cost of business entertainment except where the expense is disallowed in computing your employer's tax assessment or is reasonable entertainment of an overseas trading customer.

If you are a director or a P11D employee (10.6.2) you should make a claim to the Revenue in respect of any allowable expenses that have been included by your employer in your form P11D. The claim should certify that the expenses covered were incurred 'wholly, exclusively and necessarily' in performing the duties of your employment. You will not then be taxed on payments for such expenses made by your employer whether made to you or third parties.

Any expenses that you personally incur in connection with your employment should be included on your return and these include:

Overalls, clothing and tools.
Travelling.
Business use of your own car including capital allowances (11.9.11).
Home telephone and other expenses (1.2.9).
Professional fees and subscriptions relating to your work.
Your own contributions to any approved superannuation (pension) scheme operated by your employers (10.12).
In certain employments (eg, entertainment industry) such expenses as hairdressing, make-up, clothes cleaning, etc.
Certain relocation expenses (10.6.18)

10.9 Share option and share incentive schemes

(TA 1988 Ss135–140, 162, 185–187 & Schs 9 & 10, FA 1988 Ss68 & 77–89 & FA 1996 Ss102–111 & Sch 15)

10.9.1 Unapproved share option schemes

As a director or an employee of a company, you may be granted an option to take up shares in the company. When you exercise your option, the notional 'gain' will be included in your Schedule E assessment for the tax year in which you exercise the option. (This does not apply if you exercise your option under an approved scheme — see below.) You thus pay income tax on the 'gain' (as earned income) calculated thus:

Market value of shares on day you exercise option (ie, when you take up the shares)		£A
Less: Price paid by you for the shares	£B	
Price paid by you for the option (if any)	C	D
Assessable 'gain'		£E

If you subsequently sell the shares themselves at a profit, subject to the share incentive scheme rules (10.9.3), this will be liable to capital gains tax (20.1) calculated as follows:

Net proceeds obtained on the sale of the shares		£F
Less: Price paid by you for the shares	£B	
Price paid by you for the option (if any)	C	
Gain already assessed under Schedule E	E	A
Capital gain		£G

10.9.2 Approved share option schemes
(TA 1988 S185 & Sch 9, FA 1995 S137 & FA 1996 S114)

Special rules apply to options granted after 5 April 1984 under an approved scheme, which can extend to groups. In particular, the gain will only be taxable when the shares are sold and capital gains tax (not income tax) will apply. On the grant of an option to an employee after 15 March 1993, the company's capital gain is the amount (if any) paid. Previously, the market value of the option was used. Important changes apply for options granted after 16 July 1995. However, if granted broadly before 17 July 1995, options continue to be within the old rules. The conditions for Inland Revenue approval include the following:

(1) Each participant may hold options over shares with a maximum value at the time of grant of £30,000. (Under the old rules, the limit applying to options granted before 17 July 1995 was £100,000 or four times the current or previous year's emoluments if greater.)
(2) The options may not now be granted at an exercise price which is 'manifestly' less than the market value of the shares at the date of the grant.
(3) You cannot exercise your option earlier than three years or later than ten years after its grant.
(4) You must be a full-time director or employee when the option is granted to you but may leave before its exercise. Part-timers may be included in schemes approved from May 1995.
(5) You can only exercise approved options once every three years.
(6) No participant has a 'material interest' (broadly 10 per cent of the shares) in the company or group if close (13.17).
(7) The options must be non-transferable and the shares, fully paid ordinary shares. These shares must form part of the capital of the company (G) granting the option, or its parent, or a consortium company owning at least 5 per cent of the ordinary shares of G.

(8) Shares subject to special restrictions may not be used. However, employees may now be required to sell their shares when their employment ends.

(9) Where a company has two classes of issued ordinary shares, most of the class of shares used in the scheme needed to be held by outsiders. However, a class of shares can now be used of which the majority is held by directors or employees and gives them control of the company.

(10) Redeemable shares cannot be used, except now in the case of registered worker co-operatives.

(11) Where a company with an approved share scheme is taken over by another company, it is now possible for the options to be exchanged for options over shares in that other company. Certain conditions must be satisfied, including having the replacement options governed by the rules of the original scheme.

(12) With retrospective effect back to 1984, where loans are obtained by employees to exercise their options, conditions regarding security and repayment are not regarded as 'restrictions'. Thus the shares are not debarred on this account.

10.9.3 Savings related share option schemes
(TA 1988 S185 & Sch 9 & FA 1996 S113)

Any notional or real gains from an approved savings related share option scheme will be free of income tax. However, some capital gains tax may be payable. Under such a scheme you are given an option to buy shares in the company which employs you or its controlling company. (You would not be eligible if you controlled more than 25 per cent of the shares and it is a close company — 13.17.)

You must save the money to buy the shares through a special SAYE contract set to produce the required cost of the shares on its maturity. (The proceeds from SAYE linked schemes set up under earlier legislation may also be used.) SAYE contracts may now be arranged by banks, as well as building societies and the Department for National Savings. However, the latter are withdrawing from the field and the Treasury are providing a model scheme for guidance.

Early exercise of the option is normally only allowed in special circumstances, such as death, disability, retirement or redundancy. Early exercise is also now allowed if the company or part of its business in which you work leaves the group operating the scheme.

A new rule allows you to exercise an option at the due time, even though you then work for a company which is only associated with the company granting the option, providing it is under its control.

The maximum permitted monthly contribution is £250 and no minimum monthly contribution below £5 can be stipulated. Also, the future purchase price of the shares must not be manifestly less than 80 per cent of the market value of the shares when the option is granted. You must normally exercise the option within six months of reaching pensionable age. However, this becomes an age between 60 and 75 specified for the scheme, where it is approved after 25 July 1991.

10.9.4 Share incentive schemes

(TA 1988 Ss138–139, FA 1988 Ss77–89 & F2A 1992 S37)

These are schemes under which you are allowed to purchase shares in the company where you work because of your employment or directorship and not simply because of a general offer to the public. If you obtain shares under certain incentive schemes, you are broadly assessed to income tax under Schedule E on the increase in the market value of your shares between their acquisition date and the earliest of the following:

(1) Seven years from when you bought the shares;
(2) the time when you cease to be a director or an employee of the company;
(3) the time when you sell the shares; and
(4) the time when your shares cease to be subject to any special restrictions.

The above rules apply to shares from incentive schemes acquired before 26 October 1987. Certain *profit sharing schemes* (10.9.6) were excluded provided various conditions were satisfied.

Special rules operate regarding acquisitions of shares or interests in shares after 25 October 1987. Broadly, the previous rules apply in essence with some changes. However, those not charged under Schedule E Case I in respect of the employment are excluded. Also excluded are acquisitions arising from public offers.

Income tax may be chargeable in certain circumstances, such as the removal or variation of restrictions over the shares; or the creation or variation of rights in the shares owned or other shares in the company. However, this does not apply if the company is employee-controlled because of holdings of shares of the same class, nor if it is a subsidiary (but not a 'dependent subsidiary' — see below); nor if a majority of the shares of the same class are held other than by directors and employees, associated companies, etc. The tax is levied on the value increase resulting from the removal of restrictions, etc.

Special benefits, such as a capital distribution, or the sale of rights in a rights issue may be taxable. However, from 12 November 1991, unless the company is a 'dependent subsidiary' wider exemption applies. Broadly, employee shareholders are not taxed on their special benefits where they are available to at least 90 per cent of shareholders and a majority of the shares are held by non-employees.

A 'dependent subsidiary' is one whose business is mainly carried on with group members. Furthermore, any increase in the value of the company during its accounts period must be limited to 5 per cent. The directors must give the Inland Revenue a certificate within two years of the end of the accounts period. You are liable on shares in a 'dependent subsidiary' in the same way as other shares (see above).

10.9.5 Employee shareholdings
(TA 1988 S162 & FA 1988 S68)

Special rules apply if you are a director or *higher paid* employee (10.6.2) and you acquire shares at an undervalue by reason of your employment. The shares need not be in the company which employs you.

You are treated as obtaining shares at an undervalue if you pay less than the market value of fully paid shares of the same class at that time. This applies whether or not you are under any obligation to pay more at a future time. You are taxed on the shortfall of what you pay for the shares compared with market value when you bought them. This shortfall is treated as an interest free loan (10.6.9) and you are treated as if your taxable earnings were increased by the benefit of such a loan. This continues until the shortfall is ended or the shares are sold, even if you cease your employment.

If you obtain shares through a priority allocation to the employees of your company, when it offers shares to the public, special rules apply. You will not be assessed on any benefit provided no more than 10 per cent of the offer goes to employees, all entitlements are on similar terms and the arrangement is not exclusively for directors or highly paid employees. In the case of a fixed price issue, the employees must subscribe at that price whilst for a tender issue, the lowest price successfully tendered applies.

Certain relaxations apply from 11 October 1988. For example, relief is not completely withdrawn if the price is too low; it simply does not apply to the benefit represented by the difference in price. Also, if there are several offers to the public of shares of the same class, a 10 per cent overall limit applies but up to 40 per cent of the shares comprised in one offer may go to employees. Furthermore, from August 1990, different directors or employees can obtain a different mix of shares offered to the public at the same time, provided the aggregate benefit is similar. The exemption was further extended from 16 January 1991 to cover a public offer comprising a package of shares in more than one company and also 'special benefits' such as bonus shares.

10.9.6 Profit sharing schemes

(TA 1988 Ss186–187 & Sch 9, FA 1994 Ss100 & 101 & FA 1996 Ss116–118)

Tax relief is available for employees participating in a company share scheme which has been approved by the Revenue. Under such a scheme, trustees are allowed to acquire shares in the company to the value of up to £3,000 or 10 per cent of salary, subject to a ceiling of £8,000. For this purpose you take your salary for the current or previous year, whichever is the higher. If the trustees receive qualifying corporate bonds from May 1994, as the result of a takeover or reconstruction, they can keep these. Alternatively they can distribute them in due course to the participants.

A participant must agree to his shares remaining with the trustees for at least two years unless he dies, becomes redundant or reaches normal retirement age. However, for schemes approved after 25 July 1991 an age must be specified between 60 and 75 for all members. For schemes approved earlier, whose rules are changed appropriately, men who become chargeable to income tax after reaching retirement age on shares allocated to them, will not be chargeable on more than for women of the same age. This applies from 30 November 1993.

The scheme must be open fairly to all employees within the company or group with five years' service or more. The employers may allow those with shorter service to join, however. Any dividends on the shares are paid over to the participants.

When the trustees sell any of a participant's shares after two years, a percentage will be charged to income tax. (Broadly from May 1996, shares held for at least 3 years give rise to no income tax charge.) The percentage is calculated on the original value (less any capital receipts already charged to income tax as below), or the proceeds of the shares if less, as follows:

Period held — years	*% taxable post 7.85*	*% taxable post 4.96*
2–3	100	£100
4–5	75	Nil
5 or more	Nil	Nil

The appropriate percentage (see previous page) of capital receipts less an allowance is charged to income tax. The allowance is £20 for each year until disposal plus £20 in addition, with a maximum of £100 (£60 from 1997–98). There is a special 50 per cent abatement of the charge for employees leaving due to injury, disability, redundancy or reaching pensionable age.

10.9.7 Setting-up costs of employee share schemes *(TA1988 S84A)*

From 1 April 1991, the costs of setting up various types of employee share schemes are allowable for tax purposes. These include all-employee profit sharing schemes (10.9.6), all-employee savings-related share option schemes (10.9.3) and discretionary share option schemes (10.9.2). If Revenue approval is obtained more than 9 months after the end of the period of account when the expenditure was incurred, allowance is given for the period when approval is given.

10.10 Employee Share Ownership Trusts (ESOTs) *(TA 1988 S85A, FA 1989 Ss67–74 & Sch 5, TCGA 1992 Ss227–235 & FA 1996 Ss119 & 120)*

Tax relief for ESOTs applies to contributions made to qualifying trusts from 27 July 1989. The main features are:

(1) ESOTs may borrow to acquire their shares rather than relying on funds provided by the employer company.
(2) ESOTs may provide a market in unquoted shares and may distribute larger amounts of shares than under Profit Sharing Schemes (10.9.6).
(3) All employees of the company and its subsidiaries, who work 20 or more hours weekly and have been employed for at least five years must be beneficiaries of the ESOT.
(4) Beneficiaries may also include ex-employees and ex-directors within 18 months of leaving; and employees and directors who work at least 20 hours weekly. (Part-timers may be included in trusts established from May 1995.) However, those with a 'material interest' in the company (broadly 5 per cent) must be excluded.
(5) Funds from the company must be used within nine months after the end of the company's accounting period in which they were received. The funds must be used in buying ordinary shares in the company, servicing and repaying borrowings, paying benefits and paying expenses.

(6) The shares must be distributed within seven years of their acquisition to all accepting beneficiaries on similar terms. This period is twenty years for ESOTs set up after April 1994.
(7) Payments to an ESOT by the company or a subsidiary are allowed for corporation tax. However, the trust itself is taxable on its income and capital gains. Also, employees receiving shares at less than market value will be liable to income tax.
(8) Capital gains tax roll-over relief (20.25) is available, subject to certain conditions, for disposals of your company shares to an ESOT. Replacement assets must be purchased within six months of the sale. (Broadly, your dwelling house and BES shares are not allowed as replacement assets qualifying for relief.) If the replacement assets are disposed of without other assets being acquired, the deferred gain will be brought into charge.
(9) From 1 April 1991, the costs of setting up an ESOT are an allowable deduction for tax purposes.
(10) Prior to 1 January 1992, a tax charge could arise from a share-for-share exchange. Subsequently, there is no tax charge provided the new holding stands in place of the old for capital gains tax purposes (20.18.6).
(11) Broadly from May 1996, it is possible to operate savings related share option schemes in conjunction with qualifying ESOTs.

10.11 Retirement pension schemes

(TA 1988 Ss590–617 & 630–655; FA 1989 Ss75–77 & Schs 6 & 7, FA 1993 S112, FA 1994 Ss103–110 & FA 1995 Ss58–60 & Sch 11)

Any national insurance contributions that you pay as an employee are not deductible from your taxable income. Your employer, however, deducts his share of such contributions from his taxable profits. On your retirement your state pension is taxable as earned income, on the basis of the actual amount for the tax year, and any widow's pension payable to your wife is also taxable in this way. There is an Earnings Related component in the State Scheme, out of which you may be contracted (14.2.1). 'Contracting-out' using an occupational scheme relieves you and your employer of the obligation to pay higher rate National Insurance contributions (25.2).

Any pension paid to you out of your employer's own staff superannuation scheme is taxable as earned income. The same applies to any retirement pension paid by your employer that has not been provided for under any scheme. Reference should be made to Chapter 14 for a fuller treatment of pensions.

Retirement schemes are either 'contributory' or 'non-contributory'. In the latter case the employer bears the entire cost and in the former case the employee makes his own regular contributions to the scheme. If you work for a big company it may run its own exempt approved pension scheme which will put aside funds to provide pensions for its employees. A separate pension trust is set up and investments are made on which generally no UK tax is payable either on income or capital gains. The employees' contributions (if any) are deductible from their taxable earnings, subject to certain limits and amounts paid by the company are deductible from its taxable profits. Furthermore no 'benefit in kind' assessments are made on the employees. To qualify for this taxation treatment Revenue approval must be obtained (14.3.2).

Instead of managing their own exempt approved pension scheme many employers arrange for it to be operated by an insurance company. In return for annual premiums paid to it based on the salaries of the employees covered, the insurance company provides retirement pensions and also sometimes lump sum payments in the event of the death in service of any employee. Subject to Revenue approval (see below) the company deducts the contributions that it pays from its taxable profits and the employees deduct their contributions (if any) from their taxable earnings.

From 1 July 1988, *personal pension schemes* (14.5) have been available for those not in staff superannuation schemes (or for the purposes of 'contracting-out'). Contributions may be paid by the employer or employee. From October 1987, 'free standing' AVC contracts operate (14.4).

If a new scheme is to obtain Revenue approval it must satisfy various conditions (14.3.2). Separate rules apply to personal pension schemes. For further details please refer to Chapter 14 (14.5 and 14.6).

10.12 Compensation for loss of office *(TA 1988 Ss148 & 188)*

If a 'golden handshake' payment is made to you on your retirement, resignation, redundancy or removal from that office, etc at least the first £30,000 will normally be tax free. (Prior to 6 April 1988 this figure was £25,000.) However, this exemption depends on the payments being not otherwise taxable.

From 1 November 1991, Inland Revenue practice has changed regarding *ex gratia* payments made on retirement or death. These may now be taxed under the rules relating to pension schemes (Chapter 14). However, Revenue (PSO) approval will be available if the normal retirement benefits scheme requirements are satisfied and the lump sum *ex gratia* payment is the only lump sum relevant benefit potentially payable from your employment. The tax treatment of *ex gratia* termination payments other than on retirement or death is generally unchanged and the excess (if any) over £30,000 will be taxed as your earned income. (Prior to 6 April 1988 certain additional reductions were made apart from the £25,000 exemption (10.12.1).)

The employer is usually able to deduct 'golden handshake' payments from his taxable profits unless for example they are abnormally high payments to controlling directors or are made in connection with a sale of the actual business or made just before its cessation.

If you have a service contract that provides for a lump sum payment to be made to you when you leave your employer this payment will not be tax free because it is treated as arising out of your employment. This point should be borne in mind when service contracts are drawn up.

Any payments received by a former employee in the following circumstances are normally tax free:

(1) *Ex gratia* payments on the death or permanent disability of the employee.
(2) Terminal grants to members of HM Forces.
(3) *Ex gratia* payments on the termination of a job where the employee worked abroad either:
   (*a*) for three-quarters of his entire term of service; or
   (*b*) for the whole of the last ten years; or
   (*c*) where the total service is more than 20 years, for half the total service period including any ten of the last 20 years.

10.12.1 Tax treatment — termination before 6 April 1988

Under the rules which applied for terminations after 5 April 1981 and before 6 April 1988, the first £25,000 which you received was exempt. For 1981–82 the balance was taxed at half your marginal rate on it. After 5 April 1982, the relief was restricted. The first £25,000 was still exempt, but only £25,000 attracted the 50 per cent relief and then tax on the next £25,000 was reduced by 25 per cent, the remainder being fully taxed.

For periods before 6 April 1981, the treatment of 'golden handshake' payments depended on whether they were '*ex gratia*' or compensation payments. Fuller details are given in the 1988–89 and earlier editions of this book.

10.12.2 Counselling services
(TA 1988 Ss589A & B)

From 16 March 1993, counselling services provided by your employer on your redundancy are tax free. (Previously, they would normally have counted towards the £30,000 exemption.) The services include advice on adjusting to job loss, writing CVs, interview skills, job searches and providing office equipment.

10.13 The assessment basis
(FA 1989 Ss36–45)

Up to 5 April 1989, many directors and certain others were assessed to income tax on their emoluments on what was known as the 'accounts basis'. This involved paying tax for a tax year based on your director's remuneration, etc, for the accounts year ending therein. Thus, if your remuneration for the year to 31 December 1987 was £25,000, this was assessed for 1987–1988.

From 6 April 1989, the earnings of *all* directors and employees are assessed for the year in which they are received and not for the year for which they were earned. (Certain pensions are to be assessed under Schedule E on an accruals basis.) However, transitional provisions deal with situations where income was either taxed twice or not at all. In general, the earnings were taken out of assessment for the year when earned and taxed only in the year received, provided relief is claimed.

Where the accounts basis had operated, income may have escaped assessment altogether. This applied to income for 1988–89 relating to that part of the year falling after the accounting date and before 6 April 1989. Where earnings for 1989–90 or later were received before 6 April 1989, these may have escaped assessment. However, such earnings were taxed as if received on 6 April 1989.

Where emoluments for an accounting period ending after 5 April 1989 are paid more than nine months after the end of that period, they must be added back in the employer's tax computations and only allowed as a deduction when paid. This applies where the remuneration relates to any period after 5 April 1989.

10.14 The PAYE system
(TA 1988 S203)

Most of the Schedule E income tax payable on earnings from employments in this country is collected under the 'pay as you earn' system (PAYE), which covers both basic rate and higher rate income tax. Your employer is responsible for administering the PAYE on your own wages and that of your fellow employees. From each wages payment that you receive, whether it be weekly or monthly, your employer must deduct the relevant income tax and National Insurance contributions, paying to you the net amount. (If income tax has been previously over-deducted by your employer or if you suddenly become entitled to higher relief you may be due to receive a repayment which your employer will make to you.)

10.14.1 Payment

Your employer has to pay over to the Collector of Taxes the total PAYE income tax deductions (less refunds) and National Insurance contributions in respect of the previous month. The time limit is by the nineteenth day of the following month. If payment is not made, it is now open to the Collector to send an estimated demand which must be paid within seven days unless:

(1) The correct PAYE is paid.
(2) The Collector is satisfied that nothing further is due.
(3) The Collector is invited to inspect the PAYE records.

For 1992–93 and subsequent years, interest is due on any amounts outstanding after the following 19 April (ie, 19 April 1993, etc).

After 5 April 1992, employers whose monthly payments of PAYE and national insurance contributions are less than £600 are allowed to pay quarterly. (The figure for 1994–95 was £450.) Payments are then made to the Inland Revenue for the quarters ending 5 July, 5 October, 5 January and 5 April, and each is due within 14 days.

10.14.2 Records

Prior to 6 April 1981, your employer was required to keep a separate tax deduction card for each of his employees (including directors but not partners). From 6 April 1981 he is allowed to use his own records which may be computerised. Otherwise he may use the official Deductions Working Sheet (form P11). This can be used for weekly or monthly paid employees. For a weekly paid person the following particulars are entered and calculated:

(1) National insurance contributions.
(2) Statutory sick pay and statutory maternity pay.
(3) Gross pay for the week.
(4) Cumulative pay for the tax year to date.
(5) Total 'free pay' to date (see below).
(6) Total taxable pay to date (3–4).
(7) Total tax due to date (see below).
(8) Tax to be paid or repaid for the week (see below).

(Similar details for each month are entered for monthly paid employees.) The total 'free pay' to date is obtained from 'Table A' in the tax tables provided by the Revenue. This table shows for each week the 'free pay' applicable to each code number (see below). If your total pay is less than your 'free pay' to date then you pay no more tax for that week and would normally get a refund.

From 6 April 1993, 'Tables A' are known as 'Pay Adjustment Tables' and also give the amounts to add to your pay where you have a K code (10.14.3).

The tax to be paid or repaid for the week (see (7) above) is calculated by subtracting the total tax due to date for the previous week from that for the current week (see (6) above). The total tax due to date is found each week from the tax deduction tables. These show the tax attributable to the relevant total taxable pay to date.

The tax deduction tables in use are designated tables LR, B, C and D. Table LR shows the amount of tax due at the lower rate of 20 per cent. Table B shows tax due at the basic rate. Table C shows for each week or month (see below) the amounts to be taxed at the higher rate.

If you have only one employment your tax is calculated from table B if your earnings are below the higher rates level, unless only the lower rate applies. Should your earnings make you liable for higher rate income tax, however, your PAYE tax payable is calculated from table C which is in fact supplementary to table B.

Where your earnings are substantial and you have more than one employment the Revenue will normally direct that tables B and C are used for your main employment. For your other employments, however, they might issue you with code D0. This means that tax at 40 per cent is applicable to those employments. The 'D' codings merely provide the Revenue with a very approximate method of taxing at source your salaries from employments other than your main one.

The Revenue provide monthly tax deduction tables for use where salary payments are made on a monthly basis. The Deductions Working Sheet has a column in which to enter the amount deductible for earnings-related National Insurance contributions, which are collected through the PAYE system.

10.14.3 Your code number

Your code number is calculated from your income tax allowances and reliefs. It is allocated to you by the Inspector of Taxes and takes into account all the reliefs to which you are entitled against which some of your other income may be set off. Account may also be taken of any Schedule E income tax underpaid or overpaid for the previous year.

Coding notices are only sent to cover changes. Otherwise the code for the previous year must be used. The notice itemises the various allowances and reliefs to which you are entitled (3.0.1). Any other necessary adjustments are also shown on your coding notice which shows at the bottom the adjusted balance of your allowances and also the code number which corresponds to that figure. The Inspector will probably obtain the details for your coding notice from your last income tax return.

In order to convert your total allowances and adjustments into your code number, you simply divide by ten and round down to the nearest whole number. Thus if your allowances, etc for 1997–98 total £4,045, your code number is 404. For administrative purposes, your code number will normally end in L, H, P, T or V depending on your main personal reliefs (single, married couple's, age, etc). There are also K codes (see below). When these reliefs increase instructions are issued by the Revenue to employers to augment codes ending in L, H, P, T or V accordingly. In these cases revised coding notices are not needed.

The above remarks normally apply to your coding in respect of your main employment. If you have other employments and the Revenue consider that your taxable earnings after deductions for the year 1997–98 will not exceed £26,100, you will be coded 'BR' in respect of each of your other employments. This means that table B (10.14.2) is applied to your total earnings from each employment except your main one. No deductions are normally made for your allowances, etc because these are included in your coding for your main employment. If, however, your earnings are likely to exceed £26,100 then the Inspector of Taxes is likely to allocate you with 'D' codings (10.14.2) in respect of your supplementary employments.

From 6 April 1993, a system of K codes operates. These cover car and other benefits etc, which increase your taxable pay. Another application is where your state retirement pension exceeds your personal allowances. It is hoped that this arrangement will facilitate the collection of tax on benefits. If you have a K code instead of a normal one, your employer simply adds the appropriate amount to your taxable pay rather than deducting it.

10.14.4 Employers' PAYE returns

At the end of each tax year your employer must complete a form P35 and send this to the Revenue. End of year returns P14 must be completed for each employee and sent with the P35. The P14s are completed from the Deductions Working Sheets (P11) or other records and include National Insurance number, date of birth, final tax code, total pay, tax and National Insurance contributions, as well as any Statutory Sick Pay and Statutory Maternity Pay. Also any forms P11D required for the year (10.7) should be sent to the Revenue.

The form P35 is a summary of the total tax due to be deducted for the tax year in respect of all of the employees. The earnings-related National Insurance contributions are also entered for each employee. The total Statutory Sick Pay and Statutory Maternity Pay details are also included. The details are obtained from the tax deduction cards. The total income tax due to be paid over for the year by the employer is then found by adding up all of the tax entries on the form P35 and from this is deducted the total of the actual payments made. A similar procedure is followed regarding the earnings-related National Insurance contributions except that the amount to be paid over also includes the employer's contributions.

The balances shown by the form P35 represent underpayments or overpayments of PAYE income tax and earnings-related contributions: if the employer has underpaid he should send a cheque with the form and if he has overpaid a repayment will subsequently be received.

There are time limits for submitting the forms which must be carefully watched. Penalties (16.9.3) may arise on forms P14 and P35 not submitted by 19 May following the tax year. Thus the 1995–96 forms should be submitted by 19 May 1996. (By concession, the Revenue allow the forms to be received on the last business day within seven extra days.)

At the end of each tax year the employer should issue to each of his employees a form P60 which is a certificate of gross earnings for the year and of income tax deducted under PAYE and now forms part of the P14 pack (P14/P60). This must be done by 31 May.

10.14.5 Change of employer

If you leave your employment your old employer should complete for you a form P45 in triplicate showing your name, district reference, code number, week or month number of the last entries on your tax deduction card, total gross pay to date and total tax due to date. Your old employer sends part 1 of the form P45 to his Inspector of Taxes and hands to you parts 2 and 3 which you must give to your new employer. The latter enters your address and date of starting on part 3 and sends it to his Inspector. From 6 April 1997, a four-part form P45 came into operation, with one part for you to keep.

Your new employer should prepare for you a tax deduction card in accordance with your form P45 and deduct PAYE tax from your wages in the normal way.

If you are not able to give a form P45 to your new employer, he will normally deduct tax under the 'emergency' system which assumes you are single and gives you no other allowances. If this happens you should make an income tax return to the Inspector of Taxes or supply the necessary details to him, so that he can issue you with your correct code number which your employer will then use, making any necessary tax repayment to you.

Form P46 is available for you to complete if you do not have a P45 when you start a new job. It covers whether you are a school leaver or whether it is your main job or an additional one which you are starting. The P46 enables you to indicate your circumstances so that your employer will know whether to deduct basic rate tax from your salary or use an emergency code. (There is also a coding claim form P15 for use in establishing your coding.)

10.14.6 Extension of scope of PAYE

(FA 1994 Ss125–133)

New rules were introduced operative from May 1994 to prevent employers avoiding PAYE by paying staff in assets. Payments through third parties such as offshore trusts are also targeted. Similar rules operate in relation to National Insurance contributions from 1 December 1993.

If you are paid income by an intermediary, this is treated as paid by your employer for PAYE purposes. Also, if you are given part of your income as 'tradeable assets', this is now caught by the PAYE net. Examples of 'tradeable assets' are gold and commodities. The rules extend to vouchers and credit tokens used to provide these assets.

10.15 Profit Related Pay

(TA 1988 Ss169–184 & Sch 29, FA 1995 Ss123 & 137 & FA 1997 S63)

Valuable tax relief operates from 6 April 1987 in respect of Profit Related Pay (PRP). The main features are as follows:

(1) For profit periods beginning after 31 March 1991 and before 1 January 1998, all of your PRP is free of income tax up to the lower of £4,000 or 20 per cent of your PAYE pay for the year. Subsequently, the relief is being phased out (see (10)).

(2) For periods of account before 1 April 1991, half of your PRP was free of income tax up to the point where it was 20 per cent of your PAYE pay or £4,000 a year, if lower. (For periods of account before 1 April 1989, this figure was £3,000.)

(3) Relief only applies to PRP payments made under a scheme registered by the Inland Revenue before the start of the first profit period it is to cover. Tax relief is given by your employer through the PAYE system.

(4) PRP schemes can be registered for profitable groups, companies, firms or sub-units of any of these. Also, central (eg, headquarters) units can be included with PRP based on the profits of the whole undertaking. However, there are certain excluded employers, mainly under the control of central or local government.

(5) New rules relate to PRP schemes for particular units within a business, which are registered after 30 November 1993. Broadly, the object is to ensure that the PRP payable in such schemes is not disproportionately greater than that paid under other schemes to employees in the same business.

(6) The rules of any PRP scheme must provide a clear relationship between PRP and profits. Normally, there is a pool representing a stated percentage of the profits for distribution between eligible employees. This is known as the upper percentage limit (UPL). Alternatively, a fixed sum might be stipulated which varies in proportion with future profits. For PRP schemes registered after 30 November 1993, the basic UPL (160 per cent or more) must be increased where taxable pay for the employees covered is less than for the previous year.

(7) A PRP scheme must exclude controlling directors (with 25 per cent or more interest in the company). Recruits with less than three years' service and part-timers (less than 20 hours per week)

may be excluded. However, part-timers are included for schemes registered from May 1995. Otherwise, the general rule is that at least 80 per cent of the employees in an employment unit at the beginning of each period must be eligible for PRP.

(8) Independent audits are needed for both the registration application and the operation of the scheme.

(9) Profits for PRP purposes should relate to employees' efforts. In computing such profits, certain 'extraordinary items' may be entirely included or excluded. These include profits or losses on terminating an operation, re-organisation and restructuring costs relating to the unit and profits or losses on fixed asset disposals.

(10) The relief is being phased out by reducing the £4,000 ceiling as follows:

Profit period beginning	*Ceiling for relief*
1 January 98 — 31 December 98	£2,000
1 January 99 — 31 December 99	£1,000
From 1 January 2000	NIL

11 Income from businesses and professions

11.1 Trades, professions and vocations

The profits from trades, professions and vocations are normally assessed under Schedule D Case I (trades) and Schedule D Case II (professions and vocations). There are certain special rules which apply to partnerships (Chapter 12) and companies (Chapter 13).

Trade includes manufacturing, retailing, wholesaling and all kinds of trading ventures.

A profession is defined as an occupation requiring special intellectual skills, sometimes coupled with manual skills (eg, doctor of medicine, architect, accountant, barrister).

A vocation has been defined as the way that a person passes his life (eg, composer, author, actor, singer).

11.2 What is trading?

Your regular business will normally be treated as a trade requiring assessment under Schedule D Case I. There are, however, certain other activities which might constitute trading depending on the circumstances. The following are some general guidelines:

(1) Regular buying and selling normally constitutes trading although this does not usually apply to purchases and sales of shares by an individual.
(2) An isolated transaction might be held to be trading if it is by its very nature commercial. For example, a single purchase and sale of a quantity of unmatured whisky is normally treated as a trading transaction. This is because the ownership of unmatured whisky is mainly for commercial purposes.

(3) Isolated transactions involving the purchase and sale of works of art are not normally trading. Here the works of art are owned to be admired and not exclusively (if at all) for commercial purposes. Capital gains tax, however, might be payable on sales of works of art for over £6,000 each (20.24).
(4) Isolated transactions in income producing assets are not usually treated as trading. Capital gains tax would normally apply (20.1).
(5) If you do something to your purchase before selling it the sale might be considered to be trading. For instance, if you buy a ship, convert it and then sell it you will be treated as trading.
(6) Repetition of the same transaction is evidence of trading.
(7) If you deal in property this is likely to be treated as trading (7.10).
(8) The possession of expert business knowledge in connection with a transaction that you carry out will increase your chances of being treated as trading.

11.3 What business expenses are allowed?

In computing the amount of your profits to be charged under Case I or Case II of Schedule D you are allowed to deduct any sums wholly and exclusively incurred for the purposes of the trade, profession or vocation, subject to various special rules (see below). Only expenses of a revenue nature are deductible, however, and these must be distinguished from capital expenditure (2.6).

11.3.1 Table: Allowable business expenses

To the extent that they are incurred wholly and exclusively for business purposes the following are deductible (the list is not exhaustive):

(1) The cost of goods bought for resale and materials used in manufacturing.
(2) Wages and salaries paid to employees, together with National Insurance payments. This includes employees seconded on a temporary basis to charities (TA 1988 S86) and to certain educational bodies including local authorities.
(3) Pensions paid to past employees and their dependants.
(4) Redundancy payments to employees including certain voluntary payments on business cessation, up to three times the statutory amount (TA 1988 S90).

(5) The running costs of any premises used for the business including rent and rates, light and heat, repairs (not capital improvements), insurance, cleaning, etc.
(6) Discounts allowed on sales.
(7) Carriage, packing and delivery costs.
(8) Printing, postage, stationery and telephone.
(9) Repairs to your plant and machinery.
(10) Staff welfare expenses.
(11) Insurance regarding loss of profits, public liability, goods in transit, burglary, etc.
(12) Advertising.
(13) Trade subscriptions.
(14) Professional charges of a revenue nature — eg, audit fees.
(15) Legal charges of a revenue nature, eg, debt collection, preparing trading contracts and settling trading disputes.
(16) If you pay a premium for the lease of your business premises and the recipient is taxed under Schedule A you can claim the cost of the premium as a deduction from your business profits spread over the term of the lease.
(17) VAT on your purchases and expenses if you are not registered for VAT. (If you are registered you set this VAT against that on your sales and only charge your purchases, etc excluding VAT.)
(18) Travelling expenses including hotel bills and fares on business trips but excluding the cost of travelling between your home and business (unless you also do business from home).
(19) The entertaining of overseas customers prior to 15 March 1988 (but not subsequently) and your own staff but not entertaining UK customers.
(20) Gifts which incorporate an advertisement for your business provided that the value for each recipient each year does not exceed £10 (TA 1988 S577).
(21) Bad debts which arose in the course of trading. Also provisions made for specific debtors whom you anticipate may not pay. Also, any debt which you release after 29 November 1993 as part of a formal voluntary arrangement (FA 1994 S144). Special rules limit the relief available for doubtful sovereign debt due from overseas governments, etc normally to banks. Broadly, the allowable amount for 1990–91 is limited to the 1989–90 level and scaled up by 5 per cent annually thereafter (FA 1990 S74).
(22) A trader's expenses of obtaining patents are normally allowable. The outright purchase of a patent is a capital expense, however, which normally qualifies for capital allowances.
(23) Running expenses of motor vehicles excluding such proportion as is attributable to private use.
(24) Interest payments including hire purchase interest. Relief for bank and other interest is normally given on the basis of payments rather than accruals.
(25) The incidental costs of obtaining loan finance which carries deductible interest (TA 1988 S77). Costs concerning repayment, providing security and abortive exercises are covered; but not stamp duty, foreign exchange losses, issue discounts or repayment premiums. This relief extends to certain convertible loan stocks.

(26) Pre-trading expenditure, of a revenue nature, incurred within seven years before starting to trade (TA 1988 S401 & FA 1993 S109). For companies it is treated as falling on the first day of trading; for individuals it was regarded as a separate loss (11.22). However, for businesses set up after 5 April 1995, individuals are treated like companies in this respect (FA 1995 S120).

(27) Contributions before 1 April 2000 to local enterprise agencies approved by the Secretary of State. However, you obtain no relief if you (or those connected with you) are entitled to benefits from the agencies (TA 1988 S79, FA 1990 S75 & FA 1994 S145).

(28) Similar rules apply to contributions to training and enterprise councils made from 1 April 1990 to 31 March 2000 (FA 1990 S76 & FA 1994 S145).

(29) Work training provided by an employer for employees about to leave their current jobs, or who have just left. Training courses must provide improved skills or knowledge for use in new jobs or business and the employee is not taxed on the benefit. Courses must not exceed one year and must take place within the UK (TA 1988 S588).

(30) Security expenditure (FA 1989 Ss112 & 113). This is allowed for the self-employed (including partners) regarding assets or services to meet personal security threats arising from their businesses.

(31) Certain revenue expenditure incurred concerning waste disposal sites from 6 April 1989 (FA 1990 S78 & FA 1993 S110). Expenditure on preparing a site is allowed according to the proportion of its capacity filled with waste in the accounts year. Expenditure on making good a site is given in the year of payment or on commencement of trade if later. However, no allowance is given for expenditure on which capital allowances (11.8) are given.

(32) Certain payments for football ground improvements made by pool promoters (FA 1990 S126).

(33) Gifts of equipment, manufactured, sold or used in the trade, to schools and other educational establishments (FA 1991 S68).

(34) The setting-up costs of certain employee share schemes from 1 April 1991 (10.9.6).

(35) Contributions from 30 November 1993 to 31 March 2000 to a Business Links organisation (FA 1994 S145).

(36) Class 1A National Insurance contributions on car benefits for employees (FA 1997 S65).

11.3.2 Table: Expenses not deductible from business profits

(TA 1988 S74)

(1) Any payments or expenses not wholly and exclusively laid out for the purposes of the business.

(2) Expenses incurred for the private or domestic purposes of yourself or family.

(3) Where expenses contain some business and some private element the proportion attributable to the latter is not deductible. In the case of a private dwelling house used for business purposes the deductible proportion is not normally allowed to exceed two-thirds of the rent and other costs.

(4) Any capital used for improvements to your business premises.
(5) Any loss not connected with the business.
(6) Any reserves and provisions made for anticipated expenses such as repairs, retirement benefits, etc including general bad debts reserves but not reserves for specific bad debts (nor contributions under approved pension plans).
(7) Any annuity or other annual payment (other than interest) payable out of the profits (4.2).
(8) Payments of income tax, capital gains tax and corporation tax, etc.
(9) Your own drawings as the owner or part owner of the business.
(10) Depreciation and amortisation of plant and machinery, motor vehicles, buildings, etc. Capital allowances are normally available however (11.9).
(11) Any royalty payment from which you deduct income tax.
(12) Entertaining expenses unless in connection with overseas customers and their agents before 15 March 1988 (FA 1988 S72) or your own staff.
(13) Professional charges of a capital nature. For example legal fees in connection with a new lease, architects' fees for designing a new building, accountants' fees connected with the purchase of a new business. These expenses can often be added to the cost of the assets for capital gains tax purposes (20.10).
(14) Fines for illegal acts and connected legal expenses.
(15) Charitable donations, unless wholly for business purposes (TA 1988 S577). (Note special rules for non-close companies (15.2.1) and gifts each exceeding £250.)
(16) Political donations.
(17) The cost of acquiring capital assets such as plant and machinery, motor vehicles, buildings, etc. Capital allowances are frequently available however (11.9).
(18) Expenditure after 10 June 1993 involved in payments which are criminal offences (FA 1993 S123).
(19) Payments after 29 November 1993 resulting from extortion by terrorist groups or other criminals (FA 1994 S141).

11.4 The computation of your assessable profits for Schedule D Cases I and II *(TA 1988 Ss74–112)*

If you conduct a business or profession you will normally have annual accounts prepared on a commercial basis including a profit and loss account or an income and expenditure account. Your annual accounts should normally be drawn up to the same date in each year but need not coincide with the tax year (which ends on 5 April).

From April 1990, simpler accounts are permitted from 'small businesses'. These were individuals and partnerships with a turnover less than £10,000 a year. This figure is increased to £15,000 for accounts submitted after 6 April 1992. A simple three line account is needed showing total turnover, purchases and expenses and net profit. Tax returns from April 1991 allow the three line account to be incorporated therein. However, accurate business records must still be kept.

The profit shown by your annual accounts will form the basis of your assessment under Case I or Case II of Schedule D, but it will normally require adjustment in some or all of the following ways:

(1) Add to your profit any non-deductible expenses that have been charged in your accounts (11.3.2).

(2) Deduct from your profit any items included in your accounts which are not taxed under Cases I and II of Schedule D either because they are non-taxable or because they are liable to tax under another Case or Schedule. Examples are:
Capital profits liable to capital gains tax (20.1).
Interest receivable taxed under Schedule D Case III (8.4).
Rents receivable taxed under Schedule A (7.1).
Interest received net, income tax having been deducted at source (8.2); also dividends (8.1).
Amounts originally set aside as reserves and now recredited in your accounts provided the original amounts were not allowed against your taxable profits.

(3) Deduct from your profit any allowable expenses not already charged in your accounts.

(4) Exclude from your profits government grants towards the cost of specified capital expenditure or compensation for loss of capital assets. Other grants under the Industries Act 1972, etc are now generally taxable. However, regional development grants under the Industrial Development Act 1982 and certain grants to assist industry in Northern Ireland are normally exempt.

(5) If you have recently left the unemployment register to set up a business you may be receiving Enterprise Allowances. These are paid for one year at a weekly amount and are now taxable under Schedule D Case VI (15.1). They should therefore be eliminated from your profits assessable under Case I or II of Schedule D. (However, Enterprise Allowances are liable to Class 4 National Insurance.)

(6) Add to your profit any trading profits not already included.

(7) From your profits adjusted as above, deduct your capital allowances for the year (11.8).

(8) Under the new current year basis (11.7.4 and 11.8.2) capital allowances are based on the accounting period and treated as deductible expenses. This starts from 1997–98 for businesses existing on 5 April 1994 and from commencement for newer ones.

11.4.1 Example: Schedule D Case I computation

Mr A carries on a manufacturing business. His accounts for the year to 31 December 1997, which show a net profit of £39,000, include the following:

Expenses			
Depreciation of motor vehicles	£4,300	Entertaining expenses	£2,250
Depreciation of plant and machinery	6,700		
Bad debts provision (5% × sales debtors)	1,650		
Legal expenses *re* debt collection	200	**Income** Bank deposit interest	£70
Legal expenses *re* new lease (not a renewal)	270	Profit on sale of motor car	1,050
Charitable donations (non business)	90	Bad debts provision no longer required (general)	200

Assuming capital allowances of £10,500 for the year ended 31 December 1997, compute Mr A's adjusted Case I profit.

Mr A — Schedule D Case I computation based on accounts for year ended 31 December 1997

Net profit per accounts		£39,000
Add: Disallowable expenses:		
Depreciation (£4,300 + £6,700)	£11,000	
General bad debts provision	1,650	
Legal expenses *re* new lease	270	
Charitable donations	90	
Entertaining expenses	2,250	15,260
		£54,260
Less:		
Bank deposit interest	£70	
Profit on sale of motor car (capital)	1,050	
Bad debts provision no longer required	200	
Capital allowances	10,500	11,820
Adjusted profit		£42,440

11.5 Stock valuation

An important factor in the preparation of business accounts is the valuation of stock and work in progress. This is the amount of unsold raw materials, finished goods and work in progress that was owned at the end of the accounts period. The stock, etc must be valued at each accounting date and the profits are augmented by the excess of the closing stock over the opening stock or decreased by the deficit. It is clear that if the closing stock is valued on a more generous basis than the opening stock then the profits shown will be higher than the true profits and vice versa.

The Revenue pay careful attention to the manner in which businesses value their stock and they normally insist that for tax purposes the opening and closing stocks are valued on the same basis. The usual basis adopted is that each item in stock is valued at the lower of its cost or net realisable value. The exact cost to be included may or may not contain an addition for expenses depending on the exact basis adopted. The general rule in ascertaining cost is that identical items should be identified on the basis that the earliest purchases were sold or used first (FIFO). In all cases the method chosen must be used consistently. 'Net realisable value' is what it is estimated will be obtained from disposing of the stock in the ordinary course of business at the balance sheet date, after allowing for all expenses in connection with the disposal.

Rules operate from 29 November 1994 to prevent the manipulation of stock values for discontinued businesses. These are to stop tax advantages being obtained from selling the stock to a connected party at an untrue valuation (FA 1995 S140).

11.6 Stock relief
(FA 1981 S35, Schs 9 & 10 & FA 1984 Ss48–49)

Stock relief was brought into effect by the Finance Act 1975 and withdrawn for periods of account beginning after 12 March 1984. Relief was broadly based on average price increases as reflected in an 'All Stocks' index. Fuller details are given in previous editions of this book.

11.7 Basis of assessment
(TA 1988 S60 & FA 1994 Ss200–205)

A new system operates from 1996–97 (11.7.4). The assessment for that year is based on the average profits for the two years ending in 1996–97.

After that, the assessment for any year is based on the accounts for the year ending within the year of assessment. Thus, if your accounting date is 31 December, your 1997–98 assessment will be on your profits for the year to 31 December 1997.

The normal basis of assessment under Cases I and II of Schedule D was previously the profits of the accounts year ending in the preceding tax year. This applied for 1995–96 and earlier years of assessment.

Thus if a business makes up its annual accounts to 30 September its 1995–96 Schedule D Case I assessment was based on the profits for the year to 30 September 1994 (ie, ending in the preceding tax year 1995–96). Special rules apply to the opening and closing years (see below) and also where you change your accounting date.

11.7.1 Opening years
(TA 1988 Ss61 & 62)

(1) If your business commences after 5 April 1994, the new current year basis applies throughout (11.7.4). *The following applies where you commenced to trade on an earlier date.*

(2) In the first tax year of a business, profession or vocation the assessment was based on the profits from the starting date until the following 5 April. If accounts had been prepared for the first full year or other period to bridge that date, then the profits were apportioned on a time basis. Thus if a business started on 6 July 1993 and made up its accounts to 5 July 1994 showing a profit of £24,000 for that year, the assessment for 1993–94 was based on the period 6 July 1993 to 5 April 1994, ie, £24,000 × 9/12 = £18,000.

(3) The assessment for the second tax year of a business trade or vocation was normally based on the profits for the first complete 12 months of operations. Thus in the above example the assessment for 1994–95 would be based on the profits for the first complete year, ie, to 5 July 1994 and would therefore be £24,000.

(4) The third year's assessment was normally on the preceding year basis subject to the election option mentioned under (4). In the example above the 1995–96 assessment was thus £24,000 (profits for the accounts year ending in the preceding tax year).

(5) The taxpayer has the option to elect that the assessment for both the second and third tax years (but not only one of them, nor subsequent years) should be based on the actual profits for those years. The election should be made to the Inspector of Taxes within seven years of the end of the second year of assessment. Thus you may still be in time if you are eligible to elect.

(6) Special rules applied to commencements following certain partnership changes after 19 March 1985 (12.5).

11.7.2 Closing years
(TA 1988 S63)

(1) For the tax year in which a trade, profession or vocation is permanently stopped the assessment under Schedule D Case I or II is based on the actual profits from the previous 6 April until the date of cessation. This also applies under the new basis, subject to 'overlap relief' (11.7.4).

(2) Regarding the two years prior to the tax year in which the cessation takes place, under the old system, assessments normally will have been made on a preceding year basis. The Revenue has the right, however, to make additional assessments to cover any excess of the actual profits for those two tax years. The adjustment only works in favour of the Revenue and if your profits for the two tax years preceding that in which your business ceases are less than the original assessments for those years, you will not be able to obtain any reduction.

11.7.3 Example: Schedule D Cases I and II — assessments for closing years — old rules

Mr E ceases to trade on 31 July 1995 having made adjusted profits as follows:

Year ended 31 July 1992	£2,500
Year ended 31 July 1993	£2,400
Year ended 31 July 1994	£3,600
Year ended 31 July 1995	£3,000

What are Mr E's final assessments on these profits?

Before it was known that Mr E was ceasing to trade, his assessments would be as follows:

Tax year	*Basis*	*Base period*	*Schedule D Case I assessment*
1993–94	Preceding year	Year to 31.7.92	£2,500
1994–95	Preceding year	Year to 31.7.93	2,400
Total for 1993–94 and 1994–95			£4,900

When cessation on 31.7.95 is notified to the Revenue they will adjust the assessments for 1993–94 and 1994–95 as follows:

1993–94				
Actual	6.4.93–31.7.93	£2,400 × $3\frac{5}{6}$/12	767	
	1.8.93–5.4.94	£3,600 × $8\frac{1}{6}$/12	2,450	3,217
1994–95				
Actual	6.4.94–31.7.94	£3,600 × $3\frac{5}{6}$/12	1,150	
	1.8.94–5.4.95	£3,000 × $8\frac{1}{6}$/12	2,042	3,192
Revised total for 1993–94 and 1994–95				£6,409
Less: Already assessed				4,900
Additional assessments 1993–94 and 1994–95				£1,509
1995–96				
Actual	6.4.95–31.7.95	£3,000 × $3\frac{5}{6}$/12		£958

11.7.4 The new current year basis

(FA 1994 Ss200–205 & 209–218 & Sch 20 & FA 1995 S122 & Schs 21 & 22)

(1) If your business commences *after 5 April 1994*, the new basis applies at once. Otherwise, it applies for 1997–98 and future years, with special rules for 1996–97.

(2) The basic rule is that you are assessed on the adjusted profits for your accounts year which ends in the year of assessment. Thus if you make up your annual accounts to 30 September, your 1997–98 assessment is based on your profits for the year to 30 September 1997.

(3) For 1996–97, your assessment is normally based on the average of your profits for the two years ending in 1996–97. Thus if your taxable profits for the year to 30 September 1995 are £20,000 and for the year to 30 September 1996 they are £30,000, your 1996–97 assessment is £25,000. This is subject to certain anti-avoidance rules (11.7.6). Normally, you have the option of preparing one set of accounts for the 24 month period ending in 1996–97. Half of the profits for this period will then be assessed for 1996–97.

(4) Exceptionally, your transitional base period may cover more or less than 24 months, perhaps due to a change of accounting date. Your 1996–97 assessment is then based on the proportionate profits for one year. Thus if the period is 30 months for which your profits are £60,000, your 1996–97 assessment is $\frac{12}{30}$ × £60,000 = £24,000.

(5) Under the new rules, the first year of assessment for a business will be based on the profits to the next 5 April (apportioned in days). Say you commenced trading on 1 July 1995, your 1995–96 assessment is based on your profits from that date to 5 April 1996.

If 30 June is your accounting date, your 1996–97 assessment normally will be on your profit for the year to 30 June 1996.

(6) When your business ceases, the assessment for the final period from 6 April will be on an actual basis. Thus suppose you stop trading on 30 June 1998: your 1998–99 assessment will be on the profits from 6 April 1998 to 30 June 1998.

(7) Where a business changes its accounting date the aim will be to tax 12 months' profits for all years except the first and last. This may mean that some profits are taxed twice. However, the intention is that over the lifetime of a business, its profits are fully taxed, but only once. Hence 'overlap relief' will be given where the business ends or a basis period exceeds 12 months, in respect of profits taxed more than once.

(8) 'Overlap relief' often results where a business starts after 5 April 1994. For instance, if you started to trade on 1 July 1994 with a 30 June accounting date, the period 1 July 1994 to 5 April 1995 would be taxed twice. Supposing your proportionate profits for that period are £20,000, you will get relief of this amount when your business eventually ceases.

(9) Special rules cover such areas as losses (11.22.1), capital allowances (11.8.2) and partnerships (12.2).

11.7.5 Transitional provisions — anti avoidance *(FA 1995 Sch 22)*

Since your assessment for 1996–97 is normally based on the average of your profits for the two years ended in 1996–97, there is apparant scope for saving tax. You switch profits into those two years from the adjoining ones so that only half counts. However, this has been legislated against.

The basic rule is that where you artificially shift income or profits into your transitional periods (2 years ending in 1996–97) you will be additionally taxed on $1\frac{1}{4}$ times the amount on which you tried to save tax. However, you will not be taxed if you can show that the main benefit which you expected was not a tax one or that the sole purpose was a bona fide commercial one. A *de minimus* exemption will also apply, with details due shortly before 6 April 1997.

11.7.6 Example: Schedule D Cases 1 and II — assessment for transitional year 1996–97

Mr B has been trading since before 6 April 1994. He prepares his annual accounts to 30 June and his adjusted profits are:

Year ended 30 June 1995	£20,000
Year ended 30 June 1996	£24,000

Mr B's capital allowances (11.8.3) for 1996–97 (based on the 2 years to 30 June 1996) are say £6,000. His assessment for 1996–97 is:

Adjusted profits — year ended 30 June 1995		£20,000
year ended 30 June 1996		24,000
		£44,000
Adjusted profits assessable for 1996–97	50%	22,000
Less capital allowances 1996–97		6,000
		£16,000

11.8 Capital allowances
(CAA etc)

You are not normally allowed to deduct from your taxable profits the cost or depreciation of capital assets. You can, however, deduct capital allowances in respect of the cost of certain assets used in your business or profession including the following:

(1) Plant and machinery (11.9) — this category also includes furniture, fittings, office equipment and motor vehicles, together with the thermal insulation of industrial buildings and of making certain buildings comply with the fire regulations. Other categories of included expenditure relate to safety at sports grounds and stadia (11.9.9) security (11.9.10) and computer software (11.9.15).
(2) Industrial buildings (11.11) — this includes factories and some warehouses, etc.
(3) Agricultural and forestry buildings, etc (11.14).
(4) Hotel buildings, etc (11.15).
(5) Scientific research expenditure (11.17).
(6) Patents and know-how (11.18).
(7) Mines, oil wells, etc (11.20) and dredging (11.19).

If you have expenditure which qualifies for allowances under more than one of the above heads, you will be able to make an irrevocable choice. This applies for accounting periods ending after 27 July 1989 (FA 1989 Sch 13).

11.8.1 Base period

(CAA S160)

For a business, profession or vocation (including partnerships) the capital allowances are computed according to the assets purchased and those used in the annual accounts period (ie, the base period). For these purposes, you must take the date when the expenditure was incurred. This is now generally when the obligation to pay becomes unconditional, unless, for example, part of the capital expenditure is payable more than four months later. Under the old system, a deduction was made from the Schedule D Case I or Case II assessment in respect of the total capital allowances for that tax year.

For example, if a business made up its accounts to 31 December each year then its Schedule D Case I assessment for 1995–96 was based on its accounts for the year to 31 December 1994 (ending in the preceding tax year). Similarly its 1995–96 capital allowances were based on the year to 31 December 1994. (See 11.8.2 below for the new rules introduced with the current year basis.)

Under the old system, special rules applied where there were base periods of less than one year. Where one base period applied to two tax years, the additions during the base period were allocated to the earlier tax year for the purposes of calculating the allowances. If there was a gap between base periods, it was added to the second base period unless this marked a cessation of trading — in this case you added the gap to the first period.

11.8.2 New current year assessment rules

(FA 1994 Ss211–212 & Sch 20)

New capital allowances rules were introduced in line with the current year basis (11.7.4). These take full effect for 1997–98 and future years, regarding businesses existing at 5 April 1994. Capital allowances are treated as trading expenses. Similarly, balancing charges are regarded as trading receipts. Capital allowances have to be claimed in the tax return.

Capital allowances are now related to the period for which accounts are drawn up, rather than the year of assessment. However, any unrelieved amounts from 1996–97 and earlier years are to be included with the allowances for the first accounts ending after 5 April 1997.

For the *transitional year of assessment, 1996–97*, capital allowances are normally to be based on a two year period ending therein. This corresponds with your assessment basis. Thus if your accounting date is

30 September, your 1996–97 capital allowances are based on the two years to 30 September 1996. You use the opening balances, additions and disposals attributable to that period, taking writing down allowance (11.9.2) for one year.

11.8.3 VAT Capital Goods Scheme adjustments
(FA 1991 S59)

Extra VAT paid under the VAT Capital Goods Scheme qualifies for capital allowances in the year of payment. Similarly, VAT repaid from that date reduces the appropriate expenditure pool for capital allowances purposes in the year of receipt. This particularly affects businesses which are partly exempt (23.3) from VAT such as those in banking, finance, insurance and property.

The items covered are limited to computers and computer equipment worth at least £50,000 and land and buildings worth at least £250,000. The VAT adjustments generally arise on changes of use.

11.9 Capital allowances on plant and machinery

In general, expenditure after 31 March 1986 only qualifies for 25 per cent writing down allowance each year, however, special rules apply to long-life assets (11.9.8), motor vehicles (11.9.11) and plant which you lease out (11.9.14). Expenditure in the year to 31 October 1993 may also have qualified for first-year allowance at 40 per cent for plant and 20 per cent initial allowance for industrial and agricultural buildings, etc. Balancing charges and allowances can arise when plant is sold (11.9.4). The main allowances available on plant purchased new or second-hand between 26 October 1970 and 1 April 1986 were normally a first-year allowance for the year of purchase and a writing down allowance for each subsequent year.

To claim relief, you must notify the Revenue within two years after the chargeable period when you incurred the expenditure. (For chargeable periods ended before 30.11.93, you are allowed at least 3 years.) This applies unless the expenditure was incurred and notified to the Revenue before 30 November 1993. If you still own the asset, you can claim relief for a later period within two years of its end (FA 1994 S111).

11.9.1 First-year allowances
(CAA Ss22 & 23 & FA 1993 S115 & Sch 13)

Special relief applied where you incurred expenditure on plant and machinery during the year to 31 October 1993. You obtained a first-year allowance of 40 per cent of the cost for the base period when this was incurred. However, if you wished you could disclaim all or part of this. If first-year allowance was taken, writing down allowance was not available until the second year. The 40 per cent first-year allowance applied to most plant and machinery. Excluded were cars (11.9.11), most assets acquired from connected persons and those sold and leased back; also acquisitions aimed at avoiding tax by obtaining the allowance.

First year allowance was available in previous years as below and further details are given in the 1989–90 and earlier editions of this book.

Expenditure date	*Rate of allowance*
After 21.3.72 and before 14.3.84	100%
After 13.3.84 and before 1.4.85	75%
After 31.3.85 and before 1.4.86	50%
After 31.3.86 and before 1.11.92	nil
After 31.10.92 and before 1.11.93	40%

11.9.2 Writing down allowance *(CAA S24 & FA 1997 S83 & Sch 14)*

Each asset is put into a 'pool' at its cost price (less any first-year allowance obtained) and a writing down allowance of 25 per cent is given on the balance. You can take less than 25 per cent in any year and this also applies to companies (13.10). Writing down allowance was not normally given for the first year, if first-year allowance was obtained. Only 6 per cent may be available on long-life assets bought after 25 November 1996 (11.9.8).

The 'pooling' rules normally apply to Schedule D businesses. However, from 6 April 1997 (1 April for companies) capital allowances are also to be computed on a 'pooling' basis regarding machinery and plant used for a property letting business. This will normally relate to all your Schedule A income (7.1).

Expenditure after 31 March 1986 (apart from during the year to 31 October 1993) generally qualifies for no first-year allowance, but writing down allowance runs from the first year. Unlike first-year allowances, writing down allowances previously only applied when the assets concerned were brought into use. However, from 1 April 1985, they are available from when the expenditure is incurred.

If the base period is less than a year, the rate of writing down allowance is proportionately reduced. Thus, if the base period for a business is only six months for a given year of assessment, then any writing down allowances for that period would be at the rate of 25% × 6/12 = 12.5%.

For 1996–97, there is normally a 2 year base period (11.8.2). However, only one year's writing down allowances are taken.

11.9.3 Ships

(CAA Ss30–33, FA 1995 Ss94–98 & FA 1996 S179 & Sch 35)

Free depreciation by postponing first-year allowances was available with regard to new ships. This extended to expenditure on second-hand ships incurred after 31 March 1985. The same principle still applies regarding writing down allowances on expenditure on new ships after 13 March 1984 and second-hand ships after 31 March 1985. The allowances can be 'rolled-up' and used at will. These rules do not apply, however, to certain leasing situations where capital allowances are restricted (11.9.14).

You can claim to defer a balancing charge on a ship disposal. It is now necessary that you reinvest the proceeds in other shipping within six years and relief is available across groups of companies.

11.9.4 Sales of plant and machinery — balancing allowances and charges

(CAA Ss24, 26, 152, 157, 158 & 161, FA 1990 Sch 13, F2A 1992 S67, FA 1993 S117 & FA 1994 S119)

If you sell an item of plant from your 'pool' of purchases, you simply deduct the sale proceeds from the 'pool' balance. If the proceeds exceed the original cost of the plant, however, you only deduct the cost from the pool and the excess is a capital gain. Should the sale proceeds exceed your 'pool' balance, the excess is treated as a balancing charge and it is added to your assessment for the relevant year. By means of the balancing charge, the Revenue recoup the excess of capital allowances that would otherwise have been given to you.

Note that your time of sale is taken as the earlier of completion or when possession is given. This rule is of general application for most capital allowance purposes regarding sales from 6 April 1990.

Regarding plant, etc (apart from some motor cars) purchased after 26 October 1970, balancing allowances normally only occur in the event of a cessation. If you cease permanently to trade during a period then you receive for that period a 'balancing allowance' equal to the remainder of your 'pool' (of expenditure on assets after 26 October 1970 less allowances already obtained) less its disposal value.

If assets are sold from one person (company, etc) to another, both being under common control, both may elect within two years that the tax written down value is passed from one to the other. The effect is that there is no balancing allowance or charge. (These provisions must now be assumed always to have had effect regarding qualifying hotels, scientific research assets and commercial buildings in enterprise zones, providing both parties are entitled to capital allowances.) A similar election may be made within two years after the succession of a trade between connected persons (for example where a trade passes from one company to another under common control).

With effect from 1 January 1992 balancing charges and other balancing adjustments are not applicable regarding certain transfers of UK trades from a company situated in one EC member state to a company situated in another. The consideration must consist of shares or securities and the transfer must be for commercial reasons and not with a main purpose of saving tax.

11.9.5 Example: Capital allowances on plant and machinery

A has been carrying on a manufacturing business for many years and makes up his accounts to 31 December each year. At 31 December 1991 the capital allowances written down value of his plant, etc was £8,100. Mr A purchased the following new plant:

Date	*Description*	*Cost*
on 2 February 1992	Typewriters	£1,000
on 1 March 1992	Machinery	5,000
on 30 June 1992	Machinery	2,000
on 30 September 1993	Office furniture	1,925

During the year to 31 December 1991, Mr A sold machinery costing £1,000 for £450.

Compute Mr A's capital allowances from 1993–94 to 1997–98.

	'Pool'	*Total allowances*
Balance forward	8,100	
1993–94 (base period year to 31 December 1992)		
Additions:		
2 February 1992	1,000	
1 March 1992	5,000	
30 June 1992	2,000	
	16,100	

Writing down allowance 25% × £16,100		(4,025)	£4,025
Balance forward		12,075	
1994–95 (base period year to 31 December 1993)			
Additions: 30 September 1993	1,925		
First-year allowance 40%	(770)	1,155	770
Writing down allowance 25% × £12,075		(3,019)	3,019
Balance forward		£10,211	£3,789
1995–96 (base period year to 31 December 1994) Writing down allowance 25% × £10,211		(2,553)	£2,553
Balance forward		£7,658	
1996–97 (base period 2 years to 31 December 1996) Writing down allowance 25% × £7,658		(1,915)	£1,915
Balance forward		£5,743	
1997–98 (base period year to 31 December 1997) Writing down allowance 25% × £5,743		(1,436)	£1,436
Balance forward		£4,307	

11.9.6 Short-life assets

(CAA Ss37 & 38)

A special rule applies to short-life plant and machinery which you buy for your trade after 31 March 1986. You can elect to have the writing down allowances on that plant calculated separately from your 'pool' (de-pooling). The election must be made within two years of the year of acquisition. De-pooling does not normally apply to assets leased to non-traders, or to cars or ships.

When you sell the assets, there will be a balancing allowance or charge, not normally otherwise arising. However, if the machinery or plant has not been sold within five years, it must be transferred to your 'pool' at its tax written-down value.

11.9.7 Example: Short-life assets — de-pooling

Mr B makes up his business accounts to 31 December and bought plant for £100 on 30 June 1992, for which he made a de-pooling election. The plant is sold for £10 on 15 May 1996. The capital allowances computations are as follows:

Year ended 31 December		£
1992	cost	100
	25% writing down allowance	25
		75
1993		19
		56
1994		14
		42
1995		10
		32
1996	Sale proceeds	10
	Balancing allowance	£22

Note: If the plant had not been disposed of by 31 December 1996, the written down value would be transferred to the general plant pool.

11.9.8 Long-life assets
(FA 1997 S84 & Sch 14)

On assets bought after 25 November 1996, your writing down allowance will be only 6 per cent, subject to the following:

(1) The 6 per cent rate applies to plant and machinery with an expected life when new of at least 25 years.
(2) Your business will be outside the rules if it spends no more than £100,000 each year on such assets (reduced pro rata for associated companies).
(3) Other exclusions are motor cars and machinery and plant in a building used as a dwelling house, shop, showroom, hotel or office.
(4) Ships continue to attract 25 per cent as do railway assets bought before 2011.

(5) Expenditure before 2001 under contracts effected before 26 November 1996 continues to attract 25 per cent relief.
(6) If applicable, a separate pool is needed for your long-life assets.
(7) Where you sell a long-life asset for less than its tax written down value, in order to gain a tax advantage, it is treated as sold for that value.

11.9.9 Safety at sports grounds
(CAA S70)

If relief is not otherwise available, you can claim capital allowances at 25 per cent on the reducing balance on certain safety expenditure at sports grounds. You must be trading and the grounds designated under the Safety of Sports Grounds Act 1975. From 1 January 1989 this is extended to include 'regulated stands' (broadly providing covered accommodation for 500 or more spectators).

11.9.10 Security assets
(CAA Ss71 & 72)

Expenditure after 5 April 1989 on 'Security assets' may qualify for capital allowances (25 per cent on reducing balance). You must acquire the assets to meet a special threat to your personal security which arises by virtue of your trade or profession. Partnership and sole traders are covered by the rules.

11.9.11 Motor vehicles
(CAA Ss34–36 and 41)

If you buy a car for use in your business you will obtain the 25 per cent writing down allowance for every year including the first. Special rules apply, however, to cars costing over £12,000 in which case your allowance for any year is restricted to 25 per cent × £12,000, ie, £3,000. Each car that costs over £12,000 must be treated as a separate 'pool' which, when sold, gives rise to its own balancing allowance or balancing charge. For cars purchased before 11 March 1992 the limit was £8,000.

Cars purchased for no more than £12,000 are all put into a separate pool (CAA S41). This pool also includes assets acquired before 1 April 1986, which you lease out and which did not qualify for first-year allowance (11.9.14). Prior to being withdrawn, first-year allowances were not given on motor vehicles unless they were designed to carry goods; or were of a type unsuitable for use as private vehicles; or were vehicles for hire to the public such as taxis or certain hire cars; or were provided for the use of the recipients of certain mobility allowances and supplements.

If your car is leased through your business (or company) and its equivalent retail cost price exceeds a given limit, the rental deduction from the taxable business profits is correspondingly restricted. The limit is £12,000 retail cost equivalent if the car was first rented after 10 March 1992 and £8,000 if earlier. This restriction is not to apply to hire purchase arrangements where there is an option to purchase for 1 per cent or less of the original retail cost (FA 1991 S61).

The actual deductible rental is found by multiplying the true rental by $(12{,}000 + \frac{RP-12{,}000}{2})$ and dividing it by the RP (retail price of the car when new).

11.9.12 Example: Higher priced motor cars

On 31 January 1992 and 21 June 1992 Mr C purchased for use in his business two cars costing respectively £9,000 and £14,000. The second of these is sold on 30 June 1994 for £7,000. The Revenue direct that 20 per cent of the use of each car should be treated as being for private purposes. Mr C prepares his annual accounts to 31 July each year. Compute the capital allowances available on the cars up to 1997–98 on the basis that no cars are then purchased or sold up to 31 July 1997.

	(1)	*(2)*	*Total allowances*	*Allowances available to business (80%)*
1993–94				
Additions 31 January 1992	9,000			
21 June 1992		14,000		
Writing down allowance (restricted)	2,000	3,000	£5,000	£4,000
	7,000	11,000		
1994–95				
Writing down allowance	1,750	2,750	£4,500	£3,600
	5,250	8,250		

1995–96				
Proceeds 30 June 1994		7,000		
Balancing allowance		£1,250	1,250	
Writing down allowance	1,313		1,313	
	3,937		£2,563	£2,050
1996–97				
Writing down allowance	984		£984	£787
	£2,953			
1997–98				
Writing down allowance	738		£738	£590
Carried forward	£2,215			

Notes: (1) Car (1) is subject to the £8,000 restriction being pre-11.3.92 and car (2) to the £12,000 restriction being post 10.3.92.

(2) Because the business use is restricted to 80 per cent the balancing allowance is restricted in this way.

(3) The basis period for 1996–97 is the 2 years to 31 July 1996.

11.9.13 Hire purchase
(CAA S60)

If you buy plant or machinery on hire purchase you are entitled to full capital allowances as soon as you bring it into use in your business. You receive allowances on the capital proportion of the total instalments — the interest proportion is allowed against your business profits in the year that the respective instalments are paid. Thus if you buy under hire purchase a machine whose cash cost would be £1,000 and you are paying a total of £1,600 over three years, you get capital allowances on £1,000 as soon as you start to use the machine (ie, 25 per cent writing down allowance). You would also deduct the interest of £600 from your profits for the three years during which you are paying off the instalments (ie, about £200 each year).

11.9.14 Machinery for leasing
(CAA Ss39–50 & 61 & FA 1993 Ss115 & 116)

You are normally able to obtain 25 per cent writing down allowance (11.9.2) on expenditure to buy assets which you lease out. However, subject to the rules, 40 per cent first-year allowance may have been available on expenditure during the year to 31 October 1993. A separate pool is used for all such assets purchased before 1 April 1986 and certain cars (11.9.11). Prior to 1 April 1986 plant purchased for leasing qualified for first-year allowance, subject to various rules noted in earlier editions of this book. One requirement was that the assets were used for 'qualifying purposes' for the 'requisite period' (four years of use or earlier disposal).

Where an asset ceased to be used for qualifying purposes during the *requisite period* (above), the capital allowances were recomputed as if no first-year allowance had been given. This normally gave rise to a balancing charge when use for *qualifying purposes* ceased.

Anti-avoidance legislation operates concerning leasing partnerships from which a loss benefit otherwise would be obtained from first-year allowances (15.10.6). Wider provisions prevent your offsetting capital allowances from casual leasing activities against other income (15.10.6). For expenditure incurred after 10 March 1982 on assets leased outside the UK and ships or aircraft let on charter further restrictions apply (15.10.6). Special capital allowances rules also apply to film production costs (11.21).

11.9.15 Computer software
(F2A 1992 S68)

A 25 per cent writing down allowance is available for capital expenditure on the outright acquisition of computer software. (If the expenditure is during the year to 31 October 1993, a 40 per cent first-year allowance is due in year one.) From 10 March 1992, this extends to capital expenditure on software licences and access to electronic transmission.

11.9.16 Definition of plant and machinery
(FA 1994 S117)

New rules have been introduced which provide that buildings and structures do not qualify as plant for capital allowances purposes, nor does land. These rules cover expenditure incurred from 30 November 1993, unless under a contract made before that date and incurred before 5 April 1996. Earlier expenditure is not affected and established exceptions under case law are preserved.

The expression 'building' includes such items as walls, gates, main services, waste disposal and fire safety systems, sewerage, drainage and lift shafts. Items not affected include electrical and water systems provided for the trade, manufacturing equipment, furniture and fittings, cookers, dishwashers, etc. other machinery, movable partition walls, decorative assets for hotels, etc and advertising displays.

'Structures' include tunnels, bridges, pavements, roads, inland navigations, dams, sea walls and weirs. Items not affected include altering land to install machinery, dry docks, jetties, etc, to carry plant, pipelines, indoor and outdoor swimming pools, fish tanks and railway lines. The rules only mention what is not plant; otherwise, existing law must be followed.

11.10 Fixtures — entitlement to capital allowances

(CAA Ss51–59 & FA 1997 S86 & Sch 16)

Detailed rules apply to clarify who is entitled to capital allowances where machinery or plant is installed in a building or on land and becomes a fixture. The rules may treat the plant as belonging to you for capital allowances purposes even though you are not the owner. Except for payments under certain existing leases or other contracts, the new rules apply to expenditure after 11 July 1984.

If you lease a piece of equipment and it becomes a fixture at a building, you will obtain capital allowances if you jointly elect with the lessee. Where you pay to be granted a lease including a fixture on which the lessor would obtain capital allowances, you can jointly elect that you receive the allowances.

Modifications to the rules take effect from 24 July 1996 with a view to:

(1) Provide for a joint election of purchaser and vendor as to the amount of the sale price to be apportioned to fixtures,
(2) Prevent the acceleration of allowances on fixtures,
(3) Stop allowances exceeding the original cost of a fixture, and
(4) Bar allowances on fixtures leased to non-taxpayers if the lessor has no relevant interest in the land.

11.11 Industrial buildings

(CAA Ss1–21, FA 1993 S113 & FA 1995 Ss87–89)

The cost of new industrial buildings that are used in your business (ie, factories, warehouses, etc and some repair shops) qualify for industrial buildings allowances. Qualifying expenditure also includes additions and improvements to industrial buildings. From 6 April 1991, industrial buildings allowance extends to the construction of toll roads (FA 1991 S60).

Now also included are import warehouses which store goods or materials imported into the UK. From 6 April 1995, the relief covers privately financed public roads under the Design Build Finance and Operate initiative.

Each year (including the first) a writing down allowance of 4 per cent of the original cost is obtained. (The allowance is 2 per cent if the expenditure was incurred before 6 November 1962.) Up to 25 per cent of the capital cost of an industrial building may relate to a non-qualifying use without restricting the allowances.

Prior to 1 April 1986 and for the year to 31 October 1993, expenditure qualified for initial allowance as follows:

Date of expenditure		*Rate*
After	*and before*	
12 November 1974	11 March 1981	50%
10 March 1981	14 March 1984	75%
13 March 1984	1 April 1985	50%
31 March 1985	1 April 1986	25%
31 March 1986	1 November 1992	Nil
31 October 1992	1 November 1993	20%

Building costs after 31 March 1986 normally do not attract initial allowances apart from in Enterprise Zones (11.12). However, 20 per cent initial allowance was available for qualifying buildings constructed under a contract entered into between 1 November 1992 and 31 October 1993. Also, the buildings must have been brought into use for the purposes of the trade by 31 December 1994. In cases where the expenditure was in the same year as the building was brought into use, both initial and writing down allowance were available.

If a building on which industrial buildings allowances have been obtained is sold then the sale proceeds must be compared with the balance of original cost less initial allowances and writing down allowances obtained. Any excess proceeds will be assessed as a balancing charge and any deficit will be allowed as a balancing allowance. This now applies even if you had ceased to use the building for industrial purposes. Any excess of the proceeds compared with the original cost must be disregarded for this purpose but may give rise to a capital gain (20.2).

11.12 Enterprise Zones

(CAA Ss1, 6, 10A & 10B & FA 1994 Ss120–121)

The Government have designated a number of Enterprise Zones. One of their attractions is that expenditure on industrial and commercial buildings including hotels qualifies for 100 per cent initial allowance. Unusually shops and offices are included. Less than the full initial allowance may be claimed in which case 25 per cent writing down allowance (straight line) is available on the original expenditure until used up.

Enterprise Zone allowances are now restricted to exclude expenditure incurred more than ten years after the expiry of the zone. Expenditure payable after 15 December 1991 on an unused building is no longer denied Enterprise Zone allowances because it is bought after the expiry of the zone's ten-year life. Also, allowances are to be available on used buildings sold, within two years of being brought into use after that date. (The time limit is 31.8.94 if it would have expired from 13.1.94 to 31.8.94.) In this case, the purchaser obtains limited relief where part of the expenditure was incurred when the site was in an Enterprise Zone and part was not.

Where you own the freehold and sell a long lease in your property for a capital sum, this has not given rise to a balancing charge. However, buildings purchased by you in enterprise zones on or after 13 January 1994 may produce balancing charges if disposed of in this way. The new rules provide for balancing charges on sales of the long leases within seven years (25 years in cases with guaranteed exit arrangements).

11.13 Small workshops

(FA 1980 S75 & Sch 13, FA 1982 S73 & FA 1984 S58)

Expenditure on small workshops (no more than 2,500 square feet of floor space) incurred after 26 March 1980 and before 27 March 1983 obtained special relief. For small workshops of no more than 1,250 square feet relief extended until 26 March 1985. The reliefs were the same as those available for certain buildings in Enterprise Zones (see above).

11.14 Agricultural buildings allowance
(CAA Ss122–133 & FA 1993 S114 & Sch 12)

If you are the owner or tenant of any farm or forestry land, you will obtain allowance for your expenditure on certain constructions on that land. These include farmhouses, farm or (generally only up to 19 June 1989) forestry buildings, cottages, and fences, etc.

The allowance is given in the form of an annual writing down allowance of 4 per cent on your original expenditure. (Previously, an initial allowance of up to 20 per cent could also be claimed. The balance was eligible for writing down allowance of 10 per cent of the original cost for each year including the first.) With the exception of the year to 31 October 1993, for expenditure incurred from 1 April 1986, there is no initial allowance and the writing down allowance is reduced to 4 per cent. (The old rates applied if expenditure was incurred before 1 April 1987 under a contract effected before 14 March 1984.)

To obtain the 20 per cent initial allowance, the buildings must have been constructed under a contract entered into between 1 November 1992 and 31 October 1993. Also, they must have been brought into use by 31 December 1994.

Expenditure after 31 March 1986, attracting 4 per cent writing down allowance is generally written off over a 25 year period. However, if you sell or demolish the building within that time, you can elect for a balancing adjustment (ie, balancing allowance or charge — 11.9.4). This also applies if the building is destroyed. The election must be made within two years after the end of the relevant year of assessment (accounting period for a company).

If your expenditure is on a farmhouse, then your allowance will normally be based on only one-third (maximum) of the total cost to take account of the personal benefit.

11.15 Hotel buildings
(CAA Ss6, 7 & 19 & FA 1990 Sch 13)

Expenditure incurred on the construction or improvement of certain hotel buildings qualifies for an annual writing down allowance of 4 per cent of the original cost. If the hotel is in an Enterprise Zone (11.12), expenditure qualifies for relief at special rates (100 per cent initial allowance, etc). To qualify for the allowance, the hotel must have at least ten bedrooms for letting to the public and provide breakfast and an evening meal. Also, it must be open for at least four months in the season from April to October inclusive.

11.16 Assured tenancies

(CAA Ss84–97 & FA 1990 Sch 13)

A 75 per cent initial allowance followed by 4 per cent writing down allowance was available on qualifying expenditure incurred between 9 March 1982 and 14 March 1984. From 14 March 1984, the initial allowance was phased out in exactly the same way as for industrial buildings (11.11), but the writing down allowance remains for expenditure incurred before 1 April 1992. (The land or property must be acquired under a contract entered into before 15 March 1988.) The allowances are given on dwellings let on assured tenancies by bodies approved by the Secretary of State for the Environment under the Assured Tenancies Scheme. Only approved bodies obtain the allowance.

Although not previously classified as capital allowances for chargeable periods beginning before 6 April 1990, assured tenancies allowances are now so treated. This enables them to be included in group relief claims (13.13).

The expenditure on each house or flat qualifying for allowance is limited to £40,000 (£60,000 in Greater London). Regarding expenditure after 4 May 1983 (unless under existing contracts) only landlords which are companies qualify for the allowance.

11.17 Scientific research allowance

(CAA Ss136–139 & FA 1990 Sch 13)

Capital expenditure incurred on scientific research for the purposes of your trade is wholly allowed in the year that the expenditure arises. Any revenue expenditure will be allowed as a charge against your taxable profits provided that it is related to your trade or it is medical research related to the welfare of your employees.

One hundred per cent allowance is given on capital expenditure excluding the cost of land and houses. However, scientific research allowance and industrial buildings allowance are not given on the same expenditure. Disposal proceeds of scientific research assets are normally treated as taxable trading receipts, to the extent that together with any allowances, they exceed the original cost.

11.18 Patent rights and 'know how'

(TA 1988 Ss520–533 & FA 1989 Sch 13)

The 1985 Finance Act changed the allowance basis for both patent rights and 'know how', so that from 1 April 1986, only a 25 per cent writing down allowance applies.

Prior to 1 April 1986, if you purchased a patent to use in your business then you obtain a writing down allowance of 1/17th of the expenditure for each of the 17 years starting with that in which you made the purchase. If you sell the patent then the excess or deficit of the proceeds compared with the unexpired balance of cost (after writing down allowances) is treated as a balancing charge or allowance (11.9.4). If, however, the proceeds exceed the original cost, then you are assessed to income tax under Schedule D Case VI on this excess (normally spread over six years or the remainder of the patent if less). Note that costs in connection with creating and registering your own patents are treated as deductible revenue expenses (TA 1988 S83).

If you purchase patent rights from a connected person, your allowances may be limited, by reference to the vendor's disposal value for capital allowance purposes. Otherwise, it is necessary to use your capital expenditure, or if smaller, the market value of the rights on your acquiring them, or normally the original acquisition costs of the vendor.

Any payments that you made before 1 April 1986 to obtain 'know how' for your business or profession entitle you to a writing down allowance of one-sixth of such expenditure for each of the first six consecutive years. If you sell 'know how' that had been used in your business, the proceeds are taxed as trading receipts. If, however, you cease to trade within the six years, you may charge the balance of your 'know how' expenditure against the taxable profits of your final trading period.

11.19 Dredging

(CAA Ss134 & 135)

For dredging expenditure after March 1986, an annual writing down allowance of 4 per cent on the original amount is due. Previously an initial allowance of 15 per cent applied, together with writing down allowance at 4 per cent each year on a straight line basis.

11.20 Mineral extraction
(CAA Ss98–121)

Expenditure before 1 April 1986 attracted initial and writing down allowances related to output, etc. These have now been replaced by writing down allowances at 25 per cent or 10 per cent, depending on the nature of the expenditure. Pre-1 April 1986 balances qualify for the new reliefs, but you can claim initial allowances on qualifying expenditure incurred up to 31 March 1987 under a contract entered into before 16 July 1985.

Balancing allowances or charges arise under the present system where mineral deposits cease to be worked or the mine, etc is sold.

11.21 Films, etc
(CAA S68 & F2A 1992 Ss41–43 & 69)

Films, tapes and discs with at least a two-year life normally qualified for capital allowances. However, this was withdrawn from 10 March 1982 for overseas films but continued for British made films (including those for television). Unless the film, etc is trading stock, the rules provide for the production expenditure not qualifying for capital allowances to be written off over the film's income-producing life. Film investment is sometimes made by means of limited partnerships. However, relief for limited partners' losses after 19 March 1985 was severely restricted (12.4).

The production of qualifying films (those with sufficient EC content) obtains special relief from 11 March 1992. Pre-production costs incurred from that date attract relief at once, up to a limit of 20 per cent of total budgeted cost; production expenditure on films completed after 10 March 1992 is to be written off as to one-third each year starting with the completion of the film, as is the cost of acquiring qualifying films.

11.22 Relief for losses

11.22.1 Losses under the new current year basis
(FA 1994 Ss209 & 210 & FA 1995 Ss118 & 119)

The previous system under which relief was allowed for business losses is outlined on the next page (11.22.2). Broadly, this system still applies but with some alterations.

Among the changes relating to the move to the current year basis (11.7.4) are the following:

(1) Losses are computed on the basis of the periods for which the accounts of the business are prepared, instead of the present fiscal year basis. However, businesses, etc set up before 6 April 1994 may continue to set 1995–96 trading losses against other income for that year or 1996–97.
(2) Relief for trading and professional losses under S380 (11.22.2) is allocated differently. It is now to go against your income either of the year of loss or the preceding year and you can choose which has priority.
(3) Similarly, the rules regarding losses on certain unquoted shares (20.14) have changed, as have those for terminal losses (11.24) and losses in new businesses (11.23). (Losses on qualifying unquoted shares suffered in 1993–94 can be relieved against 1993–94 or 1994–95 income).
(4) In general, the new rules take effect from 1997–98 for businesses existing at 5 April 1994 and otherwise from commencement.

11.22.2 The previous system
(TA 1988 Ss380–390 & 397 & FA 1991 S72)

If the adjusted results for your business, profession or vocation showed a deficit of income compared with expenditure for a particular year then your assessment under Case I or Case II of Schedule D was nil for the related tax year. Thus, if your accounts run to 31 December and you made an adjusted loss of £1,000 for 1994, your 1995–96 assessment was nil. The loss of £1,000 for the year to 31 December 1994 should be augmented by your 1995–96 capital allowances (say £600) and the resultant total loss of £1,600 was available for relief. This was first given against (*a*) your other income for the tax year in which you suffered the loss and (*b*) that for the following tax year. ((*a*) includes your business assessment on the profits for the year prior to the loss.)

A useful rule was introduced for 1991–92 and future years. If you make a trading loss in the year and have insufficient other income for the year to offset it, you can claim relief against capital gains for that tax year. If there are still unused trading losses after absorbing other income for the following year, relief is available against the capital gains for that year (20.13).

Strictly speaking under the previous system, you apportioned your loss to the actual tax years that span your accounts year: thus, if your loss (excluding capital allowances) for the year to 31 December 1994 was £1,600, this was allocated as follows: £1,600 × 3/12 = £400 to 1993–94 and £1,600 × 9/12 = £1,200 to 1994–95. Except in the first years of trading, however, the Revenue normally allowed you to allocate the loss for a given accounts year to the tax year in which it ends. Thus the £1,600 loss for the year to 31 December 1994 was allocated to 1994–95 and your relief was set against other income for 1994–95 and 1995–96.

A strict order of set-off needed to be followed — the loss was first set against your other earned income for the year, then against your unearned income. Prior to 6 April 1990, it was then possible to set any balance of the loss against your spouse's earned income and then his or her unearned income. However, following the introduction of independent taxation from that date, this is no longer permitted.

The above loss relief is given under TA 1988 S380 and you must claim it by making the required election to your Inspector of Taxes within two years of the end of the tax year to which it relates. However, under the new rules (11.22.1) notice is needed within 12 months from 31 January following the year of assessment. If your loss is not entirely relieved as above then you can claim that the balance should be carried forward and set off against future profits from the *same* trade, profession or vocation (TA 1988 S385).

Note that for the transitional year, 1996–97, your assessment is normally based on your average profits for the two years ending with your accounting date within 1996–97 (11.7.4). If you make a loss for one of those years, this counts as nil and the loss is available for relief as above. Thus if you make a £12,000 loss for the year to 30 September 1995 and a profit of £20,000 for the year to 30 September 1996, your 1996–97 assessment is 1/2 × £20,000 = £10,000. Also, you will have £12,000 available for loss relief.

Note that you are not allowed to carry a loss forward from one trade to another. You should remember this if you change businesses. A move to a nearby shop in the same trade may be in order, however.

Your loss in the first year of assessment of a new business includes *pre-trading expenditure* of a revenue nature (11.3.1). This applied to individuals and partnerships regarding such expenditure within three years before trading commences (TA 1988 S401). For trades beginning after 31 March 1989, the period is five years (FA 1989 S113).

Income tax relief is claimable for certain losses on disposals of *unquoted shares in trading companies* by original subscribers (20.14). These losses take precedence over claims under S380.

Loss relief is given before personal reliefs and allowances (3.0.1, etc) which cannot be carried forward. Thus these may be lost through your income being absorbed by losses. If possible, carry the losses forward in these circumstances so that your allowances are not wasted.

11.22.3 Example: Relief for losses

Dr D makes a loss of £20,000 in his practice for the year to 31 December 1998 having made a profit of £6,000 for 1997. For 1999 his profit is £22,000. His only other income is taxed dividends, which including tax credits amount to £5,000 for 1997–98 and £6,000 for 1998–99. What loss relief can Dr D obtain?

Dr D's loss of £20,000 for the year to 31 December 1998 will be allocated to the tax year 1998–99(11.22.2).

1997–98 loss relief (S380)	
Against 1997–98 Schedule D Case II assessment	£6,000
Against 1997–98 dividends	5,000
1998–99 loss relief (S380)	
Against 1998–99 dividends	£6,000
1999–00 loss relief (S385)	
Against 1999–00 Schedule D Case II assessment	£3,000
	£20,000

(Case II assessment for 1999–00 becomes £22,000 – £3,000 = £19,000)

11.23 Loss in new business
(TA 1988 S381 & FA 1994 S209)

If you carry on a business or profession personally or in partnership, a special relief is available. This applies to any loss which you make in your first year of assessment, or in any of the next three years. A written claim is required within two years of the end of the year of assessment.

The losses include capital allowances, and certain pre-trading expenditure (see above). They are offset against your income for the three years of assessment prior to the year in which the losses are made, taking the earliest first.

11.24 Terminal losses
(TA 1988 Ss388 & 389 & FA 1994 S209)

If you cease to carry on a trade, profession or vocation and make an adjusted loss in your last complete year of trading, you get relief for this so-called 'terminal loss'. The relief is augmented by your capital allowances apportionable to your last 12 months of trading. The terminal losses are allowed against your business assessments for the three years of assessment prior to that in which you cease to trade. Under the new rules (11.22.1) this is extended to include the tax year of cessation.

11.25 Business Expansion Scheme

(TA 1988 Ss289–312, FA 1988 Ss50–53, Sch 4, FA 1993 S111, FA 1995 S68 & FA 1997 S74 & Sch 8)

Under the Business Expansion Scheme, subject to the rules, you obtained income tax relief in a year of assessment in respect of amounts subscribed for shares in a qualifying company during that year up to £40,000 in total. A qualifying company exists to carry on one or more *qualifying trades* — broadly, manufacturing, wholesale and retail business but not leasing and financial activities, etc (11.26(5)).

The Business Expansion Scheme operated regarding shares issued from 6 April 1983 up to 31 December 1993. From 1 January 1994, the Enterprise Investment Scheme (EIS) operates (11.26). This has many common features such as mainly similar rules for qualifying trades.

The following features of the Business Expansion Scheme should be noted and further details are given in previous editions of this book:

(1) As well as covering investment in new companies, shares issued by established unquoted trading companies satisfying certain conditions were included.
(2) The scheme excluded employees, paid directors and 30 per cent + shareholders.
(3) Shares on which relief was claimed must in general be held for at least five years.
(4) Claims for relief were normally needed within two years after the end of the year of assessment to which the claim related.
(5) The relief did not normally reduce the cost for capital gains tax purposes. Furthermore shares issued after 18 March 1986 are exempt from capital gains tax when first disposed of.
(6) Share capital issued in excess of £50,000 in total in any year did not qualify for relief if the company broadly had more than half its assets consisting of land and buildings (net of certain liabilities and excluding fixed plant and machinery). This test does not apply after 28 November 1994.
(7) Regarding BES shares issued on or after 1 May 1990, a maximum amount of £750,000 capital raised by a company qualified for

relief in any period of 12 months. (£5,000,000 for certain ship chartering and private rented housing.)

(8) BES relief extended to investment in companies' properties for letting under *assured tenancies*. The company needed to provide tenancies over at least a four-year period from when the BES shares were issued.

(9) From 10 March 1992, BES companies were allowed to buy properties from owner-occupiers and grant qualifying tenancies to the former owners.

(10) Tax relief for interest on loans to buy shares in a close company (13.17) issued after 13 March 1989 was not available if BES relief was available.

11.26 Enterprise Investment Scheme

(FA 1994 S137 & Sch 15, FA 1995 Ss66 & 67 & Sch 13 & FA 1997 S74 & Sch 8)

Regarding new investment from 1 January 1994, the Enterprise Investment Scheme (EIS) has replaced the Business Expansion Scheme. The EIS is available for purchases of ordinary shares in 'qualifying' unquoted trading companies. Important features are:

(1) You obtain income tax relief at 20 per cent on your investment.

(2) For 1994–95 and subsequent years, you are allowed to invest up to £100,000 in EIS companies. However, for 1993–94, a combined limit of £40,000 applied for BES and EIS investment.

(3) Subject to a maximum of £15,000, half of the amount that you invest between 6 April and 5 October in any year can be carried back to the previous tax year.

(4) There is a limit of £1,000,000 on the amount that a company can raise in a year on which EIS relief will be given. (The limit is £5,000,000 for certain shipping companies.)

(5) 'Qualifying companies' are unquoted trading companies which carry on a qualifying activity for at least three years. The range of qualifying activities is broadly similar to that for BES (11.25), but does not include private rented housing. The following rules regarding qualifying trades and companies apply broadly both for BES and EIS:

    (a) A trade whose income is mainly from royalties and licence fees does not qualify but exceptions are film production and distribution.

    (b) Companies whose business consists of research and development in general qualify.

(c) Ship chartering is a qualifying trade. Charters must not exceed one year and the ships must be UK registered and owned, managed and navigated by the company. (Pleasure craft are excluded.)
(d) Wholesaling or retailing goods normally collected or held as investments is not a qualifying trade, unless the company actively tries to sell them. Examples are fine wines and antiques.
(e) Certain parent companies are qualifying companies if all their subsidiaries are wholly owned. This extends to tiers of companies provided they are each at least 90 per cent owned. Subsidiaries can even be resident abroad if the group's trade is mainly within the UK.

(6) You must hold your EIS shares for at least five years or else your relief will be withdrawn.
(7) For EIS shares on which relief has not been withdrawn, there is capital gains tax exemption when they are first sold. Any loss you make in these circumstances is available against capital gains or on election against income.
(8) From 27 November 1996, investment in the parent of a group of companies may qualify where non-qualifying activities only form a minor part of the group activities as a whole. Previously, all group companies needed to qualify.
(9) To obtain relief, you need to be a 'qualifying investor'. That means that during the period you are not 'connected' with the company (holding over 30 per cent of the shares or an employee). This applies from incorporation (or if later, two years before issue) to five years after the issue of the shares.
(10) You can become a paid director and still qualify for EIS relief, provided you were not connected with the company or its trade before the shares were issued.
(11) The scheme extends to companies trading in the UK, whether or not incorporated and resident here. Furthermore, you will be entitled to relief on EIS shares, provided you pay UK income tax, even if you are not UK resident.
(12) The land content test (11.25(6)) originally applied for EIS purposes as for the BES. However, as from 29 November 1994 it no longer operates.
(13) Also from 29 November 1994, the parallel trades rule denying relief in certain circumstances ceased to have effect.
(14) If you subscribe for EIS shares you will be entitled to reinvestment relief where you realise capital gains on other assets after 28 November 1994, when you are UK resident and ordinarily resident. The EIS shares must be purchased within one year before and three years after the disposals and a claim to the

Revenue is needed. Subject to the rules, your gains are deferred until you dispose of the EIS shares.

11.27 Earnings basis and cash basis

If you are carrying on a trade, you will normally be taxed on an 'earnings basis'. This means that your sales for each accounts period are included as they arise and not when you receive the money. Sales normally arise when they are invoiced. In a retail shop the sales usually arise as the customers pay over the counter. Your expenses are also deductible on an arising basis and the actual date of payment is not relevant.

If you are carrying on a profession or vocation, however, the Revenue may tax you on a 'cash basis', which means by reference to the actual cash received, taking no account of uncollected fees at the end of each accounts period. (Sometimes a mixed earnings and cash basis is allowed.)

The cash basis is usually used for barristers. Other professions must prepare their opening accounts on an earnings basis but have the option of later switching to a cash basis. Often the expenses are calculated on an arising basis but in some small cases the actual expense payments are used ignoring accruals.

11.28 Post-cessation receipts
(TA 1988 Ss103–110)

If, after you permanently cease your trade, profession or vocation, you receive amounts relating to those activities, they are known as 'post-cessation receipts'. An example is a late fee payment that had not been included in your accounts because they are prepared on a cash basis or the fee was not included in your outstandings.

Post-cessation receipts are usually taxed under Schedule D Case VI (15.1). They are normally treated as earned income and you can set off unrelieved losses and capital allowances from before the cessation. You can, however, elect that any post-cessation receipts for the first six years after cessation should be added to your income from the business, etc on its last day of trading.

Relief is available for those born before 6 April 1917 and in business on 18 March 1968 who are taxed on a fraction of their post-cessation receipts varying between 19/20ths and 5/20ths. The latter fraction applies if you were born before 6 April 1903; if you were born before 6 April 1904 the fraction is 6/20ths and so on.

11.29 Class 4 National Insurance contributions

(TA 1988 S617 & FA 1996 S138)

You will be liable to pay the contributions if you are self-employed in accordance with the rules in Chapter 25 (25.5). For 1985–86 and subsequent years up to 1995–96, you could claim relief for half of your Class 4 contributions. Your total income (5.2) was reduced accordingly. However, this relief was withdrawn for 1996–97 and subsequent years, the Class 4 rate being reduced from 7.3 per cent to 6 per cent to compensate.

12 Partnerships

Special rules relate to the taxation of partnerships and these are covered in the following sections. However, a new system operates generally from 1997–98 and for partnerships *starting after 5 April 1994* (12.2).

12.1 What is a partnership?

Partnership is the relationship which exists between two persons in business together with the object of making profits. There does not necessarily have to be a written partnership agreement but the partnership must exist in fact. If no partnership is in fact operating then, even though there may be a written agreement, it would not make the partnership exist.

Since the assessment of a partnership differs from that of an individual in certain respects, the Revenue will seek to establish whether a partnership in fact exists. Points to consider include:

(1) Is there a written partnership agreement?
(2) Can the partners close down the business and are they liable for its debts?
(3) Do the partners' names appear on business stationery?
(4) What arrangements exist for dividing the profits (and property on dissolution)?

12.2 Partnerships under the new current year system

(FA 1994 Ss184–189, 215 & 216, FA 1995 S117 & FA 1996 S123)

In line with the new current year basis, changed rules apply broadly from 1997–98 for partnerships carrying on business on 5 April 1994.

These apply at once for partnerships commencing after that date. Points to note under the new system include the following:

(1) You are assessed on your share of the profits individually, rather than the partnership being assessed on the total.
(2) All partnership expenses and capital allowances are deducted from its profits.
(3) The profits are allocated to the period of account of the partnership, rather than the year of assessment.
(4) Your assessment is computed as if your profit share were derived from a trade or profession carried on by you alone. This deemed trade or profession runs from when you joined the partnership until you leave it (or it ceases). If you had originally commenced trading by yourself, the deemed trade goes back to when you started.
(5) New rules apply regarding a change of partners after 5 April 1994. This is no longer regarded as a cessation (12.5), provided there is at least one person who was a partner both in the old partnership and the new one. Consequently, the continuation basis election (12.6) is no longer needed and is withdrawn.
(6) With effect from 1996–97, new self-assessment rules take effect. These include new partnership returns for 1996–97 and enquiry procedures.
(7) Your partnership assessment for 1996–97 is on the *transitional basis*, provided it was carrying on business on 5 April 1994. For example:

Adjusted profits for the year to: 30 June 1995	£30,000
30 June 1996	40,000
	£70,000
Average for 1996–97	35,000
Capital allowances for 1996–97 (say)	5,000
Divisible between partners in 1996–97 profit sharing ratios	£30,000

(8) One partner may be made responsible for partnership tax returns, etc. If he or she is not available, a 'successor' may so act.
(9) The 1996–97 partnership assessment will normally be payable on 1 January and 1 July 1997. For 1997–98 (and subsequently), you will make payments on account on 31 January and 31 July 1988 of normally half your liability for 1996–97, with a balancing payment by 31 January 1999.

12.3 How partnership income is taxed — old system
(TA 1988 S111)

The following describes the system prior to the current year's system (12.2) including some basic points which continue.

A joint assessment to income tax under Case I or Case II of Schedule D (11.1) is made on the partners in respect of the partnership profits. This includes lower rate (20 per cent), basic rate (23 per cent) and higher rate income tax (if any) on the profits. The rules for the opening (11.7.1) and closing years (11.7.2) are generally followed as for individuals, as are those for capital allowances (11.8). However, there were special rules covering partnership changes (12.5). The 'precedent partner' (normally the senior partner), had to make a joint return of the partnership income each year.

Partnership investment income is split between the partners in their profit-sharing ratios and they personally pay any income tax arising.

When the partnership income has been determined for the purposes of Schedule D Case I or Case II, it must be split between the partners according to the proportions in which they share profits during the tax year. These proportions were not necessarily the same as the profit sharing ratios during the year when the profits were actually made. Thus if A and B made £10,000 in the year to 30 April 1994 when they split their profits 60 : 40 their partnership assessment for 1995–96 is on the preceding year basis, ie, £10,000. This was split in the ratio in which they divide profits for the year to 5 April 1996. Suppose the ratio was altered to 50 : 50 on 1 May 1994 then they were each assessed on £5,000 for 1995–96. For 1996–97, a transitional basis applies (12.2)

If a partner is remunerated partly by way of a salary and partly by receiving a share of the profits, the salary is normally not assessed under Schedule E but is included in his profit share assessable under Schedule D Case I or Case II. Interest paid to partners in respect of their capital is also treated as part of the profit share of each partner and is assessed under Schedule D Case I or Case II. Such interest is not an annual payment (4.1), nor is it taxed as investment income (8.1).

12.3.1 Example: Partnership assessments — old system

A, B and C trade in partnership sharing profits equally after the interest and salary allocations shown below. They prepare accounts to 5 April showing the following:

		Interest		*Salary*	
Year ended	*Profits*	*A*	*B*	*B*	*C*
5 April 1995	£9,000	£500	£500	£1,000	£2,000
1996	£10,000	£400	£600	£1,500	£1,500

The 1995–96 assessment under *Schedule D Case I* is as follows:

				Total	*A*	*B*	*C*
Net profit (preceding year) — year ended 5 April 1995				£9,000			
Add:	Interest	A		500			
		B		500			
	Salary	B		1,000			
		C		2,000			
				£13,000			
Less:	Interest	A	400		£400		
		B	600			£600	
	Salary	B	1,500			1,500	
		C	1,500				£1,500
				4,000			
Balance split equally				£9,000	3,000	3,000	3,000
Total assessment				£13,000	£3,400	£5,100	£4,500

Notes:

(1) In addition to the above, the normal Schedule D Case I adjustments must be made (11.4).

(2) The interest and salaries for the year to 5 April 1995 are added back to the profits.

(3) The 1995–96 assessments split includes the interest and salaries for the year to 5 April 1996.

(4) For 1997–98 and subsequently, all adjustments will relate to only one accounts year.

12.4 Partnership losses
(TA 1988 Ss380–381 & 387)

Where a partnership has an adjusted loss for any accounting period, that loss is apportioned between the partners in the same ratio as a profit would have been split. Thus the loss is split according to the profit sharing ratios applying to the year of assessment corresponding to the tax year in which the loss is made. For example, if a loss was made in the year to 5 April 1995 this was split between the partners according to their profit sharing ratios for the tax year 1995–96 (assuming that the preceding year basis of assessment applies). However, a loss made in the transitional year 1996–97 was split in the profit sharing ratios for that year and similarly for 1997–98 and future years.

Each partner can use his partnership losses as he chooses according to the various rules for obtaining loss relief (11.22). Thus he can claim for the loss to be relieved against his other income tax assessments for the tax year in which the loss is actually made or the previous year. (Under the old system, relief for the loss was available for the year of the loss and the following one). Also he can carry forward any unused balance of the loss to be set off against future profit shares from the same partnership; this applies even if the partnership had been treated as discontinued because of a partnership change (see below).

If you are a limited partner, so that your risk is limited to the capital which you have invested, your loss is also restricted in the same way. This applies broadly to losses after 19 March 1985.

12.5 Changes of partners
(TA 1988 Ss61–63 & 113)

If there was any change in the make up of a partnership caused either by a partner leaving or dying or a fresh partner joining, the partnership was treated as ceasing for taxation purposes unless the continuation election described below was made. However, different treatment applies under the new rules for changes after 5 April 1994 (12.2). A complete change in the ownership still triggers a deemed cessation. However, a partial change in the identity of the partners is treated as a continuation.

Previously, the effects of cessation caused by a change of partners were similar to any other Schedule D Case I or Case II cessation (11.7.2). Thus the assessment for the final tax year was based on the actual profits for that year and the Revenue have the option to increase the assessments for the two previous tax years to the actual profits for those years.

Up to 19 March 1985, the first years of a changed partnership were assessed in accordance with the normal commencement rules (11.7.1). However, for changes after that date, the first four years were assessed on an actual basis and then the previous year basis applied, unless you elected for years five and six to be on an actual profit basis. This was subject to a continuation election (12.6).

12.6 Election for continuation basis
(TA 1988 Ss113 & 116)

Within two years of the date of a change in the members of a partnership an election could be made to the Revenue that the partnership should be taxed on a continuation basis. The election applied for changes before 6 April 1994 (12.2). It could be made provided that at least one of the partners in the old partnership remained as a partner in the new partnership. All of the partners in both the old and the new partnership signed the election.

The effect of the election was that the partnership was not treated as ceasing for taxation purposes at the date of the change. Instead the Schedule D Case I or Case II assessment for the tax year in which the change took place was apportioned to the date of the change. Then the old partners were assessed on their share of the assessment apportioned up to the change and the new partners were assessed on the proportion after the change.

For example, suppose that the adjusted profits of a professional partnership for the year to 31 December 1992 were £12,000 and until 5 October 1993 there were three equal partners A, B and C. If with effect from that date B and C sold their partnership shares to D and assuming A, B, C and D all made the necessary election before 5 October 1995, the following Schedule D Case II assessments arise for 1993–94 (on a preceding year basis):

	6 April 1993 – 5 October 1993	*6 October 1993 – 5 April 1994*	*Total*
A	£2,000	£2,000	£4,000
B	2,000	—	2,000
C	2,000	—	2,000
D	—	4,000	4,000
	£6,000	£6,000	£12,000

There are some special rules governing partnerships between individuals and a company (TA 1988 Ss114–115).

12.7 Partnership capital gains
(TCGA S59)

When a partnership asset is sold in circumstances that if owned by an individual capital gains tax would have been payable, this tax is assessed on the partners according to their shares in the partnership asset. Thus if a capital gain of £1,000 is made from the sale of a partnership asset on 1 January 1997 and A, B, C and D share equally in the partnership assets, a capital gain of £250 each must be added to the capital gains tax assessments for 1996–97 of A, B, C and D respectively (20.1).

Where a share in a partnership changes hands, a share in all of the partnership assets is treated for capital gains tax purposes as changing ownership and this might give rise to capital gains or capital losses for the partner who is disposing of his share. Thus if A, B and C are equal partners and A sells his share to D, A is treated for capital gains tax purposes as disposing of a one-third share in each of the partnership assets to D.

12.8 Overseas partnerships
(TA 1988 S112)

If you are in partnership carrying on a trade or business and the control and management of the trade or business is outside the UK then the partnership is treated for tax purposes as being non-resident. This follows even if you or some of your other partners are resident here (17.3.4) and some of the business is conducted in this country.

Any profits arising from the partnership trade or business in this country are assessed here under Schedule D Case I. The firm is assessed in the name of any partner resident in the United Kingdom. Regarding the partnership profits earned abroad, these are assessable in respect of any profit shares of the partners resident here under Schedule D Case V according to the special rules outlined in Chapter 18. This now generally applies even if under a double tax agreement, the profits of the overseas partnership arising abroad are exempt from UK tax. From 1997–98 each partner will be assessed separately (12.2).

12.9 European economic interest groupings
(FA 1990 S69 & Sch 11)

Tax rules regarding European Economic Interest Groupings (EEIGs) operate from 1 July 1989. Such 'groupings' are business entities set up by two or more European community member states with simpler rules than traditional company law bodies—they are more akin to partnerships in some respects. EEIGs may not be formed to make profits for themselves but rather benefit all of their members. Likely activities are packing, processing, marketing and research.

An EEIG is transparent, so far as tax on income and capital gains is concerned. Thus these will only be charged to tax in the hands of the members. However, this does not apply to the deduction of tax. Thus an EEIG based in the UK is responsible for operating PAYE.

13 Companies

13.1 Introduction

The following is a general outline of the taxation of companies that are resident in the UK or are trading here through a branch or agency. In the latter case it is normally only the profits arising in this country that are taxable here. It must be stressed that the actual provisions are lengthy and many details have been omitted in this summary.

13.2 Corporation tax on profits, etc
(TA 1988 S6 & FA 1997 Ss58 & 59)

The tax on the profits, etc of companies is called corporation tax which is charged at the present rate of 33 per cent, subject to special relief for companies with profits under £1,500,000 (13.7). Full corporation tax is now charged both on a company's profits and its capital gains (13.15).

Corporation tax applies not only to limited companies, but also to certain associations and unlimited companies. A company's income must be considered for each accounting period (13.4). It is charged to corporation tax on the basis of the actual income assessable for each accounting period according to the rules of the various cases of Schedule D (2.3.1) or other Schedules if applicable.

The rate of corporation tax was fixed by Parliament in the Finance Act each year for the preceding 'financial year'. A 'financial year' commences on 1 April and for example the financial year 1997 is the year to 31 March 1998. The Finance Act 1991 retrospectively reduced the rate for 1990 from 35 per cent to 34 per cent and the rates for subsequent years have been fixed at 33 per cent. The following table shows the rates of corporation tax over the years.

13.2.1 Table: Full corporation tax rates

Financial year	*Tax rate*	*Taxable fraction of capital gains*
1973–1982	52%	15/26
1983	50%	3/5
1984	45%	2/3
1985	40%	3/4
1986	35%	6/7*
1987–1989	35%	All
1990	34%	All
1991–1997	33%	All

* All if gains after 16 March 1987

13.3 The imputation system

If a company pays dividends, these are paid gross to the shareholders, and tax of 20/80ths of the dividend must be paid over to the Revenue as what is known as 'advance corporation tax' (13.6). Before 6 April 1994, the ACT rate was 22.5/77.5ths.

From 6 April 1988 to 5 April 1993 the ACT rate was 25/75ths. The ACT can be deducted from the company's corporation tax bill, so that effectively a lower rate than 33 per cent is paid. Before 6 April 1993 the shareholders were 'imputed' with tax of 25/75ths of their dividends, being only liable for tax at the higher rate.

From 6 April 1993, UK shareholders obtain a tax credit of 20/80ths of their dividends but (if liable) pay the higher rate on their dividends plus tax credits. Thus a dividend of £80 carries a tax credit of £20 and you pay higher rate tax on £80 + £20 at 40 per cent making £40. But you deduct the credit of £20 and only pay £20. If your top tax rate is the basic rate (23 per cent) you pay no extra tax on your dividends, under the rules (FA 1993 S77).

Before 6 April 1993, you got a tax credit of 25/75ths of your dividends. Thus, if you received a dividend of £75, you were imputed with a tax credit of 25/75ths × £75 = £25. You paid higher rates of tax on £75 + £25 = £100, but you deducted the £25 tax credit from your total tax bill. The imputation of income tax in the shareholders' hands on their dividends has resulted in the present system being known as the 'imputation system' of corporation tax.

13.4 Accounting periods for corporation tax
(TA 1988 Ss8, 10 & 478 & Sch 30)

Corporation tax is charged in respect of accounting periods. These usually coincide with the periods for which the company prepares its annual accounts but cannot exceed 12 months in duration. Thus, if a company prepares accounts for a period of 18 months, the first 12 months will constitute one accounting period and the remaining six months are treated as another accounting period.

The actual tax is payable nine months after the end of each accounting period, or within 30 days from the date of issue of the assessment if this is later. This is subject to changes made by the 'pay and file' system (13.4.1).

Interest may arise on overdue corporation tax in accordance with the rules (16.8.2). Interest rates are as follows:

From	*Rate per cent*	*From*	*Rate per cent*
6 February 1996	$6\frac{1}{4}$	6 July 1989	$12\frac{1}{4}$
6 March 1995	7	6 January 1989	$11\frac{1}{2}$
6 October 1994	$6\frac{1}{4}$	6 October 1988	$10\frac{3}{4}$
6 January 1994	$5\frac{1}{2}$	6 August 1988	$9\frac{3}{4}$
6 March 1993	$6\frac{1}{4}$	6 May 1988	$7\frac{3}{4}$
6 December 1992	7	6 December 1987	$8\frac{1}{4}$
6 November 1992	$7\frac{3}{4}$	6 September 1987	9
6 October 1991	$9\frac{1}{4}$	6 June 1987	$8\frac{1}{4}$
6 July 1991	10	6 April 1987	9
6 May 1991	$10\frac{3}{4}$	6 November 1986	$9\frac{1}{2}$
6 March 1991	$11\frac{1}{2}$	6 August 1986	$8\frac{1}{2}$
6 November 1990	$12\frac{1}{4}$	1 May 1985	11
6 November 1989	13		

13.4.1 The pay and file system
(TA 1988 Ss8, 10, 419 & 826, FA 1990 Ss91 & 93–100 & Schs 16–17, FA 1993 Sch 14 & FA 1994 Ss181–183)

The Keith Committee made various proposals on filing accounts interest and penalties which were enacted in 1987. These take effect starting with the first accounting period of each company which ends after 30 September 1993. However, the new filing arrangements only apply where notices to make corporation tax returns are issued after 31 December 1993. The scheme is called the 'pay and file system'. Particular points are:

(1) Companies must pay corporation tax nine months after their accounting dates, whether or not assessments have been raised.

(2) Tax paid late or repaid by the Revenue carries interest from the required payment date.
(3) Accounts (and normally, subject to notice being issued, a return) are required to be submitted to the Revenue within 12 months from the accounting date.
(4) If accounts are filed late without excuse, penalties are as follows:

	Penalty		*% of unpaid tax*
	Basic	*Persistent Failure*	
Return overdue by:			
Up to 3 months	£100	£500	
Over 3 months	£200	£1,000	
Delay from end of return period:			
Over 18 months			10%
Over 24 months			20%

(5) Companies should ensure that their accounting systems provide adequate information to comply with the new rules.
(6) If a company cannot supply actual figures, estimated ones will be accepted provided all reasonable steps have been taken to provide correct ones. These must then be supplied shortly.
(7) Losses are formally determined by assessment, in the same way as profits. Formal determinations also apply to capital allowances, management expenses and charges available for surrender as group relief.
(8) From a date to be announced, corporation tax returns will require companies to make self-assessments of their tax. Also from that date, a new scheme for the Revenue to make enquiries into returns, subject to giving notice, will begin. It has been announced that the changes will not apply to accounting periods ending in 1998 or earlier.

13.5 Repayment supplement and interest on overpaid corporation tax *(TA 1988 S825 & 826)*

This applies for a company if it receives a tax repayment more than a year after the date that corporation tax is due for the relevant accounting period and after 31 July 1975. However, no repayment supplement is due for accounting periods ending after 30 September 1993, although interest is payable. The repayment supplement is tax free, and is calculated from the date one year after the due date for paying corporation tax until the end of the tax month (ending fifth day of next month) in which the repayment is made. If the original tax had not been paid, by the anniversary of the due date, the interest runs from the anniversary following the payment of the tax. Where loss relief is claimed (13.11), repayment supplement may arise with reference to the accounting period of the loss, rather than any earlier period when the original profits were made. The rates are as on overdue corporation tax payments (13.4).

For accounting periods ending after 30 September 1993, tax-free interest is paid on overpaid tax. For corporation tax, interest normally runs from the payment date (or due and payable date, if later) to the date of repayment. The rates are as follows:

From	*Rate per cent*
1 October 1993	3.35
6 January 1994	2.5
6 October 1994	3.25
6 March 1995	4
6 February 1996	3.25

13.6 ACT on dividends, etc

(TA 1988 Ss14, 209, 238 & 239, FA 1993 Ss77–81, Sch 6 & FA 1997 Ss69–71 & Sch 7)

Companies have to pay 'advance corporation tax' (ACT) at 20/80ths on their payments of dividends (13.3). This tax is also payable on other 'qualifying distributions'. The rate was 3/7ths from 6 April 1979 to 5 April 1986, then 29/71sts to 5 April 1987 and 27/73rds to 5 April 1988, following which 25/75ths applied until 5 April 1993 and 9/31sts to 5 April 1994.

13.6.1 Distributions

Under the present system there are two different classes of distribution known as qualifying and non-qualifying distributions. Qualifying distributions are dividends and similar payments. Other examples are interest on certain securities and after 14 May 1992 on Equity Notes. Non-qualifying distributions are those which are really distributions of special sorts of shares, etc which carry a potential future claim on the company's profits: for example, bonus debentures or bonus redeemable shares. Whereas qualifying distributions are subjected to ACT, in the case of non-qualifying distributions, no ACT is payable by the company. The shareholder gets no tax credit (20 per cent) and is not liable to such tax on the non-qualifying distribution. He is, however, liable to the excess of his higher rate tax over the tax credit rate (20 per cent) on the actual value of the non-qualifying distribution.

With effect from 8 October 1996, new treatment applies to certain distributions which are linked to transactions in securities. These include where companies purchase their own shares. (FA 1997 Sch 7.) The distributions are now treated as foreign income dividends (13.6.7), so as to deny the recipients any repayment of the tax credits. (Share dealers take such distributions into their trading profits from 26 November 1996.)

Distributions generally exempted from the new rules include cash alternatives to stock dividends and certain dividends paid before a company is sold. Furthermore, group income elections (13.16(2)) can be made to pay dividends within the new legislation gross, provided the paying company is wholly owned by the recipient.

13.6.2 Accounting periods for ACT

(TA 1988 Sch 13 & 16 & FA 1996 Schs 23 & 24)

Companies must account to the Revenue for ACT on a three-monthly basis. Returns are made for each three months to 31 March and 30 June, 30 September and 31 December respectively — and so on. Also if the company's accounting period does not end on one of these dates, the period of three months during which it ends is divided into two separate periods for which returns must be submitted. Thus if a company's accounts run to 30 November each year, it submits ACT returns for the period 1 October to 30 November and 1 December to 31 December, as well as for the other three quarters each year.

The ACT return must show for the relevant period the 'franked payments' (see below) and 'franked investment income' received (see below) as well as the amount of ACT payable and certain other details. A cheque in settlement of the ACT due should normally be sent with the return. This is due within 14 days of the return period. In computing the ACT due for payment, companies may deduct tax credits on receipts of 'franked investment income' during the relevant period. Minor modifications to returns will be made when self assessment for companies takes effect.

13.6.3 Franked payment

(TA 1988 S238)

This is defined as being a qualifying distribution made by a company together with the relevant ACT. Thus, a qualifying distribution of £8,000 represents a franked payment of £10,000 (ie, £8,000 + £8,000 × 20/80).

13.6.4 Franked investment income
(TA 1988 S238)

This consists of income from a UK resident company (17.3.3) being distributions in respect of which tax credits are obtained. A company's franked investment income is the amount including the relevant tax credits. Thus if a company receives a dividend of £800, this is treated as being franked investment income of £1,000 (ie, £800 + £800 × 20/80).

13.6.5 Setting off ACT against 'mainstream' corporation tax
(TA 1988 Ss238–246)

As its name suggests, advance corporation tax is a pre-payment of the main or mainstream corporation tax bill of a company. The latter is only ascertained when accounts are submitted to the Revenue after the end of the accounting period.

There is a limit to the amount of ACT which can be off-set against a company's 'mainstream' corporation tax liability. This limit is the amount of ACT which would be paid on a full distribution of the company's income excluding capital gains but before the deduction of any tax. In computing this full distribution, account is taken of the notional ACT payable.

For example, if a company makes adjusted revenue profits of £2,000,000 before tax for the year to 31 March 1997, the maximum set-off for ACT is £400,000. Thus, if the company distributed £1,600,000 it would pay ACT of £1,600,000 × 20/80 = £400,000 and so its entire profit would be absorbed. After the end of its accounts year it would be assessed to £2,000,000 × 33 per cent corporation tax (£660,000) from which £400,000 ACT would be deducted leaving a net amount payable of £260,000 (13 per cent). (This is of course an arbitrary calculation because after taking account of all of the corporation tax payable in this example, the distribution would produce a deficit.)

For accounting periods beginning on or after 17 March 1987, but not before, ACT may be set off against corporation tax on capital gains (13.15). Where an accounting period straddled 17 March 1987, only corporation tax on gains after that date qualified for set-off.

A company obtains relief for overseas tax suffered by deducting it from the corporation tax falling on the same income. For accounting periods ending after 31 March 1984, the overseas tax is deducted before any relief is taken for ACT. However, for accounting periods beginning after

2 June 1986, the rules ensure that the net corporation tax charge on foreign income, after double tax relief and ACT, is at least the now 13 per cent minimum (see previous page).

13.6.6 Carry-back and carry-forward of ACT
(TA 1988 Ss239 & 245)

Any ACT which is not relieved against corporation tax payable for the accounting period in which the relevant distribution is made, because of the restriction mentioned above, is known as 'surplus ACT'. This surplus ACT can be carried back and off-set against corporation tax payable for any accounting periods beginning in the six years preceding that in which the relevant distribution is made. A claim to this effect must be made within two years of the end of the period for which the surplus ACT arises.

If a claim as above is made to the Revenue, the surplus ACT will be allocated to one or more earlier periods and a reduction in corporation tax payable or a repayment of corporation tax will result.

Any surplus ACT which is not carried back as above may normally be carried forward without time limit to be set off against future corporation tax payable.

Relief is restricted if within three years there is both a change in the ownership of the company and a major change in the nature or conduct of its trade (or this becomes negligible). ACT relating to an accounting period before the change in ownership cannot be carried forward to a period after that change. Furthermore, ACT arising after such a change cannot be carried back before the change, where this occurs after 15 March 1993.

13.6.7 Foreign income dividend scheme
(TA 1988 S246A, FA 1994 S138 & Sch 16 & FA 1996 Sch 27)

Under the foreign income dividend (FID) scheme, from 1 July 1994, a company can elect to pay an FID. ACT is payable, but FIDs carry no tax credit. If the dividend is paid out of foreign income profits, the company is able to recover surplus ACT. The FID scheme is aimed at the surplus ACT arising when UK corporation tax is reduced or eliminated by relief for foreign tax.

Broadly from 8 October 1996, certain distributions linked to transactions in securities and companies purchasing their own shares are treated as if they were FIDs (13.6.1). As a result, they earn no tax credit. However, shareholders subject to income tax are treated as though the FIDs have bourne income tax at 20 per cent.

An FID may be paid without ACT by an 'international headquarters company'. At least 80 per cent of the share capital of such a company must be owned by non-residents with no shareholder owning less than 5 per cent. Among improvements operating for accounting periods ending after 28 November 1995, ownership by such a company can be through any number of tiers.

13.7 Small companies rate

(TA 1988 S13 & FA 1997 S59)

This is the term used to describe the special reduced corporation tax rate which is charged on company profits which do not exceed certain limits for a given accounting period. The profits in question comprise those on which corporation tax is paid together with 'franked investment income' (13.6.4) for the period. The rate is 23 per cent from 1 April 1997. However, small companies rate does not apply to close-investment holding companies for chargeable accounting periods beginning after 31 March 1989 (13.18).

The small companies rate applies to periods after 31 March 1973 and previous rates have been as follows:

	%
3 years to 31 March 1986	30
Year to 31 March 1987	29
Year to 31 March 1988	27
8 years to 31 March 1996	25
Year to 31 March 1997	24

The rate is to be charged on the profits of a company with no 'associated companies' (see 13.8) provided these do not exceed £300,000. If the profits are between £300,000 and £1,500,000, some marginal relief is given. These figures have been fixed for the year to 31 March 1995 and subsequently. Prior to this they were £250,000 and £1,250,000 for the 3 years to 31 March 1994, £200,000 and £1,000,000 for the year to 31 March 1991, £150,000 and £750,000 for the year to 31 March 1990 and previously £100,000 and £500,000.

The tax is then broadly the full corporation tax rate (13.2.1) on the profits less a fixed fraction (currently 1/40) of the amount by which they fall short of £1,500,000, etc. Thus there is now a marginal rate of 35.5 per cent within the £300,000–£1,500,000 profit band. This assumes there are no 'associated companies' (see 13.8). For financial year 1990, the fraction was 9/400. For financial years 1991–1995, the fraction was 1/50 with 9/400 applying for 1996.

If a company has 'associated companies', then the above-mentioned figures of £300,000 and £1,500,000 must be divided by one plus the number of 'associated companies' connected with the company under consideration. Thus, if five associated companies comprise a group, they will each pay 23 per cent on their profits for the year to 31 March 1998 if these are no more than £60,000 (£300,000/5) each. If any of the companies has profits between £60,000 and £300,000 (£1,500,000/5), some marginal relief is obtained.

13.8 Associated companies

(TA 1988 Ss416 & 417)

These are companies which are either under common control or one controls the other. Control broadly comprises voting power or entitlement to the greater part of either the profits, or the assets on liquidation.

In considering whether two companies are under common control, shares held by a husband and wife and their minor children are considered as one. If, however, one company is controlled by an individual and another company is controlled by a more distant relative such as his brother, the two companies are not normally treated as being 'associated'.

Also 'associated' are the settlor of a trust and its trustees. Furthermore, if you are interested in any shares held by a trust, you are 'associated' with the trustees. Two companies can be associated if both are interested in the same shares.

13.9 The computation of assessable profits

(TA 1988 Ss8–9 & 337–341)

It is strictly speaking necessary to compute the income assessable under each Schedule (and Case of Schedule D) and aggregate these to find the total amount chargeable to corporation tax. All corporation tax assessments are made on an 'actual' basis, however, instead of the preceding year basis that sometimes applies for income tax purposes; for example, Schedule D Case I.

The adjustments to the accounts profits that are required for corporation tax purposes follow with some modifications of the normal rules for income tax assessments described earlier in the book. The following are some of the necessary adjustments:

(1) Deduct any franked investment income (13.6.4).
(2) Add back payments made for non-business purposes (11.3.2).
(3) Add back capital losses and payments and deduct capital profits and capital receipts. The capital gain less capital losses of the company must be computed for the accounting period according to the capital gains tax rules (20.1).
(4) Add back legal and other professional charges relating to capital projects.
(5) Add back business entertaining unless in connection with the company's own staff or, before 15 March 1988, overseas customers (11.3.2). Gifts of advertising articles such as diaries, pens, etc of less than £10 value to each customer are also allowable.
(6) Add back depreciation and amortisation charged in the accounts in respect of fixed assets.
(7) Adjust the interest payable and receivable to the actual gross payments and receipts during the accounting period (if this is different from the amount shown in the accounts).
(8) Deduct capital allowances for the accounting period (see below and 11.8).
(9) Add back any balancing charges and deduct any balancing allowances (11.9.4).
(10) Add income tax at 20 per cent to any building society interest received. This income tax is calculated by multiplying the actual interest received by 20/80 (2.7). The tax must then be deducted from the total corporation tax payable. (Prior to 6 April 1996 the rate was 25 per cent).
(11) Add accruals of rent from members of the same group of companies who have already obtained tax relief (15.10.11). This applies to rent accruing on or after 10 March 1992.

13.10 Special capital allowances rules for companies

The normal capital allowances rules for businesses, etc (11.8), apply to companies subject to a number of special rules including the following:

(1) An individual in business can claim that his writing down allowances should be at a lower rate than the normal rate of 25 per cent. Companies also have this right (CAA S24).

(2) Where there is a 'company reconstruction without change of ownership' as a result of which one company takes over all of the assets and business of another company, the former continues to receive exactly the same capital allowances on the assets transferred as the old company would have got. A reconstruction without change of ownership takes place if at any time during the two years following the reconstruction, no less than 75 per cent of the acquiring company belongs to the same people who owned no less than 75 per cent of the old company. (This is treated for all corporation tax purposes as a continuation of the trade (TA 1988 Ss343–344).)

(3) Special rules now apply where a UK trade is transferred in exchange for shares from one EC company to a company in another EC state. Balancing adjustments are not made, subject to certain conditions (11.9.4).

(4) Under the 'pay and file' system, operating for the first accounting period ending after 30 September 1993, a formal claim for capital allowances is needed. This is included in the new corporation tax return. You no longer need to disclaim allowances, since you simply claim the required amount.

(5) From 6 April 1995, companies starting further trades may have their capital allowances on plant etc restricted for the first accounting year (FA 1995 S102).

13.11 Losses

(TA 1988 Ss393–396, 768 & 768A–C & FA 1995 S135 & Sch 26)

The loss carry-back rules were improved for accounting periods ending after 31 March 1991. Losses made in such accounting periods can be relieved against profits for the three previous years, provided the same trade has been carried on during that time. Relief is also denied where there is a change of ownership after 13 June 1991 and a major change in the nature or conduct of the trade. Thus if your company has a loss for the year to 30 April 1993, it can claim to offset this against profits going back to the year to 30 April 1990. A claim to the Revenue is needed within generally two years of the end of the accounting period when the loss was incurred. However, the Revenue are empowered to allow extra time.

If, for an accounting period of a company ending before 1 April 1991, a trading loss resulted after the necessary corporation tax adjustments, then a repayment of the tax on an equal amount of the profits (of any description) for the same period could be obtained. A claim was required and this could also extend to the profits for the previous period. The loss could only be carried back over a period equal in length to that in which it arose. A claim to the Revenue was needed within two years of the end of the accounting period in which the loss occured.

As an alternative to the above, a repayment of tax deducted at source from interest received and tax credits on dividends can be obtained. Otherwise the losses will be carried forward and relieved against future profits. (This is subject to possible restriction if the ownership of the company changes, similar to above.) Losses on shares in qualifying trading companies sold by investment companies can be set off against their surplus franked investment income. This follows the general relief against income now available for such losses made by investment companies (20.14).

The anti-avoidance provisions applying to losses carried forward by a company whose ownership changes, relate in modified form to capital losses and ACT. Investment companies are normally covered, where there is a change in the ownership of such a company after 28 November 1994. Excess management charges and charges on income brought forward from before the change will not be allowed against subsequent income and gains if:

(1) During the three years afterwards, the capital (as defined) increases by at least £1m or more than doubles, compared with in the year before, or
(2) There is a major change in the nature or conduct of the business within 3 years before and 3 years after the change, or
(3) The business had become small or negligible before the change and subsequently revived.

Under the 'pay and file' system, a trading loss in an accounting period ended after 30 September 1993 is normally automatically set off against future profits in the same trade. However, an exception is where claims already have been made to relieve the loss in other ways. The new corporation tax return form includes spaces to keep track of the losses. The company will be able to set aside the automatic carry-forward, so as to use part or all of the losses as group relief.

13.12 Reconstructions

(TA 1988 Ss343 & 344)

A 'company reconstruction without change of ownership' (13.10(2)) has other advantages apart from capital allowance continuity. In particular where a company takes over the trade and assets of another and they are under at least 75 per cent common ownership, any trading losses are carried over with the trade. However, the unused tax losses may be restricted if the original company is insolvent when its trade is transferred.

13.13 Group loss relief
(TA 1988 Ss402–413 & Sch 18 & FA 1997 S68)

In a group of companies (ie, parent and subsidiaries) the trading losses (including capital allowances, etc) of respective group members can be offset by way of group relief against the profits of others provided that:

(1) The necessary claim is made within two years of the end of the accounting period.

(2) The group relationship exists throughout the respective accounting periods of the loss making and profit making companies. Otherwise the relief is only obtained for the period during which the group relationship exists; profits and losses being apportioned on a time basis if necessary.

(3) The parent and subsidiary companies are all resident in the UK and the parent has at least a 75 per cent interest in each of the subsidiaries. Also the parent company must be entitled to at least both 75 per cent of the distributable profits of each subsidiary and 75 per cent of the assets available on the liquidation of each subsidiary. Option arrangements, etc made after 14 November 1991 are to be taken into account in calculating the percentages, as if they had been exercised.

(4) Subject to certain special rules group relief also applies to a consortium where UK companies own between them ordinary shares of a loss making company or of a holding company which owns 90 per cent of a loss making company. It is necessary for 75 per cent or more of the ordinary shares to be owned by the consortium with no less than 5 per cent held by each member (thus the maximum number is 20). Losses for accounting periods made by consortium companies can be surrendered down to a company which is jointly owned.

(5) Where a company joins or leaves a group during its accounting period the time apportionment basis (see above) may be set aside if it operates unfairly. A 'just and reasonable method' is then used. A similar rule applies in consortium situations.

(6) Subject to certain conditions, a loss can be claimed partly as group relief and partly as consortium relief. Also, consortium relief can

flow through to other companies in a consortium member's group.

(7) It should be noted that no group relief is available for the losses of dual-resident investment companies (15.10.15).

13.14 Terminal losses

(TA 1988 S394)

These were available to a company in a similar way to an individual who ceases trading (11.24). Thus, a company was entitled to claim to set off a terminal loss incurred in its last 12 months of trading against its profits for the three preceding years.

The terminal loss rules only apply for companies incurring losses in an accounting period ending before 1 April 1991. Losses in subsequent periods may in any event be relieved against profits for the three previous years (13.11).

13.15 Companies' capital gains and capital losses

(TCGA Ss8 & 170–192, TA 1988 Ss345–347, 400 & 435 & Sch 29, FA 1993 S88 & Sch 8 & FA 1994 S94)

The capital gains of companies are now charged to corporation tax at the normal rates. This applies for gains realised from 17 March 1987. (Prior to this, effectively companies paid 30 per cent on their net gains.) Thus a gain made by a company with £1.25m profits bears 33 per cent tax. However, a gain of £20,000 made by a company with £50,000 other taxable profits pays the 23 per cent small companies rate on the gain (13.7).

An exception concerns the capital gains which life assurance companies make for their policyholders. These remain taxed at 30 per cent. This only applies to the policyholders' funds; any shareholders' profits are now taxable under the new arrangements.

Capital losses in accounting periods may be set off against gains, so that the net gains are taxable. Chargeable gains can be relieved by means of capital losses in the same period or those brought forward from previous periods. Trading losses can be set off against capital profits of the same period or the previous period. Trading losses in accounting periods ending after 31 March 1991 can be set off against gains going back three years (13.11). Capital profits can also be set off by group loss relief claims (13.13). Trading losses brought forward from previous periods, however, can only be set off against future trading profits and not against future chargeable gains.

Capital losses (20.13) incurred by a company can only be set off against any capital gains of the company in the same accounting period or a future accounting period. Unused capital losses can be carried forward to future years even if the company has ceased trading whereas a cessation prevents trading losses from being carried forward. Companies are prevented from manufacturing capital losses by sales from large holdings (2 per cent upwards) of another company's shares and buying them back within a month if quoted and six months otherwise.

Under TCGA S13 UK resident and domiciled shareholders of an overseas company can have its capital gains apportioned to them if the company would have been close if UK resident. This rule also covers overseas trusts with shares in such companies. The effect is that UK beneficiaries of the trusts could then be taxed, if they receive any benefit (20.32). The apportionment of gains accruing after 27 November 1995 will depend on the extent of each UK shareholder's participation in the overseas company (FA 1996 S174).

As from 15 March 1988, the exploitation of capital gains tax indexation allowance through inter-group financing was countered. From the same date, the rules were amended to ensure that share exchanges by companies in the same group do not result in capital gains or losses being charged or allowed more than once.

As from 1 January 1992, F2A 1992 introduced various rules concerning capital gains tax where a trade owned by one EC company is transferred to another in exchange for shares or securities. Of particular importance is where a UK trade is transferred in this way from a company resident in one EC country to one resident in another. Under these circumstances, the assets are treated as being transferred at values giving no capital gain or loss, provided certain anti-avoidance provisions are not infringed.

Previously, it was possible for a group of companies to buy a company with unused capital losses and then introduce their own assets prior to sale. Any gains on sale would then be offset against the losses. This was stopped for sales after 15 March 1993 regarding losses from a company which joined the group after 31 March 1987. Losses it subsequently realises on assets it held on joining the group after that date are also restricted. Post-11 March 1994 disposals of these assets are included, even if first transferred within the group.

13.16 Groups of companies

(TA 1988 Ss240, 247 & 248 & 402–413, FA 1989 Ss97–102 & FA 1995 Ss47 & 48)

Various special provisions relate to groups of companies (broadly parent and subsidiaries). A subsidiary company is classified according to the percentage of its ordinary capital owned (directly or indirectly) by its parent. Thus a 51 per cent subsidiary is over 50 per cent owned by its parent; and a 75 per cent subsidiary is not less than 75 per cent so owned. For these purposes, loan financing may play a part in calculating the percentage owned, unless 'normal commercial loans' (TA 1988 Sch 18).

Some of the main rules relating to groups of companies are as follows:

(1) Group loss relief is available in respect of a parent company and its 75 per cent subsidiaries subject to various rules (13.13).

(2) Provided the necessary election is made to the Revenue, dividend payments from 51 per cent subsidiaries to the parent may be made without having to account for ACT. A similar rule relates to inter-group interest payments. These provisions only apply to companies resident in the UK. Also included are payments from a consortium-owned trading or holding company to the consortium members, where the consortium owns at least 75 per cent of the ordinary shares. Each consortium member must own at least 5 per cent; before 1 January 1985, consortia were limited to five members, but from that date there is no limit apart from the 5 per cent minimum.
From 27 July 1989, there needs to be a group relationship in an economic sense between the companies. For example, one company needs not only more than 50 per cent of the other but also to be entitled to more than 50 per cent of the distributable profits and of the assets in a winding up.

(3) Transfers of assets within a group consisting of a parent and its 75 per cent subsidiaries (all resident in the UK) do not generally give rise to capital gains tax. This excludes certain dual resident companies. The parent must be effectively entitled to over 50 per cent of the profits of the subsidiary and of its assets on winding up.) When the asset leaves the group, however, capital gains tax is paid on the entire chargeable gain on the asset whilst it was owned by any group company (TCGA S171). Also, rules restrict schemes to reduce tax on selling subsidiaries (15.10.17).

Assets are charged when a company leaves the group. Also, since 29 November 1994, capital gains tax on an asset can be charged where two companies are degrouped together (FA 1995 S43).

(4) Capital gains tax 'roll-over relief' (20.25) applies to a UK group consisting of a parent company and its 75 per cent subsidiaries. The gain on an asset sold by one trading company may be 'rolled over' against the purchase of an asset by another trading company (excluding certain dual resident companies) in the group (TCGA S175 & FA 1995 S47). (Property holding and non-trading companies which hold assets used for trade by trading companies in the group are also included.) After 28 November 1994, relief applies for disposals under compulsory purchase orders where another group company acquires replacement land.

(5) If a parent company holds more than 50 per cent of the ordinary shares of a subsidiary and is entitled to more than 50 per cent of its distributable profits and more than 50 per cent of its assets on liquidation, the parent can transfer to its subsidiary relief for ACT. Thus if the parent pays a dividend of £8,000 it gets £2,000 ACT relief, but instead of taking this itself it can surrender the relief to its subsidiary which then deducts £2,000 from its corporation tax bill. If the subsidiary ceases to be owned by the parent, any unused ACT will be lost. However, for accounting periods ending after 13 March 1989, this does not apply if the companies remain in the same overall group.

(6) A special rule applies to interest payments between companies under common control, including a parent and 51 per cent (or more) subsidiaries. To prevent relief for the payer occurring in one year and tax being paid the next, the interest is to be treated as received on the day when paid. This rule applies where the paying company obtains relief for the interest as a charge on income and the recipient is taxed under Case III (8.4).

(7) ACT surrendered from one group company to another, which remains unused is lost if there is a major change in the recipient company's business within three years.

13.16.1 Group rules introduced with 'pay and file'
(FA 1989 S102 & FA 1990 Ss101–103 & Sch 16)

With the introduction of 'pay and file' (13.4.1) for accounting periods ended after 30 September 1993, revised rules operate for groups, including the following:

(1) In a group of companies, a refund of tax in one company can be set off against liabilities in other companies by election. The object is to avoid companies being penalised by the differential between interest payable and receivable under the new system.

(2) Improved and more flexible procedures are introduced concerning group relief claims.
(3) Claims may be made and be capable of being withdrawn within two years of the end of the accounting period. If later, this is to be extended to the date that the profits and losses for the period are determined, but no more than six years from the end of the period.
(4) Trading losses which have been relieved against the profits of a later period will be allowed to be reallocated and surrendered as group relief.
(5) New rules applying for accounting periods ending after self-assessment is introduced will make it easier for companies to make and withdraw ACT surrenders (FA 1996 Sch 25).

13.17 Close companies

(TA 1988 Ss414–430 & Sch 19 & FA 1989 Ss103–107 & Sch 12)

Special provisions relate to 'close' companies, more particularly, for periods beginning before 1 April 1989 and are described in greater depth in previous editions of this book. Close companies are broadly those under the control of five or fewer persons and their 'associates'. The latter term includes close family such as husband, wife, child, father, mother, brother, sister, etc. A quoted company is not 'close', however, if not less than 35 per cent of its voting shares are owned by the general public.

There is also an alternative test by reference to whether five or fewer persons and their 'associates' would receive broadly the greater part of the company's assets on liquidation which would be available for distribution.

A UK subsidiary of an overseas parent company is 'close' if the latter would have itself been 'close' if resident here. It is thus seen that most small or medium companies are likely to be 'close' companies unless they are subsidiaries of non-close companies. The majority of 'family' companies are 'close'.

13.17.1 Apportionment of income under the imputation system

(TA 1988 Ss423–430 & Sch 19 & FA 1989 S103 & Sch 12)

For periods beginning *before 1 April 1989*, the Revenue could apportion among the shareholders the excess of the 'relevant income' of a close company over its distributions. In the case of a company which was a trading company or member of a trading group, no apportionment was made if the excess was under £1,001. For property investment companies the threshold was £251. Subject to the rules, such as abatement, 'relevant income' consisted of not more than the company's 'distributable investment income' plus 50 per cent of its property income.

If a close company ceased to trade, its distribution requirement included all of its trading and property income after abatement for its final chargeable accounting period and any other chargeable accounting periods ending within a year of the date of cessation and prior to 27 March 1980. For subsequent periods, trading income was excluded from the distribution requirement. The company could not claim to retain money for business purposes in these circumstances. However, for accounting periods beginning after 31 March 1989, there is no distribution requirement.

13.17.2 Loans and distributions for close companies *(TA 1988 Ss418–422 & FA 1996 S173)*

A special provision regarding close companies which remains operative is that if they make loans to their 'participators' (see below) or associates of the latter, the companies are charged tax at the ACT rate on the amounts. (If the loan is repaid to the company, the tax will be repaid.) Thus if a loan of £8,000 is made to a participator the company will be assessed to tax of 20/80 × £8,000 = £2,000. Loans by companies controlled by or subsequently acquired by close companies are also covered by this rule.

Under new rules which apply for loans made in accounting periods ending on or after 31 March 1996, the tax is due 9 months after the end of the accounting period. If the loan is repaid before the tax is due, it is not necessary to pay the tax. Previously, the due date was only 14 days after the end of the accounting period in which the loan was made and the Revenue could assess loans even if repaid.

Should a close company lend money to a participator or his associate and then release the debt, higher rate tax is assessed on the recipient in respect of the grossed up equivalent of the loan. Thus in the above example, if the company releases the participator from his debt he will pay higher rate tax on £10,000 (£8,000 + £2,000). A deduction of £2,000 will be made, however, from the total tax payable.

The meaning of the term 'distribution' (dividend, etc) is extended in the case of close companies to include living expenses and accommodation, etc provided for a 'participator' (or his associate). A 'participator' means broadly a person having a share or interest in the capital or income of a company, including, for example, a shareholder or loan creditor.

The effect of treating a payment as a distribution is that it is not deductible from the taxable profit of the company. ACT on any 'qualifying distributions' (13.6.1) including the above is paid to the Revenue.

13.18 Close investment holding companies (CICs)

(FA 1989 Ss90, 105 & 106 & Sch 12)

(1) Provisions having effect for accounting periods beginning after 31 March 1989 imposed harsher taxation on certain Close Investment Holding Companies (CICs).
(2) A CIC is a close company which is neither a 'trading company' nor a member of a trading group, nor a property investment company (which lets to non-connected persons).
(3) Broadly, a trading company is one which exists wholly or mainly for the purpose of trading on a commercial basis.
(4) Dealing in property or shares does not cause a company to be a CIC. Similarly, mixed property dealing and investment companies are not CICs.
(5) CICs are subject to 33 per cent corporation tax regardless of their level of profits. They do not obtain the benefit of the 23 per cent small companies rate.
(6) If a shareholder waives, or does not receive a dividend, the extent to which someone else is entitled to be repaid a tax credit may be restricted. The Revenue may request information and make 'just and reasonable' restrictions. This does not apply where, for example, there is only one class of shares.
(7) Where a CIC takes out a life assurance policy after 13 March 1989, profits subsequently realised will be taxed, subject to the rules.

13.19 Non-resident companies trading in the UK

(TA 1988 S11)

Where a non-resident company (17.3.3) carries on a trade in this country through a branch or agency here, corporation tax is charged in respect of the profits of the branch or agency. If those profits are also subject to tax in the country of residence of the company, double tax relief may be available (18.6). (Special rules apply where companies become non-resident (17.3.3).)

13.20 UK companies with overseas income

Any overseas income of a company that is resident in this country is subject to corporation tax on the gross amount of such income. Double tax relief is frequently available in respect of overseas income that is taxed both in the UK and abroad.

If a UK company receives a dividend from an overseas company from which withholding tax has been deducted, the gross dividend is included in the taxable profits subject to corporation tax. Normally, double tax relief for the withholding tax suffered is given against the corporation tax payable. (Withholding tax is tax that is 'withheld' from the dividend when the latter is paid. It is thus a form of tax deducted at source.) In addition, if at least 10 per cent of the voting capital of the overseas company is owned by the UK company, relief is given for the 'underlying tax' (ie, the proportion of the total tax paid by the foreign company attributable to its dividends). Also in these circumstances, in certain cases no basic rate tax is to be charged on the paying and collecting agents (F2A 1992 S30). In no case, however, can the double tax relief rate exceed the rate of UK corporation tax (33 per cent, etc).

13.21 Controlled foreign companies (CFCs)

(TA 1988 Ss747–756 & Schs 24–26, FA 1995 S133 & Sch 25 & FA 1996 Sch 36)

The Revenue are able to impose extra tax on UK companies with interests in CFCs, subject to certain rules including the following:

(1) The overseas company must be under overall UK control.
(2) The overseas company must be subject to tax in its country of residence which is less than 75 per cent of that payable if it were UK resident. For profits arising before 16 March 1993, the fraction was one-half.
(3) A UK company (together with associates, etc) has at least a 10 per cent interest in the overseas company.
(4) Acceptable dividend payments which are made by a company not resident at the time of payment, will exclude the charge. For accounting periods beginning after 27 November 1995, the requirement for trading companies is 90 per cent (previously 50 per cent) of the profits, calculated as for UK tax purposes. For investment companies this figure has always been 90 per cent but

capital profits and foreign tax are deducted from the profits for accounting periods ending after 29 November 1993. Also, investment companies are now able to make distributions for such periods out of profits of earlier periods not yet taxed under the CFC rules.

(5) The charge is excluded if the controlled foreign company satisfies an 'exempt activities' test. For this, the company must have a business establishment where it is resident and be managed there. Also it must broadly be a trading or qualifying holding company rather than an investment company.

(6) Exclusion is also available through a motive test. The foreign company's transactions must be carried out for commercial reasons and not for the main purpose of saving UK tax nor diverting profits from the UK.

(7) Certain foreign companies quoted on foreign stock exchanges are also excluded.

(8) There is no charge if the foreign company's profits for the year are less than £20,000.

(9) A list has been published of excluded countries which will not be regarded as low tax countries for the purposes of the above rules. In general, the list excludes tax havens and normally applies where at least 90 per cent is 'local source' income.

(10) Where applicable, the profits of the overseas company are apportioned to any UK companies with at least a 10 per cent interest and corporation tax is charged at the appropriate rate for each. A deduction is then made for any 'creditable tax' (overseas tax, etc) which is similarly apportioned. Appropriate relief is then given where dividends are paid by the overseas company.

(11) Various anti-avoidance provisions have been introduced (15.10). For example, CFCs can include dual resident companies from 20 March 1990.

(12) From 23 March 1995, where profits need to be calculated for the CFC rules, they are expressed in the currency used in the company's accounts.

(13) It is planned to bring CFCs into the self-assessment framework in the future.

13.22 Stock relief for companies

(FA 1976 Sch 5; FA 1984 S48 etc)

The system for companies was similar to that for individuals and partnerships (11.6). For accounting periods ending after 13 November 1980, the relief was found by taking the opening stock (less £2,000) and applying the increase in the 'All Stocks Index' over the accounting period. Stock relief ceased completely for periods of account beginning after 12 March 1984. Reference should be made to previous editions of this book for further details.

13.23 Demergers

(TA 1988 Ss213–218)

Special rules assist two or more trading businesses in 'demerging' where they are carried on by a single company or a group. In demergers, subject to the detailed provisions:

(1) Where a company distributes shares in a 75 per cent subsidiary (13.6.1) to its shareholders this is not treated as a distribution and so no ACT or income tax arises for the company or its shareholders.
(2) Relief also applies where one company transfers a trade to a second company which in turn distributes its shares to the shareholders of the first.
(3) Capital gains tax relief applies to any distribution which you receive in the above circumstances until you sell the actual shares.
(4) There was also certain relief from development land tax and stamp duty in demergers.
(5) The provisions only apply to the genuine splitting off of trades or trading subsidiaries. There are anti-avoidance provisions to counter, for example the extraction of tax-free cash from companies subject to an advance clearance procedure.

13.24 Unquoted company purchasing its own shares

(TA 1988 Ss219–229 & FA 1997 S69 & Sch 7)

The 1981 Companies Act enables companies to purchase their own shares and issue redeemable equity shares. If the proceeds exceeded the original cost, the excess would be treated as a distribution under existing law and taxed in the same way as a dividend. Thus the company would pay ACT on the excess and an individual receiving the payment would pay higher rate tax on the grossed up excess less a tax credit (13.6.5). However, with effect from 8 October 1996, these distributions are treated as foreign income dividends (13.6.7). As a result, recipients will not be able to obtain any repayment of tax credit.

In order to remove the disincentive of this heavy taxation, relief is provided in certain circumstances so that the company pays no ACT and the shareholder's liability will be restricted to capital gains tax (unless he is a share-dealer, in which case the gain is treated as his income). Stamp duty relief applied up to 27 October 1986, but not subsequently. Broadly, the conditions for relief are as follows:

(1) The company must not be quoted nor be the subsidiary of a quoted company. (Shares dealt with on the Unlisted Securities Market are not treated as quoted.)
(2) The company must be a trading company or the holding company of a trading group.
(3) The purchase or redemption of the shares must be mainly to benefit a trade of the company or its 75 per cent subsidiary.
(4) The shareholder must be UK resident and ordinarily resident, having normally owned the shares for at least five years (three years in specified cases such as inherited shares, where ownership by the deceased is also counted).
(5) If the shareholder keeps part of his shareholding in the company (or its group) his shareholding must be substantially reduced. Broadly, this means reducing his interest by at least 25 per cent and not being 'connected' (ie, holding with 'associates' 30 per cent of the shares, etc).
(6) If the payment is used for capital transfer tax or inheritance tax within two years after a death, (4) and (5) above do not apply and relief is due, provided that to pay the tax out of other funds would have caused undue hardship.
(7) Advance clearance application may be made to the Revenue.
(8) As indicated, the above rules do not apply where a company buys back its shares from a dealer. Instead, the company remains liable for ACT on the excess of the proceeds over the original cost and the dealer is taxed under Schedule D Case I or II (11.4), receiving no tax credit.

13.25 Foreign exchange gains and losses
(FA 1993 Ss92–96, 122–170 & Schs 15–18 & FA 1995 Ss130 & 132 & Sch 24)

A new tax system for company foreign exchange transactions applies to companies for their first accounting periods starting after 22 March 1995. This replaces the previous system which lacked certainty. Particular features in the new scheme include the following:

(1) Exchange gains and losses on monetary assets (cash bank deposits and debts, etc) and liabilities are taxed or relieved as income as they accrue.

(2) Capital gains tax is no longer to be charged on any monetary assets in foreign currency.
(3) Exchange differences on monetary items are recognised as they accrue.
(4) Where certain conditions are met, the calculation of trading profits before capital allowances, in currencies other than Sterling, is permitted.
(5) Unrealised exchange gains above certain limits may be deferred, where they arise on long-term capital items.
(6) Where a borrowing matches a monetary asset, exchange differences may be deferred until the asset is disposed of.
(7) For the purposes of the rules, the ECU is to be regarded as a foreign currency.
(8) Transfers of assets by way of security are ignored and the company continues to be regarded as holding them.
(9) Exchange differences on debts must be computed from when the obligation to pay arises rather than when payment is due (if later).

13.26 Interest rate and currency contracts and options

(FA 1994 Ss147–177 & Sch 18)

The tax treatment of financial instruments to manage interest rates and currency risks for companies is being reformed. The new rules apply for accounting periods beginning on or after 23 March 1995. Profits and losses on 'qualifying contracts' are normally to be taxed or relieved on an income basis when they accrue. These broadly include currency or interest rate contracts or options acquired under the new rules.

13.27 Loan relationships

(FA 1996 Ss80–105 & Schs 8–15 & FA 1997 S83 & Sch 13)

Detailed new rules apply for companies with effect from 1 April 1996, regarding 'loan relationships'. This applies to debts which are loans under general law and whether owed to or by the company. In general, the rules treat all profits and losses on loans made by companies as income, interest payments being taxed or relieved as they accrue rather than are paid. Assets covered are taken out of the capital gains tax regime. Certain revised transitional rules apply from 14 November 1996.

The new rules apply to corporate bonds, Permanent Interest Bearing Shares and other corporate debt. Gilts held by companies are also covered, apart from profits and losses on 3.5% Funding Stock 1999/2004 and 5.5% Treasury Stock 2008/12.

14 Pensions

14.1 Introduction

With the increase in life expectancy and the decrease in the average age of retirement, pension planning grows in importance. You will need to plan for a longer retirement and should aim to receive an adequate pension during that period.

This chapter is mainly concerned with the tax aspects of pension arrangements as they will affect you. There are three main divisions:

(1) The State scheme (14.2)
(2) Occupational pension schemes (14.3)
(3) Personal pension schemes (14.4)

So far as you are concerned, these categories are not necessarily mutually exclusive. You can certainly expect some State pension. If you belong to an occupational scheme provided by your employers and have no other income, then you will not be able to make contributions to personal pension schemes. However, if you have other earnings outside your main employment, you will be eligible to contribute to one or more personal pension schemes. You can also do so if you do not belong to an occupational scheme covering your main employment.

The main tax benefits of personal pension and occupational pension schemes are relief on the contributions, growth in a fund which is usually free of UK tax and the option of taking a lump-sum (currently tax free) on retirement. In addition, substantial life cover can be included and the cost allowed for tax.

14.2 The State scheme

The State pension scheme provides a basic pension. Employees may also qualify for a graduated pension on contributions from April 1961 to

April 1975 and payments under a State Earnings Related Pension Scheme (SERPS).

The basic pension is shown later (25.3.1). To obtain the maximum, you need to have paid or been credited with National Insurance contributions for roughly 9/10ths of your anticipated working life.

SERPS is comprised in your National Insurance contributions (25.2.2), unless you are contracted out (14.2.1). Your employers will account for their contributions, and your own, with their PAYE remittances (10.14).

You only pay contributions on a part of your earnings (25.2.2). Broadly, your SERPS pension will be between 20 and 25 per cent of an earnings band, depending on when you retire. The lowest percentage is planned to apply to people retiring in the 2030s and thereafter.

You are taxed on your State pensions. If you paid the contributions, the income is regarded as 'earned'.

14.2.1 Contracting out of SERPS

Contracting out enables you to redirect some of your National Insurance contributions to a personal or occupational pension scheme so that it can provide an alternative to SERPS.

Some occupational pension schemes will undertake to provide a benefit which is roughly equivalent to SERPS whilst others simply require a 'minimum contribution' to be paid each month. This minimum contribution will comprise a payment by your employer supplemented at older ages by a DSS contribution. The DSS will pay the total annual minimum contribution to your chosen personal pension.

Where the minimum contribution is required, it is invested in a 'protected rights fund', but this in itself does not offer guarantees nor match SERPS benefits foregone.

14.3 Occupational pension schemes

(TA 1988 Ss590–617, Sch 23 & FA 1989 Sch 6, FA 1994 Ss103–108 & FA 1995 S61)

14.3.1 Introduction

Your employers may operate an occupational pension scheme for some or all of the employees. However, you cannot be compelled to join or remain in the scheme. You could, for instance, opt out in favour of a personal pension scheme (14.6.1) although you would generally be unwise to do so.

If an occupational pension scheme is non-contributory, employees will not be required to make contributions to the funds. Otherwise it will be known as a contributory scheme. Directors can be members but there are some restrictions on controlling directors of investment companies (14.3.5).

The schemes have their own trustees and the funds are separate from those of the employer. Smaller schemes are more likely to be run by life assurance companies; larger ones may well have their own investment managers.

In general, your scheme is likely to be 'approved', in which case it obtains favourable tax treatment. However, unapproved schemes may be established providing greater benefits than those permitted under an approved scheme.

An *unapproved scheme* may be funded, in which case your employers get tax relief on their contributions but you are taxed on them as benefits. Contributions do not generate a National Insurance liability. Your own contributions (if any) are not deductible for tax purposes. You will be taxed on your pension from a funded scheme but not on lump sums.

FA 1994 S108 taxes part of the benefits received under arrangements made or varied after 30 November 1993 from a funded unapproved retirement benefits scheme (FURBS) which has not been taxed in the UK.

If the scheme is unfunded, your pension will simply be paid out of your employers' general resources at the time. You will be taxed on any pensions and lump sum payments you receive.

14.3.2 Obtaining approval

The Inland Revenue department with responsibility for pensions is now called the Pension Schemes Office (PSO), formerly the Superannuation Funds Office (SFO). To qualify for favourable tax treatment, approval must be sought from the PSO. It takes two forms, 'approval' and 'exempt approval'.

'Approval' simply prevents you from being taxed on the contributions that your employer makes for you. Most schemes apply for 'exempt approval' which allows a wider range of reliefs. Additional tax benefits include tax relief on your own and your employer's contributions and investment growth in a fund which will usually be free of UK tax. Exempt approval will only be granted to schemes established under irrevocable trusts.

The PSO have wide powers to approve schemes. To begin with, certain conditions (TA 1988 S590(2)) must normally be satisfied concerning the pension scheme and these include:

(1) The sole purpose should be the provision of 'relevant benefits' in respect of the service of an employee. These would include any kind of financial benefit, such as pensions or lump sums, connected with your leaving your employment; paid to yourself, your executors, widow, widower, children or dependants. (Benefits given in connection with genuine redundancy are excluded.)
(2) The employer and employees must recognise it and written particulars of the scheme must be given to you if you are a present or potential member.
(3) The scheme must be established in connection with a trade, etc carried on in the UK by a UK resident person. (However, discretionary approval can be extended to a scheme established by an overseas resident company carrying on part of its trade in the UK.)
(4) A UK resident person must be responsible for administering the scheme according to the rules. Such 'administrator' is normally a trustee or sponsor.
(5) The employer must contribute to the scheme.

Provided the above mandatory rules are satisfied, together with certain other conditions, the PSO are obliged to approve a scheme. Alternatively, they are able to grant approval on a discretionary basis if certain less stringent requirements are satisfied, and this is the more usual approach. The following are the main features that approved pension funds are likely to have:

(1) Pensions are paid at a specified age which may be within the range 50 to 75. However, discretionary approval is often granted by the PSO to schemes allowing retirement at any age due to permanent incapacity caused by illness or accident.
(2) Your pension may be calculated by reference to your length of service and final remuneration. This is known as the *final salary* basis and your pension will be calculated as a fraction of this, typically 1/60th for each year of service up to 40. This produces a maximum pension of two-thirds of final remuneration. Under

their discretionary powers, the PSO often allow a shorter service requirement for the maximum pension.

(3) Since April 1988, *money purchase* schemes are becoming increasingly popular. Broadly, within Inland Revenue limits, your pension is related to the value of the fund created from contributions rather than your final remuneration. This fund will be used to provide your pension and other benefits. Typically, an annuity might be purchased for you on your retirement.

(4) On your death after retirement, a pension may be payable to your widow or widower or dependent children. However, the pension will be limited, for instance to two-thirds of your own pension where payable to a surviving spouse. Should you die within five years of taking your pension, a tax free lump sum may also be available.

(5) On retirement, you are normally allowed to commute part of your pension, thus receiving a lump sum and a lower pension. The lump sum is the greater of 3/80ths of final remuneration (capped if necessary — 14.3.4) for each of the first 40 years of service and $2\frac{1}{4}$ times the initial pension before commutation.

(6) Your scheme may include a lump sum payment of up to four times your final remuneration, should you die in service.

A special charge arises where certain small occupational schemes (mainly those with fewer than 12 members), cease to be 'approved' after 1 November 1994. 40 per cent tax is charged on the value of the funds (FA 1995 S61).

14.3.3 Contributions

Your employer is obliged to contribute to the scheme and, as indicated, such contributions are in general allowable business expenses. In some cases the employer may pay a 'special' contribution in order to buy benefits in respect of past service. If these special contributions are at least £$\frac{1}{2}$ million and exceed the employer's total contribution to the pension scheme for all members then tax relief may be spread over a few years. The contributions must actually be paid for your employer to obtain tax relief (FA 1993 S112).

In some circumstances, you may make a salary or bonus sacrifice to fund your employer's contributions, but of course this will reduce your pensionable remuneration.

Whether or not your scheme is contributory (14.3.1) you will have a facility to pay additional voluntary contributions (AVCs) provided that your total personal contribution does not exceed 15 per cent of your total remuneration and that you will not exceed the Inland Revenue benefit limit. Additional voluntary contributions may either be deducted from your pay (net pay arrangement) and invested in your employer's scheme or paid directly by you to a free-standing AVC (14.4).

14.3.4 Benefits

As mentioned above (14.3.2), the standard pension scale of one-sixtieth of your final remuneration for each year of service with up to 40 years to count may be increased so that the maximum pension at retirement date (two-thirds of final remuneration) can be achieved with less than 40 years' service. Just what length of service will be required depends on when you joined a scheme with your employer. It could be as little as 10 years if you joined before 17 March 1987, but since then has been 20 years.

Final remuneration includes benefits taxable under Schedule E and could therefore include, for instance, a taxable car benefit. It is unusual for employers to pension anything other than basic salary although bonuses and other taxable benefits can be pensioned by top-up arrangements including free-standing AVCs (14.4). Final remuneration may be based on the average of three or more consecutive years ending in the last 10 preceding retirement or the best year in the last five. If one year is taken as the basis then any fluctuating earnings such as bonuses must be averaged over at least three years ending with the selected year. The one year basis is not available for directors who control 20 per cent or more of shares in their companies who must always average total remuneration.

If you retire after 16 March 1987 with a salary over £100,000, you can only use the first basis or use £100,000 as your final remuneration. Should you have joined your scheme after 16 March 1987 and before 14 March 1989, your maximum final remuneration for calculating lump sums is £100,000.

Where your scheme was established after 13 March 1989 or if you joined an older scheme after 31 May 1989, income capping rules apply. The effect is that your benefits are limited to those appropriate to a given 'cap'. This started as £60,000 for 1989–90 and increases in line with the Retail Prices Index unless otherwise directed. For 1992–93 and 1993–94, it was £75,000, with £76,800 applying for 1994–95, £78,600 for 1995–96, £82,200 for 1996–97 and £84,000 for 1997–98. (Unapproved schemes (14.3.1) are not caught by the income capping rules and so offer scope for the highly paid.)

If you are caught by the income capping rules, your early retirement benefit position will be improved. Provided you have had at least 20 years of service with your employer, you can have the maximum two-thirds pension on retirement between 50 and 75.

14.3.5 Schemes for directors

Should you be a director, you are normally eligible to join your company's approved pension scheme and enjoy its full benefits. Alternatively, a separate arrangement might be made for you.

There are certain restrictions. If you control at least 20 per cent of the company's shares your final salary is calculated on a less favourable basis (14.3.4). Furthermore, if you have at least 20 per cent control of an investment company and are a director or you are a director and your family owns over 50 per cent, your benefits from its approved pension scheme will be further restricted. (The restrictions on controlling directors of investment companies do not necessarily apply where the company is a holding company.)

14.4 Free-standing additional voluntary contribution (FSAVC) schemes

(TA1988 S591(2)(h))

As mentioned above (14.3.3), you are permitted to make pension contributions of up to 15 per cent of your remuneration each year. If this is not fully used, you can put all or part of the balance into an FSAVC scheme of your own. Some people are ineligible for membership of an FSAVC, most notably directors who control 20 per cent or more of a company's shares. Furthermore, you may only contribute to one FSAVC in respect of each employment in a tax year (although you can contribute to a main scheme AVC and FSAVC at the same time).

Your FSAVC will be free-standing and independent of your employer. However, it is considered together with your occupational scheme when calculating your maximum benefit entitlement. You should note that the FSAVC pension cannot be commuted to produce a lump sum (14.3.2), nor can the pension under a main scheme AVC taken out after 8 April 1987.

FSAVC contributions are paid net of basic rate income tax. If you are a higher rate payer, you will normally obtain the extra relief after you submit your tax return.

When you retire, your combined FSAVC and occupational scheme arrangements may be over-funded. If so, your benefits from the latter are not reduced and your over-funding is repaid to you from your

FSAVC scheme, subject to a tax charge. This is 33 per cent if you are a basic rate payer and an effective rate of roughly 47 per cent if you pay higher rate income tax.

14.5 Personal pension schemes and retirement annuity contracts

(TA 1988 Ss618–655, FA 1989 Sch 7, FA 1994 Ss109 & 110 & FA 1995 S58 & Sch 11)

For many years, there have been pension schemes available where your employer does not operate a scheme for you, or alternatively if you are self-employed. Subject to the rules, full tax relief is available.

The arrangements prior to 1 July 1988 consisted of retirement annuity contracts (14.7). Subsequently, personal pension schemes (14.6) have taken over. New retirement annuity contracts are no longer available after 30 June 1988. However, it is still possible to make further contributions under contracts existing at that date.

Retirement annuity and personal pension schemes are broadly similar. However, there are some important differences, which might cause you to pick one avenue or the other, if you have the choice. For example, higher percentage contributions are sometimes permitted for personal pensions, whereas 'income capping' applies to them but not to retirement annuity contracts.

14.6 Personal pension schemes

There are many rules to be satisfied. These include eligibility, contributions, tax relief and benefits. Details are given below.

14.6.1 Are you eligible?

(1) In order to make contributions to a personal pension scheme, you need to have 'relevant earnings'. These are earnings from any employment, in respect of which you do not belong to an approved pension scheme. For these purposes, schemes providing only death in service benefits are ignored.

(2) Earnings are also 'relevant' if they are taxed under Schedule D Cases I and II. Thus self-employed earnings from businesses and professions are included.

(3) You can have two sources of income, one consisting of relevant earnings and the other being from an employment where you belong to the pension scheme. You will then be able to make

personal pension contributions only by reference to the first-mentioned earnings.

(4) If you leave an approved scheme and take out a personal pension but remain in employment, you will be able to have a transfer payment from the scheme.

(5) You are allowed to arrange a personal pension scheme to receive a transfer, even though you are not eligible to contribute to it.

(6) If you are a controlling director of an investment company, any remuneration which you receive from it will not constitute 'relevant earnings'.

(7) Your maximum permitted contributions are related to your *net relevant earnings*. These are your 'relevant earnings' less various deductions. Examples are capital allowances, expenses of your employment and losses in your trade.

(8) 'Minimum contributions' paid by the DSS when you contract out (14.2.1) do not count towards your limit. Furthermore, you may set up a personal pension to receive minimum contributions only, even if you are a member of an occupational pension scheme provided that it is not contracted out.

14.6.2 Tax relief

(1) Subject to the rules, your contributions under an approved personal pension scheme during a tax year are set against your relevant earnings assessed for that year. You thus obtain full income tax relief at the basic rate and higher rate if applicable.

(2) If you are an employee, you will normally pay your contributions net of basic rate tax. Any higher tax rate relief will be obtained later; perhaps through your coding. If your employer makes contributions, they are not regarded as your taxable income. However, they are counted towards the maximum contributions that you can make.

(3) Your permitted contributions are calculated as a percentage of your net relevant earnings for the tax year. If you are less than 36 at the beginning of the year of assessment, the percentage is 17.5. Otherwise a higher scale applies (14.6.3).

(4) Up to 5 per cent of your net relevant earnings can be applied in purchasing life cover through a personal pension scheme. A lump sum is payable on your death during the period of cover but no later than 75. These contributions count towards the total (17.5 per cent, etc).

(5) Since 1989–90 there has been a limit on the maximum net relevant earnings that you can use to calculate your contributions. Originally it was £60,000, but is broadly indexed up, being £84,000 for 1997–98 (£82,200 for 1996–97). Thus if you are 30

years old on 6 April 1997, your maximum contributions for 1997–98 total £84,000 × 17.5 per cent = £14,700.

(6) Each of you and your spouse, being independently taxed, has a separate personal pension scheme position. You can each make contributions up to your respective limits.

(7) Paying contributions into personal pension and retirement annuity schemes at the same time may restrict the amount you can put into the former. However, if you have income from pensionable employment and net relevant earnings, you can make full contributions to a personal pension scheme for the latter.

(8) If you ask the Department of Social Security to pay minimum contributions to your personal pension scheme, this enables you to be contracted out of SERPS. Such contributions do not count towards the total (17.5 per cent, etc).

(9) If you pay contributions before the end of a tax year, you may make an election by the following 5 July to have some or all of your contributions paid in that year carried back to the previous one. The effect is that they are treated for tax purposes as if paid in the earlier year. Thus your total tax relief is restricted to your entitlement for the earlier year. If you have no net relevant earnings for that tax year, you can carry the contributions back to the year before, but no earlier.

(10) There is also a carry-forward facility, but this works in a different way. If your contributions in a tax year are less than the maximum you could have made, you automatically carry forward the balance for six years, if not used earlier. You are thus able to make extra contributions in future years. However, in no year should your contributions exceed your relevant earnings.

14.6.3 Table: Contribution limits

Age at start of year of assessment	*Personal pensions*	*Retirement annuities*
	% of net relevant earnings	
Under 36	17.5	17.5
36–45	20	17.5
46–50	25	17.5
51–55	30	20
56–60	35	22.5
61 and over	40	27.5

14.6.4 Benefits

The benefits available under a personal pension scheme are broadly similar to those provided under an approved occupational pension scheme of the 'money purchase' type. However, there is more flexibility. Thus you obtain a pension and have the option of commuting part as a lump sum. This sum may not be more than 25 per cent of the fund providing your pension. The various choices considered apply separately for each of the schemes to which you belong.

You do not actually need to retire before receiving your pension. You can arrange to start receiving it at 50 or over, but not after you reach your 75th birthday. However, an earlier date may be allowed if accident or illness prevent you carrying out your job or one for which you would be suited, or if your occupation is one where it is usual to retire young, such as most sports.

Your pension takes the form of an annuity. This is either provided by the life company which arranged the scheme or your fund is used to purchase an annuity on the open market. Either way, it is fully taxable (from 6 April 1995 under PAYE). However, if you buy an annuity with your lump sum, the capital part is tax free (9.14).

If you have included an element of life cover, the lump sum on your death could be written in trust and so be free of inheritance tax. If you die before your pension commences, your estate might be paid a lump sum to cover your original contributions, together with interest and bonuses, etc. More usually, the value of the fund might be paid. Alternatively, an annuity might be paid to your widow or other dependants whom you nominate.

The 1995 Finance Act has enabled you to defer buying your personal pension scheme annuity until up to age 75 (FA 1995 Sch 11). Even so, you are allowed to draw taxable income from the pension fund. The amount must be no less than 35 per cent, nor more than 100 per cent of what the Government Actuary says you would have obtained by buying an annuity. The new rules apply whether or not you opt for a tax-free sum at pension date. If you die within the deferral period, your spouse and dependants can either continue to make income withdrawals, buy an annuity or take the fund in cash (FA 1996 S172).

14.7 Retirement annuities

As indicated, although no fresh contracts may be made after 30 June 1988, if you have any already in existence at that date, you can make further contributions. The following points should be noted about retirement annuity contracts:

(1) Lower percentages of net relevant earnings can be contributed from age 36 (14.6.3).
(2) No income capping applies to net relevant earnings.
(3) The maximum lump sum which may be taken is three times the pension subsequently payable. However, for each contract you entered into after 16 March 1987, there is a maximum of £150,000.
(4) You must pay the contributions gross and your employer will not be allowed to contribute to your scheme.
(5) Benefits must not normally become payable before age 60.
(6) Most retirement annuities include a facility to take an open market option. This allows the plan holder to move his fund when he takes his benefit to the company offering the best annuity rate. However, if the open market option is taken, then funds must be transferred to a personal pension scheme and the maximum lump sum will be restricted to 25 per cent of the total fund. Retirement annuities can also be transferred to personal pension schemes before age 60 which enable benefits to be taken from the lower age of 50.

15 Miscellaneous aspects

15.1 Miscellaneous profits — Schedule D Case VI

(TA 1988 Ss18, 69 & 392 & FA 1994 S208)

Miscellaneous profits not falling within any of the other cases of Schedule D are charged to income tax under Case VI. Such income includes:

(1) Profits from furnished lettings (7.5) (generally assessed under Schedule A from 1995–96).
(2) Income from underwriting (if not a business). However, Lloyd's underwriting profits (15.9) are assessed under Schedule D Case I.
(3) Income from guaranteeing loans.
(4) Income from dealing in futures. However, this is now more likely to be subject to capital gains tax (20.31).
(5) Certain capital sums received from the sale of UK patent rights.
(6) Post-cessation receipts (11.28).
(7) Certain 'anti-avoidance' assessments (15.10).
(8) Enterprise allowance payments after 17 March 1986. Previously Case I or II applied. Case VI also applies to payments before 18 March which continue subsequently (11.4).
(9) Profits on the disposal of certificates of deposit.
(10) Gains on certain life policies held by companies (FA 1989 Sch 9).

The basis of assessment under Schedule D Case VI is the actual income arising in the tax year. (Occasionally, the Revenue opt for an average basis but this will no longer apply from 1996–97, when the new current year system takes effect.) Expenses incurred in earning the income can be deducted in ascertaining the assessable profits.

Losses sustained in any Case VI transaction can be set off against Case VI profits of the same or any subsequent year; they cannot, in general, be set off against income assessable under any other Case or Schedule (TA 1988, S392). However, pre-1995–96 furnished lettings losses may be carried forward to set against the Schedule A pool of income (7.6).

15.2 Tax-free organisations

(TA 1988 Ss338–339, 460, 505–506 & 683, FA 1990 S25, FA 1991 Sch 9 & FA 1996 S109)

15.2.1 Charities

Approved charities are exempt from tax on any income that is used only for charitable purposes from:

(1) Land and buildings.
(2) Interest dividends and annual payments.
(3) Trades carried on by the beneficiaries of the charity or trades exercised in the course of executing the actual purposes of the charity. Certain lottery income is included from April 1995 (FA 1995 S138).

Approved charities are also exempt from capital gains tax.

Since charities are exempted from tax on dividend income, they are able to reclaim the normal tax credit of 20 per cent (25 per cent prior to 6 April 1993). In addition, extra amounts of credit are available to alleviate the sudden drop from 25 per cent to 20 per cent. The transitional tax credit rates are approximately 1993–94 24 per cent, 1994–95 23 per cent, 1995–96 22 per cent and 1996–97 21 per cent (FA 1993 S80).

Gifts to charity out of both capital and income are often afforded favourable tax treatment as described elsewhere in this book. In particular, note capital gains tax (20.29.1), and inheritance tax (22.1).

Deeds of covenant to charities receive highly favourable tax treatment. As covenantor, you will obtain higher rate tax relief on your gross payments, subject to the rules (6.5). An approved charity (15.2.1) is able to reclaim the basic rate income tax that you will have deducted in making a payment to it under a deed of covenant.

Thus if you covenant to pay a charity £100 gross each year, you will deduct income tax at the basic rate (23 per cent) and only pay £77. The charity will then reclaim the income tax amounting to £23. The charity thus gets a total of £100 each year. Even if the basic rate of income tax is changed, the charity will still get a total of £100 each year from your payment. (By way of contrast, if the covenant is 'net', the charity benefits more when the basic rate is higher.)

Deeds of covenant which are written to last four years or until some later event (eg, giving up membership of the charity) previously ceased to be effective for tax purposes after four years. (New deeds of covenant were then required.) However, the rules have now changed to allow tax relief for such covenants to run on, provided you are not empowered to stop payment within the initial four-year period.

From 1 April 1986, single donations by companies which are not close (13.17) are allowable for tax purposes subject to certain conditions. Basic rate income tax (23 per cent) must be deducted on payment which the charity reclaims. The company accounts to the Revenue for this tax but obtains corporation tax relief (normally 33 per cent). Donations qualifying for relief are limited to 3 per cent of ordinary share dividends in the accounting period (TA 1988 Ss338 & 339). A new single-donation relief applies from 1 October 1990 as follows. However, for appropriate companies, the above still applies if more favourable.

Certain charitable gifts qualify for '*Gift Aid*'. This is income tax or, for companies, corporation tax relief for charitable donations of at least £250 net each. Previous minimum net amounts were £400 before 16 March 1993 and £600 from 1 October 1990 to 6 May 1992. There was an annual maximum of £5,000,000. (Associated companies shared the £5,000,000 maximum.) However, the maximum was abolished for donations from 19 March 1991. Basic rate income tax is deducted by the donor and reclaimed by the charity. The donor obtains full tax relief at the higher rate, if applicable. Similarly a company deducts the gross donation from its taxable profits and obtains relief at its corporation tax rate (33 per cent, etc).

Thus, suppose you give under 'gift aid' £1,000 gross to a charity, you deduct 23 per cent basic rate and pay £770, the charity reclaiming the £230. You will also obtain £170 further relief if you are a higher rate income tax payer. Your net cost will then be £600.

A payroll deduction scheme operates from 1987–88. Employees are able to contribute up to £1,200 each year to charities (£900 from 1993–94 to 1995–96) through an approved agent and obtain tax relief (TA 1988 S202 & FA 1990 S24). Employers' expenses in running schemes are allowable business deductions, as are those paid to charitable agencies (FA 1993 S69).

Certain anti-avoidance provisions (TA 1988 Ss506–507 & Sch 20) restrict a charity's tax relief if its *funds* are used for non-charitable purposes, or passed to an overseas body without ensuring that it will use the money for charity. Relief is also restricted if the charity lends or invests the funds for the benefit of the original donor unless for charitable purposes. Note that higher rate relief for covenanted donations may be restricted where the charity's own relief is limited. These rules do not generally apply if a charity's taxable income and gains are no more than £10,000 in a year. If you pay more than £1,000 of donations under covenant in a year to charities whose relief is limited as above, your own higher rate relief may be restricted.

From 14 March 1989, the rules for tax relief on covenanted membership subscriptions to heritage and conservation charities were relaxed. The right to free or cheap entry to view the property of the charity no longer prevents the member from obtaining tax relief (FA 1989 S59).

15.2.2 Other tax-free organisations

Other organisations whose income in certain circumstances may be free of tax include registered and unregistered friendly societies, registered trade unions, mutual associations and pension funds.

Registered friendly societies are exempt from tax on profits from life assurance business subject to certain limits. The maximum annual premium payable on such a life assurance policy is now £270. The previous limit was based on annual premiums of £200 (FA 1991 Sch 9). Premiums under existing Friendly Society policies may be increased to the new limit without affecting the tax benefits. In addition, the previous restriction that the cash value on early surrender cannot exceed the premiums paid has also been removed. There remains a limit of £156 annually for each annuity (TA 1988 S464).

Since 31 May 1984, the life business of friendly societies has been treated for tax purposes as being more akin to that of life assurance companies (TA 1988 S466 & FA 1996 S171). The 1992 Friendly Societies Act allows societies to incorporate. The legislation regarding tax exemption now extends to incorporated societies.

Provident benefits paid by *trade unions* to their members are tax-exempt up to certain limits. (Such payments might cover sickness, injury, etc.) The limits which apply from 1 April 1991, are £4,000 for lump sums and £825 for annuities (TA 1988 S467 & FA 1991 S74). (The previous limits were £3,000 and £625.)

Depending on the exact circumstances, tax exemption may apply to government bodies, foreign diplomats and United Nations Organisation officials in this country and the salaries of the members of visiting forces.

15.3 Patent holders

(TA 1988 Ss520–528)

If you own a patent (11.18) and you grant the right to use it to somebody else he will normally pay you a periodical royalty in respect of the patent user. This royalty is normally subject to tax by deduction at source at the basic rate (23 per cent). If, however, the payer does not deduct tax then you would generally be assessed to income tax under Case VI of Schedule D.

The gross equivalent of any patent royalties that you receive must be included in your total income for income tax purposes (5.2), but you get a credit for the basic rate tax already suffered by deduction at source. Where you receive a lump sum payment, in respect of royalties for the past user of your patent, you can spread the payment backwards over the period of use in order to calculate your income tax liability.

If you sell any patent rights for a capital sum, this will normally be chargeable under Case VI of Schedule D provided you are resident in this country. You can, however, spread the payment forward over a period of six years in computing your income tax liability. If, however, you are non-resident, the payer should deduct income tax at 23 per cent in paying you (subject to possible double tax relief and exemptions).

15.4 Authors' copyright sales and royalties

(TA 1988 Ss534–537)

Unlike patent royalties, copyright royalty payments to authors, etc are made gross without the deduction of any income tax. If you have such receipts and you are an author or composer, etc by profession, then your royalties will be taxed under Schedule D Case II as part of your professional earnings (11.4). Otherwise, any royalties that you receive may be assessed under Schedule D Case VI.

Where you assign the copyright in the whole or a part of a work, any sum that you receive is taxable by reference to the tax year or accounting period in which it is received. If you make the required claim to the Revenue, however, you can normally obtain relief by spreading the payment as follows:

(1) If it took you more than 12 but less than 24 months to prepare the work of art, one half of your proceeds is taxed as if received when paid to you and the other half of the proceeds is taxed as if received one year earlier. If you took more than 24 months over the writing, composing, etc of the work, then you are taxed on one third of the proceeds as if received when paid to you, another third is taxed as if received one year earlier and the remaining third is taxed one year earlier still. Thus a three-year spread is obtained.

(2) If you are the author of an established work and not less than ten years after the first publication you wholly or partially assign your copyright or grant an interest therein, for a period of at least two years, you can spread any lump sum received. The period over which the sum is spread is the lesser of six years or the duration of the grant or licence.

15.5 Sub-contractors

(TA 1988 Ss559–567, FA 1995 S139 & Sch 27, FA 1996 S178 & FA 1997 S54)

If you are an independent or self-employed contractor and are not engaged under a contract of employment, you will be taxed under Schedule D Case I and not under Schedule E. This will normally be advantageous to you because you will be able to deduct various expenses such as travelling from your home or other base of operations to the site, etc where you are working for the time being.

Special rules apply to payments made by a building contractor or similar organisation in the building trade to a sub-contractor in connection with building and construction work. These extend to non-building firms which spend substantial amounts on construction operations (over £250,000 on average for the last three years).

The contractor must deduct tax at the rate of 24 per cent (23 per cent from 1 July 1997 (from each payment made to the sub-contractors who work for him excepting those with exemption certificates (see next page). The tax deducted must be paid over to the Revenue. Each sub-contractor then prepares accounts under Schedule D Case I which include the gross equivalents of the payments made to him. Income tax is computed on the basis of the accounts (11.4) and the tax already suffered is deducted. If the income tax liability is less than the tax deducted a repayment is obtained. Interest is charged where formal assessments are made on contractors for under-deductions from payments to sub-contractors.

The scheme also applies to certain companies, whilst other rules require the deduction of tax from payments made to temporary agency workers. Companies with a sub-contractor exemption certificate (see below) will need to notify the Revenue of any change in company control.

If you are a sub-contractor in the building trade you will normally be able to obtain an exemption certificate from your Inspector of Taxes if you complete the necessary application form and can satisfy certain conditions including having a regular place of business in this country. Also you must have been either employed (including full-time education or training) or in business in the UK and made full tax returns for a qualifying period of three years up to your application.

Up to six months are allowed in the three-year qualifying period for unemployment, etc at the Inland Revenue's discretion. Relaxations are made to cover periods of working overseas — the three-year qualifying period being allowed to be within the last six years. If you obtain an exemption certificate and show it to a building contractor for whom you do work, then he will be permitted to pay you gross without the tax deduction described above.

The 1995 Finance Act makes certain changes to the above rules, from a day or days to be announced, not earlier than 1 August 1998. For example, the £250,000 level, above which non-building firms come into the scheme will increase to £1,000,000 of construction work. Also from no earlier than that date, mandatory registration cards will be introduced for subcontractors unable to qualify for exemption certificates.

15.6 Farming

If you carry on a farming or market gardening business in this country you will be treated as carrying on a trade. You will be assessed to income tax under Schedule D Case I (11.4).

In addition to the normal Schedule D Case I rules, some special ones apply, including the following:

(1) If you have more than one farm they will all be assessed as one business (TA 1988 S53).
(2) You may receive *deficiency payments* from the Government in respect of certain crops, etc. These are by concession included in your taxable profits for the year when they are received rather than when the crop is sold.

(3) If you have an eligible agricultural or horticultural holding, you may be able to benefit under one of the various Ministry of Agriculture, Fisheries and Food Grant Schemes. Grants received under these schemes are treated as either capital receipts or revenue receipts for tax purposes according to their nature. For example, field husbandry grants are revenue and grants to cover the reclamation of waste land are capital.

(4) Normally all your livestock will be treated for tax purposes as stock-in-trade. If you have any 'production herds', however, you can elect within two years from the end of your first year of assessment that the *herd basis* should apply. 'Production herds' are those kept for the purpose of obtaining products from the living animal (eg, wool, milk, etc). Where a herd basis election has been made the initial cost of the herd is not charged against your profits but is capitalised together with the cost of any additional animals. The cost of rearing the animals to maturity is also capitalised. Any sales proceeds are taxable and the costs of replacement animals are deductible from your taxable profits. If you sell your entire herd you are not charged to tax on the proceeds (TA 1988 S97 & Sch 5).

(5) A special *agricultural buildings allowance* is available (11.14).

(6) If you carry on any farming or market gardening activities without any reasonable expectation of profit on a non-commercial basis you will normally be treated as conducting merely *hobby farming*. The effect of this will be that you will not be granted tax relief for any losses from your farming against your other income. You will, however, be permitted to carry forward any losses from your hobby farming to be set against future taxable profits from the same source (TA 1988 S397). Generally, the restriction applies when you make your sixth consecutive loss.

(7) Relief is available regarding *fluctuating profits* (taken net of capital allowances if under new scheme — 11.7.4) of individual farmers or partnerships. You are able to claim to average the profits of any pair of consecutive years of assessment, provided you do so within broadly 22 months of the end of the second year. If the taxable profits for either or both years are later adjusted, the original claim is set aside but a new one can be made by the end of the year of assessment following that in which the adjustment is made. Another condition is that the profits in the lower year must be no more than 70 per cent of the profits of the better year. If the lower profits are 70 per cent to 75 per cent of the higher, however, limited spreading is allowed. Where a loss is made in any year, for the purposes of the spreading rules, the profits are treated as nil and the loss is relieved in the usual ways (11.22) (TA 1988 S96).

(8) Capital gains tax roll-over relief (20.25) was extended to include first milk and potato quotas and then ewe and suckler cow premium quotas (TCGA S151 & FA 1993 S86).

15.7 Building society arrangements

(TA 1988 S476, FA 1990 S30 & Sch 5, FA 1991 S53 & FA 1996 S65)

From 6 April 1991 building societies (as well as banks, etc) deduct income tax from interest payments and account for it to the Inland Revenue. The rate was 25 per cent upto 5 April 1996 and then 20 per cent. Non-taxpayers are able to reclaim tax deducted. However, building societies may pay interest and dividends gross to individuals ordinarily resident outside the United Kingdom (8.6). This also applies to payments to charities, friendly societies and pension funds, etc.

Prior to 6 April 1991, if you received any building society interest you were not assessed to basic rate income tax on it. However, you included the grossed up equivalent in your total income for tax purposes (5.2) as if income tax at the basic rate (25 per cent) had been deducted on payment of the interest to you (8.6). This 'notional' tax deduction could not be reclaimed by you, as a general rule. (An exception was made, where a UK resident or ordinarily resident individual (17.3.1) or charity had an absolute interest in the residuary estate of a deceased person (21.10.1) and the income included building society interest.)

Before 6 April 1991, building societies paid a special composite tax rate based on the interest payable to individual investors, depositors and certain others. This partially compensated the Revenue for the basic rate income tax not directly assessed on the investors in respect of their interest.

15.8 Insolvents

When a person becomes bankrupt, a bankruptcy or interim order is made on a certain date and all income tax and capital gains assessments that have been made by that date for previous years are treated as debts in the bankruptcy. Also any assessments made for the tax year ending on the following 5 April will rank as debts in the bankruptcy provided the assessments were made before the date of the receiving order. PAYE and sub-contractors' deductions made within the previous year will rank as preferential debts. This means that they will be paid in full before any payment is made on the non-preferential debts. The remaining assessments will rank as non-preferential debts.

In the case of VAT (23.11.9) tax payable for the 6 months prior to the date of the order, etc ranks as a preferential debt.

Any future income of the bankrupt individual will be charged to tax in the normal way. Thus any salary would be subjected to PAYE (10.14) — also income tax would be payable on other income.

15.9 Lloyd's underwriters

(FA 1993 Ss171–184 & Schs 19–20, FA 1994 Ss219–230 & Sch 21 & FA 1995 S143)

The special rules which apply to the taxation of Lloyd's underwriters were substantially altered by FA 1993 (and FA 1994 for companies), the main changes being:

(1) There is a new tax deductible reserve, to replace the limited special reserve. This enables you to put aside profits free of tax to meet future losses. Up to 50 per cent of your profits can be transferred in this way each year, provided the value of the reserve fund is no more than half your overall premium limit. Income and gains within the reserves will be tax-free.

(2) Gains on assets representing your invested premiums will no longer be specially treated. In future, they will be incorporated in trading profits.

(3) In general, your taxable receipts and allowable expenses will be within Schedule D Case I (11.1), together with gains and losses on assets in premium trust funds.

(4) Because of the Lloyd's three year accounting basis, the new rules will take effect slowly. For example, the first profit transfers to the new reserve will be for the 1992 underwriting year but not made until around July 1995.

(5) Although syndicate accounts for each trading year are drawn up annually, they are closed off after the third year to allow members to join and leave. At that stage the members for that year pay those for the new year appropriate insurance premiums and the new year's syndicate members take over the outstanding liabilities. This is known as 'reinsurance to close'.

(6) Starting with the 1985 account, 'reinsurance to close' is tax deductible only to the extent that it is shown not to exceed a fair and reasonable assessment of the liabilities. This means aiming at having neither a profit nor loss accrue to the recipient of the

premium. These rules were introduced in 1987 and were modified in 1988 and 1993.

(7) For accounting periods beginning after 31 December 1993, profits from corporate membership of Lloyd's are charged to corporation tax under FA 1994. In general, these are treated as trading income except for non-syndicate profits otherwise taxable as income. 'Reinsurance to close' relief is available as for individuals (above).

15.10 Anti-avoidance provisions
(TA 1988 Ss703–787, etc)

There is an important distinction between *tax evasion* and *tax avoidance*. Tax evasion refers to all those activities illegally undertaken by a taxpayer to free himself from tax which the law charges upon his income, eg the falsification of his returns, books and accounts. This is illegal and subject to very heavy penalties (16.9.2). Tax avoidance, on the other hand, denotes that the taxpayer has arranged his affairs in such a way as to reduce his tax liability legally — for example, by investing in tax free securities such as national savings certificates.

Tax avoidance is also attempted in more complicated and devious ways with particular use being made of overseas trusts and companies. In order to prevent abuse of the UK tax rules in this way various anti-avoidance provisions have been introduced. Also, certain Court decisions such as *Ramsay* and *Furniss v Dawson* have barred tax relief from artificial circuitous schemes.

Unfortunately, some of the rules introduced to counter sophisticated avoidance schemes penalise quite innocent commercial activities, not carried out with a view to tax saving. It is thus important to consider the anti-avoidance provisions, particularly when involved in overseas operations and company reorganisations or takeovers. The following are some of the more important provisions to consider.

15.10.1 Transactions in securities
(TA 1988 Ss703–709, FA 1996 S175 & FA 1997 S73)

These provisions charge you to income tax under Schedule D Case VI in respect of any 'tax advantage' that you obtain as a result of one or more 'transactions in securities'. For these purposes a 'tax advantage' is a saving of income tax or corporation tax (including, from 11 October 1996 the payment of a tax credit), but it does not apply to capital gains tax. 'Transactions in securities' include the formation and liquidation of companies as well as purchases and sales of shares, etc. A frequent application of this legislation is to prevent tax savings being effected by obtaining the use of the undistributed profits of companies by means of schemes involving 'transactions in securities'.

You can avoid being assessed under these provisions if you can show that the transactions concerned were carried out for commercial purposes and one of your main objects was not tax saving. If you are planning to carry out certain transactions which you fear may be covered by these provisions you have the right to apply for clearance to the Revenue giving all relevant facts and they must let you know within one month whether such clearance is granted.

15.10.2 Transfer of assets abroad *(TA 1988 Ss739–746 & FA 1997 S81)*

The object of these provisions is to prevent you from avoiding tax by transferring some of your assets abroad. The provisions normally, but not exclusively, apply to transfers of assets made by persons ordinarily resident in this country (17.3.1). If as a result of such transfer of assets, income is payable to persons resident or domiciled abroad (to avoid UK income tax) then if anyone ordinarily resident in the UK has the 'power to enjoy' any of the income, he can be assessed to income tax under Schedule D Case VI on all or part of the income. 'Power to enjoy' the income is widely defined.

For income arising from 26 November 1996, confirming normal practice, the legislation applies whatever your ordinary residence status is when you make the transfer, and where a purpose is to avoid any form of direct tax.

There are no provisions under which clearance can be obtained and this particular legislation must be most carefully considered regarding all overseas schemes. You can even be assessed on a benefit if you did not make the original transfer. However, no income can be assessed more than once.

15.10.3 Sales at undervalue or overvalue *(TA 1988 Ss770–774)*

Important rules apply where any sale takes place between people who are connected with each other (this can include partnerships and companies) and the price is less than the open market value of the goods. Then in calculating the tax liability on the trading income of the seller, the sales proceeds must be adjusted to the true value of the goods if the Revenue so direct. This does not apply if the purchase is made by a taxable business in this country as a part of its trading stock. If the purchaser is an overseas trader, however, the sale is not exempted from these provisions.

A similar adjustment must be made for the buyer if the price is more than the open market value of the goods. Other provisions cover capital gains on sales between connected persons. At some future time, it is planned to bring the above transactions within the self-assessment framework.

15.10.4 Sale of income derived from personal activities

(TA 1988 Ss775, 777 & 778)

The object of these provisions is to prevent you from saving tax by contriving to sell your present or future earnings for a capital sum, thereby paying no tax or only capital gains tax instead of income tax at basic and higher rates. Subject to the precise rules, any such capital sum is to be treated as earned income arising when it is receivable and is chargeable under Case VI of Schedule D.

These provisions might apply if you receive a capital sum from the sale of a business which derives part of its value from your personal services. From 6 April 1988, the provisions are not so penal because broadly the same tax rates apply to income and capital gains.

15.10.5 Artificial transactions in land and 'sale and leaseback'

(TA 1988 Ss776–780)

These provisions are considered in detail in the chapter which deals with income from land and property (see 7.11). Note that tax advantages from sales of land with the right to repurchase are also countered.

15.10.6 Leasing & capital allowances

(TA 1988 Ss384 & 395, etc & CAA 1990 Ss39–50 & FA 1997 S82 & Sch 12)

Complicated anti-avoidance provisions operate concerning the claiming of relief for capital allowances in certain contrived situations. These provisions were designed to counter certain tax saving schemes involving leasing arrangements in group situations and consortia; also leasing partnerships between individuals and companies.

Wider provisions prevent your setting off losses created through claims for capital allowances on leasing assets, against non-leasing income. The rules cover capital expenditure after 26 March 1980 by individuals and partnerships (unless under previous contracts and the assets are used by 27 March 1982). An exception is made for a leasing trade to which you devote substantially all your time, provided this trade continues for at least six months.

Leasing assets normally qualifies for a 25 per cent writing down allowance (11.9.14). However, the rate is restricted to 10 per cent where the assets are leased to non-residents. Similarly, a writing down allowance of only 10 per cent is available on expenditure after 9 March 1982 where *ships* or *aircraft* were let on charter to non-residents in order to obtain first-year allowances.

Two new measures counter tax-saving through finance leasing schemes. Under a finance lease, a bank, etc, buys an asset and leases it to you so that you have substantially all the benefits of outright ownership.

Also hit are new leases made after 26 November 1996, where the rentals are concentrated towards the ends of their terms. In both cases from that date, for tax purposes, the rentals are as appears in the lessor's commercial accounts, rather than the rentals receivable. Furthermore, the assets concerned will not attract capital allowances (FA 1997 S82 & Sch 12).

15.10.7 Group relief restrictions
(TA 1988 Ss409–413 & FA 1989 Ss97–102)

These provisions can act to restrict or prevent group loss relief being available for one group company (13.13) in respect of trading losses of another. A particular point to watch is that if a group of companies has arranged to sell a loss-making company, relief for the losses of that company may not be available to the other group members for periods prior to the accounting period in which the sale actually takes place.

Special rules apply where companies join or leave a group. Instead of the normal time apportionment to fit the losses or profits to the respective old and new groups, a just and reasonable basis will be substituted in obviously distorted cases. This could involve separate accounts before and after the date of changing groups.

Modifications of the rules regarding groups took effect during 1989 and are mentioned elsewhere (13.16).

15.10.8 Interest schemes
(TA 1988 S787)

Complicated tax avoidance schemes were developed concerning 'manufactured' interest relief. Anti-avoidance rules operate regarding the interest payments.

15.10.9 Capital gains tax
(TCGA Ss27, 29, 137, 138 & 169 & Sch 7A)

Various rules were introduced for countering the avoidance of capital gains tax in certain situations. The latter include 'value-shifting' schemes, where an allowable loss has been created artificially by moving value out of one asset and possibly into another.

There are also anti-avoidance rules concerning capital gains tax resulting from company reconstructions, takeovers and amalgamations (20.18.6). A clearance procedure applies, however, which is similar to that applying for transactions in securities (15.10.1). Also, the rules do not apply if you can show that the arrangements were carried out for commercial, rather than tax-saving purposes.

Provisions prevent the artificial creation of capital losses by inflating the purchase price of assets for capital gains tax purposes above their true value, so that by selling for the true worth a capital loss results. This artificial effect sometimes resulted from the rule that transactions between connected persons are treated as being for a consideration equal to market value and sometimes through reorganisations of share capital (20.18.6). The capital gains tax cost of the purchaser is only increased to the extent that the capital gains tax position of the vendor is affected.

Gifts relief (20.28) does not apply to non-resident donees. This was being avoided by using certain dual-resident trusts, but from 18 March 1986 these are regarded as non-resident for this purpose.

Capital gains tax roll-over relief is not available where a non-resident replaces a business asset within the UK charge with one which is outside it. In general, this new rule applies where the old asset is disposed of, or the new one purchased after 13 March 1989.

With effect from 16 March 1993, tax benefits from buying capital loss companies (13.15) have been legislated against. From the same date, capital gains are no longer to fall out of charge where shares are exchanged for debentures which are outside the tax net.

15.10.10 Commodity and financial futures
(TA 1988 S399 & TCGA S143)

Losses created by means of certain artificial dealing partnerships may not be relieved against general income. (Note that a commodity deal not forming part of a trade is liable to capital gains tax rather than Case VI income tax as previously.)

15.10.11 Rent between connected persons

(F2A 1992 S57)

A new rule applies to rent accruing after 9 March 1992 between connected persons (broadly close relatives and companies belonging to the same group or under common control). This covers those connected after both that date and when the lease was made. Previously, where the payer obtained tax relief, this was normally on an accruals basis and the recipient was only taxed on the basis of the rent receivable in the period, thus being able to defer tax. Under the new rules, the recipient will be charged on the rent accruing. This applies where the payer obtains tax relief on the rent and this is paid in arrears.

15.10.12 Bank lending, etc

(TA 1988 S798)

There are rules to prevent certain tax advantages being obtained by exploiting the double tax relief system. Also, the creation of 'equity loans' where the interest paid is partly dependent on a company's results no longer produces a 'distribution'. This affects banks and the loss-making companies they were able to lend money to at lower rates. The double taxation rules relate mainly to banks.

15.10.13 Controlled foreign companies

(TA 1988 Ss747–756 & Schs 24–26 etc)

From 6 April 1984, the Revenue are given powers to assess additional tax on certain UK resident companies with interests in controlled foreign companies. Fuller details are given earlier (13.21) but the circumstances where a charge might arise are where a foreign subsidiary in a low tax area is paying insufficient of its profits as dividends, etc to its UK parent company.

15.10.14 Offshore funds

(TA 1988 Ss757–764 & Schs 27–28, TCGA S102 & FA 1995 S134)

Broadly, if you dispose of an investment in an offshore fund which does not distribute enough of its income, you will be taxed on your entire gain as if it were income under Schedule D Case VI (15.10.2). Gains on switches of holdings in offshore 'umbrella' funds by UK investors, attract capital gains tax. Since 29 November 1994 only 'collective investment schemes' are covered by legislation and the distribution test is waived if the income is no more than 1% of the average value of the assets.

15.10.15 Dual resident companies
(TCGA Ss159, 160 & 188)

Special provisions apply to prohibit a dual resident investment company from surrendering losses to other members of a UK group (13.13). The companies concerned are UK resident and also taxed in another country because of place of incorporation, management or residence. Furthermore, the definition of such dual resident investment companies extends to those which either do not trade or are mainly used to borrow or to purchase or hold shares in another group member.

Where an asset of a dual resident company ceases to be within the UK capital gains tax charge due to a double tax agreement, the company is deemed to have disposed of the asset. Regarding replacements of business assets (either the disposal or replacement) roll-over relief is not available if a UK asset within the capital gains tax charge is replaced by an asset which is not.

From 20 March 1990 certain dual resident companies are treated as resident outside the UK for some tax purposes. This is to counter avoidance of tax through controlled foreign companies (13.21) and transfers of assets abroad.

Also from 20 March 1990, rules operate which are designed to prevent a company transferring assets tax-free to a dual resident company in whose hands any gain would be outside the UK tax charge. Similarly, from that date, roll-over relief (20.25) is denied on the replacement of business assets where one member of a group disposes of an asset and a dual resident group member replaces it with an asset outside the UK tax charge.

15.10.16 Migration of companies, etc
(TA 1988 S765)

Taxes Act 1988 S765 contains penal provisions to prevent a UK company from becoming non-resident without Treasury consent being obtained. Such consent is also required to transfer part or all of its business to a non-resident and for certain share transactions. From 15 March 1988, such consent is no longer needed (except for certain share transactions) and it is replaced by a tax charge on unrealised gains. Companies intending to emigrate must notify the Inland Revenue in advance providing an estimate of their UK tax commitments including tax on unrealised gains, and details of arrangements to settle such tax. If the tax is not paid, penalties may be charged. Furthermore, former directors and group companies can be held responsible for tax and interest.

After 30 June 1990, Treasury consent is no longer needed regarding certain transactions relating to companies within the European Community. This applies to issues and transfers of shares and debentures of overseas subsidiaries within the EC. Where *special* Treasury consent was previously needed, reporting to the Revenue is now required with non-compliance penalties of up to £3,000.

15.10.17 Capital Gains Tax — sales of subsidiaries *(TCGA Ss31–34 etc)*

With effect from 14 March 1989, certain schemes to save tax on capital gains where a group disposes of one or more subsidiaries are curbed. For example, the value of a subsidiary may be reduced before sale by distributing assets to fellow group members at less than market value; such undervalue will be added to the sale proceeds in calculating the capital gain on the sale of the subsidiary. However, the new legislation is not intended to catch distributions which could be made out of normal profits and reserves.

Another situation which has been countered, is where the commercial control of a subsidiary is sold, whilst keeping it within the group for capital gains relief on inter-group transfers etc through using special shares. From 14 March 1989, the benefits of group membership only apply if the parent company of the group has, directly or indirectly, an interest of over 50 per cent in the income and assets of the company.

The sale of a subsidiary can also give rise to capital gains on assets previously transfered to it from other group companies. This and similar anti-avoidance rules are considered earlier (13.16).

15.10.18 Capital Gains Tax — non-resident trusts *(TCGA Ss80–98 & Sch 5)*

From 19 March 1991, sweeping changes have effect regarding the capital gains tax rules relating to offshore settlements. The rules (20.32) involve the settlor and beneficiaries. Among other changes, the use of such settlements to delay the onset of capital gains tax has been much curtailed.

15.10.19 Interest within multinational groups *(FA 1993 Ss61–66)*

Special rules apply to interest payable within multinational groups to UK companies by non-resident associated companies on certain loans, etc. The interest is taxable as it accrues, rather than when it arises as hitherto. This applies to interest accruing from 1 April 1993.

The rules apply where under the financial arrangements, the interest payable in any 12 month period is less than the amount accruing pro rata to the lender in that period. However, if you can satisfy the Inspector of Taxes that saving tax was not the main motive for using the arising basis and similar terms would have been agreed at arm's length, exemption is available from the new rules.

16 Returns, assessments and repayment claims

This chapter covers administrative matters, largely to be found in the Taxes Management Act 1970 (TMA). With effect from 1996–97, radical changes take effect, with the introduction of a new self-assessment system. This is dealt with below.

16.1 Self-assessment — an overview *(FA 1994 Ss178–199 & Sch 19, FA 1995 Ss103–116 & Sch 20 & FA 1996 Ss121–136 & Schs 17–22)*

FA 1994 contains the framework for a self-assessment system which applies for 1996–97 and future years. FA 1995 and FA 1996 contain further relevant provisions. Points to note include the following:

(1) Individuals and trustees need to submit their returns to the Revenue by the filing date. This is 31 January after the end of the tax year of the return or if later, three months after its issue. You must include a self-assessment of your tax liabilities.
(2) You need not work out your tax bill if you submit your return by 30 September after the tax year or if later, two months after its issue.
(3) New tax returns are being sent to partnerships to show the income and its division between the partners.
(4) Late returns may give rise to penalties including £100 at once and again after six months; also if the Commissioners agree, £60 per day.
(5) The Revenue are able to correct minor errors within nine months of your sending in a return. You are able to make amendments within one year and the Revenue have the same time for notifying you that they are making enquiries. They may then delay making any repayment reflected in your return.
(6) The Revenue will issue you with a formal notice after completing an enquiry. You are then able to appeal.

(7) If you have not submitted your return in time, the Revenue are able to make an estimated assessment and you cannot appeal against the tax charge. However, this is displaced when you send in your return and self-assessment.

(8) Your income tax and capital gains tax is normally due for payment on 31 January after the year of assessment. However, except where most of your income is taxed at source, you normally make income tax payments on account on 31 January in the tax year and the following 31 July. These will generally be of equal amount and based on the final liability for the previous year, but may be reduced to reflect circumstances.

(9) Interest runs from the due date. Also you may incur a 5 per cent surcharge on your unpaid tax for a year of assessment if it is not paid by the next 28 February. A further 5 per cent surcharge may arise on any tax outstanding at the following 31 July. However, the Revenue pay interest on tax over-payments from the original tax payment dates (or due dates if later).

(10) Where a settlement has more than one trustee, each is able to make a return and be accountable for errors and omissions. Any liable trustee can be required to meet liabilities to income tax and capital gains tax.

(11) Your return and self-assessment needs to reflect the taxable position after allowing for claims to reliefs and tax credits. Where the necessary conditions exist for a relief, you are able to claim it in your self-assessment without prior Revenue approval.

(12) You must claim any allowable loss for capital gains tax purposes in relation to the year when it accrues. This means you can include it in your tax return and must claim it within 5 years 10 months of the end of the year of assessment when the loss arises.

(13) Your employers must provide you and the Revenue with details of your expenses payments and benefits in kind, including cash equivalent calculations, unless a dispensation has been given by the Revenue. The deadline is 31 May following the end of the tax year.

(14) In general, in cases where previously the time limit for income tax and capital gains tax claims has been two years, this becomes 31 January after the year following the year of assessment. Thus a claim for 1996–97 will be needed by 31 January 1999 instead of 5 April 1999. During this period you are also allowed to revoke or amend any claims and elections made ahead of this time limit.

(15) Various reliefs, such as loss relief, farmers' averaging (15.6), spreading of literary and artistic receipts (15.4) and post-cessation receipts may relate to more than one year. Where this is the case, relief is given in the assessment for the later (latest) year when the claim is made but taking account of the tax figures of the earlier year(s). This will avoid re-opening the earlier years.

(16) There is a wide range of revised time limits applying for income tax and capital gains tax but not corporation tax. In general, the changes involve reductions of just over two months. Thus two years from the end of the year of assessment will become 31 January in the next year but one. Similarly six years thereafter becomes 31 January in the sixth year.

(17) You are required to keep and preserve adequate records on which to base your tax return.

16.2 Your tax return

(TMA S8 & FA 1990 S77 & S90)

The Revenue will normally send to you periodically a tax return for completion. If your income includes Schedule A and/or Schedule D income you will usually have to submit a tax return each year. If, however, all your income is taxed under PAYE (10.14) you may only be required to complete a return about every three years. Husbands and wives must submit separate returns. (Normally, up to 5 April 1990, your wife's income was included in your return.)

Apart from individuals, trusts, partnerships and companies, etc also have to submit tax returns. In the case of companies, hitherto, provided the Revenue received the annual accounts and tax computations they did not normally insist on the submission of corporation tax returns. However, with the introduction of 'pay and file', for the first accounting periods ending after 30 September 1993 (13.4.1), corporation tax returns are mandatory if notices are issued.

If no return is submitted, sources of income and capital gains must broadly be notified to the Inland Revenue. The time limit is one year from the end of the year of assessment or accounting period and there is a penalty of up to the amount of the unpaid tax (FA 1988 Ss120–122).

If you have not been sent a tax return for the previous tax year and you have received income for that year apart from your wages or salary, you should request that the Revenue sends you a return form for completion. This request should be made to the Inspector of Taxes who deals with your affairs — if you are employed it will be the tax district that handles your employer's PAYE affairs.

As well as including details of your income for the previous tax year your tax return also constitutes a claim for income tax allowances and reliefs in respect of the current tax year. Thus your 1997 tax return must show your income for the year to 5 April 1997 and the income tax allowances that you are claiming for the year to 5 April 1998. A further reason for you to request a tax return from your Inspector of Taxes is thus to ensure that you are granted all of the income tax reliefs to which you are entitled.

Under the previous system, when a tax return was issued to you it normally stipulated that it must be completed and sent back within 30 days but the Revenue usually allowed further time if required. (However, if you delayed beyond 31 October and had new sources of income unknown to the Inland Revenue, you could be charged interest on the eventual assessment, if this is held up.) However, your return for 5 April 1997 is normally due by 31 January 1998 (16.1).

Your 1996 tax return was probably sent to you early in April 1996 and requested details as follows:

Income:	Year ended 5 April 1996
Outgoings:	Year ended 5 April 1996
Capital gains:	Year ended 5 April 1996
Allowances:	Claim for year ending 5 April 1997.

The 1996 and earlier tax returns were comprehensive and consisted of up to 12 pages. Fuller details are included in earlier editions of this book.

Note that your 1997 tax return will be the first to be completed under the self-assessment rules. You will probably have received this more detailed form in April 1997 and it is described below.

16.2.1 Your Tax Return for the Year to 5 April 1997

The basic return consists of an eight page form, together with supplementary pages where needed. Green arrows and instructions are provided to guide you through the form.

Page 1 is informative, reminding you that the form should reach the Revenue by 30 September 1997 for them to calculate your tax bill, or include any tax you owe up to £1,000 in next year's tax code. Otherwise, the due date is 31 January 1998.

The following warnings are given:

(1) Automatic penalties if your return is late.
(2) Late tax payments attract interest and penalties.
(3) Tax returns to be checked — penalties for false information.

Page 2 is designed to find out if you have the right supplementary pages. There is a series of questions with yes/no boxes for your answers. Each 'yes' means using particular *supplementary pages*, which are colour-coded and are as follows:

		Circumstances
1)	Employment	Employee, director or agency worker.
2)	Share schemes	Taxable share options/share related benefits.
3)	Self-employment	You are self-employed but not a partner.
4)	Partnership	You are a partner.
5)	Land and property	You receive UK income from land etc.
6)	Foreign	You have taxable overseas income.
7)	Trusts etc	Income from Trusts and deceased's estates.
8)	Capital gains	Gains (losses) above the exemptions (20.6).
9)	Non-residence etc	You were not resident/ordinarily resident/domiciled in the UK in all or part of 1997–98.

Page 3 requests details of income on UK savings and investments. This includes interest from banks, building societies, unit trusts, National Savings products and dividends. There are spaces for the amounts after tax, tax deducted tax credit or notional tax and gross income. (The notional tax is not repayable and relates to income such as scrip dividends and foreign income dividends from UK companies).

Page 4 covers the remainder of your income. The first section applies if you received UK pensions, retirement annuities or Social Security benefits. You must enter the taxable amounts for 1996–97 of any state pensions and benefits. These include State Retirement Pension, Widow's Pension, Unemployment Benefit, Invalid Care Allowance, Statutory Sick Pay and Maternity Pay and Incapacity Benefit.

The remainder of Page 4 has spaces for the following:

(1) Taxable maintenance or alimony.
(2) Gains on life assurance policies (with/without notional tax).
(3) Refunds of additional voluntary contributions (regarding pensions).
(4) Other income not entered elsewhere.
(5) *Losses* brought forward; used in 1996–97; sustained in 1996–97.

Page 5 is for claiming reliefs. The first part relates to pension contributions and includes retirement annuity contracts and self employed/employee contributions to personal pension plans. There are spaces for payments made in 1996–97, used in an earlier year, now to be carried back and brought back from 1997–98.

The following other reliefs are covered, with spaces for the amounts:

(1) Payments for vocational training.
(2) Interest to purchase your main home (other than MIRAS).

(3) Interest on other qualifying loans.
(4) Maintenance or alimony payments under a court order etc.
(5) Subscriptions for Venture Capital Trust shares (up to £100,000).
(6) Subscriptions under the Enterprise Investment Scheme (up to £100,000).
(7) Charitable covenants or annuities.
(8) Gift Aid payments.
(9) Post-cessation expenses and losses on relevant discounted securities.
(10) Payments to a trade union or friendly society for death benefits.

Page 6 is for claiming allowances and the various personal allowances are covered (3.0.1, etc). Also, spaces are provided for transitional relief (3.2.1), shared claims and transfer of surplus allowances.

Pages 7 & 8 are headed 'other information'. First, you must give the amount of tax refunded to you directly. Next comes the section relevant if you wish to *calculate your own tax*. If so, you must enter the following:

(1) Unpaid tax for earlier years included in your 1996–97 tax code.
(2) Tax due for 1996–97 included in your tax code for a later year.
(3) Total tax due for 1996–97 (put in brackets if an overpayment). A tax calculation working sheet is provided.
(4) Unpaid tax for earlier years.
(5) Overpaid tax for earlier years.
(6) Your first payment on account for 1997–98.
(7) 1997–98 tax you are reclaiming now.

If you are claiming to reduce your payments on account you must tick a box provided and give your reasons in the 'additional information' box which is on Page 8.

A repayments section allows you to indicate where and to whom (an agent, etc) they should be sent and a section for personal detail (date of birth, etc) follows.

Boxes are provided on Page 8 to tick if you expect to receive a new pension in 1997–98, or do not want tax you owe collected through your tax code. Certain other boxes are to be used together with the 'additional information' section. These cover such matters as provisional figures in your return; details of anyone to whom you have paid rent to outside the UK; claims for trading loss relief; and backwards/forwards spreading of literary or artistic income (15.4).

The final part of your tax return comprises a declaration for you to sign. You must certify that the return is correct and complete to the best of your knowledge and belief. Also, there are spaces to tick, indicating the supplementary pages which you have completed and enclosed.

16.3 The Tax Inspectors and Collectors
(TMA S1 & FA 1990 S104)

The overall control and management of income tax, corporation tax and capital gains tax is exercised by the Board of Inland Revenue. They are responsible for administering the relevant law as contained in the 1988

Income and Corporation Taxes Act and the various Finance Acts. The latter were normally enacted annually about July, the main items having been announced by the Chancellor of the Exchequer in his budget speech in March or April. Budgets are now in November. However, in 1993, there was a budget in March and a second one in November. Finance Acts are now to be enacted by 5 May each year.

The Board of Inland Revenue is made up of the Commissioners of Inland Revenue. The day-to-day administration, however, is carried out by various Inspectors of Taxes and Collectors of Taxes who are civil servants, appointed by the Board. Inspectors and collectors may be appointed for general purposes or specific purposes, at the discretion of the Board.

The Inspectors of Taxes are organised into various tax districts to one of which you will have to send your income tax return. A district inspector heads each district under whom are a number of inspectors and clerks, who obtain and verify as they think fit the information that is necessary to raise assessments to income tax, capital gains tax and corporation tax.

The Collectors of Taxes have the responsibility of collecting the tax that has been assessed. They normally issue demands for the tax that is due (16.8).

The office of the Inspector of Foreign Dividends handles various matters in connection with double tax relief claims.

16.3.1 The assessment mechanism
(TMA S29 & FA 1988 S119)

When you have submitted your income tax return for 1995–96 and earlier years, the Inspector of Taxes issues a ‘notice of assessment’ to income tax in respect of your various types of income. A separate assessment is raised in respect of Schedule E earnings. Since the latter normally will have been taxed already under PAYE the assessment shows whether any additional payment of income tax is required or whether a repayment is due (16.7). Your capital gains tax assessment is also raised by your Inspector of Taxes (20.15).

If the Revenue have not received sufficient information to raise accurate tax assessments prior to the date on which the tax is due for payment, they will normally make estimated assessments in respect of the tax-payer’s sources of income. Estimated capital gains tax assessments will also be raised if appropriate.

For 1996–97 and subsequent years, a self-assessment system applies (16.2). (If you submit your return by 30 September 1997, the Revenue can be asked to calculate your 1996–97 tax; otherwise you must do so.)

16.3.2 Due dates for payment of tax

(TA 1988 S5)

The due date for payment of income tax assessed under the various Schedules and Cases (2.3.1) is normally 1 January in the year of assessment. This applies for years up to 1996–97. For subsequent years the dates are revised (16.1).

Thus your Schedule D Case III income tax for 1995–96 including higher rates was payable on 1 January 1996. Schedule D Case I and Case II assessments on your profits from a trade or profession were payable, however, in two instalments on 1 January in the year of assessment and the following 1 July.

Higher rate income tax on your 'taxed' investment income was payable on 1 December following the year of assessment. This includes tax on interest, etc taxed at source and dividends. Higher rate income tax on other investment income, however (including rents, etc), was normally payable on 1 January in the year of assessment. (For due dates of payment of corporation tax see 13.4.)

For assessments issued later than 30 days before the respective date above, however, the date when the tax becomes due and payable is delayed to a later date. This is normally 30 days after the issue of the assessment. Note, however, the effect of appeals (16.4).

For 1996–97 and subsequently, the due dates for paying income tax and capital gains tax are generally 31 January following the year of assessment. For 1997–98 and subsequently, you make payments on account on 31 January and 31 July, each based on half the self-assessed amount for the year before (excluding tax paid at source). (Generally you will not make payments on account if your tax for the previous year is less than £500.) A similar basis applies for 1996–97, except that all tax under Schedule A and Schedule D Cases III to VI is normally covered by the instalment due on 31 January 1997. Due to Inland Revenue error, many were told to pay half their liability on 31 January and half on 31 July 1997. Such payments will be accepted without penalty.

16.3.3 Discovery

(TMA S29 (3))

The estimated assessments will be made by the Revenue to as great a degree of accuracy as possible according to any information in their possession such as particulars for previous years. If, however, the Revenue make a *discovery* that:

(1) profits which ought to have been assessed to tax have not been assessed, or
(2) an assessment to tax is or has become insufficient, or
(3) excessive relief has been given

the Revenue may make an assessment in the amount or further amount which ought in their opinion to be charged.

16.3.4 Time limits for assessments *(TMA Ss34 & 36)*

Normally an assessment to tax may be made at any time not later than six years after the end of the chargeable period to which the assessment relates. This means that any income tax assessment for 1996–97 may be made on or before 5 April 2003.

In cases, however, of any fraudulent or negligent conduct by the taxpayer (16.9.1) the Revenue have more time to make assessments.

A special rule applies to the recovery by the Revenue of excessive repayment claims, etc. The time limit is then six years from the end of the tax year when the original repayment, etc was made.

16.3.5 Tax remission — official error

If you send in full returns of your taxable income and you receive no assessments, so that you are led to believe that your tax affairs are in order, it is the practice of the Revenue to excuse you all or part of the tax.

For tax arrears notified prior to 11 May 1996, income limits applied as shown in the following table. However, from that date there are no such limits.

16.3.6 Table: Tax remission limits from 17 February 1993 to 10 March 1996

Gross income limits	*Fraction of arrears collected*
£15,500	None
18,000	$\frac{1}{4}$
22,000	$\frac{1}{2}$
26,000	$\frac{3}{4}$
40,000	$\frac{9}{10}$
above 40,000	All

16.4 Appeals against assessments
(TMA S31 & F2A 1975 S45)

If you are not in agreement with an assessment to income tax, capital gains tax or corporation tax you may appeal to the Inspector of Taxes within 30 days of the date of the assessment. Your appeal must be in writing and state the grounds on which you object to the assessment; most frequently these are that 'the assessment is estimated and excessive'. Should you not be able to appeal within 30 days for some good reason such as absence from home or ill-health, the Revenue will normally allow you to make a late appeal.

The majority of appeals are settled by agreement. This normally follows when the accounts and/or returns have been submitted to the Inspector of Taxes and any queries that he raises are answered. If, however, you are not able to agree with the Revenue or if you or your accountants have not submitted all of the required information, the appeal will be listed for personal hearing before the Commissioners (16.5).

All the tax charged by an assessment is treated as due and payable (16.3.2) unless, within 30 days, you estimate how much you are being overcharged and apply to the Inspector for the balance to be postponed.

The 30-day time limit is extended where your circumstances change so that your tax liability reduces. It will then be determined by agreement with the Inspector or otherwise by the Commissioners how much of the tax should be held over with only the balance being collected. This collectable balance is payable within 30 days after the Inspector or Commissioners have dealt with the application for postponement. Any unpaid tax normally becomes due 30 days after the date on which, following the agreement of the assessment, the Inspector issues a notice of the tax payable. An interest charge could run from an earlier date, however (16.8.2), especially in the case of a long drawn out appeal.

16.5 The Special and General Commissioners
(TMA Ss2–6, F2A 1992 Ss75, 76 & Sch 16 & FA 1994 S254)

The Commissioners before whom tax appeals are heard are of two kinds, General and Special.

The General Commissioners are not normally paid. They are similar to lay magistrates and the majority of them have no special legal or accountancy qualifications. General Commissioners are appointed in England and Wales by the Lord Chancellor. They are appointed for specific districts each of which has a Clerk to the Commissioners, who is usually a solicitor, to assist them.

The Treasury previously appointed the Special Commissioners who usually had practical experience of taxation matters gained either in private practice or with the Inland Revenue. Now, under rules in the 1984 Finance Act, the Lord Chancellor appoints them only from barristers, solicitors or advocates of at least ten years' standing. The Special Commissioners are full-time civil servants.

Appeals will automatically be heard before the General Commissioners in the district which deals with the tax assessment, except that:

(1) When appealing, you may request that any resulting hearing should be in another district which is more convenient to you.
(2) You may elect within 30 days of the assessment that the appeal should be brought before the Special Commissioners. This does not apply, however, to questions regarding personal reliefs and (under the new rules) delay cases which are always dealt with by the General Commissioners.
(3) Appeals against certain income tax assessments are always heard by the Special Commissioners including those on annual payments not covered by income, transactions in securities (TA 1988 S703) valuations of unquoted securities and transfers of assets abroad (TA 1988 S739).

In many cases you will thus have a choice as to whether the Special or General Commissioners should hear your appeal. As a general rule if your case is good in equity and its justice would commend it to average honest men, you should choose the General Commissioners. If you have a good legal case (ie, one sound according to a strict reading of the law) you should choose the Special Commissioners. However, if you elect for your appeal to be heard by the Special Commissioners this can be opposed by the Revenue if they prove you have no case to present.

New rules include giving the Special Commissioners powers to publish their decisions and to award costs where either party has acted wholly unreasonably in pursuing a tax appeal. Also, the Commissioners are given powers to require any party involved in an appeal, including the Revenue, to furnish information.

16.6 Investigatory powers of the Revenue
(TMA Ss20, 20A, 20B, etc & FA 1988 S127)

The powers of the Revenue to obtain papers and search premises were strengthened by the 1976 and 1989 Finance Acts. Subject to the consent of the Board of Inland Revenue, the Inspector may require you by notice in writing to supply him with documents in your possession or power, which he considers have a bearing on your tax liability. From 27 July 1990, the Board are not to consent unless you have failed or may have failed to comply with any provisions of the Taxes Acts; and as a result your tax position has been seriously affected.

The Inspector may also require documents from certain other people. These other people include your spouse and any of your children. In general these rules do not apply to pending appeals, but they do include access to computer records.

If any of your income comes from a business which you either carried on yourself or you managed, then any person who is or was carrying on a business may be directed to provide documents concerning their dealings with your business. The same applies if your wife carries on a business or manages one.

These rules also apply to a past business and any companies of which you or your spouse are, or were, directors. From August 1988, such companies need not be carrying on business. Furthermore, the Director of Savings is within the net.

In order for your Inspector of Taxes to obtain information about your affairs from other people, he must obtain the consent of a General or Special Commissioner (16.5) and the latter must ensure that the Inspector is justified in his request. FA 1994 S255 provides that the same Commissioner cannot later hear an appeal involving the same information. The inspector must tell you why he requires documents unless he can convince a commissioner that disclosure might prejudice collecting the tax.

A barrister, advocate or solicitor cannot be compelled to yield up documents without your consent provided these are covered by professional privilege. This even applies to such a lawyer acting as your tax accountant (see below).

From 27 July 1989 various changes took effect including:

(1) the protection of personal records and journalistic material from disclosure;

(2) a requirement for the Inland Revenue to allow not less than 30 days for requested information to be produced;
(3) the putting of written questions to the taxpayer;
(4) it being a criminal offence to falsify, conceal or destroy documents called for under the Revenue powers.

16.6.1 Tax accountants' papers

Your tax accountant is not obliged to reveal his working papers to the Revenue subject to the following.

Where a tax accountant is convicted of an offence in relation to tax by a UK court or has a penalty awarded against him for assisting in making incorrect returns, etc subject to certain rules, an Inspector of Taxes may require him to surrender documents relating to the tax affairs of any of his clients. Notice is required in writing and the permission of a circuit judge, Scottish sheriff or Irish county court judge must be obtained. The power of the Revenue to give this notice generally ceases 12 months after the conviction or penalty award, and does not have effect whilst an appeal is pending.

Not less than 30 days must be allowed for a convicted tax accountant to deliver documents required by the Revenue. Also from that time, personal records and journalistic material are protected as are, in general, audit papers and records of tax advice. At the same time, taxpayers must be notified of requests for information from third parties, unless fraud is involved.

16.6.2 Entry warrant to obtain documents

If the Revenue obtain an entry warrant in a case of suspected fraud they may enter specified premises, seizing and removing any documents or other things required as evidence for relevant proceedings.

A warrant is valid for 14 days and can only be granted by a circuit judge, etc who is satisfied on information given on oath by an officer of the Board of Inland Revenue, that evidence concerning a tax fraud is to be found on the premises in question.

The Inland Revenue search powers are broadly restricted to the investigation of 'serious fraud' and are subject to a detailed code of conduct. Also, taxpayers have rights of access to property removed under the search powers.

16.6.3 Returns of information
(TMA Ss13–19)

The Revenue are empowered to request returns of certain information from traders and others. For example, you may be required to give particulars of any lodgers you may have.

Your bank may be required to return details of interest paid to you during a tax year. Furthermore, the Revenue are empowered to obtain from any business details of its payments of fees, commissions, royalties, etc exceeding £15 to any person during a tax year.

There is a three-year time limit regarding many of the Revenue powers to request information returns. However, they can extend their enquiries to certain government departments and public authorities.

16.6.4 Appeal hearings
(TMA Ss44–59)

The Clerk to the Commissioners will advise you of the time and place for your appeal hearing. If you are unable to attend for some good reason or if you or your accountants have not completed the required accounts, etc it will normally be possible to have the matter adjourned at least once until a later time. If you would like an adjournment you or your agent should raise the question with your Inspector of Taxes who will usually be prepared to arrange this for you if your reasons are in order.

At the appeal hearing you may represent yourself or be represented by an accountant or a solicitor or barrister. If your appeal is on a point of law which you anticipate may go to the Courts (see below) it is wise to be represented at the outset by a barrister who can act for you in the Courts.

The Revenue are normally represented by an Inspector of Taxes but on difficult legal points a person from the Solicitors' Office may act. The proceedings before the Commissioners resemble those in the Courts in many ways — for example, witnesses may be summoned under oath to be examined and cross-examined.

When the hearing has been completed the Commissioners will withdraw to consider their decision. They may confirm or reduce or increase the original assessment. The decision of the Commissioners is final regarding questions of fact.

If either the taxpayer or the Revenue are dissatisfied with their decision on a point of law, they should immediately 'express dissatisfaction'. The

Commissioners should then be requested to supply a 'case stated' which is a document signed by them setting out their decision. A fee of £25 is now charged.

The case will then be taken on appeal to the Courts where it will first be heard before a single judge in the Chancery Division. (It is possible for certain appeals against decisions of the Special Commissioners to be referred direct to the Court of Appeal.) The decision of such a court can be appealed against, following which the case will be heard before the Court of Appeal and on further appeal it may go before the House of Lords.

Before you request a 'case stated' from the Commissioners you should weigh very carefully the strength of your case and the potential tax saving if you succeed in the higher Courts against the high legal costs which would be involved.

16.7 Repayment claims

(TMA Ss42–43B & TA 1988 S281)

Repayment claims arise in connection with many different facets of taxation. You will normally, however, find that any income tax repayment to which you become entitled arises in one of the following ways:

(1) Most of your income has been taxed at the source and your personal reliefs and allowances exceed your other income. (Also, you may not have received the full benefit of the £4,100 20 per cent lower rate income tax band for 1997–98.) If your income tax return reveals this position and you send in the required simple repayment claim form together with dividend vouchers, etc in respect of the income tax credits, you will receive an income tax repayment. The repayment will reduce your income tax bill for the tax year to its correct level.

(2) Some of your income has been taxed both in the UK and in another country. You are frequently able to make a double taxation relief repayment claim of either UK tax or overseas tax depending on the circumstances (18.6).

(3) You may have already paid a Schedule A or Schedule D assessment for a tax year and, as described elsewhere in this book, you make an election to the Revenue which results in your assessment for that year being reduced. An example of such an election is where you elect that the second and third years of your business should be assessed on an actual basis (11.7.3).

(4) You make a business loss which you claim to be offset against your other income for the year (11.22). Some of this income has suffered income tax by deduction at the source and on making the required claim and submitting the tax vouchers or receipts you will be repaid an appropriate amount of such tax, as well as tax credits on dividends.

(5) You discover that an 'error or mistake' has been made in a return or statement or schedule that you have previously submitted as a result of which you have been over-assessed to tax. Within six years after the end of the tax year in which the original assessment was made, you may make a claim to your Inspector of Taxes for the repayment of the tax previously overpaid.

(6) Repayment claims often arise in respect of minors (under 18) all of whom are taxpayers in their own right and so are entitled to at least the personal allowance for a single person (£4,045). Thus if a minor's only income for 1997–98 consists of dividends of say £400 and none of the investments were gifted to him by his parents, then he can reclaim all of the relevant tax credits (ie, 20/80 × £400 = £100). Similarly, if the trustees of a settlement apply income for the education and maintenance of a minor, that income is treated as belonging to the child. The income is treated as having suffered basic rate income tax at the source (and additional rate tax if applicable). This enables an income tax repayment claim to be made for the minor unless he has already obtained the full benefit of his tax reliefs and allowances or the settlement had been actually created by one of his parents.

(7) The Revenue may raise an additional assessment and if this is not related to fraud or negligent conduct, you may be able to claim additional reliefs as a result. Such claims, elections, etc, even though out of time according to the normal rules, are valid if made within one year of the end of the tax period in which the assessment is made.

The procedure for making repayment claims is normally very simple. If the Revenue have already received a full return of your income, or in the case of a business or company its accounts and tax computations, it will generally only be necessary to sign a short form in which you claim the tax repayment to which you are entitled. You should also send dividend vouchers or tax deduction certificates or receipts to cover the amount of your repayment.

Special forms are usually required for double tax relief claims on which you must enter particulars of the dividends. Special forms are also provided by the Revenue for use in connection with various other repayment claims, for example, concerning minors.

Income tax repayment claims should normally be made to your local Inspector of Taxes. If you are, for example, a British subject resident abroad your repayment claims should be made to the Chief Inspector (Claims) at Bootle. The Inspector of Foreign Dividends, however, deals with applications from those residing abroad for the recovery of United Kingdom tax suffered on overseas dividends, etc.

16.7.1 Example: Income tax repayment claim

Miss A is 24 years of age and during the year to 5 April 1998 she only had occasional employment from which her gross earnings were £2,000, no PAYE being deducted. During 1997–98 she pays allowable loan interest of £155. Miss A's only other income for 1997–98 consists of £2,000 dividends (tax credit £500) and an income distribution of £660 (net) from a discretionary trust. Calculate the amount of the income tax repayment claim of Miss A for 1997–98.

Miss A — Income tax repayment claim 1997–98

Details		*Gross income*	*Tax credits*
Earned income		£2,000	
Taxed dividends including tax credit		2,500	£500
Trust income — net	£660		
Grossed up equivalent at 34%		1,000	340
		£5,500	
Less: Personal allowance	£4,045		
Loan interest (paid gross)	155		
		4,200	
Taxable amount		£1,300	
Total tax credits			£840
Less: Income tax liability £1,300 at 20%			260
Income tax repayable for 1997–98			£580

16.7.2 Repayment supplement
(TA 1988 Ss824–826 & FA 1989 S158)

This used to apply if you received a tax repayment more than a year after the end of the year of assessment to which it relates. You also have to be resident in the UK. Interest at the appropriate rate(s) free of tax normally runs from the later of the end of the assessment year in which the tax was paid or 5 April following the year for which repayment is made, until the end of the tax month of repayment.

The interest rate before 6 February 1997 and after 5 February 1996 was 6.25 per cent, prior to which it was 7 per cent. Prior to 6 March 1995, the rate was 6.25 per cent, before 6 October 1994, the rate was 5.5 per cent, earlier than 6 January 1994, 6.25 per cent and before 6 March 1993, it was 7 per cent.

Similar rules and rates applied for companies and a fuller rate scale appears earlier (13.4). Identical rates also applied for interest on overdue tax (16.8.2) prior to 6 February 1997.

From 6 February 1997, separate repayment supplement and overdue tax rates apply. These are 4 per cent and 8.5 per cent respectively. An important change is that the repayment supplement runs from when you paid the tax.

16.8 The collection of tax

(TMA Ss60–68)

The collection of income tax, corporation tax and capital gains tax is done by the Collectors of Taxes (16.3).

On being notified of an assessment by the Inspector of Taxes the Collector will send out a first demand. If this is not paid within about a month of its 'due date' a second demand will be sent and after about another ten days a final demand will follow. The final demand requests payment within seven days under the threat of legal proceedings against the taxpayer concerned. It is usual for the first demand to be integrated with the notice of assessment and the payslip should be detached from the rest of the form when you make your payment.

The Revenue are empowered to take action in Magistrates' Courts for the recovery of tax up to a limit which is currently £250 (FA 1984 S57). Otherwise, action must be in the County Courts (up to the 'County Court limit') or the High Court.

16.8.1 Payments on account

If you receive a large tax demand which you find difficult to meet out of your available funds the Collector of Taxes will in cases of hardship allow you to settle the outstanding tax by instalments payable at say monthly or quarterly intervals. You should contact the Collector of Taxes and explain the position to him. Interest will probably be payable, however (see next page). A standard payments on account system has come in with self-assessment (16.1).

16.8.2 Interest on overdue tax
(TMA Ss86–92; F2A 1987 Ss85–88 & FA 1989 Ss156–159)

The following rules apply to assessments issued after 31 July 1975 concerning 1995–96 and earlier years. Assessments issued earlier are covered by different rules (even if still unpaid), and details are given in previous editions. The rules have been clarified and modified by the 1989 Finance Act. For example, the mechanics for altering the interest rate have been made more automatic, rather than needing a statutory instrument, as previously.

Interest is payable at the appropriate rate(s) from the 'reckonable date' until the tax is settled. Some recent rates are:

From	*Rate per cent*
6 February 1997	$8\frac{1}{2}$
6 February 1996	$6\frac{1}{4}$
6 March 1995	7
6 October 1994	$6\frac{1}{4}$
6 January 1994	$5\frac{1}{2}$
6 March 1993	$6\frac{1}{4}$
6 December 1992	7
6 November 1992	$7\frac{3}{4}$
6 October 1991	$9\frac{1}{4}$
6 July 1991	10
6 May 1991	$10\frac{3}{4}$
6 March 1991	$11\frac{1}{2}$
6 November 1989	$12\frac{1}{4}$

The 'reckonable date' for 1995–96 and earlier assessments, is the date when the tax becomes due and payable (16.3.2) unless you appeal and obtain a deferment of tax. In that case the 'reckonable date' is when the tax becomes due and payable or the date given by the following table whichever is earlier:

	Description of tax	*Date applicable*
(1)	Schedules A or D	1 July following the end of the year of assessment.
(2)	Additional rates of income tax	1 June following the end of the next year of assessment.
(3)	Capital gains tax	1 June following the end of the next year of assessment.
(4)	Corporation tax	Usually the normal payment date (13.4).

The above table applies to all amounts, even if not covered by the original assessment if this was issued after July 1982. Otherwise, such additional amounts were only charged to interest from 30 days after the issue of the revised notice of assessment.

The Revenue could excuse at their discretion the payment of interest not exceeding £30 in total for any one assessment. Since 19 April 1993, this rule no longer applies. No interest paid on overdue tax is allowed as a deduction from your taxable income or business profits nor is it allowed as a deduction for corporation tax or capital gains tax purposes.

From 20 April 1988, interest arises on overdue formal assessments, which have to be raised for PAYE and sub-contractor deductions (15.5). The interest charge runs from 14 days after the end of the tax year to which the assessment relates. With effect from 19 April 1993, interest is chargeable on late payments to the Revenue of PAYE deductions made by employers.

For 1996–97 and subsequently the self-assessment rules apply (16.1). These normally direct that interest runs from the due date for the tax. In general, this means that interest at currently 8.5 per cent applies to overdue income tax and capital gains tax from each due date (31 January, 31 July, etc).

16.8.3 Surcharge on unpaid tax
(TMA S9c)

An additional charge has been introduced under the self-assessment system. Any *balancing* payments unpaid after 28 days from the due date (31 January 1998, etc) will normally carry a surcharge of 5 per cent. An additional 5 per cent will be levied on tax still unpaid after 6 months.

16.9 Back duty investigations

If you have not disclosed to the Revenue your true income or if you have claimed tax reliefs and allowances to which you were not entitled the discovery of such facts by the authorities might give rise to a 'back duty' case.

It is open to the Revenue to take criminal proceedings against you resulting in a fine and/or imprisonment but this is rare. The normal course will be for the Revenue to obtain full particulars of the income omitted by you and raise assessments on you in respect of the further tax that is due. You will also normally be charged interest on the tax from when it should have been paid if your income had been properly declared. The Revenue may also charge you to penalties (see 16.9.2) depending upon whether your omissions were due to pure carelessness or ignorance or on the other hand were due to some fraudulent intention.

In order to ascertain the amount of your undisclosed income the Revenue will frequently require that capital statements be drawn up at the beginning and end of the period under review. The increase in your net worth between those two dates is then added to your living expenses for the period to give your total income (subject to adjustments for known capital profits, purchases and sales, betting winnings, etc). Your total income less income already taxed will give your total income requiring still to be taxed. This should be split between the various intervening tax years by considering your assets and living expenses, etc for each tax year.

16.9.1 Fraud, wilful default or neglect; fraudulent or negligent conduct

(TMA S36)

Tax lost through the 'fraudulent or negligent conduct' of a taxpayer may be assessed up to 20 years after the end of the period to which it relates. This rule was introduced by the 1989 Finance Act and it also applies to partners and where agents are culpable. These provisions apply to assessments for 1983–84 onwards and, regarding companies, for accounting periods ending after 31 March 1983.

For years of assessment prior to 1983–84 and accounting periods ending before 1 April 1983, the normal six-year time limit for making assessments (16.3.4) is extended indefinitely in any case where there is fraud or wilful default. This does not apply, however, in the case of the personal representatives of a deceased person (21.2).

In a case of 'neglect' by a taxpayer, the Revenue are empowered to make assessments for 1982–83 and earlier, for six years prior to a tax year for which an assessment has already been made. The latter must be not more than six years ago and the Revenue must obtain the leave of the Special or General Commissioners. 'Neglect' is defined as 'negligence or a failure to give any notice, make any return or to produce or furnish any document or other information required by or under the Taxes Acts'.

16.9.2 Interest and penalties

(TMA Ss86–107 & FA 1989 Ss156–170)

Where an assessment has been made for the purpose of making good a loss of tax through fraud, wilful default or neglect, interest at 8.5 per cent (6.25 per cent prior to 6 February 1997) is charged on the underpaid tax from the date that the tax should have been paid. This also covers tax lost through 'fraudulent or negligent conduct' and was extended from 27 July 1989 to tax assessed late as the result of an incorrect return.

Prior to 6 February 1996, various other interest rates applied as for overdue tax (16.8.2).

The maximum penalties are laid down in the legislation but frequently the Board of the Inland Revenue are prepared to accept less according to the particular facts of each case.

Regarding tax years after 1987–88 (or accounting periods ending after 31 March 1989 for companies), relief is given where more than one penalty arises on the same tax. In no case is the total amount of penalty to exceed the maximum possible amount for any one of the penalties involved.

The 1989 Finance Act introduced a simpler procedure for charging default interest and penalties. The Revenue may make formal determinations of the amounts due rather like assessments. You have full rights of appeal to the Appeal Commissioners and Courts. These new rules do not apply to the initial penalties under the compliance rules which continue to be awarded by the Appeal Commissioners.

16.9.3 Table: Penalties—current rules

(TMA Ss93–107, FA 1989 Ss162–170 & FA 1991 S70)

The following are examples of some of the *maximum* penalties:

Offence	*Penalties*
Failure to submit personal tax returns.	£300 plus £60 per day after a court declaration.
Under the new system (limited to tax due).	£100 after the filing date (31 January) and £100 after 31 July (and £60 per day etc).
Failure to submit return continuing beyond tax year following that in which issued.	Additional penalty of up to the amount of tax on income and gain, for year. However, if there is no assessable income or gains, the maximum *total* penalty is £100.
Incorrect returns.	100% of tax lost.
Assisting in the preparation of incorrect returns or accounts.	£3,000.
Supplying incorrect information to the Revenue.	£3,000.

Failure to keep records under self-assessment	£3,000
Failure to give notice of liability to tax.	From 6 April 1989 the penalty is the amount of tax if notice is more than one year overdue.
Failure to make (when required) a return of information for the Revenue.	£300 plus £60 for each additional day in default.
Late submission of employers' year-end PAYE returns (10.14.4).	Initial penalty of up to £1,200 per 50 employees and £100 per 50 employees per month for further delays up to one year; beyond which up to 100% of tax underpaid or paid late.
Fraudulent or negligent certificate of non-liability to tax re building society or bank deposit.	Up to £3,000.
False statement made by sub-contractor to obtain exemption from tax deduction (15.5)	£5,000.

16.9.4 Penalties—previous rules
(TMA Ss93–107 & FA 1988 Ss120–122A)

Many of the selected penalties shown in the previous table, (16.9.3), operate from 1989 and others came in with the self-assessment system (16.1). Details of penalties for earlier years are given in previous editions of this book. In general, the fixed penalties were lower. Also, failing to give notice of liability to tax before 6 April 1989 attracted only a £100 penalty, but now if notice is more than one year overdue, the penalty can go up to the amount of the tax.

17 Domicile and residence

17.1 The importance of domicile and residence

Your domicile and residence have a considerable effect on your liability to UK income tax, capital gains tax and inheritance tax. The position is summarised in the following table and dealt with in more detail in Chapters 18 and 19. (Domicile is defined in 17.2 and residence in 17.3.)

17.1.1 Table: The tax effects of domicile and residence

Tax	*Situation of assets or where income arises*	*Tax treatment depending on taxpayer's residence and domicile* — *Taxed on arising basis*	*Taxed on remittance basis (18.1.1)*	*Tax free*
Income Tax				
Schedule D				
Cases I & II	UK	All classes		
	Abroad	Not normally applicable		
Case III	UK	Normally all classes		
	Abroad	Not normally applicable		
Cases IV & V other than trades, professions, pensions, etc	UK	Not applicable	Not applicable	
	Abroad	UK domiciled resident and ordinarily resident	Non-domiciled, UK domiciled resident but not ordinarily resident	Non-resident

Case V relating to trades, professions, pensions, etc	UK Abroad	Not applicable UK domiciled resident and ordinarily resident (90% pensions)	Not applicable Non-domiciled, UK domiciled resident but not ordinarily resident	Non-resident
Case VI	UK Abroad	All classes Not normally applicable apart from anti-avoidance rules (15.10)		
Schedule E		See 10.1–10.4		
Capital Gains Tax	UK or Abroad	UK domiciled and resident or ordinarily resident	Non-domiciled but resident or ordinarily resident (UK assets on arising basis)	Neither resident nor ordinarily resident
Inheritance Tax (residence is normally immaterial)	UK	UK domiciled or non-domiciled		
	Abroad	UK domiciled or deemed domiciled (22.4)		Non-domiciled

17.2 What is domicile?

Your domicile is the country which you regard as your natural home. It is your place of abode to which you intend to return in the event of your going abroad. For most people it is their country of birth. Everyone has one domicile only. Unlike dual nationality, it is not possible to have two domiciles under English law. There are three main categories of domicile:

(1) Domicile of origin.
(2) Domicile of choice.
(3) Domicile of dependency.

17.2.1 Domicile of origin

You receive a domicile of origin at birth; it is normally that of your father at the date of your birth. In the case, however, of an illegitimate child or one born after the death of his father, his domicile of origin is that of his mother.

Your domicile of origin can be abandoned and you can take on a domicile of choice (see below). You will quickly revert to your domicile of origin, however, if you take up permanent residence again in that country.

17.2.2 Domicile of choice

If you abandon your domicile of origin and go and live in another country with the intention of permanently living there, the new country will become your domicile of choice. You will normally have to abandon most of your links with your original country of domicile (above). However, from 6 April 1996, registration for and voting in UK elections as an overseas elector is disregarded (FA 1996 S200).

If you lose or abandon your domicile of choice, your domicile of origin automatically applies once again, unless you establish a new one.

17.2.3 Domicile of dependency

Certain dependent individuals are deemed incapable of choosing a new domicile and the latter is always fixed by the operation of the law. Dependants for this purpose include infants, married women before 1 January 1974 and mental patients.

A child under 16 years of age automatically has the domicile of his father if he is legitimate, and otherwise that of his mother. If, however, a girl of under 16 marries then she takes on her husband's domicile. (Prior to 1 January 1974 the relevant age was 18.) In Scotland a boy has an independent domicile from age 14 and a girl from age 12.

Prior to 1 January 1974 a wife assumed the domicile of her husband while they were married. After the end of the marriage (by death or divorce) the woman kept her former husband's domicile unless she took on a fresh domicile of choice. Since 1 January 1974, however, a wife's domicile is independent of that of her husband. If married before that date, the husband's domicile remains as the wife's deemed domicile of choice until displaced by positive action.

17.2.4 Future changes

A new Domicile Bill was expected which would alter the domicile rules. In particular, it would have been easier for your domicile to be changed and your domicile of origin displaced. However, in May 1993 the Government said that it had no immediate plans to change the rules.

17.3 What is residence?

Your residence for tax purposes is something which is fixed by your circumstances from year to year and you may sometimes be treated as being resident in more than one country at the same time.

Residence depends on the facts of each case and is determined by the individual's presence in a country, his objects in being there and his future intentions regarding his length of stay. The main criterion is the length of time spent in the country during each tax year. Another important point was whether a 'place of abode' is kept in the country (17.3.6).

17.3.1 What is ordinary residence?

If you have always lived in this country you are treated as being ordinarily resident here. Ordinary residence means that the residence is not casual and uncertain but that the individual who resides in a particular country does so in the ordinary course of his life. It implies residence with some degree of continuity, according to the way a person's life is usually ordered.

If you come to this country with the intention of taking up permanent residence here, it is Revenue practice to regard you as being both resident and ordinarily resident in the UK from your date of arrival. If, however, you originally did not intend to take up permanent residence here, you would not be considered ordinarily resident unless you stay here for two complete tax years and keep a place to live in this country.

17.3.2 The residence of an individual *(TA 1988 Ss334–336)*

If a person visits this country for some temporary purpose only and not with the intention of establishing his residence here, he is not normally treated as being a UK resident unless he spends at least six months here during the tax year.

An overseas visitor, however, might be treated as acquiring UK residence if he pays habitual substantial visits to this country. The normal requirement would be to come here for at least four consecutive years and stay for an average of at least three months each year. If you wish to remain non-resident you must avoid such habitual visits.

If you come to this country during a tax year with the intention of staying for two years or more, a Revenue concession will apply. You will only be treated as UK resident from your date of arrival, rather than from the beginning of the tax year when you come. A similar concession applies for your year of departure if you leave the UK for permanent overseas residence.

If you pay only short casual visits abroad you will not lose your UK residence, but if an entire tax year is included in any continuous period spent abroad you will normally be treated as being non-resident for at least the intervening tax year (17.3.7).

17.3.3 The residence of a company
(TA 1988 Ss747, 765–767, FA 1988 Ss66 & 130–132 & Sch 7 & FA 1994 Ss249–251)

Subject to transitional provisions (see below), a company which is incorporated in the UK is treated for tax purposes as being resident here. Prior to 15 March 1988, a company was deemed to be resident where its central control and management were carried out. This was not necessarily where the company was registered although normally the central control and management would be exercised in the country in which the company was registered.

Where a company simply had its registered office here but carried on all its business from offices abroad and held its board meetings abroad, it was non-resident. Such companies did not come within the new rules for determining residence until 15 March 1993, provided they were already non-resident on 14 March 1988 or became non-resident later with Treasury consent. (In general, such companies needed to continue to carry on business.)

Under the controlled foreign company rules (13.21), where a company is resident abroad, it is necessary to establish in which country. Broadly, it is regarded as resident in the country where it is liable to tax because of its domicile, residence or place of management.

If a company registered abroad transacts some of its business in this country, it will not normally be treated as being UK resident provided its management and control are exercised abroad, which includes all board meetings being held abroad.

Taxes Act 1988 S765 contains certain penal provisions to prevent a UK company from becoming non-resident without Treasury consent being obtained. Fuller details are given earlier (15.10.16).

Where a company is resident in two countries, the double tax agreement often determines which residence applies for its purposes. If such a dual resident company is non-UK resident under the double tax agreement, it is so regarded for all UK tax purposes from 30 November 1993.

17.3.4 The residence of a partnership
(TA 1988 S112)

Where any trade or business is carried on by a partnership and the control and management of the trade is situated abroad, the partnership is deemed to be resident abroad. This applies even if some of the partners are resident in this country and some of the trade is carried on here (12.8).

17.3.5 The residence of a trust

A trust is generally treated for capital gains tax purposes as being resident and ordinarily resident in the UK unless its general administration is ordinarily carried on outside this country and a majority of the trustees are neither resident nor ordinarily resident here. Stricter rules generally apply for income tax. For these purposes, broadly from 1989–90 (with some exceptions), special rules apply where at least one trustee is UK resident and one is not, depending on the settlor's status when he created the settlement or introduced further funds. If the settlor was then resident, ordinarily resident or domiciled in the UK, for determining the residence of the trust, all of the trustees are treated as being UK resident. Otherwise, they are all treated as being resident outside the UK. (A similar rule concerns the residence of executors, etc.) For 1989–90 only, a trust was non-resident if none of the trustees were UK resident from 1 October 1989 to 5 April 1990 (FA 1989 Ss110 & 111).

17.3.6 Place of abode in the UK
(TA 1988 S335 & FA 1993 S208)

Prior to 6 April 1993, if you maintained a house or flat in this country available for your occupation this was usually a factor towards deciding that you were resident here. Your residence position, however, was decided without regard to any place of abode maintained for your use in the UK in the following circumstances.

(1) You worked full-time in a trade, profession or vocation no part of which was carried on in this country.

(2) You worked full-time in an office or employment, all the duties of which (ignoring merely incidental duties) were performed outside the UK.

For 1993–94 and subsequent years of assessment, your residence position may not be affected by your having a place of abode here. Such accomodation will be ignored in considering whether or not you have come to the UK for a temporary purpose (17.3.2). However, if you leave the UK and retain a home here, your reasons for this may be a factor in deciding your residence.

17.3.7 The effect of visits abroad

(TA 1988 S334)

If you are a citizen of the Commonwealth or the Republic of Ireland and your ordinary residence has been in the UK you are still charged to income tax if you have left this country if it is for the purpose of only occasional residence abroad. In order to obtain non-residence for UK tax purposes your overseas residence must be more than merely occasional, it must have a strong element of permanency. The normal Revenue requirements are as follows:

(1) A definite intention to establish a permanent residence abroad.
(2) The actual fulfilment of such intention.
(3) Normally a full tax year should be spent outside this country before you are considered non-resident. Short periods in the UK may be disregarded by the Revenue, however. Thus if you left the country permanently on 30 September 1995 you will only be confirmed as non-resident after 5 April 1997. If you go abroad for the purposes of employment or to carry on a trade, once you are accepted by the Revenue as being no longer resident here, your non-residence is made retrospective to the day after your date of departure. In other cases of permanent departure, non-residence will normally run from the day after departure, but in some instances may run only from the following 6 April. In general, the Revenue have less stringent rules regarding those working abroad under contracts of employment.

17.4 How to change your domicile and residence

As has been already indicated, domicile and residence normally run together but domicile is much more difficult to change.

The way in which to change your residence is summarised on the previous page. You simply establish a permanent residence abroad and remain out of this country for a complete tax year. (In certain circumstances short visits to the UK are allowed.) After that you must avoid returning to this country for as much as six months in any one tax year, averaging less than three months here every year. Even if you do not work abroad, it is now less necessary to avoid having a place of abode available for you in the UK (17.3.6).

The general rule is that you will be charged to UK tax for the entire year of assessment as being either resident here or non-resident. However, in certain circumstances, by Inland Revenue Concession, the year of assessment is split for this purpose, namely where, being not ordinarily resident:

(1) You come to the UK to take up permanent residence or stay at least two years (previously three years),
(2) You cease to reside in the UK because you have left for permanent residence abroad.

The concession (A11) also applies if you go abroad under a contract of employment which includes a complete tax year. However, you may not spend 183 days or more in the UK in any tax year, nor an average of 91 days over a maximum period of 4 years.

In order to establish a fresh domicile, you should take as many steps as possible to show that you regard your new country as your permanent home.

The following points are relevant to establishing a particular country as your new domicile:

(1) Develop a long period of residence in the new country.
(2) Purchase or lease a home.
(3) Marry a native of that country.
(4) Develop business interests there.
(5) Make arrangements to be buried there.
(6) Draw up your will according to the law of the country.
(7) Exercise political rights in your new country of domicile (17.2.2).
(8) Arrange to be naturalised (not vital).
(9) Have your children educated in the new country.
(10) Resign from all clubs and associations in your former country of domicile and join clubs, etc in your new country.

(11) Any religious affiliations that you have with your old domicile should be terminated and new ones established in your new domicile.
(12) Arrange for your family to be with you in your new country.

The above are some of the factors to be considered and the more of these circumstances that can be shown to prevail, the sooner you will be accepted as having changed your domicile.

18 Tax on foreign income

18.1 Overseas income from investments and businesses

(TA 1988 Ss18 & 65–67 & FA 1994 S207)

If you obtain any income from investments and businesses situated overseas, you will normally be charged to income tax under Case IV or Case V of Schedule D. Case IV applies to income from 'securities' unless the income has already been charged under Schedule C or its successors (8.2). Case V applies to income from 'possessions' outside the UK. This includes businesses but does not cover emoluments from any overseas employment (18.5).

Your income assessed under Case IV and V of Schedule D will be included in your total income for tax purposes (5.2).

Frequently your overseas income will have already suffered tax in its country of origin. If you also have to pay UK income tax on this income you will normally be entitled to some relief to limit the extent that you are taxed doubly on the same income (18.6).

From 1997–98, the normal basis of assessment under Cases IV and V of Schedule D is the amount of income arising in the year of assessment. For 1996–97, a transitional basis may apply (18.2). Before that, for sources of income existing prior to 5 April 1994, there was a 'previous year' basis. In the opening and closing years of a source of income, however, special rules applied (18.2.1 and 18.2.2).

In certain special circumstances the 'arising basis' is not used and the normally more favourable 'remittance basis' applies. If you are UK domiciled and ordinarily resident, however, your assessments on overseas pensions are based on only 90 per cent of the income arising.

18.1.1 What is the remittance basis?

Under the remittance basis you are only taxed on the amount of income actually brought into this country, in the year of assessment (whilst you still possess the source of overseas income). Remittances from sources opened before 6 April 1994 were assessable on the basis of the amounts for the previous tax year. However, 1996–97 is a transitional year, for which you are assessed on half your remittances in 1995–96 and 1996–97. If you are assessed on the remittance basis and bring income into the UK in a tax year after the source has come to an end, you are not liable to UK tax on it at all (18.1.2). Remittances can be made in cash or kind (18.1.3).

If you make no remittances you will have no liability to UK tax on your overseas income that is taxable on the remittance basis, no matter how high your income is in any year, although you might well suffer foreign tax.

18.1.2 When does the remittance basis apply?
(TA 1988 S65)

Your Case IV and V assessments will be based not on the 'arising' basis but on the remittance basis:

(1) If you are resident in this country but not domiciled here (17.3.2); or

(2) If you are a British subject or a citizen of the Republic of Ireland and are resident in this country but not ordinarily resident here.

You may have some overseas income that is taxed on a remittance basis and some that is taxed on an arising basis. In this case you should clearly segregate the two sources of income by using separate bank accounts since income from the latter can be brought into this country without paying any additional tax here because it has already been charged to UK tax.

If you are not resident in this country (17.3.2), you will not normally be charged to tax in respect of your Case IV and Case V income, even if it is remitted here.

18.1.3 What are classed as remittances?
(TA 1988 S65)

Whilst you have any continuing sources of overseas income in respect of which income arising abroad has not been fully transmitted to this country, any sums brought into the UK will normally be first considered to be remittances of overseas income.

The above will not apply if you keep separate bank accounts for income and capital, bringing in funds from the latter only (possibly giving rise to capital gains tax).

As well as cash and cheques, any property imported or value arising here from property not imported will be classed as remittances. Thus if you buy a car abroad out of your overseas profits and bring it into this country this is a remittance (although strictly speaking the second-hand value of the car at the time of importation should be used instead of the cost of the car). Similarly, if you hire an asset abroad out of unremitted overseas income, any use that you get from the asset in this country should be valued and treated as a remittance.

If you borrow money against sums owing to you for overseas income and bring the former into this country, this is a remittance. Similarly, if you borrow money here and repay it abroad out of overseas profits, this is known as a 'constructive remittance' and is taxable. Other forms of 'constructive remittances' include the payment out of overseas income of interest owing in this country, and the repayment out of such income, of money borrowed overseas which was made available to you in this country.

If you use non-remitted overseas income to buy shares in UK companies this is normally treated as a remittance unless a third party abroad actually acts as the principal in the transaction.

You are able to use non-remitted overseas income to cover the costs of overseas visits (including holidays) and provided you bring none of the money back to this country there is no taxable remittance. For this purpose the Revenue allow you to receive traveller's cheques in this country provided they are not cashed here.

If overseas profits are remitted to the Channel Islands or the Isle of Man this is not treated as a taxable remittance since those countries are not regarded as part of the UK for taxation purposes. They were, however, treated as being part of the UK for the purposes of exchange control. This was most important since it was a UK exchange control rule that income earned abroad should be remitted to the UK. This rule was satisfied by sending the money to, say, Jersey or Guernsey without in turn incurring any UK income tax liability. The UK exchange control rules were generally withdrawn from 24 October 1979 and you are now free to keep money in other countries, subject to their own regulations. Furthermore, the legal framework, the Exchange Control Act 1947, was abolished in 1987. However, tax planning should allow for the possible reintroduction of exchange control under a future government.

18.2 The basis of assessment under Schedule D Cases IV and V

(TA 1988 Ss65 & 391, FA 1994 S207 & FA 1995 S41)

As previously mentioned the normal basis of assessment was the amount of income arising in the tax year preceding the year of assessment. In certain cases, however, the assessment is based on the remittances in the previous tax year (18.1.2).

Legislation in the 1994 Finance Act has abolished the preceding year basis from 1996–97. The assessment for each subsequent tax year will be based on your actual income within it. Your 1996–97 assessment is normally based on half your income (or remittances) for that year and 1995–96. However, new sources arising after 5 April 1994 are immediately assessed on the new (actual) basis.

Under the new system, income from property outside the UK has been aligned with that within the UK by importing some of the new Schedule A rules (7.6). Thus interest payable on a loan to purchase property is allowed as a deduction. Income from overseas property remains assessable under Schedule D Case V and separate from your UK property income pool. However, after 5 April 1997, your overseas property income will be pooled.

A few deductions are allowed in computing the income arising including the following:

(1) Any annuity paid out of the income to a non-resident of this country.
(2) Any other annual payment (not being interest) out of the income to a non-resident.
(3) Normal trading expenses against the income from any trade, etc which you have abroad.
(4) Normal maintenance costs against rental income arising abroad.
(5) Ten per cent of any pensions.
(6) If you pay any overseas taxes for which you get no form of double tax relief then you can deduct such payments in computing your overseas income arising.
(7) If your overseas pension (or part of it) arises under the German or Austrian law relating to victims of Nazi persecution, the deduction was 50 per cent up to 1985–86. Subsequently such income is totally exempt. This includes cases where refugees from Germany were later credited with unpaid social security contributions thereby getting higher pensions.

18.2.1 Special rules for fresh income — old system
(TA 1988 S66)

If you have a new source of Schedule D Case IV and V income which arose before 6 April 1994, your assessments were as follows:

(1) For the tax year in which the income first arose on the income for that year.
(2) Unless the income first arose on 6 April, the assessment for the second tax year was on the actual income arising in that year.
(3) Your assessment for the third tax year was based on the income arising in the preceding tax year. Also if income first arose on 6 April your assessment for the second tax year was based on the income arising in the previous year.
(4) You had the option of electing that your first assessments falling to be made on a preceding year basis as in (3) above should instead be on the income actually arising in the respective tax year.
(5) In case of income assessable on a remittance basis (18.1.1) the above rules were applied by substituting the remittances during the tax year for the income arising during that year.
(6) These rules do not apply for sources of income taxed under the new system (18.2).

18.2.2 Special rules where source of income ceases — old system
(TA 1988 S67 & FA 1995 Ss124 & 125)

(1) If an overseas source of income ceases in a given tax year then your assessment for that year was (and still is) on the income arising in it.
(2) Your assessment for the tax year preceding that in which the source ceases was increased to the actual income arising if this was greater than the original 'preceding year' assessment.
(3) If you obtained no income from the terminated source during its last two years then if you so elect within two years after the end of the tax year in which the source ceased, your assessment for the last tax year in which any income arose is adjusted to the actual income for that year. Also the assessment for the following year is cancelled — this would otherwise have been on the preceding year's income.
The assessment for the tax year prior to the one in which income last arose is increased to the actual amount arising if this is greater than the original 'preceding year' assessment.
(4) If you have obtained no income from an overseas source for six years, you can elect that it should be treated as having ceased in

the last tax year in which income arose. Your assessment for that year is then adjusted to 'actual' and the following year's assessment is cancelled. The previous year's assessment may require to be increased to the actual income arising as in (2).

(5) The above rules apply to income assessed on a remittance basis — you simply consider the remittances during the tax year instead of the income arising. Rules (3) and (4) (previous page) are of particular application to situations where the assessments are on a remittance basis since you may choose to make no remittances for a number of years so that you incur no UK tax on the relevant overseas income for those years.

(6) Where you are assessed on the remittance basis (18.1.1) you will not be liable to UK tax on any income that you bring into this country during a tax year later than the one in which your overseas source ceases.

(7) Under the new system (18.2), some of the above rules are not needed, since assessments are generally on an actual basis.

(8) A new rule covers where you trade overseas in whole or part and cease being UK resident. This will result in your being taxed as if your trade or profession ceases and recommences. It takes effect generally from 1997–98 and if your business started after 5 April 1994, for 1995–96 and 1996–97 also. A similar rule will apply for partnerships (FA 1995 Ss124 & 125).

18.3 Professions conducted partly abroad

If you are engaged in any profession or vocation that is conducted partly within this country and partly overseas, you will normally be assessed on your entire 'global' profits under Case II of Schedule D. It is only if you conduct a separate profession or vocation entirely abroad that Schedule D Case V will apply.

This rule is particularly applicable to actors and entertainers, etc who travel widely in the conduct of their professions. The rule does not apply, however, to income from an office or employment the duties of which are conducted entirely abroad.

18.4 Relief for overseas trading by individuals

(FA 1978 S27 & Sch 4 & FA 1984 S30)

From 1978–79 to 1984–85 inclusive special relief applied against assessments under Schedule D Cases I and II on trades, professions or vocations including partnerships. If you carried on such a trade, etc, resided in the UK and were absent from it for at least 30 'qualifying days' in a year of assessment, you were able to claim the relief. You deducted from your assessment a percentage of the proportion relating to your total 'qualifying days' working abroad. From 1978–79 to 1983–84, the relief was 25 per cent, for 1984–85 it was 12.5 per cent and nil thereafter.

18.5 Earnings from overseas employments

(TA 1988 Ss19, 132, 192 & 193 & F2A 1992 S54)

From 6 April 1974 to 5 April 1984, you were normally assessed to tax under Case I of Schedule E on 75 per cent of your earnings from any overseas employments. For 1984–85, the taxable proportion was 87.5 per cent, after which the relief was totally abolished. However, subject to certain rules, a 100 per cent deduction still applies for extended periods of absence (18.5.1).

18.5.1 The 100 per cent deduction

You are not normally liable to UK tax on any income from *overseas employments* which you earn during a 'qualifying period' of absence from this country of at least a year. This does not need to be a tax year and you are allowed to spend here up to one-sixth of the period, but no more than 62 days in any one visit. Otherwise the required continuous 'qualifying period' is broken. This means that you must start reckoning your qualifying period from when you return overseas again.

Also, the one-sixth test is applied to all periods cumulatively from the start of your 'qualifying period' until the end of each overseas visit. Thus if you start your overseas service by being away for 20 days, come back for 20 days and return for 20 days, your 'chain' is broken because you have spent one-third of the 60 days in the UK instead of the maximum of one-sixth.

An *overseas employment* is one the duties of which are performed outside this country. If an employment is performed partly here and partly abroad, you will normally be taxed on the income arising under Case I of Schedule E (10.1). Special rules (19.1.7) apply, however, if you are not domiciled here (17.2). Any duties that you perform in this country which are purely incidental to the performance of your overseas employment are normally disregarded and so the special treatment would apply.

If you work on a ship, from 1988–89 the 62-day period is increased to 90 days and the fraction is one-quarter (FA 1988 S67). Seafarers have longer permitted periods in the UK which apply where at least part of a UK visit between two periods of absence is after 5 April 1991. The new limits are respectively 183 days and half the total period (FA 1991 S45).

There are special rules for *workers in Kuwait or Iraq* who were engaged in an office or employment there at any time during the 62 days to 2 August 1991. Any who returned to the UK after that date but could prove that apart from the Gulf crisis, they would have remained or returned and qualified for the 100 per cent relief, will obtain this (FA 1991 S46).

From 6 April 1992, your overseas earnings must be calculated net for the purposes of the relief. Deductions must be made for appropriate pension contributions, expenses and capital allowances. Previously, faultily drawn legislation allowed gross earnings to be used and the Revenue will agree assessments on that basis for 1990–91, 1991–92 and certain prior assessments which are still open (F2A 1992 S54).

18.5.2 Remittances

The rules concerning the remittance of Schedule E Case III income are exactly the same as for income assessable under Cases IV and V of Schedule D (18.1.2). The remittance basis now broadly only applies for overseas employments if you are UK resident and not domiciled here and/or not ordinarily resident.

Remittances of income from overseas employments are not taxable here in any of the following circumstances:

(1) If made later than the tax year in which the employment ceases but before 6 April 1990. You are assessed on remittances made after 5 April 1990 whether or not the employment has ceased.
(2) If made during a tax year in which you are not resident here (whether or not you are ordinarily resident in this country).
(3) If made when you are UK domiciled and ordinarily resident (normally taxed on an arising basis).

18.5.3 Expenses concerning work overseas
(TA 1988 Ss80–81 & 193–195)

Provided your employer ultimately bears the cost, normally you are not taxed as a benefit on any of the following expenses concerning overseas employments:

(1) Travelling to take up your overseas employment or returning on its termination. (Expense relief is available if you bear the cost yourself.)
(2) Board and lodging overseas.
(3) Certain visits by your family (10.6.4).
(4) Unlimited outward and return journeys between your overseas employment and the UK.

Similar rules apply to the travel and subsistence of UK residents with businesses carried on wholly abroad. The rules cover travel between overseas trades as well as between the UK and abroad.

18.6 Double taxation relief
(TA 1988 Ss788–816)

The UK government has entered into agreements with the governments of other countries for the purpose of preventing double taxation under the UK tax law and under the tax law of such other countries in respect of the same income. A further object of certain of those agreements is to render reciprocal assistance in the prevention of tax evasion.

Under particular double taxation conventions certain classes of income are made taxable only in one of the countries who are party to the agreement, for example, that in which the taxpayer resides. Certain other income is taxable in both of the countries concerned but in the case of UK residents, the overseas tax is allowed as a credit against the UK tax.

Double tax relief is restricted for UK banks lending to non-residents to 15 per cent of the gross interest. However, it is now necessary to look at each loan separately. Foreign tax credit relief is only to be offset against the corporation tax on a particular loan.

If there is no double tax convention between this country and another one then 'unilateral relief' may be available. This means that if you are a UK resident and obtain income from the other country, you are normally allowed to set off any overseas tax suffered against your UK tax liability on the same income. If you are not allowed to do so then you can deduct the overseas tax in computing the overseas income taxable in this country.

Double tax agreements may include provisions for the exchange of information about taxpayers, between the UK and overseas country concerned. This is particularly aimed at countering tax evasion.

18.6.1 Table: Double taxation relief — list of countries which have General Agreements with the UK

Antigua
Australia
Austria
Azerbaijan
Bangladesh
Barbados
Belarus
Belgium
Belize
Bolivia
Botswana
Brunei
Bulgaria
Burma (Myanmar)
Canada
China
Cyprus
Czechoslovakia
Denmark
Dominica (terminated 1987)
Egypt
Estonia
Falkland Islands
Faroe Islands
Fiji
Finland
France
Gambia
Germany
Ghana
Gilbert Islands (Kiribati and Tuvalu)
Greece
Grenada
Guernsey
Guyana
Hungary
Iceland
India
Indonesia
Irish Republic
Israel
Italy
Ivory Coast
Jamaica
Japan
Jersey
Kazakhstan
Kenya
Korea
Latvia
Lesotho
Luxembourg
Malawi
Malaysia
Malta
Isle of Man
Mauritius
Mexico
Mongolia
Montserrat
Morocco
Netherlands
Netherlands Antilles (ceased 31.3.89)
New Zealand
Nigeria
Norway
Pakistan
Papua New Guinea
Philippines
Poland
Portugal
Romania
Russian Federation
St Kitts & Nevis
St Lucia (terminated 1988)
St Vincent (terminated 1987)
Seychelles (terminated 1993)
Sierra Leone
Singapore
Solomon Islands
South Africa
South West Africa (Namibia)
Spain
Sri Lanka
Sudan
Swaziland
Sweden
Switzerland
Tanzania (terminated 1980)
Thailand
Trinidad & Tobago
Tunisia
Turkey
Uganda
Ukraine
USA
USSR*
Uzbekistan
Venezuela

Vietnam	Zambia
Yugoslavia (Croatia & Slovenia)	Zimbabwe

* The convention with the USSR has become known as being with the Russian Federation, but also applies to virtually all other states which used to make up the USSR until superseded by new agreements.

Note: In addition to the above general agreements, arrangements of a more restricted kind have been entered into with Argentina, Brazil, Jordan, Lebanon and Zaire covering the double taxation of profits from shipping and air transport. Agreements with Algeria, Cameroon, Ethiopia, Iran, Kuwait and Saudi Arabia cover only air transport.

19 Non-residents, visitors and immigrants

19.1 On what income are non-residents liable to UK tax?

If, for a given tax year, you are not a UK resident (17.3.2) you will normally be liable to UK income tax only on income arising in this country. If your income arising here is also taxed in your country of residence you will in many cases be entitled to double taxation relief (18.6). Should there be a double taxation agreement between your country of residence and the UK (18.6.1) this agreement may provide that certain categories of income arising in this country should only be taxed in your own country and not here. The following paragraphs cover the position if such relief is not obtained.

19.1.1 Business profits in the UK
(TA 1988 S18 & FA 1995 S126 & Sch 23)

If you are non-resident but carry on a business in this country you will be charged to tax here on your profits. You will be assessed to income tax under Schedule D Case I (11.2) at the lower rate (20 per cent), basic rate (23 per cent) and higher rate (40 per cent) if your total income liable to UK tax is sufficiently high (2.2).

If your UK business is operated by a manager, etc he is charged to the tax on your behalf but if your only business in this country consists of selling through a broker or agent who acts for various principals, you will not be chargeable. From 6 April 1996, your branch or agent in the UK is made jointly responsible with you for all that needs to be done concerning the self-assessment of the profits.

19.1.2 Income from property and land in the UK
(TA 1988 S15)

Income tax under Schedule A (or Schedule D Case VI) is charged on this income (7.1). If you are non-resident you will nevertheless have to pay UK income tax on this income; the basic rate normally should be deducted at source by the tenant or agent in paying you. Furthermore such income is frequently not covered by the relevant double taxation agreement.

19.1.3 Interest received from sources in the UK
(TA 1988 Ss18, 66 & 67 & FA 1993 S59)

You are liable to income tax under Schedule D Case III on this income (8.5). However, if you are ordinarily resident in the UK, the composite rate scheme might have applied up to 5 April 1991 (8.7). If you are not ordinarily resident, you can sign a declaration and obtain your interest gross from banks and building societies. From this year, other deposit takers are also included.

19.1.4 Interest on UK securities
(TA 1988 Ss44–52)

Income tax at 20 per cent (25 per cent before 6 April 1996) will be withheld from interest payments made to you unless some lower rate (or nil rate) is specified in any double taxation agreement (18.6). (See also exempt gilts, 19.2.)

19.1.5 Dividend payments to non-residents
(TA 1988 Ss232, 811 & 812 & FA 1993 S77)

If you are non-resident, your dividends from UK companies normally carry no tax credits unless you get relief under TA 1988 S278 (19.7), or under certain double taxation arrangements (see below). Thus if you receive a dividend of £80, you will normally pay overseas tax on this amount with no deduction for the £20 tax credit which you would have got, if you were a UK resident. You may be liable, however, to the excess of the higher rate income tax over the tax credit (5.0.1) on the actual dividend payments. Such tax would qualify for relief against your overseas tax subject to the relevant double tax arrangements (18.6).

Provided the relevant double tax agreements have been revised to permit it, special arrangements can be made between UK companies and the Board of Inland Revenue. These enable a UK company, when paying a dividend to an overseas resident, also to pay him an amount representing the excess over his UK tax liability on the dividend, of the UK tax credit to which he is entitled under the relevant double tax agreement (18.6.1). Comparable rules apply to companies. However, from a date to be fixed, the right of certain non-resident companies to payments of tax credits will be subject to withdrawal. This broadly covers various situations involving 'unitary taxation'.

19.1.6 Investment managers acting for non-residents
(TMA S78, FA 1991 S81 & FA 1995 Ss126 & 127)

Casual agents and brokers, investment managers, such as banks and other financial concerns, are exempted from any tax liability as agents for non-residents. The exemption applies provided, for example, the agent is in the business of providing investment management services to a number of clients, on a normal commercial basis. It extends to stocks and shares, interest on deposits and futures. From 6 April 1991 (1 April for companies), the exemption extends to commodities, financial futures and options contracts (not involving land).

Generally from 6 April 1996 (and in some cases 1995) a Revenue concession became law, which may be of benefit to you if you are non-resident. Your UK income tax is then limited to that deducted at source regarding investing and trading through a broker, investment manager, etc. A condition is that the investment manager acts as your independent agent.

19.1.7 Income from employments in the UK
(TA 1988 S19, etc)

If you are not resident in this country (or not ordinarily resident) you are assessed to UK tax under Case II of Schedule E in respect of any emoluments during the relevant tax year regarding duties performed here.

For 1984–85 and subsequently, non-domiciled employees obtain relief for travel expenses between their UK jobs and their countries similar to that afforded to UK personnel working abroad (10.6.4). With effect from 6 April 1986, the relief is only available for five years from the arrival of the employee in the UK (TA 1988 S195).

19.1.8 Higher rate income tax

If you are not resident in this country but are liable to UK income tax on part or all of your income, this may be taxed at the lower, basic and higher rate. This will depend on the amount of your income liable to UK income tax. Thus if for 1997–98 this comes to £26,500 after allowable deductions, you will pay income tax at 20 per cent on £4,100, 23 per cent on £22,000 and 40 per cent on £400. Thus your total UK income tax will be £820 + £5,060 + £160 = £6,040 (subject to possible double tax relief).

19.2 Interest paid to non-residents in respect of certain UK government securities
(TA 1988 S47 & FA 1996 S154 & 155 & Sch 26)

The interest on certain specified UK government securities (19.1.4) can be paid to you gross without the deduction of any UK income tax provided the following conditions are satisfied:

(1) You are not ordinarily resident in this country (17.3.1).
(2) A claim has been made on your behalf to the Revenue requesting that payment is made to you without the deduction of any UK income tax.

If the above conditions are satisfied then the Bank of England will be instructed to remit to you overseas the gross amounts of interest as they become payable, without the deduction of any UK income tax at source.

19.3 Rules for taxation of visitors' income
(TA 1988 S336)

If you come to this country as a visitor only and you do not intend to establish your residence here, you will not normally be charged to UK income tax on income arising elsewhere. This applies provided you have not actually been in this country for more than six months during the relevant tax year.

As a general rule you are not subject to UK income tax unless you are chargeable as a person resident here (17.3.2).

Even if you are not resident in this country during a given tax year you will normally be chargeable to UK income tax on your income arising from sources within the UK. However, interest on certain government bonds is exempted if you make the required application to the Revenue (8.2). You may also be entitled to double taxation relief in respect of your income arising in this country (18.6).

19.4 When does a habitual visitor become a UK resident?

If you are a visitor to the UK you are treated as resident here for tax purposes in any year of assessment in which you spend more than six months in this country.

Even if you do not stay for six months in any tax year, you will be regarded as becoming resident if you come here year after year (so that your visits become in effect part of your habit of life) and those visits are for a substantial period or periods of time. The Revenue normally regard an average of three months as being substantial and the visits as having become habitual after four years. Further, if your arrangements indicated from the start that regular visits for substantial periods were to be made the Revenue would regard you as being resident here in and from the first tax year.

If, however, a place of abode was maintained for you in this country, subject to certain specified exceptions, you were regarded by the Revenue as being resident here for any year in which you paid a visit to the UK. This was relaxed from 1993–94 (17.3.6).

19.5 The position of visiting diplomats *(TA 1988 Ss320–322)*

Special tax exemptions are given to visiting diplomats including agents-general, high commissioners, consuls and official agents. Consular officers and employees of foreign states who visit this country are afforded certain tax exemptions here, even if they stay in the UK for sufficiently long normally to be treated as resident here.

Regarding consular officers and employees of foreign states, the conditions for the exemptions to apply are that:

(1) the individual is not a citizen of the UK or colonies;
(2) he is not engaged in any trade, profession or employment in this country (apart from his diplomatic duties); and
(3) he is either a permanent employee of the foreign state or was not ordinarily resident in the UK immediately before he became a consular officer or employee here.

The tax concessions which apply when appropriate arrangements have been made with the foreign state concerned, include the following:

(1) Any income of the individual which falls under Cases IV and V of Schedule D (18.2) is not subject to income tax here.
(2) Certain overseas dividends and interest on securities are not taxed in this country.
(3) Emoluments of the individual from his consular office or employment are not taxed here.
(4) No capital gains tax (20.3) is payable on disposals of assets situated outside the UK.

19.6 Visiting entertainers and sportsmen

(TA 1988 Ss555–558)

Rules apply from 1 May 1987 under which UK appearances by non-resident sportsmen and entertainers are taxed at once. Payments of £1,000, or more, are subjected to basic rate (23 per cent) income tax at source. However, it is possible to agree a lower or nil rate with the Inland Revenue where it can be established that the eventual UK tax liability will be less than 23 per cent.

19.7 The entitlement of certain non-residents to UK tax reliefs

(TA 1988 S278 & FA 1996 S145)

Unless you are resident here or fall within the categories listed below, you will not obtain any UK personal reliefs and allowances (3.0.1) against your income tax liability in this country.

If you fall within the undermentioned categories, however, you will qualify for personal relief against your income taxable in this country.

(1) Subjects of Great Britain or the Republic of Ireland.
(2) Employees of the Crown or Crown protectorates or missionary societies.
(3) Residents of the Isle of Man or the Channel Islands.
(4) Previous residents of the UK who have gone abroad for reasons of their own health or that of a member of their families.
(5) Widows of Crown servants.
(6) From 6 April 1996, a national of any European Economic Area state.

To get this relief, you must submit a claim to the Revenue giving details of your UK and world income. From 6 April 1990 with the introduction of independent taxation of husband and wife, full personal allowances are available for those in the above specified categories.

Prior to 6 April 1990, the relief was restricted, however, so that your UK tax liability was not less than the proportion (A/B) of what it would have been if UK tax had been charged on your world income less UK allowances. (A was your total income subject to UK tax and B was your total income throughout the world. Any income on which you obtained double tax relief was excluded from A but included in B.)

19.8 Immigrants

If you come from abroad to this country with the intention of taking up permanent residence here the following tax consequences will result:

(1) You will normally get full UK personal reliefs and allowances for income tax for the entire tax year during which you arrive.
(2) If you have any British government securities on which you had been receiving interest gross as a non-resident (8.2) as soon as you arrive here you will be liable to tax on this interest.
(3) You will not be taxed here on any lump sum payment that you receive from a former employer or overseas provident fund in respect of termination of an overseas employment.
(4) If you have any income assessable under Case IV or V of Schedule D on a remittance basis (18.1.1) and the source ceases before you arrive here, you will have no liability on any sums remitted. If the source ceases in your year of arrival but after you take up permanent residence here, your liability is on the lower of your total remittances in the tax year and the income arising from your date of arrival until the date that the source closed.
(5) If you had a source of income outside this country before coming here, this source is not treated as being a fresh one on your arrival. Thus if you had possessed the source for some years the preceding year basis will normally apply.
(6) Subject to the above comments, you will generally be taxed here only in respect of income arising from your date of arrival.

20 Capital gains tax

20.1 Introduction

Subject to the specific rules that are summarised in the following pages, you will be charged to capital gains tax in respect of any chargeable gains that accrue to you on the disposal of assets during a given tax year. You deduct from your capital gains any allowable capital losses (20.13). For individuals, capital gains tax is charged at the same rates as income tax (20 per cent, 23 per cent and 40 per cent).

An annual exemption of £6,500 applies for individuals and broadly £3,250 for trusts (21.6). Companies pay corporation tax at corporation tax rates on their capital gains (13.15), subject to special rules for authorised investment trusts and unit trusts (20.18.7).

Most references throughout this chapter are to the Taxation of Chargeable Gains Act 1992 which consolidates the relevant legislation.

20.2 What is a chargeable gain?

(TCGA S15)

A chargeable gain is a gain which accrues after 6 April 1965 to a taxpayer (including a company, trust, partnership, individual, etc) such gain being computed in accordance with the provisions of the relevant legislation. There must, however, be a disposal of an asset in order that there should be a chargeable gain.

20.3 Who is liable?

(TCGA Ss2, 10 & 12)

Any taxpayer (including a company, trust, partnership, individual, etc) is chargeable to capital gains tax on any chargeable gains accruing to him in a year of assessment during any part of which he is: (*a*) resident in this country (17.3), or (*b*) ordinarily resident here (17.3.1).

Also, even if neither resident nor ordinarily resident here, a taxpayer who carries on a trade in the UK through a branch or agency is generally liable to capital gains tax accruing on the disposal of: (*a*) assets in this country used in his trade, or (*b*) assets held here and used for the branch or agency. For gains accruing from 14 March 1989, this rule extends to professions and vocations, as well as trades (20.32).

If you are resident or ordinarily resident here during a tax year you will be liable to capital gains tax on realisations of assets throughout the world. An exception is made, however, if you are not domiciled in this country (17.2); in that case you are only charged to capital gains tax on your overseas realisations of assets to the extent that such gains are remitted here (18.1). For these purposes, if you are non-domiciled and have a non-sterling bank account, this is treated as located outside the UK unless both the account is held at a UK branch and you are UK-resident (TCGA S275).

20.4 Capital gains tax rates from 6 April 1988
(TCGA Ss4–6)

Originally, capital gains tax was charged by means of a single rate of 30 per cent.This was changed from 6 April 1988 and further modified from 6 April 1992, with the introduction of the lower rate band:

(1) Individuals now suffer capital gains tax at 20 per cent, 23 per cent and 40 per cent.
(2) The rate for accumulation and maintenance trusts and discretionary settlements is 34 per cent (21.6).
(3) Other trusts in general pay 23 per cent. However if the settlor or his or her spouse has any interest in or rights relating to a settlement, any capital gains will be subjected to his or her rates (21.6).
(4) The capital gains of companies continue to bear corporation tax at the appropriate rate (13.15).
(5) To find the rate or rates payable by an individual, you take the total gains less losses (20.13) for the tax year, deduct capital losses brought forward and the annual exemption, considering this together with taxable income after reliefs and allowances. (From 1991–92, certain trading losses may also be deducted—20.13.) For 1997–98, the first £4,100 is taxed at 20 per cent, the next

£22,000 attracts 23 per cent and the remainder 40 per cent. (Your income is taxed at your lower rates first and your capital gains attract your highest rates.)

(6) Thus, if your taxable income after allowances for 1997–98 is £21,100, you have £22,000 – £17,000 = £5,000 of your 23 per cent rate band unused. This means that if your net capital gains for 1997–98 are £16,500, this is reduced to £10,000 by your annual exemption (£6,500). Your capital gains tax is thus:

£5,000 at 23%	1,150
£5,000 at 40%	2,000
	£3,150

(7) Husband and wife were considered together for the above rules for 1988–89 and 1989–90, but not subsequently. Now they are treated separately and this represents a substantial improvement which took effect from 6 April 1990.

20.5 Relief for moderate total gains before 6 April 1980
(CGTA S5 & Sch 1, etc)

From 1977–78 to 1979–80, if your chargeable gains for a year were no more than £1,000, no tax was charged. The excess over £1,000 was taxed at 15 per cent, provided your total net gains were no more than £5,000. If your total net gains were in the band from £5,000 to £9,500, your tax was £600 plus half of the excess over £5,000. For fuller details please refer to the 1984–85 and previous editions of this Guide.

20.6 Annual exemptions from 6 April 1980
(TCGA S3 & Sch 1 & FA 1994 S90)

The system for relieving small gains was changed from 6 April 1980. The following rules apply and the rates shown are for 1997–98.

(1) The first £6,500 of your net gains is exempted from capital gains tax. This applies no matter how high are your total gains for the year.

(2) Any set-off for losses from previous years (20.13) is restricted to leave £6,500 of gains to be exempted. In this way your exemption is protected and you have more losses to carry forward. All losses for the year must be deducted, however, in arriving at the net gains.

(3) These rules apply to personal representatives for the tax year of death and the next two years.
(4) The rules also apply to trusts for the mentally disabled and for those receiving attendance allowance.
(5) For other trusts set up before 7 June 1978 the first £3,250 of net capital gains each year is exempt (21.6).
(6) Trusts set up after 6 June 1978 by the same settlor each have an exemption of £3,250 divided by the number of such trusts. Thus if you have set up two trusts since that date, they each have an exemption of £1,625. In any event each trust obtains an exemption of at least £650.
(7) Any set off for trust losses from previous years is restricted so that the appropriate exemption (£3,250, etc) is not wasted.
(8) The above figures apply to future years subject to indexation in line with the increase in the Retail Prices Index in the September before the year of assessment, compared with the previous September. This applies unless Parliament otherwise directs.
(9) From 1990–91 onwards, husband and wife each have their own annual exemptions and the above rules apply to their own gains and losses alone. Previously, unless they were separated, only one annual exemption applied to their combined net gains.
(10) The corresponding annual exemption figures for previous years have been:

	Individuals, etc	*Trusts*
1980–81 & 1981–82	£3,000	£1,500
1982–83	5,000	2,500
1983–84	5,300	2,650
1984–85	5,600	2,800
1985–86	5,900	2,950
1986–87	6,300	3,150
1987–88	6,600	3,300
1988–89 to 1990–91	5,000	2,500
1991–92	5,500	2,750
1992–93 to 1994–95	5,800	2,900
1995–96	6,000	3,000
1996–97	6,300	3,150

20.7 What assets are liable?
(TCGA Ss21–27)

Subject to various exemptions (see 20.8.1) all forms of property are treated as 'assets' for capital gains tax purposes including:

(1) Investments, land and buildings, jewellery, antiques, etc.

(2) Options and debts, etc.

(3) Any currency other than sterling (special rules for companies—13.25).

(4) Any form of property created by the person disposing of it or otherwise coming to be owned without being acquired. (This would cover any article which you made or work of art created by you.)

20.8 What assets are exempted?

(TCGA—see below)

The following classes of assets are exempted from charge to capital gains tax subject to the relevant rules:

20.8.1 Table: Assets exempted from capital gains tax

(1) Private motor vehicles (S263).

(2) Certain gifts covered by an election (20.27).

(3) Your own home — this is known as your 'main private residence' (20.23).

(4) National Savings Certificates, Defence Bonds, Development Bonds, Save-as-you-earn, etc (S121).

(5) Any foreign currency which you obtained for personal expenditure abroad (S269).

(6) Any decoration for gallantry (unless purchased) (S268).

(7) Betting winnings including pools, lotteries and premium bonds (S51).

(8) Compensation or damages for any wrong or injury suffered to your person or in connection with your profession or vocation (S51).

(9) British government securities (S115). Disposals prior to 2 July 1986 were only exempt if the 'gilts' had been held for at least one year, or had passed to you on death or from a trust.

(10) Life assurance policies and deferred annuities provided that you are the original owner or they were given to you. If you bought the rights to a policy from its original owner you may be liable to capital gains tax on the surrender, maturity or sale of the policy, or death of the life assured (S210). Certain policies assigned after 25 June 1982 may give rise to income tax instead of capital gains tax, however (TA 1988 Ss540 & 544).

(11) Chattels sold for £6,000 or less (20.24).

(12) Assets gifted to charity (20.29.1).

(13) The gift to the nation of any assets (eg, paintings) deemed to be of national, scientific or historic interest; also land, etc given to the National Trust (S258).

(14) The gift of historic houses and certain other property of interest to the public, provided they are given access — also funds settled between 2 May 1976 and 6 April 1984 for its upkeep (S258). (Now covered by the gifts exemption — 20.28.)

(15) Tangible movable property which is a wasting asset (ie, with a predictable life of 50 years or less). This includes boats, animals, etc, but not land and buildings (S45) nor assets qualifying for capital allowances.
(16) Disposals by a close company (13.17) of assets on trust for the benefit of its employees (S239).
(17) If you sell a debt this is not liable to capital gains tax provided you are the original creditor and the debt is not a 'debt on a security' (a debenture, etc). Otherwise capital gains tax applies. The 'debt on security' requirements do not apply, however, to certain business loans (excluding those from associated companies) made after 11 April 1978. Loss relief may be available on such debts and also on certain business guarantees made after that date (S251).
(18) Land transferred after 5 April 1983 from one local constituency association to another, which is taking over from it, as a result of the Parliamentary constituency boundaries being redrawn (S264).
(19) Certain corporate bonds issued after 13 March 1984 which you held for more than 12 months (20.19). Disposals after 1 July 1986 are exempt without time limit (Ss115–117).
(20) Transactions in futures and options in gilts and qualifying corporate bonds after 1 July 1986 (S115).
(21) Business expansion scheme shares issued to you after 18 March 1986, provided you are the first holder of those particular shares (11.25).
(22) Certain 'deep discount' (8.8) and from 14 March 1989, 'deep gain' securities (S117).
(23) Profits from the sale of timber and uncut trees (TCGA S250).
(24) Sales of PEP units, subject to the rules (8.10).
(25) Venture Capital Trust shares held for at least five years, subject to the rules (8.12).
(26) EIS shares held for at least five years, in accordance with the rules (11.26.)

20.9 What constitutes a disposal?
(TCGA Ss21–26)

The following are examples of circumstances in which you will be treated as making a disposal or a part disposal of an asset:

(1) The outright sale of the whole asset or part of it.
(2) The gift of the asset or a part of it — the asset must be valued at the date of gift and this valuation is treated as the proceeds. An election for holding-over the gain is sometimes possible (20.28).
(3) If an asset is destroyed, eg, by fire, it is a disposal.
(4) If you sell any right in an asset, for example, by granting a lease, this is a part disposal although if you obtain a fair rent there is normally no capital gains tax liability.
(5) If any capital sum is received in return for the surrender or forfeiture of any rights, this is normally a disposal. For example, you

may receive a sum of money for not renewing a lease in accordance with a renewal option which you possessed.

(6) If you die, you are deemed to dispose of all of your assets at your date of death but no capital gains tax is payable. Whoever inherits your assets does so at their market value at your death.

(7) A part withdrawal from a life policy of the original owner and for which you gave money or money's worth (TCGA S210).

The following are not treated as disposals of assets for capital gains tax purposes:

(1) If you give or sell an asset to your spouse this is not treated as a capital gains tax disposal, provided he or she is living with you during the relevant tax year. In that case your spouse is charged to capital gains tax on any subsequent disposal that he or she makes of the asset as if bought when you originally acquired it at the actual cost to yourself (plus indexation allowance — 20.12).

(2) If you transfer an asset merely as security for a debt but retain the ownership this is not a capital gains tax disposal. This would apply, for example, if you mortgage your house.

(3) If you transfer an asset to somebody else to hold it as your nominee, this is not a disposal provided that you remain the beneficial owner.

(4) Gifts of assets to charities are effectively not treated as disposals (20.29.1).

20.10 How your chargeable gains are computed
(TCGA Ss15–20 & 37–40)

The following general rules should be followed:

(1) If the asset sold was originally acquired before 7 April 1965, special rules apply (20.17).

(2) Special rules also apply in the case of leases and other wasting assets (20.29.2).

(3) Ascertain the consideration for each of your disposals during the tax year — this will normally be the sale proceeds but in the following cases it will be the *open market value* of the assets (20.16):

    (a) Gifts of assets during the tax year.

    (b) Transfers of assets (by gift or sale) to persons connected with you including your business partner and close relations other than your wife. This also applies to other disposals of assets not at arm's length. (Anti-avoidance rules operate to prevent losses being manufactured artificially in this way (15.10).)

(c) Transactions in which the sale proceeds cannot be valued, or where an asset is given as compensation for loss of office, etc to an employee. If, for example, you give your friend a picture from your collection on condition that he paints your house each year for the next ten years, then since this service cannot be accurately valued you are treated as disposing of your picture for its market value.

(4) Deduct from the disposal consideration in respect of each asset its original cost (or value at acquisition) together with any incidental expenses in connection with your original acquisition and your disposal of each asset. For disposals after 5 April 1988, if it gives a better result, you normally deduct the value at 31 March 1982 instead of the cost (20.11). Also deduct any 'enhancement' expenditure, ie, the cost of any capital improvements to the assets not including any expenses of a 'revenue nature' (2.6).

(5) Deduct (if applicable) indexation allowance (see below).

(6) Your incidental costs of acquisition and disposal (see (4) above) include surveyors', valuers' and solicitors' fees, stamp duty, and commission in connection with the purchase and sale. Also the cost of advertising to find a buyer and accountancy charges in connection with the acquisition or disposal. No expenses are deductible, however, if they have already been allowed in computing your taxable revenue profits (2.6).

20.11 Re-basing to 31 March 1982 values

(TCGA Ss35–36 & Schs 3–4)

If you dispose of an asset after 5 April 1988, which you owned on 31 March 1982, its base value is automatically taken as its value at that date, provided this exceeds the cost. Thus, if you bought some shares for £1,000 in 1970 and they are worth £4,000 on 31 March 1982, you use £4,000 as their base value for capital gains tax purposes. Assuming you sell the shares for £10,000 in August 1996, your capital gain is £10,000 – £4,000 = £6,000 (ignoring indexation).

Re-basing to 31 March 1982 does not increase a gain or loss compared with what it would have been under the old rules. Furthermore, where there is a gain under the old system and a loss through re-basing, or *vice versa*, the transaction is treated as giving rise to neither gain nor loss. For example, if you sell an asset for £1,000 which had cost £500 and was worth £1,500 at 31 March 1982, ignoring indexation you had a gain of £500 under the old rules and a loss of £500 through re-basing; you are therefore treated as having no gain and no loss.

The existing rules for assets held at 6 April 1965 can themselves give rise to disposals being treated as producing no gain and no loss (20.17). This is not affected by re-basing.

Even if you did not hold an asset at 31 March 1982, it may still qualify for re-basing if you received it from someone else in circumstances that there was neither a gain nor loss under the rules and their acquisition was before that date. A particular example is where one spouse acquires an asset from another.

If you held assets at 31 March 1982, but subsequently realised them in circumstances such that your gain was deferred, re-basing does not apply. However, special relief is available regarding disposals after 5 April 1988 (excluding no gain/no loss disposals). Provided you make a claim to the Inland Revenue within two years of the end of the year of assessment in which the disposal is made, your original held-over, rolled-over or deferred gain is halved (TCGA S36 & Sch 4).

You have the right to elect that all of your assets are re-based as at 31 March 1982. There is a two year time limit for this irrevocable election (ie, before 6 April 1990). However, this is extended to two years after the end of the tax year in which you make your first sale after 5 April 1988.

20.12 Indexation allowance

(TCGA Ss53–57 & FA 1994 S93 & Sch 12)

If your disposal is after 5 April 1982 (31 March 1982 for companies) the original cost and enhancement expenditure may be increased by *indexation*. For disposals between 5 April 1985 (31 March for companies) and 6 April 1988, you had the option of basing indexation on the value of the asset sold, at 31 March 1982. After 5 April 1988, disposals are automatically re-based to their 31 March 1982 values if this is beneficial and so indexation is taken on the base value (20.11).

The expenditure is scaled up in proportion to the increase in the Retail Price Index from the month of acquisition (or March 1982, if later) until the month of disposal. For disposals prior to 6 April 1985, there was a one-year waiting period. Thus indexation ran from the later of 31 March 1982 and 12 months after the month of acquisition, until the month of disposal. Values for the *Retail Prices Index* are shown in 20.12.1.

For disposals from 6 April 1986 to 29 November 1993, you obtained the full benefit of indexation relief, even to the extent that it created or enlarged a loss. However, prior to 6 April 1985 (1 April 1985 for companies), indexation did not operate to create or increase a capital loss (20.13). Special rules apply regarding assets held on 6 April 1965 (20.17) and shares (20.14).

Any disposals that you make after 29 November 1993 will obtain full indexation relief if the end result is a gain. However, subject to transitional relief for individuals and trustees, indexation no longer creates or increases a capital loss. The transitional relief applies to disposals from 30 November 1993 to 5 April 1995. Up to £10,000 of loss relief due to indexation can be obtained during that period, but cannot be carried forward to 1995–96.

Transactions between husband and wife do not normally give rise to capital gains tax (20.9). Thus if you acquire an asset from your spouse, your deemed acquisition cost is taken to be his or hers, augmented by any indexation allowance attaching to it at the transfer date. When you sell the asset, you obtain full indexation allowance on your deemed acquisition cost, from the date you took over the asset from your spouse. Similar treatment applies to company intra-group transfers (13.15) and certain reconstructions. Legatees obtain indexation allowance as if they had acquired the assets at the date of death.

20.12.1 Table: Retail prices index (adjusted)

	1982	*1983*	*1984*	*1985*	*1986*	*1987*	*1988*	*1989*	*1990*	*1991*	*1992*	*1993*	*1994*	*1995*	*1996*	*1997*
January		82.6	86.8	91.2	96.2	100.0*	103.3	111.0	119.5	130.2	135.6	137.9	141.3	146.0	150.2	154.4
February		83.0	87.2	91.9	96.6	100.4	103.7	111.8	120.2	130.9	136.3	138.8	142.1	146.9	150.9	155.0
March	79.4	83.1	87.5	92.8	96.7	100.6	104.1	112.3	121.4	131.4	136.7	139.3	142.5	147.5	151.5	
April	81.0	84.3	88.6	94.8	97.7	101.8	105.8	114.3	125.1	133.1	138.8	140.6	144.2	149.0	152.6	
May	81.6	84.6	89.0	95.2	97.8	101.9	106.2	115.0	126.2	133.5	139.3	141.1	144.7	149.6	152.9	
June	81.9	84.8	89.2	95.4	97.8	101.9	106.6	115.4	126.7	134.1	139.3	141.0	144.7	149.8	153.0	
July	81.9	85.3	89.1	95.2	97.5	101.8	106.7	115.5	126.8	133.8	138.8	140.7	144.0	149.1	152.4	
August	81.9	85.7	89.9	95.5	97.8	102.1	107.9	115.8	128.1	134.1	138.9	141.3	144.7	149.9	153.1	
September	81.9	86.1	90.1	95.4	98.3	102.4	108.4	116.6	129.3	134.6	139.4	141.9	145.0	150.6	153.8	
October	82.3	86.4	90.7	95.6	98.5	102.9	109.5	117.5	130.3	135.1	139.9	141.8	145.2	149.8	153.8	
November	82.7	86.7	91.0	95.9	99.3	103.4	110.0	118.5	130.0	135.6	139.7	141.6	145.3	149.8	153.9	
December	82.5	86.9	90.9	96.0	99.6	103.3	110.3	118.8	129.9	135.7	139.2	141.9	146.0	150.7	154.4	

**Note*: At January 1987 the index base was changed to 100.0 and the above table shows figures before that date adjusted to the same base.

20.12.2 Example: Computation of chargeable gain

Mr A sells a block of flats on 15 July 1997 for £260,000. The flats were bought in May 1981 for £100,000 and subsequent capital expenditure amounted to £17,000 (all pre-April 1982). Also £10,000 had been spent on decorations and maintenance. The legal costs on purchase were £1,500 and stamp duty was £1,000. Surveyors' fees prior to purchase amounted to £500. At 31 March 1982, the market value was £115,000*. £100 was spent in advertising the sale and agents' commission amounted to £6,000. Legal costs on sale were £900. Assuming that Mr A's profit is taxed as a capital gain, what tax will he pay on it? Assume also that for 1997–98 Mr A has no other capital gains or losses and that his taxable income after all reliefs and allowances is £18,000. Assume also that the July 1997 indexation figure is 156

Cost of block of flats	£100,000
Add:	
Enhancement expenditure	17,000
(decorations and maintenance not relevant)	
Legal costs on purchase	1,500
Stamp duty on purchase	1,000
Surveyors' fees on purchase	500
Total cost	£120,000*
Add:	
Indexation £120,000 × (156 – 79.4)/79.4	115,768
	£235,768

Proceeds		260,000
Less:		
Cost and indexation as above	£235,768	
Advertising	100	
Agents' commission	6,000	
Legal fees on sale	900	
		242,768
Chargeable gain		£17,232
Less: annual exemption		6,500
		£10,732

Capital gains tax at 23% (on £26,000 – £18,000 = £8,000)	£1,840.00
at 40% £2,732	1,092.80
	£2,932.80

**Note:* if the market value at 31 March 1982 had been more than £120,000, the property would be re-based to this value and this would also be used in calculating indexation.

20.13 Capital losses

(TCGA Ss2, 16, 111 & 253–255, FA 1994 S93 & Sch 12 & FA 1995 S113)

If your capital gains tax computation in respect of any disposal during the tax year produces a loss, such loss is normally deductible from any chargeable gains arising during the year. Any remaining surplus of losses is then available to be carried forward and set off against any future capital gains. For 1989–90 and previous tax years, any unrelieved losses were offset against gains of your spouse in the same year. Any surplus losses were then carried forward to offset against your respective gains.

'Qualifying loans' made to traders which later prove irrecoverable rank as capital losses, subject to the rules. However, after 19 March 1990, any amounts subsequently recovered are taxed.

Your net capital gains are reduced by losses brought forward down to the tax free amount of currently £6,300 (20.6) and any balance of the losses is carried forward (TCGA S3(5)).

In computing your capital losses note the special rules for assets owned at 6 April 1965 (20.17). Also note that losses may be reduced by 1982 re-basing (20.11). For disposals before 30 November 1993 but (apart from transitional relief) not subsequently, indexation allowance could both create and augment a loss (20.12).

A result of indexation allowance creating capital losses was that *building society* share accounts could give rise to capital losses when closed down or reduced. This constitutes a capital gains tax disposal. No real loss is likely but for capital gains tax purposes, prior to 4 July 1987 indexation relief could produce a capital loss. However, from that date, countermanding legislation operates.

The 1995 Finance Act (S100) introduced the necessity to claim capital gains tax loss relief, which can be done through your tax return. (A special section is included in the supplementary page dealing with capital gains.) You must claim your losses within five years and 10 months of the end of the year of assessment when they arose. (For companies, this period is 6 years from the end of the relevant accounting period.)

20.13.1 Relief for trading losses against capital gains

(FA 1991 S72)

For many years, companies have been able to set off trading losses against capital gains (13.15), but not *vice versa*. A similar relief operates from 1991–92 for individuals with losses from unincorporated businesses.

If you make a loss in your trade, profession or vocation and do not have enough income to cover it, you can elect for the unused losses for say 1997–98 to be set against your capital gains for that year. Any trading losses still unused would then be carried forward to 1998–99 and any not covered by your income for that year are available against 1998–99 capital gains. The relief does not cover 'hobby farming' and other businesses not carried out on a serious commercial basis.

20.14 Losses on unquoted shares in trading companies

(TA 1988 Ss573–576 & FA 1994 S210)

Beneficial rules apply to disposals of shares in 'qualifying trading companies'. Provided you were the original subscriber, you can elect to obtain income tax relief (11.22) for any loss on a fully priced arm's length sale, liquidation, etc. For pre-1994–95 disposals, an election is required within two years after the tax year in which the relief is to be used.

For disposals in 1994–95 and subsequently, new rules apply. Losses on unquoted shares in trading companies will be available against your income of the current or preceding year. You must claim within 12 months from 31 January following the tax year of disposal.

A 'qualifying trading company' is broadly one which has always been UK resident but never quoted and has traded for at least six years, or from within a year of incorporation if less. The company is permitted to have stopped trading within the previous three years provided it has not become an investment company in the meantime. 'Trading' excludes dealing mainly in shares, land or commodity futures with retrospective effect, qualified trading companies now exclude building societies and registered industrial and provident societies. The relief applies to individuals and certain investment companies.

20.15 Assessment and payment of capital gains tax

(TMA S29, TCGA Ss7, 48 & 279–281 & FA 1994 Ss193 & 194)

Assessments to capital gains tax are raised on the taxpayer concerned in respect of each tax year as soon thereafter as the Revenue obtain the necessary information. In the case of a company, however, its gains are included in its corporation tax assessment which is due for payment according to the special company rules (13.2).

Prior to 6 April 1990, in assessing the tax, the losses of one spouse could be deducted from the gains of another. Also, the wife's gains were assessed on the husband. Both of these rules ceased to have effect from 6 April 1990, with the introduction of independent taxation.

Your capital gains tax assessment for 1994–95 was due for payment on 1 December 1995 or 30 days after the assessment was issued, if later. A similar interval applied for 1995–96 gains and those for earlier years.

Your capital gains for 1996–97 and subsequent years comes within the new self-assessment rules (16.1). Your capital gains tax is then payable by 31 January following the tax year of the gains.

The date on which a capital gain arises is the actual date of sale or gift, etc. In the case of a transaction in which a sales contract is used such as the sale of shares or property it is the date of the contract which applies. It is not the completion date if this is different. Similar considerations apply to fixing the date of acquisition for capital gains tax purposes.

Certain gifts after 13 March 1989, for which gifts relief is not available (20.28) qualify for the payment of any capital gains tax by instalments. The assets concerned are land, unquoted shares and controlling holdings of quoted shares. Subject to making an election, the tax becomes payable by ten equal yearly instalments. If the instalments are paid on time, the tax on gifts of agricultural property will carry no interest, otherwise, interest runs from the normal date when the total liability would have been due.

Normally, even if the sales consideration is paid by instalments over a number of years the gain is assessed for the tax year in which the sale arises. If, however, you can satisfy the Revenue that you would otherwise suffer undue hardship, payment of the tax can be spread over the period of the instalments (maximum eight years).

20.16 Valuations

(TCGA Ss272–274 & Sch 11)

It is necessary to value assets in various circumstances for capital gains tax purposes including gifts, transactions between connected persons, acquisitions on death and valuations at 6 April 1965. However, the most important date for valuations is 31 March 1982, for re-basing purposes (20.11).

The general rule for valuing assets for capital gains tax purposes is that you must take the 'market value' of the assets at the relevant time. 'Market value' means the price which the assets might reasonably be expected to fetch on a sale in the open market.

It is necessary to value only the assets actually being disposed of even though they form part of a larger whole. This is particularly important regarding the shares in a non-quoted company. Suppose you hold 90 per cent of the shares in such a company which are together worth £90,000. If you gift 10 per cent of the company's shares to your son you might assume that their value is £10,000. This would, however, probably not be true since your 90 per cent holding carried with it full control of the company whereas 10 per cent of the company's shares is a minority holding which would be normally worth considerably less than £10,000 in the circumstances mentioned. The true market valuation of the gifted 10 per cent holding might only be £1,000 depending on the profits of the company and dividends paid. Note that different valuation rules apply for inheritance tax purposes (22.12).

A Revenue concession applies where you acquire shares on a no gain/no loss transfer from your spouse, who had held them at 31 March 1992. It also applies to transfers in similar circumstances between group companies. Two years' written notice is needed from the end of the year of assessment or accounting period of the disposal. The 31 March 1982 value will then be taken as a proportionate part of the value of the transferor's *entire* holding at that time. This applies to disposals after 15 March 1993 and assessments open at that time. If notice is not given, the shares may be valued at 31 March 1982 as if held by the *transferee*.

Unquoted share valuations must take account of all information which a prudent arm's-length purchaser would obtain.

Particular rules relate to the valuation of quoted securities such as shares and debenture stocks. (These apply in most cases, including 31 March 1982 valuations.) In this case you must normally take:

(1) the lower of the two prices shown in the Stock Exchange Official Daily List plus one-quarter of the difference between them, or
(2) halfway between the highest and lowest prices at which bargains (other than at special prices) were recorded in the shares or securities for the relevant day.

In valuing quoted shares at 6 April 1965, however, you must take the *higher* of:

(1) midway between the two prices shown in the Stock Exchange Official Daily List (ie, the middle market price), and
(2) halfway between the highest and lowest prices at which bargains (other than at special prices) were recorded in the shares or securities for 6 April 1965.

Apart from quoted shares other valuations will normally require to be agreed with the Revenue valuation officers such as the district valuers who are concerned with valuing land and buildings.

20.17 Relief on sales of assets owned on 6 April 1965
(TCGA Sch 2)

Although a short term capital gains tax operated from April 1962 until April 1971 when it was repealed, the present-day system of capital gains tax only operates regarding sales after 6 April 1965. Rules were, therefore, introduced with the purpose of relieving such part of your capital gains as can be related to the period before 7 April 1965. Following the introduction of 1982 re-basing (20.11) these rules are of far less importance since in most cases, a lower gain (or greater loss) will result from re-basing. However, a better result sometimes results from applying the old rules and these are then used, unless you have elected for all of your assets to be valued as at 31 March 1982.

The general rule is that you assume that your asset increased in value at a uniform rate and you are relieved from capital gains tax on such proportion of the gain as arose on a time basis prior to 7 April 1965. This is known as the 'time apportionment' method. Thus if your total gain is G and you held an asset for A months prior to 6 April 1965 and B months after that date until the date of sale your taxable chargeable gain is $G \times B/(A + B)$. Your time apportionment benefit is limited to 20 years prior to 6 April 1965. Thus if you acquired an asset before 6 April 1945 you are treated as having acquired it on that date.

Where indexation relief is available, this must be applied before time apportionment. Thus the indexation benefit is reduced. This follows a case decision in the House of Lords in March 1993 (Smith v Schofield).

Instead of using 'time apportionment' you have the option of substituting for the cost of the asset its market value at 6 April 1965 (Sch 2(17)).

In order to do this you must make an election to this effect to the Revenue within two years of the end of the tax year in which you make the disposal. (In the case of a company the election must be made within two years of the end of the accounting period in which the disposal is made.) It is very rare indeed that the market value of an asset at 6 April 1965 exceeds its value at 31 March 1982. Thus 6 April 1965 valuations are mainly relevant when you disposed of assets before 6 April 1988.

The rules do not allow you to increase a capital loss by means of a 6 April 1965 election. Also, if the effect of an election is to convert a gain into a loss, you are regarded as having no gain and no loss on the transaction.

Once you make an election it is irrevocable, even if it results in your paying more tax than on a 'time apportionment' basis. If you make an election, any indexation allowance to which you are entitled (20.12) is calculated on the 6 April 1965 value and not cost. This is now subject to your right to elect for indexation to be taken on the value at 31 March 1982 (20.11).

The 'time apportionment' basis *does not* apply to quoted shares and securities (20.18). Nor does it apply to land with development value when sold (or which has been materially developed after 17 December 1973). Such land is normally automatically dealt with on the 6 April 1965 valuation basis.

In the same way that your gain is reduced by the 'time apportionment' so any loss that you make on a disposal of an asset that you owned at 6 April 1965 is also reduced in this way. Thus if you bought an investment for £6,200 on 6 April 1945 and sold it for £1,000 on 6 April 1997 your total loss is £5,200, subject to indexation. Of this only £3,200 (£5,200 × 32/52) is an allowable capital loss.

20.18 Quoted shares and securities
(TCGA Ss104–117)

The following rules do not apply to *UK government securities* which are exempt from capital gains tax if sold (or otherwise disposed of). Any disposals of 'gilt edged' securities after 1 July 1986 are exempt from capital gains tax, nor do they create allowable losses, no matter how long they are held. Previously, if you sold any such 'gilt edged' securities within a year of purchase you were liable to capital gains tax on your chargeable gain. Also, any compensation stock received on a nationalisation after 6 April 1976 may give rise to a gain or loss when sold. This includes the gain or loss on your original shares up to the date of issue of the compensation stock, together with the gain or loss on this stock if it is held for less than 12 months and sold before 2 July 1986.

20.18.1 'Pooling'

All shares of the same company and class that you held prior to 6 April 1982 (1 April for companies) were put into a 'pool'. With the introduction of indexation allowance, however, pooling no longer applied to new purchases. However, pooling was reintroduced regarding share *disposals* after 5 April 1985 (20.18.4) for individuals and trusts, etc (after 31 March 1985 for companies). You now are treated as having one pool of shares purchased after 5 April 1982 and another before that time.

The 'pool' is considered indistinguishable regarding the various numbers of shares that it comprises. Thus if you bought 100 ordinary shares in A Limited on 1 May 1976 for £200 and another 200 ordinary shares in A Limited on 30 September 1980 for £1,000 your total pool cost is £1,200 (ie, £4 per share). If you then sell 100 shares they are not treated as being the original ones which you bought for £200; they are treated as coming from your 'pool' at the average pool cost of £4 per share giving a cost of £400.

However, where you introduce shares into a single company PEP (8.10) from a 'pool', you are now able to identify the shares. This is to facilitate computing the gain on the remainder, when sold (FA 1993 S85).

'Pooling' does not apply to shares purchased on or before 6 April 1965 unless you elect for all your shares to be valued as at that date (20.18.8). In the absence of this election, you allocated any sales prior to 6 April 1982 first against your holdings at 6 April 1965 on a 'first in first out' basis. After these shares were eliminated you then went to the 'pool'.

Each separate purchase or sale of shares of the same company and class results in adjustments to the 'pool' except that if you buy and sell shares on the same day the respective sale and purchase are first matched against each other. Any surplus or deficit is then added to or deducted from your 'pool'. This rule ceased to apply for transactions from 6 April 1982 (1 April 1982 for companies — subject to a parallel pooling system), but was re-introduced from 6 April 1985.

20.18.2 Parallel pooling

(TCGA S112)

Parallel pooling applied only to companies. A formal and irrevocable election was needed which then applied to all disposals, from 1 April 1982 to 31 March 1985 of 'qualifying securities'. Fuller details are given in earlier editions of this book.

20.18.3 Identification — sales from 6 April 1982 to 5 April 1985

(FA 1982 Ss88 & 89 & Sch 13 & FA 1983 S34 & Sch 6)

If you disposed of quoted shares and securities between 5 April 1982 and 6 April 1985 special identification rules applied. Similarly, shares purchased between those dates were no longer pooled. Each of your existing share pools was treated as a separate asset with its own pool cost at 6 April 1982 and treated for indexation purposes as if acquired one year earlier. Disposals after 5 April 1982 but before 6 April 1985 were taken in order and identified first against purchases in the previous 12 months taking the earliest first. Then, you looked at previous purchases, taking the latest first.

20.18.4 Indexation and identification — sales from 6 April 1985

(TCGA Ss104–114)

Revised rules apply to share disposals by individuals after 5 April 1985 and by companies after 31 March 1985. However, securities covered by the accrued income provisions to combat bond-washing (8.3) only came within the new indexation and identification rules after 27 February 1986.

As previously mentioned indexation now runs immediately (20.12). An exception is where you buy and then sell the same shares within 10 days, your transactions are matched and you obtain no indexation relief.

Under the revised rules, you must keep separate pools of shares acquired after 5 April 1982 and those obtained from 6 April 1965 to 5 April 1982. Furthermore, acquisitions prior to 6 April 1965 must be kept separately (20.18.1), unless there is a pooling election (20.18.8), in which case they are included in the 31 March 1982 pool.

If you sell shares after 5 April 1985, they are to be identified with your acquisitions of the same shares on a 'last in first out' basis. They are thus first identified with your post 5 April 1982 pool, then with your pre-6 April 1982 holdings and finally with your unpooled pre-6 April 1965 holdings. (For companies the pools run to and from 31 March 1982 and 1 April 1982.) If it produces a better result for you, disposals out of your pre-April 1982 and pre-April 1965 pools will be re-based (20.11), the market value at 31 March 1982 being taken.

From 19 March 1991, disposals of 'business start up scheme' (11.25) shares cannot be pooled with shares of the same type.

Indexation must be calculated separately on the different parts. Holdings acquired before 1 April 1982 can be valued at 31 March 1982 for indexation purposes if you make the required election (20.12). By a concession dated 25 May 1989, the Revenue will treat holdings of the same class held at 31 March 1982 as a single holding for re-basing and indexation. This applies whether the shares, etc were bought before or after 6 April 1965. Subsequent acquisitions cannot be treated in that way. However, every additional purchase will carry indexation relief from that date until sale and so a careful record is needed to calculate relief from the respective acquisition dates. This is done on a pooled basis by adding indexation relief to the pool prior to each purchase or sale. The total indexation relief in the pool is then found by deducting the total cost and the relief on the sale is simply the proportion appropriate to the number of shares sold.

20.18.5 Example: Share identification and indexation

Mr A carried out the following share transactions in the ordinary shares of quoted company B Ltd:

	Date	*Number*	*Cost or Proceeds*
			£
Purchases	20.6.78	2,000	3,000
	10.5.80	1,000	2,000
	10.7.83	2,000	4,000
	10.9.84	4,000	11,000
Sale	20.4.96	9,000	45,000

The value of B Ltd shares at 31 March 1982 was £1.80. Calculate Mr A's capital gain assuming the following (very approximate) indexation figures:—

March 1982 to April 1996	90%
July 1983 to September 1984	10%
September 1984 to April 1996	70%

(1) The shares sold are taken first out of the post 5 April 1982 pool:

Cost of 2,000 shares 10.7.83	£4,000
Indexation July 1983 to September 1984 10%	400
	4,400
	11,000
Cost of 4,000 shares 10.9.84	15,400
Indexation September 1984 to April 1996 70%	10,780
Cost and indexation for 6,000 shares	£26,180
Proceeds of 6,000 shares	30,000
Capital gain on 6,000 shares from post 5 April 1982 pool	£ 3,820

(2) The remaining shares sold are then identified against the pre-6 April 1982 pool:

	Cost of 3,000 shares (£1.67 each)	£5,000
	Re-based to £1.80 per share	5,400
	Add indexation relief from March 1982 to April 1996 90%	4,860
		10,260
	Proceeds of 3,000 shares	15,000
	Capital gain on 3,000 shares	£4,740
TOTAL CAPITAL GAIN	£3,820 + £4,740	£8,560

20.18.6 Bonus issues, take-overs and company reorganisations

(TCGA Ss116 & 126–140, FA 1993 S84 & FA 1997 Ss88 & 89)

If you receive a free scrip (or bonus) issue of shares of the same class as those that you already hold, you must treat the additional shares as having been bought when your original shares were bought. Thus if you bought 100 shares in A Limited for £2 each in 1960 and you now receive a bonus issue of 100 shares you will have 200 shares at a cost of £1 each which are all treated as having been bought in 1960. Note, however, the special rules for scrip dividend options (8.9).

Your company may have a capital reorganisation, in the course of which you receive shares of a different class either instead of or in addition to your original shares. You are not normally charged to capital gains tax on any old shares in your company which you exchange for new ones. Any capital gains tax is only payable when you sell your new holding. The rules for reorganisations including bonus issues hold good under the new 'indexation' system unless new consideration is given.

If you take up 'rights' to subscribe for additional shares in a company of which you are a shareholder, your rights shares are treated as having been acquired when your original shares were purchased and the cost of the rights shares is added to the original cost of your holding. If you sell your 'rights' on the market without taking up the shares this is considered to be a 'part disposal' of your holding and accordingly is charged to capital gains tax (20.21). If the proceeds are small (normally no more than 5 per cent) in relation to your holding, however, you can elect not to pay tax then but set off the proceeds against the original cost of your holding. Under the indexation rules which now apply (20.18.4), however, any new consideration (for rights shares, etc) is treated effectively as a new acquisition so that indexation runs accordingly.

Anti-avoidance rules act to prevent you from obtaining capital gains tax loss relief artificially from reorganisations. Any increase in the capital gains tax acquisition value of shares which you obtain through the reorganisation is limited to the actual increase in value.

In the case of a take-over you may receive cash for your shares in which case this is taxed as an ordinary disposal. If, however, you receive shares or loan stock, etc in the acquiring company, you will not normally be liable to pay capital gains tax until you actually sell your new shares or loan stock, subject to certain conditions and anti-avoidance laws (15.10). One of the conditions is that the acquiring company already held, or obtains as a result of the take-over over 25 per cent of the ordinary share capital of the other company.

If you receive qualifying corporate bonds (20.19) on the take-over of your shares, the above relief is modified. You are treated as disposing of your shares at that time, but your gain is deferred until you sell the bonds. From 16 March 1993, these rules extend to certain debentures which are not debts on security (and so previously may have escaped tax). Securities later becoming QCBs may also be covered (20.19(11)).

Sometimes, the consideration for the sale of a company might include an element which is deferred and unascertainable, perhaps related to future profits ('earn out rights'). Broadly, from 26 November 1996, a previous concessional treatment is legislated for. This concerns an 'earn out right' being treated as a security for capital gains tax purposes including deferment.

All of the above rules concerning bonus issues, take-overs and company reorganisations apply equally to unquoted shares (20.20).

20.18.7 Investment trusts and unit trusts
(TCGA Ss99–103)

Special rules apply regarding all disposals both of shares owned *by* the trusts and of shares and units *in* the trusts by their shareholders and unit holders.

After 31 March 1980 authorised unit and investment trusts are exempt from tax on their capital gains. However, any disposals which you make of units and investment trust shares carry full capital gains tax with no credit (subject to your £6,500 annual exemption).

From 20 March 1990, capital gains tax indexation no longer applies to units in certain unit trusts and offshore funds. This mainly applies to gilt funds and sterling money funds, with at least 90 per cent invested in such funds or building society shares.

20.18.8 Holdings at 6 April 1965
(TCGA Sch 2)

'Time apportionment' (20.17) does not apply to quoted shares. Instead you must consider the mid-market price at 6 April 1965 (20.16). Subject to the election described below, your gain on any sales after 6 April 1965 of shares held at that date is the difference between the proceeds and the higher cost of the shares and their value at 6 April 1965. Similarly any allowable capital loss on such share sales is the difference between the proceeds and the lower of the cost of the shares and their value at 6 April 1965. However, for disposals after 5 April 1988, 1982 re-basing (20.11) is likely to occur. As a result, the value at 31 March 1982 is used.

If the price at which you sell the shares held at 6 April 1965 is between their value at that date and their cost then you are treated as having no gain and no loss for capital gains tax purposes (subject to the election described below). For indexation purposes, if the value at 6 April 1965 is used to compute a capital gain, then the allowance is calculated on that value (20.12). However, for disposals after 5 April 1985, you can elect for your indexation relief to be taken on the values at 31 March 1982 (20.12).

As regards disposals of quoted shares and securities which you held at 6 April 1965 you have the right to elect that any capital gains or losses on such disposals shall be calculated by substituting the 6 April 1965 values for the original costs in all cases. The election for each category is irrevocable, and has to be made within two years of the end of the tax year (or accounting year for a company) in which the first sale after 19 March 1968 is made (but see new rules below). Thus in most cases the election time limit will have expired by now. Full details are given in earlier editions of this book.

A further opportunity was introduced to allow you to elect to have pooled, quoted securities, which you acquired before 6 April 1965. The time limit is two years after the end of the year in which your first disposal occurs after 5 April 1985 (31 March 1985 for companies). The effect is that your various quoted securities become part of your respective pre-April 1982 share pools.

20.19 Exemption for corporate bonds (QCBs)

(TCGA Ss115–117 & 254–255, FA 1995 S50, FA 1996 S177 & FA 1997 S88)

The exemption for capital gains tax for gilt edged securities (20.8.1) was extended to certain QCBs satisfying the following conditions:

(1) The bonds were acquired or issued after 13 March 1984.
(2) They are debentures, loan stocks or similar securities, not necessarily secured but 'debts on security'.
(3) They are normal commercial loans, expressed in and redeemable in sterling. Denomination in foreign currency is being allowed with the introduction of the FOREX scheme (13.25).
(4) At least some of the shares or debentures of the issuing company are quoted.
(5) The bonds are capable of being marketed but are not issued by a company to another company in the same group.
(6) Disposals after 1 July 1986 are exempt regardless of the time for which the bonds have been held. Similarly losses have ceased to be available. Prior to that date, normally exemption only applied if you held the securities for at least one year before disposal.

(7) If you sustain a loss on a QCB held on or issued after 14 March 1989, you will obtain relief where part or all of the loan is irrecoverable.
(8) Regarding disposals after 18 March 1991, bonds convertible into other QCBs are exempt. However, those convertible into shares or securities of the issuing company's quoted parent are not.
(9) From 29 November 1994, the QCB capital gains tax exemption no longer applies to certain indexed securities which are linked to an index of quoted share prices.
(10) Where shares are exchanged for a mixture of cash and QCBs, the cash is liable to capital gains tax but re-investment relief (20.25.2) is available on appropriate share purchases. This relief is also available where a held-over gain comes into charge on a QCB disposal.
(11) After 26 November 1996, the change of status of a security from a non-QCB to a QCB (and vice versa) is treated as a conversion of securities (20.18.6). This could give rise to a capital gains tax charge where the terms of a security change.

20.20 Unquoted shares

(TCGA S273 & Sch 2)

Many of the above points regarding quoted shares and securities apply also to unquoted shares but the following special rules should be noted:

(1) Regarding holdings of shares at 6 April 1965 the 'time apportionment' rule normally applies to sales after that date subject to the right of election for valuation at 6 April 1965 (20.17). This is not a 'blanket' election for all your non-quoted shares as is the case for quoted shares. (For disposals after 5 April 1988, 1982 re-basing is likely to prevail — 20.11.)
(2) If after 6 April 1965 there is a capital reorganisation or take-over regarding a non-quoted company in which you have shares 'time apportionment' normally stops at that time and on any future sales you have a time apportioned gain or loss to the date of reorganisation or take-over and the full gain or loss after that time. This does not apply, however, in the case of a bonus issue of the same class of shares (20.18.6).
(3) If a reorganisation or take-over as in (2) above occurred before 6 April 1965 any shares still held at that date must automatically be valued at 6 April 1965 and the time apportionment does not apply. You still consider, however, the cost of your original holding when computing any capital gain or loss on a future sale.

(4) Prior to 6 April 1982 (1 April for companies) the 'pooling' rules (20.18.1) applied to shares acquired after 6 April 1965 but not to acquisitions before that time which must be separately considered on a 'first in first out' basis.

(5) The indexing rules (20.18.4) apply to non-quoted shares as for quoted ones. The rule in (4) above regarding shares held at 6 April 1965 was modified, however, so that the 'last in first out' basis applied for disposals between 5 April 1982 and 6 April 1985.

(6) Any relief which you obtain against your income, for business expansion scheme investment (11.25) is not also available to create a capital loss. Thus if you eventually sell the shares at a profit, you will obtain full relief for the cost in calculating your capital gain, but not if you sell at a loss.

(7) Subject to the rules (20.25.2) roll-over relief applies on reinvestment where qualifying shares in one company are sold after 15 March 1993 and qualifying shares in another are purchased.

20.21 Part disposals

(TCGA Ss42 & 242–244 & Sch 3)

Where part of an asset is disposed of (including part of a 'pool' holding of shares in a particular company) it is necessary to compute the cost applicable to the part sold. This is normally done by multiplying the original cost by the fraction A/(A+B) where A is the consideration for the part disposed of and B is the market value of the remaining property at the date of the part disposal. If indexation applies (20.12), the cost apportionment formula is applied before computing the indexation allowance. No indexation is calculated on the costs attributable to the undisposed of part (until that is sold).

For part disposals after 5 April 1988, the fraction A/(A + B) is applied to the value at 31 March 1982 if more than the cost. If a part disposal has already taken place between 31 March 1982 and 6 April 1988, the gain on a further disposal after 5 April 1988 must be computed on the basis that 1982 re-basing applied to the earlier part disposal.

A special rule applies to small part disposals of land (only a small part of the whole being sold, etc). Provided that such proceeds during the tax year do not exceed £20,000, you may deduct the proceeds from your base cost rather than pay tax now. For disposals after 5 April 1986, this rule applies where the proceeds do not exceed one-fifth of the total market value of the land.

20.22 A series of disposals
(TCGA Ss19 & 20)

Before 20 March 1985, if you acquired a series of assets (shares, etc) from one or more people connected (20.10) with you, all of the assets were valued together to find the relevant proceeds and your acquisition figure. After 19 March 1985, however, the rule operates only from the viewpoint of a person splitting up an asset or collection of assets by two or more transactions to connected persons. The transactions must be within a total period of six years.

20.23 Private residences
(TCGA Ss222–226)

The house or flat where you live is normally exempt from capital gains tax when you sell it, subject to the following rules:

(1) The house must have been your only or main residence during the time that you owned it subject to various allowable periods of absence (see below). You ignore all periods before 6 April 1965 for these purposes.

(2) You are allowed to be absent from the house for the following maximum periods without losing your exemption:
   - (a) The last 36 months of ownership. For disposals before 19 March 1991, this period was 24 months.
   - (b) Periods of absence totalling three years.
   - (c) Any period throughout which you worked abroad.
   - (d) Any periods up to four years in aggregate when you are prevented from living in your house due to your employment being elsewhere.
   - (e) Any period during which you live in job-related accommodation, but intend to return to your main residence.

   Provided you have no other residence which you claim to be exempt during the above periods they are taken cumulatively and so you could have a long period of absence and still not lose your exemption. You must, however, return to your main residence at the end of periods (b), (c) and (d) above or else you will lose part of your relief.

(3) Any periods of absence subsequent to 31 March 1982 in excess of the periods allowed (see above) result in the relevant proportion of your sale profit being charged to capital gains tax. (For disposals before 6 April 1988, all periods of absence after 6 April 1965 must be considered.) For example, if you bought your house in

June 1989 and sold it in June 1997 at a profit of £8,000 having lived elsewhere for reasons unconnected with your employment for the middle six years, your chargeable gain is £8,000 × 1/8 = £1,000. (You are only allowed three years of absence and the last three in any event, leaving one year taxable.)

(4) If a specific part of your house is set aside for business purposes then that proportion of your profits on sale of the house will be taxable. Thus if you have eight rooms of which two are wholly used for business purposes you would normally claim 25 per cent of your house expenses against your business profits and when you sell your house you will pay capital gains tax on 25 per cent of your total gain (arising after 6 April 1965). If, however, you use no rooms exclusively for business purposes you will not normally be liable for any capital gains tax if you sell your house even though you claim part of your house expenses against your business profits.

(5) If you dispose of your main residence and part has been let for residential purposes, you obtain some exemption for the let portion. This is not to exceed the exemption on the part occupied by you, or £40,000 if smaller (£20,000 before 19 March 1991). Note that you will be exempt for the periods mentioned in 2(a)–(e) in any event.

(6) If you have two residences you can give written notice to the Revenue within two years as to which of the two should be treated as your main private residence and thereby be exempted from capital gains tax. The election should be given within two years of acquiring your second residence. If you do not elect then the Revenue will decide in the light of the time that you spend at each of your residences which of these is your main private residence.

(7) For the purposes of the exemption, your main residence is taken to include land of up to half of a hectare (including the site of the house). If the house is large and its character requires a larger garden, this is likely to be allowed. (Prior to 19 March 1991, the area was one acre.) Note that the exemption covers the disposal of part of your main residence; for example a strip of your garden. However, take care not to sell the house before the garden, since this would not then be part of your main residence.

Previously, you also obtained capital gains tax exemption on no more than one residence owned by you and occupied by a dependent relative, rent-free and without any other consideration. Relief was withdrawn for disposals after 5 April 1988 unless the dependent relative had remained in occupation from an earlier date (TCGA S226).

20.24 Chattels sold for £6,000 or less
(TCGA S262)

A chattel is an asset which is tangible movable property such as a chair, a picture, or a pair of candlesticks. For these purposes a set is treated as one chattel. If you dispose of a chattel for no more than £6,000 you pay no capital gains tax and if your proceeds exceed £6,000 your capital gain is restricted to five-thirds of the excess. Thus if you sell a set of antique chairs for £6,300 (original cost £500) your capital gain is restricted to 5/3 × (£6,300 – £6,000) = £500.

If you bought a chattel for more than £6,000, and sold it for less than £6,000, your allowable loss is restricted to the excess of the cost over £6,000. (For the years 1982–83 to 1988–89 inclusive, the exemption limit was £3,000.)

20.25 Replacement of business assets — roll-over relief
(TCGA Ss152–160, FA 1993 S86 & FA 1996 S141)

You are liable for capital gains tax in respect of any sales of assets used in your business. Similarly a company is liable on any sales of its business assets. If further business assets are purchased within one year preceding and three years after the sale, 'roll-over' relief is obtained as a result of which the gain on the disposal is deducted from the cost of the new business assets. Thus, the gain is 'rolled over' and no tax is paid until the new business assets are sold, unless the latter are in turn replaced. (Note the special 50 per cent reduction for certain rolled-over pre-31 March 1982 gains — 20.11.)

To obtain roll-over relief, both your old and new assets must be 'qualifying'. This implies being within the following classes:

(1) (a) Land and buildings (but not trading stock).
    (b) Fixed plant and machinery not forming part of a building.
(2) Ships, aircraft and hovercraft.
(3) Goodwill.
(4) Satellites, space stations and spacecraft, etc after 27 July 1987.
(5) Milk and potato quotas after 29 October 1987.
(6) Ewe and suckler cow premium quotas after 31 December 1992.

Note, however, that regarding plant and machinery, roll-over relief is only available if it is fixed and so, for example, motor vans and fork lift trucks do not qualify.

To get the relief you must use the old and new assets in the same business. However, if you carry on several trades, they are treated as one for this purpose. (Relief is still available if you cease one trade and start another.) Also, roll-over relief applies regarding purchases and sales by you of personally owned assets used in your 'family company' (20.29).

If you are non-resident and replace a business asset chargeable to UK tax with one which is not, roll-over relief is generally no longer available. This covers the situation where you sell an asset used in your business in the UK and buy one overseas. This new rule normally applies where you dispose of the old asset or acquire the new one after 13 March 1989; but not if the new asset was acquired before that date and the old asset disposed of within one year.

Note that to obtain total relief, the entire proceeds must be invested, otherwise you pay tax on your capital gain up to the extent of the shortfall. Where the disposal takes place after 5 April 1988, the old asset only needs to have been used for business since 31 March 1982 for full relief to apply (if otherwise due).

If the new business asset is a wasting asset (20.29.2) it must be replaced by a non-wasting asset within ten years. Otherwise the rolled-over gain becomes chargeable. This also applies to assets which will become 'wasting' within ten years, such as a lease with 59 years to run. However, this clawback does not apply to a held-over gain arising before 31 March 1982 and becoming chargeable after 5 April 1988 (TCGA Sch 4).

'Roll-over' relief is applicable to companies (13.16). Also a special extension of the rules covers 'gilts' obtained by companies in exchange for group companies in the aircraft and shipping industries on compulsory acquisition through nationalisation. An election is required within four years of the exchange and then the normal new compensation stock rules do not apply.

For disposals or acquisitions after 13 March 1989, subject to transitional rules, dual-resident companies obtain no roll-over relief where they replace a UK business asset with one overseas. From 20 March 1990 roll-over relief is denied where the replacement asset is outside the UK tax charge and is acquired by a dual resident group member (15.10.15).

To fit in with the new self-assessment rules, provisional rollover relief claims will be allowed, including on compulsory purchase (20.25.1).

You will need to declare in your tax return that you intend to re-invest the proceeds in qualifying assets and will lose your relief unless you reinvest within 3 years of the disposal.

20.25.1 Roll-over relief on compulsory purchase *(TCGA Ss247 & 248)*

From 6 April 1982 a form of roll-over relief, similar to that available on business assets (20.25) applies to certain land which is sold to local authorities. The property must either be compulsorily bought from you or the purchasing local authority must have compulsory acquisition powers. The relief is available if your replacement property is business or non-business land but not if it qualifies for main residence relief (20.23).

20.25.2 Roll-over relief on reinvestment *(FA 1993 Sch 7, FA 1994 S91 & Sch 11, FA 1995 Ss46–47 & FA 1997 Sch 17)*

An important extension to roll-over relief (20.25) was introduced regarding the disposal of certain shares in unquoted trading companies after 15 March 1993. You needed to have owned at least 5 per cent of the voting shares (making it your 'personal company') and broadly qualify for retirement relief (apart from the age requirement) (20.29).

For disposals after 29 November 1993, the relief extends to any assets of which you dispose. Also, your new investment may be in any number of ordinary shares in the 'qualifying company'.

The following rules should particularly be noted:

(1) From 16 March 1993 to 29 November 1993, you needed to be a full time officer (including director) or employee of the old company. Also you needed to acquire at least 5 per cent of the voting shares in the new company within one year prior to and three years after the share sale. Sales of quoted shares qualified, if you had held them for at least a year before floatation.

(2) The shares purchased must be in 'qualifying' companies. These must carry on 'qualifying trades' and not be controlled by another company etc, whilst any subsidiaries must be directly owned and trading. Before 29 November 1994, the net value of its land could be no more than half of the company's chargeable assets (or half its net assets if more, after 29 November 1993). These restrictions no longer apply.

(3) From 27 November 1996, relief is available for purchases of shares in a holding company with non-UK subsidiaries provided the trades are carried on wholly or mainly in the UK. Eligibility

for relief now depends on the group activities as a whole rather than on those of each individual company.

(4) Where there is a share for share exchange, you can elect that this is a disposal so that the new relief takes effect.

(5) The definition of 'qualifying trades' is similar to that for EIS companies (11.26), with some changes. For example dealing in financial instruments is excluded but oil extraction activities are not. However, after 28 November 1994, 'qualifying trades' include property development and farming.

(6) For disposals before 30 November 1993 relief was restricted to the proportion of the gain which the company (or group's) chargeable business assets (20.29) bears to its total chargeable assets.

(7) Unlike roll-over relief on business assets (20.25) your replacement expenditure is first allocated to your gain. Thus your relief is the lower of your gain and the cost of the new asset. However, you may claim a lower amount of relief.

(8) The relief must be claimed, but will be lost if you emigrate, sell the new shares without qualifying replacement, or if within three years of your share purchase the new company's trade ceases to qualify.

(9) Anti avoidance rules apply from 20 June 1994. For example if the replacement asset comes from your spouse, the rolled-over gain cannot exceed his or her base cost.

(10) Subject to the rules, a type of reinvestment relief is available where you subscribe for EIS (11.26) and VCT (8.12) units. You can defer capital gains on other assets by investing up to £100,000 each tax year in each. Different time limits apply. For EIS relief, the capital gains must arise no earlier than 29 November 1994 and the EIS shares purchased within one year before and three years after the disposals. With VCT reinvestment, gains must be after 5 April 1995 and the VCT units purchased within one year before and one year afterwards.

20.26 Gifts of business assets

A form of 'hold-over' relief applied to certain transfers of assets, other than bargains at arm's length, made after 11 April 1978. The assets covered were any used in your trade or 'family company' (20.29); also shares in such a company. A claim was required from both parties, similar in effect to that for general gifts (next page).

A more general relief applied for individuals after 5 April 1980 and for settlements after 5 April 1981 (next page). The old relief still applied for gifts to companies. From 14 March 1989, the old rules for gifts of business assets are expanded (20.28), following the cancellation of the general relief for gifts (20.27).

20.27 General relief for gifts

(FA 1980 S79, FA 1981 Ss78 & 79, FA 1982 S82 & FA 1986 S101)

In general, transfers of assets which you made after 5 April 1980 and before 14 March 1989, other than bargains at arm's length, were covered by comprehensive 'hold-over' rules. Only UK resident or ordinarily resident individuals (17.3.1) were covered up to 5 April 1981 but after that date, gifts *to* UK trusts were included. From 6 April 1982 gifts *from* trusts were also included. There is a special 50 per cent reduction for certain held-over pre-31 March 1982 gains (20.11). A claim was normally required from you both within six years of the end of the tax year.

The general gifts relief rules were cancelled regarding gifts made after 13 March 1989. The business asset gifts provisions are expanded from that date (20.28).

20.28 Gifts relief from 14 March 1989

(TCGA Ss165–169 & Sch 7)

With the removal of general gifts relief from 14 March 1989, the business gifts relief (20.26) has been expanded so that it now includes other items. The scope is now:

(1) Business assets used in a trade profession or vocation carried on by the giver or his family company, etc.
(2) Certain agricultural property (normally where the giver has vacant possession).
(3) Shares and securities in family trading companies or non-quoted trading companies. (These categories include the holding companies of trading groups.)
(4) Gifts of heritage property and to maintenance funds.
(5) Gifts to political parties which qualify for inheritance tax exemption.
(6) Gifts which give rise to an immediate charge to inheritance tax, for example, into a discretionary settlement (22.30.2). Potentially exempt transfers (22.3) do not qualify for this relief. However, if a gift is covered by the nil rate band and exemptions for inheritance tax but would otherwise be taxed, the gifts election is available.

(7) Distributions of capital from accumulation and maintenance settlements may also qualify for the election. However, the beneficiary must not obtain the capital later than the income entitlement.
(8) Subject to an election by donor and recipient, gifts to a housing association (TCGA S259).
(9) Certain assets not mentioned above, which are not eligible for gifts relief may qualify for the tax on disposal to be paid by instalments (20.15).
(10) The relief is only available if the donee is UK resident and/or ordinarily resident.
(11) Should you receive some consideration the claim covers only the gift element, if this is less than your total gain. If you are entitled to retirement relief (below) this reduces the held-over gain.
(12) If you received a gift and made the election, then the held-over gain may be assessed on you, should you become neither resident nor ordinarily resident in the UK before having disposed of the asset. However, this only applies if emigration is within six years of the end of the year of assessment of the gift.

20.29 Business retirement relief

(TCGA Ss163–164 & Sch 6, FA 1993 Sch 7, FA 1994 S92 & FA 1996 S176)

If you are over 50 and dispose by gift or sale of the whole or part of a business which you have owned for the past ten years, you are exempted from capital gains tax on the first £250,000 of any gain arising in respect of the 'chargeable business assets' of the business. If you have several businesses your total relief is restricted to £250,000. For disposals prior to 30 November 1993 full relief extended to the first £150,000.

For disposals made prior to 28 November 1995, the age requirement was 55.

To obtain retirement relief on disposals before 19 March 1991, you normally needed to be 60 and full relief applied on the first £125,000 of proceeds. For disposals before 6 April 1987 and after 5 April 1985, this figure was £100,000.

Note that you do not actually need to retire to obtain the relief. 'Chargeable business assets' include assets used for the trade, etc of the business, and also goodwill but not assets held as investments.

For disposals after 5 April 1988, not only is the first tranche of gains exempted from capital gains tax; the second tranche is given 50 per cent relief. From 30 November 1993, the second tranche is £750,000 and from 19 March 1991, it was £450,000. (From 6 April 1988 to 18 March 1991, this tranche was £375,000.) Thus if you are over 50 and sell your business, giving rise to a chargeable gain of £650,000, £250,000 of this is exempted from capital gains tax, as is 50 per cent × (£650,000 – £250,000) = £200,000. You are taxed on only £650,000 – (£250,000 + £200,000) = £200,000. (This example assumes that you have not used any retirement relief previously.)

You are also able to obtain relief if you retire younger than the required age (50, etc.) for reasons of ill-health. You must show that you are likely to remain incapable of performing your previous work and will require a medical certificate. You must claim relief in this case and this must be done not later than 2 years after the tax year of your disposal.

The above relief also covers any disposal of shares prior to 16 March 1993 in a trading company which had been your 'family company' for at least the last ten years during which time you had been a full-time director of the company. A 'family company' was one in which you had 25 per cent of the voting rights or your immediate family had at least more than 50 per cent (at least 51 per cent before 6 April 1985) including 5 per cent held by yourself.

For share disposals after 15 March 1993, the 'family company' requirement is replaced. A 'personal company' is now necessary with relaxed shareholding requirements. It is now simply necessary to own 5 per cent of the voting shares. Also from that time, the relief extends to any 'full-time working officer or employee' who satisfies the other conditions.

Only the proportion of the gain on the shares attributable to the 'chargeable business assets' of the company compared with its total chargeable assets qualifies for the relief. Note that shares in subsidiary companies are regarded as 'chargeable business assets'.

Reduced relief is available concerning disposals of the whole or part of a business which you have owned for less than ten years. You obtain 10 per cent of the full relief if you owned the assets for at least one year prior to disposal, 20 per cent relief for at least two years of ownership and so on.

If your wife complies with the requirements, she too will be eligible for the relief if she sells her business or shares in a 'family company'.

The relief also covers disposals by a settlement of assets used by a beneficiary for his own or his family company's business. Also shares in a family trading or holding company are covered. The beneficiary must have an interest in possession in the settlement, withdraw from the business and must retire.

20.30 Charities

(TCGA Ss256 & 257)

Charities are exempted from capital gains tax in respect of any gains on the disposal of assets provided that such gains are applied to charitable purposes.

If you make a gift of an asset to a charity you pay no capital gains tax on this disposal.

20.31 Leases and other wasting assets

(TCGA Ss45, 240 & Sch 8 & FA 1996 S142)

A 'wasting asset' is defined as an asset with a predictable life not exceeding 50 years, not including freehold land and buildings, etc. Leases with no more than 50 years still to run are a special kind of wasting asset and are separately treated for capital gains tax (see below).

'Wasting assets' which are also movable property (chattels) are normally exempted from capital gains tax. In the case of other wasting assets apart from leases, you must reduce their original costs on a straight line time basis over the respective lives of the assets. Thus if you buy a wasting asset for £10,000 with an unexpired life of 40 years and sell it after 20 years for £20,000, assuming the residual value after 40 years would have been nil, your allowable cost is £10,000 × 20/40 = £5,000; thus your chargeable gain is £20,000 – £5,000 = £15,000.

In the case of a lease with no more than 50 years of its original term unexpired (including leases for shorter terms) the original cost must be written off according to a special formula under which the rate of wastage accelerates as the end of the term of the lease is reached. If you sell such an interest in property and lease back the premises at a lower rent for less than 15 years, you may be taxed on all or part of the proceeds either as a trading receipt or under Schedule D Case VI (19.1.2).

From 6 April 1996, capital sums paid to a landlord for varying, waiving or surrendering a lease, or commuting the rent are taken into account in the year when payable. Previously they were related to the year when the lease was first granted.

20.32 Traded options
(TCGA Ss115, 143, 148 & 271 & FA 1994 S96)

Options to buy or sell quoted shares are dealt with on the Stock Exchange. They are not treated as wasting assets, which means that the entire cost is deductible on sale. The abandonment of a traded option is treated as a disposal so that its cost is an allowable loss. This treatment extends to all traded options quoted on the London International Financial Futures Exchange and recognised stock exchanges.

After 1 July 1986 transactions in futures and options in gilts and qualifying bonds are exempt from capital gains tax. A further rule provides that if you write a traded option and later extinguish this obligation by buying another option, the cost is allowable against the original sale. From 30 November 1994, it is made clear that where options are settled in cash, such expenditure is fully allowable.

20.33 Commodity and financial futures
(TCGA Ss72, 143 & 271 & FA 1994 S95)

Prior to 6 April 1985, profits from futures which are not part of a trade were taxed under Schedule D Case VI (15.1). However, from that date, any profits less losses which you realise are normally covered by capital gains tax and not income tax. This rule applies to commodity futures or financial futures dealt in on a recognised futures exchange.

The 1987 Finance Act introduced broadly similar capital gains tax treatment for commodity and financial futures and qualifying options (20.32), which are dealt in 'over-the-counter'. From August 1990 income and gains from futures and options are exempt from tax in authorised unit trusts and pension schemes. From 30 November 1994, where financial and commodity futures are settled in cash, full relief is given for this expenditure.

20.34 Overseas aspects
(TCGA Ss9–14, 25, 80–98, 140, 159–160, 185–188, 275–279 & Sch 5)

As already mentioned (20.3) provided you are resident and/or ordinarily resident in this country, you are liable to tax on capital gains anywhere in the world. An exception is where assets are realised in a country which will not allow the proceeds to be remitted to the UK. You can then claim that your gain is deferred until the year when it becomes possible to remit the proceeds. If you are non-domiciled in the UK, you are only liable to capital gains tax on overseas gains to the extent that they are remitted here (18.1).

Non-residents carrying on a trade in the UK through a branch or agency are liable to capital gains tax on assets used in the business. From 14 March 1989, this also covers professions and vocations; however, assets are re-based to their values at that date. Furthermore from that date deemed disposals may take place for capital gains tax purposes. This happens if the assets are moved out of the UK or the trade, etc ceases.

If you are UK domiciled, the Revenue have powers to apportion to you the capital gains of certain overseas trusts from which you benefit (21.9) and companies. This extends to overseas companies owned by foreign trusts.

The *market value* rule (20.10) applies in general to gifts and other dispositions of overseas assets for less than full consideration involving neither resident nor ordinarily resident persons after 5 April 1983 (FA 1984 S66).

Where a company is being 'exported' (17.3.3), there is a deemed disposal of all of its assets at market value for capital gains tax purposes. This broadly applies to companies migrating after 14 March 1988, from which time only those incorporated outside the UK are able to become non-resident. Furthermore, roll-over relief (20.25.1) does not apply where assets are sold before and replaced after migration. If a company which migrates continues to trade in the UK through a branch or agency, any connected assets will be exempted from the deemed disposal.

If a foreign registered 75 per cent subsidiary of a UK company migrates, tax on the capital gains attributable to its foreign assets can be deferred. Parent and subsidiary must make a joint election and the tax becomes payable if any of the foreign assets are sold or if the parent–subsidiary relationship ceases.

After 13 March 1989, if a dual-resident company owns an asset which ceases to be within the UK capital gains tax charge through a double tax agreement, it is deemed to have disposed of the asset. Thus a capital gain may result. Also, for disposals after that date by a non-resident company, tax on the capital gains can be collected from other companies in the same group or from controlling directors. This applies if the original company does not pay within six months of the due date.

If you are a UK resident investor in an offshore 'umbrella fund' you will be subjected to a capital gains tax charge when you switch holdings. This applies to switches made after 13 March 1989.

With effect from 20 March 1990, non-resident companies may transfer their UK branch or agency business to UK resident companies without any immediate capital gains tax charge. This hold-over relief applies if the companies are in the same world-wide group.

Sweeping changes operate from 19 March 1991 regarding the capital gains tax rules for overseas trusts. These are considered later (21.9.1).

With effect from 1 January 1992, various relieving provisions came into effect regarding cross-border reorganisations of businesses within the EC. As a result, capital gains tax may be deferred where there is a share exchange and on transfers of UK and non-UK trades, subject to the rules. For a share exchange, voting control must be acquired for shares with not more than 10 per cent of the nominal value in cash. Regarding a UK trade, this must be transferred from a company situated in one EC country to one situated in another, in exchange for securities.

The FOREX legislation (13.25) came into force for the accounting periods of companies beginning after 22 March 1995. One result is that capital gains tax will no longer be charged on monetary assets in foreign currency. Legislation has been introduced for asset disposals from 1 January 1995, to block saving tax from the new rules coupled with no gain/no loss transfers (FA 1995 S131).

21 The taxation of trusts and estates

21.1 Trusts

A trust is brought into existence when a person (the settlor) transfers assets to trustees for the benefit of third parties (the beneficiaries). Another word for a trust is a settlement. A trust may also be created under a will when a person (the testator) sets aside the whole or a portion of his estate to be administered (by trustees) for the benefit of his heirs or other beneficiaries. (Where an individual declares himself to be a trustee of certain of his assets a trust will also come into existence.)

21.2 Trusts where the settlor or testator is deceased

Where the settlor or testator has died, the taxation of trusts normally follows simple rules. The trust is assessed to basic rate income tax and sometimes additional rate (5.6) on its income. Since 6 April 1993, lower rate (20 per cent) may apply for dividend income (21.2.1). From 6 April 1996, the 20 per cent rate applies more generally to savings income (2.2). Some tax will have been deducted at the source (eg, taxed interest). Capital gains tax is charged on any capital gains of the trust (21.6).

The tax assessments are normally made in the joint names of the trustees who pay the tax out of the trust funds.

No higher rate tax is paid by the trustees but when the income is distributed to any of the beneficiaries this income is added to the beneficiaries' total income for tax purposes (5.2). The income distributions are normally treated as being net of income tax at the lower (20 per cent) and/or basic rate (23 per cent). Thus they carry a corresponding tax credit. In the case of discretionary trusts, etc (21.3.4) tax must be paid to bring the tax credit up to 34 per cent. (For 1996–97, the basic rate was

24 per cent and the discretionary trusts' rate 34 per cent.) The trustees should issue with each payment a form R185E which sets out the amount paid and the relevant tax credit.

21.2.1 Dividend income of trusts from 6 April 1993
(FA 1993 Ss77–79 & Sch 6)

New rules apply for dividend income after 5 April 1993, whether or not the settlor is living. If you have an 'interest in possession' in the trust, so that for example you receive the income as of right, the trustees receive tax credits of 20 per cent and are charged no further tax on the dividends. When these are distributed to you, the net income carries with it a tax credit of the lower rate of 20 per cent. This treatment normally extends to Scottish interest–in–possession trusts with UK resident trustees.

If the trust had other income as well as dividends, this carried a credit of 25 per cent. Distributions to you were regarded as coming first out of the other income carrying 25 per cent tax credit and then out of dividend income, with a 20 per cent credit. However, with effect from 6 April 1996, a tax credit rate of 20 per cent applies to most savings income (2.2).

The trustees of accumulation and maintenance (21.4) and discretionary settlements (21.5) pay income tax of 34 per cent and set off normally 20 per cent tax credits. (From 6 April 1993 to 5 April 1996 these were 20 per cent on dividends and 25 per cent on other income.) As a beneficiary, you have a 34 per cent tax credit.

21.3 Trusts where the settlor is still living
(TA 1988 Ss660–685 & FA 1995 S74 & Sch 17)

The taxation of trusts where the settlor is still living follows the general rules outlined above except that in certain circumstances the settlor himself is assessed to tax on the income of the trust. In order to avoid such assessment various rules should be observed including the following.

From 6 April 1995, new and simplified rules apply which broadly have the same effect as the previous ones. However, material changes were proposed regarding the taxation of capital sums paid to the settlor (21.3.6), particularly concerning loans between him or her and the settlement. After widespread objections this part of the new legislation was withdrawn but is expected to reappear in modified form in the future. Meanwhile the original rules apply.

21.3.1 Period

(TA 1988 S660)

The settlement must be set up for a period which is capable of exceeding six years.

21.3.2 The settlor must not have an interest

(TA 1988 Ss673 & 683 & FA 1989 Ss108 & 109)

In the event that the settlor has retained an interest in the income or assets of the trust, he will be assessed to income tax on the income of the settlement to the extent that it remains undistributed. (The settlor has retained an interest in the trust if he or his wife can obtain some benefit from it.) Furthermore, if the income is distributed to others, subject to certain exceptions, the settlor and not the recipient will be charged to the excess of higher rate tax over the income tax on the distribution. For trusts made after 13 March 1989, in which the settlor retains an interest, with some exceptions, he or she is taxed on all of the income at the basic and higher rates. (This applies to the income from existing settlements arising from 6 April 1990.)

For 1990–91 and subsequent years, simple outright gifts and pension allocations between husband and wife are not to be treated as settlements for the purposes of these rules. However, this does not apply to gifts of property which do not carry a right to all of the income or where a right to income alone is given.

21.3.3 The settlement must be irrevocable

(TA 1988 Ss671 & 672)

If the settlor or his wife has power to revoke the settlement or partially revoke it, he is assessed to income tax on its income.

21.3.4 Discretionary settlements

(TA 1988 S674)

Discretionary settlements are those under which the application of the income and/or capital of the trust is left to the discretion of the trustees. Under such a trust the settlor or his wife must not be able to benefit from the income, or else he will be assessed to income tax on that income, whether or not any of it is actually paid to him. This does not apply if only the widow or widower of the settlor may benefit.

21.3.5 Settlements for benefit of own children

(TA 1988 Ss663–670)

Under a trust created by the settlor, his own unmarried minor children (under 18 years of age) must not receive any income nor must it be used for their upkeep or education. Otherwise the settlor will be assessed to income tax on such income. This does not apply to income which is accumulated, however (see 21.4) nor to income not exceeding £100 per child each tax year.

21.3.6 Capital sums paid to the settlor
(TA 1988 S677)

Where 'capital sums' from a settlement (including loans and loan repayments) are paid to the settlor, he is assessable to income tax. The assessments are limited to the undistributed trust income and the balance is carried forward for matching against future income. The carry forward period is limited to 11 years from the 'capital sum' payment and no income is assessable for any period subsequent to the repayment by the settlor of a loan from the settlement.

The rules extend to companies connected with the settlement (normally where the trustees are participators and the company is close — 13.17). A 'capital payment' from the company to the settlor gives rise to the assessment of trust income on him or her, if there is an associated capital payment or asset transfer within five years from the trust to the company.

Note: In all of the above cases there are rules to prevent the double taxation of the trust income so it will not be assessed both on the settlor and the beneficiaries. Usually, basic rate income tax is paid by the trust or it has already been deducted at the source as in the case of, for example, interest on government securities. Dividends received by the trust carry with them tax credits which are effectively transferred to beneficiaries who are given income distributions. Also, if the trust is subject to additional rate correspondingly higher tax credits attach to income distributions to beneficiaries (21.5).

21.4 Accumulation settlements for the benefit of the settlor's children

If you wish to create a trust for the benefit of your minor (unmarried) children without being assessed to income tax on its income (see above) this can be done by means of an accumulation settlement. The income of the settlement should be accumulated for each child until at least the age of 18 and no payments should be made for their benefit until that age. (The trust deed normally states that the trustees are empowered to accumulate income.) If it is wished to distribute income to adult beneficiaries this can be done, but the income shares of the settlor's minor children must be accumulated, or else the settlor is liable to higher rate income tax on such income.

21.5 Income of discretionary trusts, etc

(TA 1988 Ss686–687, 809 & FA 1993 Sch 6, FA 1995 S86 & FA 1996 S73 & Sch 6)

Although it no longer applies to individuals (5.6), an additional rate of latterly 10 per cent applied to all of the income of discretionary and accumulating trusts from 1988–89 to 1992–93. Thus if a discretionary trust received dividends of £750 during 1992–93 these were imputed with £250 tax to make a total of £1,000 on which additional tax of £100 was payable by the trustees. If, however, allowable expenses of say £200 were incurred then only £1,000 – £200 = £800 was liable to the additional tax and so £800 × 10 per cent = £80 was payable.

The position from 6 April 1993 to 5 April 1996 was broadly similar in effect. The settlement bore income tax of 35 per cent but obtained tax credits of 20 per cent on its dividend income and 25 per cent on other income where suffered. Trust management expenses gave rise to relief at 15 per cent (35–20) if they were allocated to dividends and 10 per cent (35–25) otherwise. The expenses were first to be allocated to dividend income. The current position (for 1996–97 and 1997–98) is that the full tax rate is 34 per cent, leaving 14 per cent to pay after allowing for 20 per cent tax credit relief.

The above applies to trusts where the income is accumulated or is payable at the discretion of the trustees but not where the income is treated for tax purposes as being that of the settlor; nor where a person is absolutely entitled to the income.

Where income distributions are made to beneficiaries, the amounts received by the latter are treated as being net of tax at 34 per cent. The recipients can reclaim part or all of this tax if their incomes are low enough. For example, if a discretionary trust pays £660 to your child (or for his maintenance) and he or she has no other income, there is a tax credit of £660 × 34/66 = £340 which is all reclaimable.

Bank interest on deposits belonging to discretionary and accumulation trusts was previously paid gross. However, from 6 April 1996, it is paid net of tax at 20 per cent. Overseas Trusts with no connection to the UK will be able to continue receiving gross interest provided the trustees give the bank a signed declaration.

21.6 Trusts' capital gains tax
(TCGA Ss5, 68–76, 165–167 & Sch 7)

Regarding realisations by trusts, a 23 per cent capital gains tax rate applies, except for discretionary and accumulation trusts. Regarding the latter, a rate of 34 per cent applies. Where the settlor (or spouse) has an interest in or rights relating to a settlement, the 23 per cent rate may be increased to the settlor's top rate. Also, the settlor's annual exemption (£6,500) would apply if not used up (TCGA Ss77 & 78).

The full (£6,500) annual exemption (20.6) applies to trusts for the mentally disabled and those receiving attendance allowance. (From 6 April 1981 only broadly half the property and income need be applied to the disabled.) Other trusts normally obtain exemption at half the rate (£3,250). However, regarding trusts formed after 6 June 1978, the exemption is split between those with the same settlor. Thus if you had settled four such trusts they each have an annual exemption of £813. If there are more than five, however, they each still have an exemption of £650.

For recent years the corresponding exemptions are:

	Disability trusts	*Other trusts*	*Minimum*
1988–89 to 1990–91	5,000	2,500	500
1991–92	5,500	2,750	550
1992–93, 1993–94 & 1994–95	5,800	2,900	580
1995–96	6,000	3,000	600
1996–97	6,300	3,150	630
1997–98	6,500	3,250	650

When any chargeable assets are introduced into the trust by the settlor this is a realisation by him on which he pays capital gains tax if applicable (20.10). For example, if A bought 1,000 shares in B Ltd for £1,000 in May 1988 and gifts them in June 1997 to a settlement that he created, the shares must be valued at that time. If the shares are then worth £2,000 he has a chargeable gain of £1,000 for 1997–98 (subject to indexation). If, however, the shares are worth only £600 at that time, he has an allowable loss of £400 (£1,000 – £600) which he can only set off against any capital gains resulting from other transactions between A and his trust. This is because they are treated as being 'connected persons' (20.10).

21.7 Trusts' capital gains tax — business assets, gifts, etc

Where, after 11 April 1978, business assets, including shares in 'family companies' were settled, the trustees and settlor could jointly claim for any gain on the assets to be held over (20.26). The effect was that the settlor had no capital gains tax to pay on the settled business assets, etc and the acquisition value for the trustees was correspondingly reduced. From 6 April 1981 to 13 March 1989, the general gifts relief (20.27) applied to disposals *to* trusts. Regarding gifts *by* trusts, the old business assets rules applied for 1981–82, after which the general gifts relief applied up to 13 March 1989. From 14 March 1989, the old business assets rules apply with some extensions (20.28), for instance concerning discretionary settlements.

From 6 April 1985 capital gains tax retirement relief was extended to cover certain trust disposals of business assets (or family company shares). This particularly applies where a beneficiary of the trust with a life interest in possession (other than for a fixed term), who previously carried on the business, withdraws from it and retires (20.29).

The new roll-over relief on reinvestment (20.25.2) applies in certain limited cases to shares sold by trusts after 15 March 1993. A typical situation would be that you are a beneficiary with an interest in possession in the shares disposed of. You would need to have been a full time working officer and own personally at least 5 per cent of the voting shares. In addition, the normal rules must be satisfied.

For disposals made after 29 November 1993 by most trusts, the wider exemption applies (20.25.2). Thus all chargeable gains of trusts will be eligible for relief if re-invested in ordinary shares in qualifying companies. The exception is where the beneficiaries include those who are neither individuals nor charities.

21.8 Trusts' capital gains tax — disposals of interests and distributions

The disposal of an interest in the trust by one of the original beneficiaries is normally exempt from capital gains tax. However, this does not apply to non-resident settlements.

Where a *life interest* ends in a settlement otherwise than on death, capital gains tax does not arise on the excess of its value over the base cost. However, on a subsequent disposal the original base value must be used. Where a *life interest* in a settlement ends on death, there is similarly no capital gains tax. However, the capital gains tax base value of the assets is adjusted to their market value at that time.

Where a capital asset of a trust is distributed to a beneficiary this is a chargeable event which can give rise to a capital gain in the trust. (This even applies for minors, etc who are not yet able to legally own the property.) Thus if a trust bought 1,000 shares in B Ltd for £2,000 in April 1983 and it distributes them to beneficiary C in July 1997 when their market value is £3,000 the trust will have a capital gain of £1,000 (£3,000 – £2,000), which is assessable for 1997–98 subject to the annual exemption and indexation. (An exception to this rule is where a beneficiary under a will receives his entitlement — 21.10.3.) The beneficiary normally has a base value equivalent to the market value of the asset.

21.9 Foreign trusts
(TCGA Ss13, 80–90 & Sch 5)

For taxation purposes a trust is generally treated as being resident abroad if a majority of the trustees are so resident and its administration and management is carried out overseas. Such a trust was generally exempt from capital gains tax on realisations of assets in the UK and elsewhere. However, sweeping changes took effect from 19 March 1991 and that rule no longer applies in certain cases (21.9.1).

For income tax purposes, broadly, for 1989–90 (with some exceptions) and subsequent years if at least one trustee is UK resident and at least one is not, special rules apply (17.3.5), depending on the settlor's status when he introduces funds into the settlement. If the settlor was then resident, ordinarily resident or domiciled in the UK, the non-resident trustees are treated as UK resident for determining the trust's residence for income tax purposes. Otherwise, all of the trustees are treated as non-UK resident.

If the settlement arises on death, the residence, etc of the deceased at the date of death applies for deeming the residence of the trustees and a similar rule applies concerning the personal representatives.

There are rules under which the Revenue can sometimes assess UK resident beneficiaries with their shares of any capital gains (provided that the settlor is UK domiciled and resident or ordinarily resident either when he made the settlement or when the capital gain is made). UK beneficiaries are only taxed to the extent that they receive *capital payments* attributable to such gains. Where the *capital payments* and trust capital gains are in different tax years the beneficiary is taxed in the later one. *Capital payments* made to beneficiaries after 5 April 1992 may attract a supplementary charge (21.9.1).

There are rules to prevent capital gains tax being avoided by transfers between settlements and by a trust changing its residence. For the purposes of the rules, the term 'settlement' includes dispositions, arrangements and agreements; whilst 'settlor' takes in those making reciprocal arrangements or undertakings to provide funds indirectly. From 19 March 1991, there are rules to charge to tax, trust capital gains on settlors who have any interest in the settlement (21.9.1).

Where a beneficiary obtains an asset from a foreign trust, his base value is taken to be the market value of the asset, as a general rule. However, from 10 March 1981 to 5 April 1983, his base value was limited to the amount of any consideration which he actually gave for the asset, except in certain cases where the foreign trust was liable to UK capital gains tax.

UK income of foreign trusts is charged to income tax here along roughly the same lines as non-resident individuals are so charged. There is no higher rate liability, however, unless distributions are made to beneficiaries resident in this country or if the anti-avoidance provisions apply regarding transfers of assets abroad (15.10.2). In the latter event, in certain circumstances, the Revenue may charge any beneficiaries who are resident in this country with basic and higher rate income tax on the trust income.

Regarding the UK dividends received by foreign discretionary and accumulation trusts after 5 April 1993, a notional tax credit of 20 per cent of the gross (20/80) is added. This is then allowed as a credit against the full 34 per cent tax leaving 14 per cent to pay. However, this tax credit is not repayable.

21.9.1 Foreign trusts — capital gains from 19 March 1991

(TCGA Ss80–87 & Sch 5 & FA 1994 S97)

Rules operate from 19 March 1991 aimed at increasing the application of UK capital gains tax to foreign trusts. These rules include a capital gains tax charge when the trustees of a settlement cease to be UK resident after 18 March 1991. This is based on the values of the assets which fall out of the UK capital gains tax net when the trustees change residence (not assets used in a UK trade). The trustees are not able to cover such gains by roll-over relief through buying new assets outside the UK tax charge.

As the settlor of a non-resident settlement, you will be charged to capital gains tax if certain conditions are satisfied including the following:

(1) You are UK domiciled and resident or ordinarily resident (17.2 and 17.3).
(2) You have an 'interest' in the settlement. This covers being able to benefit, now or in the future, from the income or property of the settlement. You are also caught if your spouse, children or their spouses can benefit.
(3) The rules apply to your settlement, if you set it up after 18 March 1991. Earlier settlements may also be caught, where, for example, property or income is provided otherwise than by way of arm's length bargains. Other instances include the trustees ceasing to be UK resident after that date and a member of your immediate family ((2) above) becoming a beneficiary for the first time.
(4) Any capital gains and losses made by your settlement before 19 March 1991 are not caught by the new rules. However, subject to the conditions being satisfied, you will be assessed on the subsequent net gains. Also, you will have an obligation to notify the Inland Revenue of events which may involve a charge to tax.

If you are a beneficiary of a non-resident settlement and receive a *capital payment* after 5 April 1992, you may be liable to pay a *supplementary charge* in addition to the normal capital gains tax. The rules include the following:

(1) You must be UK domiciled and resident or ordinarily resident (17.2 and 17.3). Also, the settlor has this status when you receive the payment or when the trust was established.
(2) Your capital payments will be matched with trust gains on a 'first-in first-out' basis.
(3) The supplementary charge runs from 1 December in the tax year following the one when the gain arose, to 30 November following the year of assessment in which your capital payment is made.
(4) You will not be charged if your capital payment fails to be matched with trust gains of the same or immediately preceding tax year.
(5) The supplementary charge will be 10 per cent of the tax for each year up to six. Thus, if the top rate remains 40 per cent, the maximum supplementary charge will be 24 per cent making a total of 64 per cent.

The Revenue must be provided with information where a non-resident trust is set up after 18 March 1991; property (other than at arm's length) is transferred to an earlier trust; or a trust ceases to be UK resident. This is normally limited to where the settlor is UK resident and/or domiciled and now applies whether or not the settlor has an interest.

21.10 Estates of deceased persons

21.10.1 The tax liability of the deceased
(TMA Ss40, 74 & 77)

When a person dies, income tax and capital gains tax must be settled on all his income and capital gains up to the date of his death. Any of this tax that is not paid during his lifetime must be settled by his executors or administrators out of his estate.

If the deceased has not been assessed to tax on all his income or capital gains prior to his death, the Revenue are allowed to make assessments on such income and capital gains within three years after the end of the tax year in which death occurred. The Revenue may make assessments in this way in respect of any tax years ending within six years before the date of death in cases of fraud, wilful default or neglect of the deceased but no earlier years can be assessed (16.9.1).

21.10.2 Income tax during the administration period
(TA 1988 Ss695–720 & FA 1995 Sch 18)

The administration period of an estate is the period from the date of death of the deceased until the assets are distributed to the beneficiaries according to the will of the deceased or according to the rules of intestacy. Where, however, a trust is set up under a will the administration period only normally lasts until the trust takes over the residue of the estate.

During the administration period, the executors or administrators pay any basic rate income tax assessments that arise on the income for that period. The tax paid by direct assessment or deduction at source is subtracted from the amounts of income paid to those entitled to the income of the estate. Non-trading expenses of the executors are also deducted, but normally, any trading expenses will have been deducted from trading income in arriving at its net taxable amount.

The beneficiaries include the income that they receive in their tax returns when the payments are made to them. They must return the gross equivalents allowing for income tax at the basic rate (23 per cent). However, any distributions of estate income out of post 5 April 1993 dividends (21.2.1) and post 5 April 1996 savings income (2.2) must be grossed up at the lower rate (20 per cent) and carry a 20 per cent tax credit.

Once the total income payable to each beneficiary has been ascertained, it is allocated to the respective tax years for which it arose and they pay (if applicable) higher rate tax on that basis. However, new rules apply to estates in the course of administration at 6 April 1995 and new ones. From that date, income payments made to the beneficiaries are taxable in the year of receipt, any balance normally being taxable on completion of the administration and not subject to spreading.

21.10.3 Capital gains tax during the administration period

(TCGA Ss3 & 62)

Although before 31 March 1971 all of the chargeable assets of the deceased were considered for capital gains tax purposes to be disposed of at the date of his death, no such liability arises regarding deaths on or after that date. The executors or administrators of the estate are regarded as acquiring the assets at their market value at the date of death and if they later sell any of the assets during the administration period, the estate is assessed to capital gains tax on any surplus. The rate was 30 per cent up to 5 April 1988, 25 per cent to 5 April 1996, 24 per cent for 1996–97 and 23 per cent thereafter.

Thus if part of the estate of A deceased consisted of 1,000 shares in B Ltd whose value at his death on say 30 June 1995 was £2,000, if those shares are sold on 1 November 1997 for £3,000 (in order to pay inheritance tax for example), the estate is assessed to capital gains tax on £1,000 (£3,000 – £2,000) for 1997–98 (subject to indexation and annual exemption).

If, however, assets of the estate are given to beneficiaries in settlement of their entitlements under the will of the deceased, no capital gains tax is charged on the estate on such transfers of assets. Instead, each beneficiary is treated for capital gains tax purposes as if he had acquired the assets at the same time as the personal representatives acquired them and at the same value.

Thus in the example mentioned above, if instead of selling the 1,000 shares in B Ltd for £3,000 on 1 November 1997 the executors gave them to C on that day in satisfaction of a legacy provided by the will of A deceased, C is treated as having acquired the shares on 30 June 1995 for £2,000 only. (The value of £2,000 was the probate value of the shares at the date of death.) Thus no capital gains tax is payable by the estate in respect of the transfer. If, however, C then sells shares on 1 December

1997 for £3,500 his chargeable gain (subject to indexation) will be £1,500 (£3,500 – £2,000), although the shares have only gone up in value by £500 since he received them. This is because his entitlement to the legacy is considered for capital gains tax purposes to extend back to the date of death.

For the year of assessment in which death occurs and the next two years, the full personal annual exemption is applied to the net gains (£6,500, etc — 20.6).

See Chapter 22 (22.30) for guidelines to the inheritance tax rules concerning settlements.

22 Inheritance tax

22.1 Introduction

This chapter deals with what was originally known as capital transfer tax, but following sweeping changes in the 1986 Finance Act was renamed inheritance tax. The name applies from 25 July 1986. However, the inheritance tax rules cover transfers on and after 18 March 1986.

The tax is highly complicated and technical. Although many of the basic capital transfer tax rules remain, important innovations such as potentially exempt transfers (PETs) were introduced (22.3). Many of its complexities are beyond the scope of this book. The following is thus only a brief outline.

The rules for inheritance tax are contained in the Inheritance Tax Act 1984 (ITA) and subsequent Finance Acts. The tax covers transfers on death and certain lifetime transfers, particularly to discretionary settlements. However, lifetime transfers between individuals and to certain trusts are only taxed if death occurs within seven years (22.3).

Before capital transfer tax there was estate duty, which did not apply to deaths occurring after 12 March 1975 (22.14). Where property passed on deaths after 12 November 1974 and before 13 March 1975, estate duty applied at capital transfer tax rates. For details of estate duty, reference should be made to Chapter 19 of the 1974–75 *Hambro Tax Guide* and earlier editions.

22.2 Property chargeable

(ITA 1984 Ss1–3 & 103–114)

Subject to various exceptions and reliefs (22.15) inheritance tax will be charged on *chargeable transfers* which you make during your lifetime, as well as on the value of your estate when you die. However, with the introduction of the inheritance tax regime, the scope for tax on lifetime gifts was much reduced by the rules concerning *potentially exempt transfers* (22.3). These escape tax unless death occurs within seven years. As a result, most inheritance tax is payable following death.

Chargeable transfers are evaluated by taking the decrease in your assets less liabilities brought about by the transfer and deducting certain exemptions (22.17). Normally, arm's length transactions are ignored if they are not intended to convey any gratuitous benefit. Any capital gains tax which you pay is ignored in calculating the decrease.

If you are domiciled (17.2) in the UK or deemed domiciled (22.4) here, inheritance tax applies to all of your property, wherever situated. Otherwise it only applies to your property in this country.

22.3 Potentially exempt transfers
(FA 1986 S101 & Sch 19 & F2A 1987 S96 & Sch 7)

If you make gifts after 17 March 1986 to other individuals, or to accumulation and maintenance settlements (22.30.1) or trusts for disabled persons, they are classed as 'potentially exempt transfers' (PETs). This means that inheritance tax will not be payable on these gifts unless you die within seven years. Should that happen, however, the PETs (less exemptions) become *chargeable transfers*. Your tax must then be recalculated as later indicated (22.5.1) but using the rate scale applying at death and subject to possible tapering relief (22.6).

From 17 March 1987, the scope of PETs includes lifetime transfers concerning interest in possession trusts. These are broadly trusts where one or more beneficiaries have the income or use of property as of right. Transfers into such trusts are PETs as are transfers out, except on death. If you make a PET, no inheritance tax return is required.

22.4 Deemed domicile
(ITA 1984 S267 & FA 1996 S200)

You are deemed to be domiciled in the UK if one of the following applies:

(1) You were domiciled here on or after 10 December 1974 and within the three years preceding the date of the chargeable transfer.

(2) You were resident here on or after 10 December 1974 and in not less than 17 of the 20 years of assessment ending with that in which you made the chargeable transfer.

22.5 Rate scale

(ITA 1984 S7 & Sch 1 & FA 1997 S93)

The inheritance tax scheme applying from 18 March 1986 has a seven year limitation on cumulation. Also, as previously mentioned (22.3) lifetime transfers (excluding transfers to discretionary settlements, etc) are not cumulated unless you die within seven years. There are, however, various exemptions from the general rules (22.17).

Capital transfer tax was charged on the cumulative total of all your lifetime transfers after 26 March 1974 together with the property passing on your death. There was a ten year limitation on cumulation (22.7).

Prior to 18 March 1986 the tax was charged at progressive rates ranging from 30 per cent to 60 per cent. A lower scale applied to lifetime gifts and a higher one to property passing on death. If you died within three years of making a chargeable transfer, additional tax was payable to bring the charge on it up to the scale applicable on death. This rule still applied where death was within three years of a pre-18 March 1986 gift.

Inheritance tax is charged according to the following table (22.5.1) which applies to *chargeable transfers* and property passing on death after 5 April 1997. For 1996–97 there was a £200,000 threshold. (Fuller details appear later — 26.4.)

There is only one scale but lifetime gifts which are not PETs (22.3) are charged at 50 per cent of the rate. This applies basically to transfers into discretionary settlements, charges on such settlements (22.30.2) and chargeable transfers arising from close company transactions. Tax is paid on such transfers soon after they are made, cumulating them with others within the previous seven years to calculate the amount. If death occurs within seven years, however, tax is adjusted using the full rates, with possible tapering relief (22.6) where death is later than three years after the transfer. However, the adjustment does not operate to reduce the original tax.

On death within seven years of a PET (22.3) inheritance tax must be calculated by treating it as a *chargeable transfer* and cumulating with any earlier chargeable transfers within seven years of the PET. Tax is calculated using the value of the gift when made but using the scale current at the date of death. On gifts more than three years before death, some tapering relief will be available (22.6).

22.5.1 Table: Inheritance tax rate after 5 April 1997

Slice of cumulative chargeable transfers	*Cumulative total*	*% on slice*	*Cumulative total tax*
The first £215,000	£215,000	Nil	£Nil
The remainder		40	

In general, the current rate scale applies to chargeable transfers and on deaths after 5 April 1997. Previously the rate scales have been modified periodically. Each time the burden has been slightly reduced. The full tables appear in Chapter 26.

22.6 Tapering relief

(ITA 1984 S7)

Where an individual dies within seven years of making a potentially exempt transfer (PET) (22.3) a proportion of the full tax is payable as follows:

Death in years	*%*
1–3	100
4	80
5	60
6	40
7	20

If a transfer is within the nil rate band, so that it attracts no inheritance tax, no benefit is obtained from tapering relief in that instance. Regarding those lifetime transfers which attract inheritance tax immediately at half the full rates (22.5), the tax is increased to full rates if death occurs within three years. Otherwise, the above tapering scale is applied to the rates current at death unless this produces a lower charge than that originally paid. In that case the original basis holds good.

22.7 The ten year cumulation period

FA 1981 introduced a ten year limitation on cumulations (superseded by a seven year limit from 18 March 1986). If you made a chargeable transfer it was added to all chargeable transfers which you made in the previous ten years and any made before that time dropped out. Thus suppose you gifted £50,000 in May 1974 and then nothing more until June 1984, your capital transfer tax on a gift then of £60,000 was calculated completely ignoring the earlier gift.

22.8 The seven year cumulation period

(ITA 1984 S3A)

Regarding chargeable transfers and deaths occurring after 17 March 1986, the cumulation period was reduced to seven years. This means that any transfers which you made in the three years to 17 March 1979 immediately fell out of cumulation regarding transfers after 17 March 1986.

Remember that only a limited category of transfers come into charge immediately (22.5). PETs (22.3) are only cumulated and charged to inheritance tax if you die within seven years. Then the PETs become *chargeable transfers* and are brought into cumulation with previous chargeable transfers within seven years of each PET (including the PETs within seven years of death). The estate left at death (22.14) is then added to the chargeable transfers in the last seven years in order to compute the inheritance tax on those assets.

22.9 Indexation of rate bands

(ITA 1984 S8 & FA 1996 S183)

For each year to 5 April, the inheritance tax rate or rates (22.5) are to apply subject to indexation. The threshold and the various rate-bands will be increased in proportion to the rise in the retail prices index from September to September and each new threshold will be rounded up to the nearest £1,000. This applies unless the Treasury otherwise directs (as regarding 1993–94 and 1994–95 when there was no indexing).

22.10 Valuation

(ITA 1984 Ss160–170 & FA 1993 S200)

For inheritance tax purposes your assets are normally valued at their open market value at the transfer date. If the value of an asset which you keep is affected by the transfer, you will need to value your 'estate' both before and after the transfer in order to calculate its resultant fall. Your liabilities must be taken into account in valuing your total 'estate'. Regarding appeals as to the value of land, the Special Commissioners are able to refer to the Lands Tribunal.

22.11 Quoted securities passing on death
(ITA 1984 Ss178–189 & FA 1993 S198)

Relief is available where quoted securities are sold for less than their probate values within 12 months of death. This applies where any quoted shares or securities or holdings in authorised unit trusts are realised within one year of death. The persons liable to pay the inheritance tax can claim that the total of the gross sale prices should be substituted for the original probate values of the investments. Where, however, the proceeds are re-invested by those persons in quoted shares or unit trusts after the death and within two months after the last sale, the above relief may be reduced or lost.

For deaths after 15 March 1992, the relief is extended to investments cancelled within 12 months of the date of death; also where quotation is suspended in the 12 months after death. It is necessary that at the date of cancellation or first anniversary, the shares are still held by the person liable for the tax.

22.12 Valuation of related property
(ITA 1984 S161)

Where the value of any of your property is less than the appropriate portion of the value of the aggregate of that and any 'related property' you must value your own property as the appropriate portion of the value of that aggregate.

'Related property' is property belonging to your spouse. It also includes property belonging to a charity, charitable trust, housing association, etc or which had belonged to it during the last five years, and came from an exempt transfer from you or your spouse after 15 April 1976.

This rule is particularly relevant to the valuation of unquoted shares. For example if you and your wife each have 40 per cent of the shares of an unquoted company, then the value of 80 per cent of the shares is normally much higher than twice the value of 40 per cent of the shares. This is because an 80 per cent holding carries with it full control of the company.

Thus the successful estate duty saving device of splitting a shareholding in a non-quoted company between your wife and yourself so that neither of you has control, is not effective (so far as the first transfer is concerned) in producing a lower aggregate value for inheritance tax purposes.

If you inherit any related property, a special relief applies where you sell the property within three years of the death for less than the value on which tax was originally paid. Subject to various conditions including the requirement that the sale is at arm's length for a freely negotiated price, you can claim for the related property in question to be revalued at death on the basis that it was not related to any other property.

22.13 Land sold within three years of death

(ITA 1984 Ss190–198)

Where the person paying the capital transfer tax or inheritance tax arising on death after 15 March 1990 on land or buildings sells them within four years of the death for less than their probate value, he can claim that the sale proceeds are substituted in the tax calculations. For sales before 16 March 1993, the period was three years.

There are a number of conditions including the requirement that the shortfall is at least the lower of £1,000 and 5 per cent of the probate value of the land. Relief is extended regarding a compulsory purchase notified before the end of three years from death.

22.14 Inheritance tax on death

(ITA 1984 S4 & FA 1986 Sch 19)

The general rule is that if you are domiciled (or deemed domiciled — 22.4) in the UK at the time of your death, all of your assets, wherever they may be situated, form part of the *gross value* of your estate for the purposes of determining the inheritance tax payable. The same applied for capital transfer tax.

If you are not domiciled in the UK at your death then the tax is only chargeable on those assets which are situated in the UK (22.28).

The *net value* of your estate is determined by making certain deductions (22.14.2) from the *gross value* of all the property passing on your death.

The tax on your death is charged as if immediately before your death you made a chargeable transfer equal to the *net value* of your estate, subject to certain adjustments and exemptions (22.15) if appropriate.

For deaths after 17 March 1986, the inheritance tax rules apply and the tax is calculated from the single scale taking account of your cumulative lifetime gifts within *seven* years of death. These gifts include PETs (22.3) on which no tax was previously paid. As previously explained, death may lead not only to tax on the estate but also on lifetime gifts (22.6).

Your executors will need to apply for probate of your will. Otherwise, if you die intestate, letters of administration must be obtained. In either case, it will be necessary for an inheritance tax account to be completed (normally on CAP Form 202 or 200). At least a provisional amount of tax will need to be paid at that time. Further administrative rules appear later in this chapter (22.24).

22.14.1 Gross value of estate
(ITA 1984 S5)

The gross value of your estate includes all your property situated anywhere in the world, such as land, shares, the goodwill of a business, debts owing to you, etc; apart from *excluded property* (22.15).

Certain other amounts must also be included in your gross estate, even though they do not belong to you or only arise after your death, such as the proceeds of a life policy held by you on your own life, or any death benefit under a pension scheme which is payable to your estate (rather than under the more usual discretionary disposal clause contained in most pension schemes).

Other amounts to be included in your gross estate are various interests in trusts (22.30). In these cases the trustees may pay the appropriate tax but the rate is calculated by reference to the value of the estate including the trust funds.

22.14.2 Net value of estate

The more common deductions which are made from the gross value of your estate in order to arrive at its net value are as follows:

(1) Certain exempt transfers (22.17.3).
(2) Funeral expenses.
(3) Debts owing by you at the date of death which are payable in the UK. However, certain debts may be disallowed in whole or part if

you had made connected gifts to the creditors, or the liability had not been incurred for full consideration for your benefit. This applies to post-17 March 1986 debts (FA 1986 S82).

(4) Debts due to persons outside the UK are normally only deductible from the value of assets situated outside this country.

(5) Whilst legal and other professional fees owing at the death may be deducted as debts, no deduction is given for probate and executors' expenses.

(6) Liabilities for income tax and capital gains tax up to the time of death, whether or not assessments were made before that time. No deduction can be made for inheritance tax payable on your death, however, nor can tax liabilities be deducted regarding income and capital gains arising for periods subsequent to your death.

22.15 Excluded property

(ITA 1984 S6)

The following 'excluded property' must be left out of the value of your estate for capital transfer tax and inheritance tax purposes, regarding both lifetime transfers and property passing on death:

(1) Property outside the UK if you are neither domiciled nor deemed domiciled in this country.

(2) A reversionary interest unless either you bought it or it relates to the falling in of a lease which was treated as a settlement (22.30). Certain anti-avoidance rules apply to prevent misuse.

(3) Cash options under approved retirement pension schemes (14.3.2), provided an annuity becomes payable to your dependants instead of the cash option itself.

(4) Certain UK government securities on which interest may be paid gross to non-residents (8.2), provided you are neither domiciled, deemed domiciled, nor ordinarily resident here.

(5) Certain overseas pensions from former colonies, etc including death payments and returns of contributions.

(6) Savings such as national savings certificates and premium bonds, if you are domiciled in the Channel Islands or the Isle of Man.

(7) Certain property in this country belonging to visiting forces and NATO headquarters staff.

22.16 Double taxation relief

(ITA 1984 Ss158 & 159)

Various other countries also operate systems of capital transfer tax/ inheritance tax and the government of the UK is empowered to enter into agreements with them for the avoidance of the double payment of such tax both here and in the other country.

Concerning capital transfer tax or inheritance tax payable on death, relief is continued for estate duty payable on the same property in other countries if there was a 'double estate duty' agreement with the countries in question as at 12 March 1975. The following countries have agreements with the UK covering estate duty and/or capital transfer tax or inheritance tax:

France	Pakistan
India	South Africa
Ireland	Sweden
Italy	Switzerland
Netherlands	United States of America

Unilateral double taxation relief is available for overseas tax paid on death or a lifetime transfer. The tax must be of a similar nature to inheritance tax and if the property is situated in the overseas country, a credit is given against the UK tax of the amount of the overseas tax. If the property is either situated *both* in the UK and the overseas country, or in *neither* of those places, the credit against the UK tax is $C \times A/(A+B)$. A is the amount of inheritance tax, B is the overseas tax and C is the smaller of A and B.

22.17 Exempt transfers
(ITA 1984 Ss18–27)

Broadly, exempt transfers can be divided between those which apply both on death and during your life and those which are only exempt if the transfers are during your life. The first category includes transfers between your wife and yourself.

22.17.1 Transfers between husband and wife

Transfers between your wife and yourself both during your lives and on death were exempt from capital transfer tax and are exempt from inheritance tax. (Thus lifetime gifts are not even treated as PETs — 22.3.)

Full exemption does not apply, however, if the recipient of the property is not domiciled (or deemed domiciled) in this country (17.2) (unless the donor is also neither domiciled nor deemed domiciled here). In this case, only the first £55,000 transferred to the non-domiciled spouse is exempt. This resembles the previous estate duty relief.

Under the estate duty rules, if you left property in trust for your wife for life, when you died duty was paid; but none was payable on her subsequent death. (If her death is after 12 November 1974, no capital transfer tax or inheritance tax applies.) If, however, the first death occurs after 12 November 1974, the new relief applies and so no tax is payable on property passing to the surviving spouse. For this reason, when the latter dies, full inheritance tax is payable on the trust property.

22.17.2 Exempt transfers — lifetime gifts

The following transfers are only exempt if made by an individual during his life. They do not normally apply to transfers made by trustees nor to assets passing on death. In any one fiscal year to 5 April, you can make all of these exempt transfers cumulatively and so can your wife. From 18 March 1986 the rules apply not only to chargeable transfers but also to PETs (22.3). Thus if a transfer which would otherwise be a PET is an exempt transfer, it will not attract inheritance tax, even if you die within seven years.

(1) *Transfers each year up to a value of £3,000*. If you do not use up the full £3,000 allowance in one year, you can carry the unused part forward for one year only. If your transfers taken against this exemption reach £3,000 in one year, you have nothing available to carry forward, even though you may have had £3,000 carried forward from the previous year.
For example if you made no chargeable transfers in the year to 5 April 1997, you have £6,000 available for exempt transfers under this category in the year to 5 April 1998. If, however, you transferred £500 in the year to 5 April 1997 you have £2,500 carried forward and so can transfer £5,500 in the year to 5 April 1998.
In any year to 5 April, your annual exemption first reduces those lifetime transfers which are not PETs; and then your PETs. (FA 1986 Sch 19) (Deaths within seven years may cause the re-allocation of your annual exemptions, particularly regarding amounts originally set against your 'non-PETs' for the following year.)

(2) *Small gifts*. Outright gifts to any one person not exceeding £250 for each year to 5 April are exempt. The £250 exemption cannot be used against gifts larger than that amount. Thus you can make an unlimited number of exempt gifts of £250 to different people but any gifts of £251 or more must be set against the £3,000 and other exemptions with the excess being potentially taxable (if the nil rate band has been exhausted).

(3) *Normal expenditure out of income*. To qualify under this exemption, a transfer must be part of your normal expenditure. This

means that there must be an element of regularity. Life assurance premiums (9.2) are particularly suited for this. Further conditions are that the transfer is out of your after-tax income and you are left with enough income to maintain your usual standard of living. Life policy premium payments will not qualify for this exemption, however, if they are made out of an annuity purchased on your life, unless you can show that the policy and the annuity were effected completely independently of each other. This rule even applies if you make gifts out of your annuity receipts and the donee pays the premiums on the policy on your life.
If you buy an annuity, and make transfers from it, only the income proportion of the annuity (9.14) is treated as your income for the purposes of the normal expenditure rule, the capital element is not.

(4) *Gifts in consideration of marriage* made to one of the partners of the marriage or settled on the partners and their children, etc. The limits are £5,000 if the donor is a parent of one of the marriage partners, £2,500 if a grandparent or great-grandparent or one of the parties themselves, or otherwise £1,000. (Eligibility for relief extends to marriage gifts from settlements where an interest in possession ends (22.30).)

22.17.3 Other exempt transfers

Subject to the particular rules, the following transfers are exempt both if made during your life and on death. They also apply to trusts (22.30).

(1) *Transfers in the course of trade, etc* are exempt if allowed as deductions in computing the profits for income tax purposes (11.3). This applies equally to professions and vocations, as well as allowable deductions against other forms of profits or gains for the purposes of income tax and corporation tax.

(2) *Gifts to charities* are exempt without limit. Gifts to settlements for charitable purposes are covered by the exemption, as are gifts to charities from other trusts.

(3) *Gifts to political parties* are wholly exempt. For these purposes, a 'political party' is one with at least two members sitting in Parliament or one member and not less than 150,000 votes for its candidates at the last General Election.

(4) *Gifts for national purposes, etc* made to the National Trust, National Heritage Memorial Fund, National Gallery, British Museum and similar organisations including universities and their libraries as well as museums and art galleries maintained by local authorities or universities.

(5) *Gifts for public benefit* of property deemed by the Treasury to be of outstanding scenic, historic, scientific or artistic merit including land, buildings, pictures, books, manuscripts, works of art, etc.
(6) *PETs (22.3) of property held for national purposes, etc.* This exemption applies where, prior to the death of the recipient, the property is sold by private treaty (or gifted) to an organisation as mentioned in (4) previously.
(7) *Gifts of shares* to an employee trust provided it will then hold at least half of the ordinary shares of the company (ITA 1984 S28).
(8) *Gifts to housing associations* or sales of land to them at undervalue (ITA 1984 S24A).

22.18 Relief for business property
(ITA 1984 Ss103–114 & FA 1996 S184)

In general, 'relevant business property' qualifies for business property relief. 'Relevant business property' includes a business or part of a business; shares and securities owned by the controller of a company; unquoted minority shareholdings and land, buildings, plant and machinery used in your partnership or a company which you control. Control of a company for these purposes includes shareholdings which are 'related property' (22.12) in relation to your own shares.

In general, investment company and land or share-dealing company shareholdings do not qualify for the relief. However, UK stockjobbing and from October 1986 'market making' qualify for the relief. You must normally own the business property, or property which has directly replaced it for at least two years prior to the transfer or else it is not 'relevant business property' and so no relief is due.

The rates of relief are 100 per cent and 50 per cent. Prior to 10 March 1992 the relief was 50 per cent and 30 per cent. The scope of the 100 per cent relief became wider on 6 April 1996.

Relief is available as follows (pre-6 April 1996 figures in brackets where different):

(1) The whole or part of a business — 100 per cent.
(2) Quoted shares or securities in a trading company which you control — 50 per cent.
(3) Property transferred by you which is used in a trade by a company controlled by you or partnership in which you are a partner —50 per cent.
(4) Unquoted shares in a trading company:—

Over 25 per cent voting power	100 per cent
25 per cent or less without control (including related property)	100 per cent (50 per cent)
(5) Holding in a USM company:—	
Over 25 per cent voting power	100 per cent
25 per cent or less without control (including related property)	100 per cent (50 per cent)

The 50 per cent relief category is extended to cover the transfer of land or buildings owned by a trust. Immediately before the transfer, the assets must have been used in his own trade by a person beneficially entitled to an interest in possession in the trust.

Business property relief is available against PETs which fall into charge following the donor's death within seven years. However, the relief is lost if the recipient disposes of the property before the donor's death. But relief is not lost if the gifted business property is disposed of, but replaced by other qualifying assets within three years. (For chargeable events such as deaths before 30 November 1993, this period was one year.) Also, the property must remain 'relevant business property' during the seven year period. If these conditions are satisfied for only part of the property, the relief is proportionately reduced. These rules also apply to other lifetime transfers within seven years of death.

Where part of an estate is left to the surviving spouse and thus attracts no tax, and part to others, the allocation of business property relief and relief for agricultural property (22.21) was open to abuse. However, from 18 March 1986 specific gifts of such property must be reduced by the relief. Otherwise, the relief is spread proportionately over the estate.

22.19 Waivers of dividends and remuneration

(ITA 1984 Ss14 & 15)

If you waive any remuneration to which you are entitled this normally does not produce any capital transfer tax or inheritance tax liability, provided the amount waived would otherwise have been assessable to income tax under Schedule E (10.1) and your employer obtains no income tax or corporation tax relief for the waived remuneration.

No inheritance tax accrues on the waiver of any dividend to which you have a right, provided you waive the dividend within the 12 months before it is due. These waiver rules apply from the inception of capital transfer tax.

22.20 Conditional exemption for certain objects and buildings, etc

(ITA 1984 Ss27, 57A, 78–79 & Sch 4)

Property similar to that mentioned in (4) and (5) above (22.17.3), is exempted from inheritance tax on death provided the recipient undertakes to keep it in the country, preserve it and allow reasonable access to the public. If it is later sold the tax is payable unless the sale is to an institution such as the British Museum, National Gallery or National Trust.

A similar relief applies to lifetime transfers subject to various conditions. The recipient must give the required undertaking. The relief extends to historical and artistic buildings and objects comprised in settlements. It also applies to settlements set up to maintain historic buildings and now objects historically associated with them, together with land of outstanding interest. Such settlements must tie up the capital for at least six years for maintenance purposes only. But after that funds may be withdrawn subject to inheritance tax in certain circumstances.

Special rules apply regarding maintenance settlements for approved objects and buildings, etc. Provided the Board of the Inland Revenue (previously the Treasury) are satisfied that the trusts and trustees comply with certain requirements, transfers to such a settlement are exempt (22.17.3) for inheritance purposes. In general the trust funds must be used for the maintenance of approved assets for at least six years.

From 17 March 1987, the exemption applies where someone with a life interest in a trust dies and within two years the property goes into a heritage maintenance fund. Heritage property can be offered in lieu of inheritance tax and, from that date, there is the option of calculating the value of the property at the date of the offer instead of acceptance.

Land is exempted which is essential to a building of historic or architectural interest. Previously exemption depended on the land touching the building, but this is no longer necessary.

22.21 Relief for agricultural property
(ITA 1984 Ss115–124 & FA 1996 S185)

Under the rules which apply after 9 March 1981 you must have either occupied the property for the purposes of agriculture for at least two years before transferring it, or owned it for seven years up to that time, with others farming. The rules are relaxed where you inherit the property or where you have replaced one agricultural property by another. Agriculture includes stud farming for the purposes of the relief and also (from 29 November 1994) the cultivation of short rotation coppice (FA 1995 S154). From 26 November 1996, farmland which has been dedicated to wildlife habitats will also be eligible for relief subject to the rules (FA 1997 S94).

The relief is 100 per cent if you enjoy the right to vacant possession or can obtain this within the next 12 months. 100 per cent relief also applies to transfers of tenanted farmland where the tenancy starts after 1 September 1995. Where a tenancy is acquired by succession following the previous tenant's death, it is treated as a tenancy starting from the date of death.

Otherwise, the relief is normally 50 per cent, which applies to existing tenanted situations, etc. Prior to 10 March 1992, the rates were 50 per cent and 30 per cent. If you qualified for the higher relief under the old but not the new rules, you still obtain this regarding property held at 9 March 1981 and transferred after that date, up to the old limit of £250,000 or 1,000 acres if more valuable. The excess is then relieved at the lower rate which is now 50 per cent.

By concession, 100 per cent relief (not 50 per cent) applies on your transfer of tenanted agricultural land, where you have the right to vacant possession within 24 months; also where the value transferred is broadly the vacant possession value of the property. This concession applies for transfers after 12 February 1995 and earlier cases which are still open. Another concession, operative from the same time, allows 50 per cent relief on certain farm cottages even though the occupier has retired.

The grant of a tenancy of agricultural property is not to be treated as a transfer of value if it is made for full consideration (ITA 1984 S16).

From 18 March 1986, similar rules to those for business property relief apply regarding lifetime gifts within seven years of death and the allocation of relief to partially exempt estates (22.18). Thus the relief is lost if the recipient disposes of the agricultural property before the donor's death unless it is replaced within three (previously one) years by other agricultural property.

22.22 Woodlands

(ITA 1984 Ss125–130)

Inheritance tax relief against the charge at death on growing timber is available, provided you either owned the woodlands for at least five years, or you acquired them by gift or inheritance.

Under the relieving provisions, provided the inheritor elects within two years of it, tax is not charged on your death. If, however, before the recipient dies, the timber is sold or given away, tax is charged on the proceeds or value of the gift. The tax rate is found by adding such proceeds to the estate at your death. Remember that the relief applies only to the timber and not the land on which it grows. However, the land may qualify for business property relief.

Where the disposal follows a change in tax rates the respective new rates (26.4) are applied, even if the death was before they took effect.

22.23 Quick succession relief

(ITA 1984 S141)

This relief applies to reduce the tax payable on death where the deceased himself received chargeable transfers on which the tax was paid within five years of his death. The deduction is broadly a proportion of the original tax, being 100 per cent, 80 per cent, 60 per cent, 40 per cent or 20 per cent, depending on whether the period between the transfer and the death is one, two, three, four or five years or less in each case. Where there are more than two transfers of the same property within five years of each other, special rules apply.

22.24 Administration and collection

(ITA 1984 Ss215–261, etc & FA 1986 Sch 18)

Inheritance tax (and capital transfer tax) are under the care and management of the Board of the Inland Revenue. Generally speaking the rules for administration, appeals and penalties resemble those for income tax (16.9.2).

Chargeable transfers must be reported to the Inland Revenue within 12 months from the end of the month of transfer or death.

The tax chargeable on death must be paid on at least an estimated figure before probate is granted (22.14). Such inheritance tax (and capital transfer tax) are payable out of the residuary estate unless there is a contrary direction in the will. However, property situated outside the UK continues to bear its own tax. Recipients of PETs are primarily responsible for the relevant tax.

Interest on unpaid tax runs from when the tax is due. The due date is six months after the end of the month in which death occurs. For lifetime transfers it is six months after the end of the month in which the transfer is made. In the case of transfers between 5 April and 1 October, the due date is 30 April in the following year.

From 16 December 1986, a single rate of interest applies to overdue inheritance tax. This is currently 5 per cent and has varied as follows:

From	*Rate* %
16 December 1986	8
6 June 1987	6
6 August 1988	8
6 October 1988	9
6 July 1989	11
6 March 1991	10
6 May 1991	9
6 July 1991	8
6 November 1992	6
6 December 1992	5
6 January 1994	4
6 October 1994	5

The interest is not deductible for income tax purposes. If you overpay inheritance tax or capital transfer tax you will get non-taxable interest at the same rates, up to the date on which the repayment of the excess tax is made.

22.25 Payment by instalments of tax on death

(ITA 1984 Ss227–229, FA 1986 Sch 19 & F2A 1992 Sch 14)

Capital transfer tax or inheritance tax on death on certain assets may be paid by annual instalments over ten years. This applies to land and buildings, controlling holdings of shares in companies and certain other unquoted shares, as well as business assets. Also, shares dealt in on the USM are included. (PETs which become chargeable only qualify for the instalments basis if the recipient had kept the property until the death of the donor.)

Instalments paid on time concerning the shares and business assets mentioned above are free of interest. Land and buildings qualify for this relief only if they are held as business assets, otherwise interest is payable, currently at 5 per cent. Tax in respect of property qualifying for agricultural relief may be paid in interest free instalments as above.

22.26 Payment of tax on lifetime gifts by instalments

The above provisions apply to lifetime transfers if the donee bears the tax and for settled property which is retained in a settlement. If interest is payable it is currently at 5 per cent. The interest free category is extended to include lifetime disposals of timber. In the case of minority holdings of unquoted shares, these must be worth at least £20,000, in order to qualify for the instalments option; also being at least 10 per cent holdings. The instalments basis may also be allowed where paying the tax in one sum would cause undue hardship and the recipient keeps the shares.

22.27 Inheritance tax and life assurance

Life assurance policies can be used to create a fund to pay future inheritance tax and to facilitate gifts to your beneficiaries.

If you effect a policy on your life for your own benefit, the proceeds payable on your death will be taxable as part of your net estate (22.14.1).

22.27.1 Policies written in trust

You may effect a policy in a non-discretionary trust for some other person or persons, such as for example your wife and children. In this case the policy proceeds will not be paid into your own estate but will be paid to the trustees for the beneficiaries. Each premium payment, however, will constitute a separate potentially exempt transfer (22.3) by you. Thus they could be taxable if you die within seven years, unless an exemption applies such as the £3,000 or £250 reliefs (22.17.2), or the normal expenditure rule (22.17.2), or the policy is for your wife. If premiums are paid to a discretionary trust, each premium will be chargeable at the time and if no exemption applies, may give rise to recalculation of tax if death occurs within seven years.

22.27.2 Gifts of policies

Where you write a policy in trust, this is one way of gifting it. Another way is to assign the policy. Unless it is covered by exemptions (22.27.1) there will usually be a potentially exempt transfer. The transfer value is normally the greater of your gross premium payments and the surrender value of the policy. Your assignment will be potentially exempt if it is to an individual or certain kinds of trust (interest in possession, accumulation and maintenance, or for the disabled). If you make cash gifts to cover subsequent premiums, these gifts will normally be potentially exempt.

However, for policies effected after 17 March 1986, the gifts with reservation rules (22.29.4) may apply. Broadly if you have a retained benefit in the policy the proceeds will form part of your estate at death.

22.27.3 'Life of another' policies

If someone else effects a policy on your life and pays the premiums, then the proceeds are not taxable on your death. This is known as a 'life of another' policy. If the person who effects the policy predeceases you, however, then the surrender value of the policy at the date of death of that person is normally included in his taxable estate.

22.28 Property outside Great Britain

Since if you are neither domiciled nor deemed domiciled (22.4) in the UK, you will only normally pay inheritance tax on your assets situated here, it is important to ascertain the situation of particular property. The situation of property for inheritance tax purposes is normally deemed to be as follows:

(1) Cash — its physical location.
(2) Bank accounts — the location of the bank or branch (see also below).
(3) Registered securities — the location of the share register.
(4) Bearer securities — the location of the title documents.
(5) Land and buildings — their actual location.
(6) Business assets — the place where the business is conducted.
(7) Debts — the residence of the debtor.

Foreign currency accounts with UK banks are exempted from inheritance tax if the deceased is not UK domiciled. This also applies if the deceased had an interest in possession (22.30) in a settlement with such an account, unless the settlor was UK domiciled, resident or ordinarily resident, when he made the settlement or the trustees were so situated immediately before the death. (ITA 1984 S158.)

22.29 Miscellaneous points

22.29.1 Close companies

(ITA 1984 Ss94–102 & FA 1986 Sch 19)

There are rules under which inheritance tax may be charged where a close company (13.17) makes a transfer of value. Broadly, tax may be charged on the company as if each of the participators (13.17.2) had made a proportionate transfer according to his or her interest in the company. The rules are extended to cover close companies being owned by trusts or being their beneficiaries.

Transfers of values arising as above from alterations in the capital and associated rights in a close company may attract inheritance tax at once. They are not PETs (22.3).

22.29.2 Free loans

(ITA 1984 S29)

From 6 April 1976 to 5 April 1981, subject to various exceptions, if you allowed someone else the use of money or property at no interest or less than the market rate, you were treated as making a chargeable transfer for each year to 5 April that the arrangement continued. These provisions ceased to have effect after 5 April 1981 although interest-free loans for a fixed stated period can still be treated as a chargeable transfer under general principles.

22.29.3 Associated operations

(ITA 1984 S268)

Special rules enable the Revenue to treat two or more transactions related to a certain property as forming one 'chargeable transfer'. Where transactions at different times are treated as associated operations, the chargeable transfer is treated as taking place at the time of the last of these transactions.

22.29.4 Gifts with reservation

(FA 1986 S102 & Sch 20)

If you make a gift after 17 March 1986 but reserve some benefit, this will normally result in the property remaining yours for inheritance tax purposes on your death. (This could also apply if you later enjoy the benefit of the gifted property.) However, if you subsequently release the reservation, you will be treated as making a PET (22.3) or chargeable transfer at that time. In contrast to PETs, the Capital Taxes Office may require a return to be made for a gift with reservation.

A particular example is where you gift a house but remain living there. The rule does not apply if your benefit is minimal (eg, you do not live in the house but only pay occasional visits). If you give full value for any benefit (eg, pay a full rent for the house), the rule is also set aside. There is also an exception where the reservation represents reasonable provision by a relative for the care and maintenance of an elderly or infirm donor whose circumstances have changed since making the gift.

The rules do not normally catch regular premium insurance policies made before 18 March 1986 and not altered since then.

22.29.5 Family maintenance

(ITA 1984 S11)

If you make any of the following gifts during your life, they are exempt:

(1) For the maintenance, education, etc of your child, former wife or illegitimate child.
(2) For the maintenance or education of a child not in his parent's care, who has been in your care during substantial periods of his minority.
(3) For the care or maintenance of a dependent relative.

22.29.6 Deeds of family arrangement

(ITA 1984 S17)

Inheritance tax is not charged on certain variations in the destination of property passing on death. Nor is it charged on the disclaimer of title to property passing on death. The variation or disclaimer must be within two years of the death. An election to the Revenue is required within six months of a variation.

This exemption operates similarly, but without time limit, where a surviving spouse's life interest under an intestacy is redeemed. It also applies if an interest in settled property is disclaimed unless there is some consideration in money or money's worth.

Disclaimers are effective for inheritance tax purposes. These involve one or more beneficiaries disclaiming their entitlement. As a result, the assets return to the estate and are dealt with according to the directions of the will or as on intestacy.

22.30 Settled property
(ITA 1984 Pt III)

The rules concerning inheritance tax (and previously capital transfer tax) in relation to settled property are most detailed and the following are just a few guidelines:

(1) Broadly any settlement is subject to the inheritance tax rules on its world-wide assets, if at the time it was made the settlor was domiciled in the UK. Otherwise only assets situated in this country (22.28) are caught.
(2) The settlement of any property after 26 March 1974 is itself treated as a chargeable transfer by the settlor. However, after 17 March 1986, settlements on accumulation and maintenance trusts (22.30.1) or for the disabled are classified as PETs (22.3). Thus any property which you settle in this way only attracts inheritance tax if you die within seven years.
(3) If you have an interest in possession in any settled property for the time being (eg, you receive the income as of right), the property itself is treated as yours for inheritance tax purposes. Thus if your interest ends, you will be treated as making a transfer of the value of the property concerned. The tax is calculated on the basis of your cumulative transfers to that time. You can deduct your £3,000 annual exemption (22.17.2) and marriage allowance if applicable (ITA S57).
(4) From 17 March 1987 lifetime transactions involving interest in possession settlements are classed as PETs. This covers gifts setting them up, transfers out and changes in the beneficial interests.
(5) No inheritance tax is payable if you obtain an absolute interest in property in which you previously had a life interest (or other interest in possession). Similarly, tax normally is not payable on the reversion to you in your lifetime (or your spouse within two years of your death) of property which you previously settled. However, this rule normally no longer applies to discretionary settlements (22.30.2).

(6) Special rules apply to trusts where there is no interest in possession—particularly discretionary trusts, etc and accumulation and maintenance settlements (22.30.1).
(7) Quick succession relief is given if an interest in possession comes to an end within five years of a previous chargeable transfer of the settled property. The relief is now allowed against the tax due on the later transfer, etc but is calculated as a *percentage of the tax payable* on the first transfer. The percentage is 100 per cent, 80 per cent, 60 per cent, 40 per cent or 20 per cent where the interval is not more than one, two, three, four, or five years respectively.
(8) Superannuation schemes and charitable trusts are normally exempted from inheritance tax as are employee and newspaper trusts (ITA Ss76, 86 & 87); also certain 'protective trusts' and trusts for the mentally disabled (treated as having a life interest in property settled for them after 9 March 1981). Where property is held temporarily on such trusts, the tax charge is proportionately reduced on a time basis (FA 1984 S102).

22.30.1 Accumulation and maintenance settlements

Accumulation and maintenance settlements with no fixed interests in possession for one or more beneficiaries up to an age not exceeding 25 are not subjected to the periodic charge (22.30.2); nor is inheritance tax charged on the capital distributed to those beneficiaries. This relief covers for example a settlement under which your son obtains an interest in possession at the age of 25 and at 35 gets the capital, the income being accumulated up to 25 apart from various payments for his maintenance. No inheritance tax is payable during the currency of the trust, nor when your son becomes entitled to the income at 25 nor the capital at 35.

Relief broadly only applies if either not more than 25 years have passed since the original settlement date (or when it first became accumulating); or if all beneficiaries are grandchildren of a common grandparent (or their widows, widowers, children, step-children, etc).

Any payments into accumulation and maintenance settlements after 17 March 1986 are PETs (22.3). Thus no inheritance tax can be payable regarding their creation unless the settlor dies within seven years.

22.30.2 Discretionary trusts, etc

The following rules apply where there is no interest in possession in *all or part of the property.*

(1) The principal charge to inheritance tax (previously capital transfer tax) is the *periodic* charge. This usually falls on every tenth anniversary of the date of the settlement occurring after 31 March 1983. (Where a transfer requiring court proceedings was made in the year to 31 March 1983, the onset of the periodic charge was delayed until after that date.) The charge is at 30 per cent of the life-time inheritance tax rate (itself now half of the full 40 per cent rate) which would apply to the assets held on discretionary trusts (taking the N/40ths fraction for additions during the ten year period — see (3) below).

(2) In calculating the rates of tax which apply, you must accumulate transfers made by the settlor in the seven years immediately prior to the creation of the settlement and other settlements made by him on the same day; but this does not apply to a pre-26 March 1974 trust. For periodic charges before 18 March 1986, you needed to accumulate transfers by the settlor in the *ten* years before the creation of the settlement.

(3) For a settlement made between 26 March 1974 and 9 March 1982, distributions of capital made in the preceding ten years are taken into account in calculating the rate of tax on the first periodic charge. An exemption applies for transfers to charities and benevolent funds for employees (this also applies to pre-27 March 1974 trusts).

(4) Interim charges are made on distributions of capital to beneficiaries between periodic charges, but only N/40ths of the full tax is charged on each distribution. (N is the number of completed three month periods for which the property has been held on discretionary trusts during the current ten year period — see (1) above.)

(5) Previously, tax was charged on the value of the trust property leaving the trust. However, after 8 March 1982, the charge is based on the reduction in the value of trust property, which could be greater.

(6) If property becomes settled under a will or intestacy it is taken to enter the settlement at death. Where the death is after 12 March 1984 any such property which is distributed within two years of death to a charity, employee trust, etc is treated as if distributed at the time of death (FA 1984 S103).

(7) Property passing directly from one discretionary settlement to another is treated as remaining in the first for the purposes of the discretionary settlement rules. However, after 14 March 1983 this does not apply to certain reversionary interests existing before 10 December 1981 (FA 1984 S104).

(8) Prior to 9 March 1982, special rules applied to non-resident trustees although these would not normally have come into force until

after 31 March 1983. Now, however, the previously planned annual charge does not operate and non-resident trustees are liable for the periodic ten-year charge (see above).

(9) Transfers into discretionary settlements are charged to inheritance tax at half the rates applicable at death. If death occurred within three years and the original transfer was before 18 March 1986, the tax is increased by using the full rates at death (22.5.1). Subsequent to that date, if death occurs broadly within five years of a post-17 March 1986 transfer, the tax is likely to be increased, subject to tapering relief (22.6). 100 per cent of tax at full rates is due if death is within three years of the transfer, 80 per cent in the fourth year and 60 per cent in the fifth year.

22.31 Avoiding double charges
(FA 1986 S104)

Rules were introduced to prevent double charges to inheritance tax on transfers of value and other events occurring after 17 March 1986. The rules in part take the place of the previous rules regarding mutual transfers. The situations covered include where a PET (22.3) becomes chargeable and immediately before the death the estate includes property acquired from the person who received the PET for less than full price.

22.32 Example: Calculation of inheritance tax payable

Mr A, having made no gifts relevant for capital transfer tax or inheritance tax, gives £56,000 to his son on 30 June 1994 and £100,000 to his wife on 15 September 1994. He dies on 31 May 1997 leaving an estate valued at £470,000, including £50,000 to his wife, £30,000 to charity and the remainder to his son, including his non-quoted shares in a family trading company valued at £120,000.

Inheritance tax is payable as follows:

30 June 1994 — gift to son		£56,000
Less Annual exemption 1993–94 brought forward	£3,000	
Annual exemption 1994–95	3,000	6,000
Potentially exempt (22.3)		£50,000

		£	£
15 September 1994 — gift to wife is exempt provided she is UK domiciled (17.2)			
Estate at death 31 May 1997			470,000
Less Bequests free of inheritance tax:			
To wife		50,000	
To charity		30,000	80,000
			390,000
Less business property relief (22.18) 100% × £120,000			120,000
			270,000
Potentially exempt transfer 30 June 1994			50,000
			£320,000
Inheritance tax on £320,000 : £215,000		Nil	—
£105,000	40%		£ 42,000

23 An outline of VAT

23.1 Introduction

VAT was introduced into the UK on 1 April 1973 with an original rate of 10 per cent. A rate of 15 per cent replaced the previous 8 per cent standard rate and $12\frac{1}{2}$ per cent higher rate on 18 June 1979. The rate was increased to $17\frac{1}{2}$ per cent from 1 April 1991. All other countries now in the European Community have introduced a similar tax and the coverage, but not the rates, has been (at least in theory) harmonised. It is beyond the scope of this book to give more than a brief outline of the provisions of VAT.

VAT in the UK is imposed:

(1) on imports of goods by any person into the UK (subject to special EC rules — 23.17);
(2) on the supply (such as sale, hire and HP) of goods and services (which together comprise virtually all supplies) by a business in the UK; and
(3) in certain circumstances the import of services by a business.

Hence the tax is payable whenever goods or services pass from one business to another or to a private consumer, although in the former case it is frequently refunded.

After the end of each accounting period for the tax (usually a period of three months) each business has to render a *return* to Customs & Excise of all its 'outputs', ie, the supplies of goods and services it has made during the period to other businesses or to consumers; and has to account to Customs & Excise one month after the end of the period for VAT on the prices (before tax) of those outputs. Each business is, at the same time, normally allowed a credit for the VAT on its 'inputs' in that period, ie, goods imported by it and goods and services supplied to it for the purposes of the business. Unlike income tax or corporation tax, no distinction is made between capital or revenue inputs; the credit generally extends to the tax on its capital purchases as well as on its purchases of stock in trade.

The total tax on the inputs of a business is ascertained from the tax invoices given to it by every other business which has supplied it with goods or services. Amongst other details a typical tax invoice shows:

Goods	£100.00
VAT at $17\frac{1}{2}$%	17.50
Price payable	£117.50

At the end of each accounting period the business will total all the tax invoices it has received for its inputs in that period, which it must keep for production to Customs & Excise when required, together with its vouchers for tax imports; it will also total all its outputs for the period (keeping copies of all tax invoices it has rendered to other businesses) and a typical return for an accounting period will show:

Total outputs during the period	£50,000	
VAT thereon		£8,750
Total inputs for the period	£20,000	
VAT thereon		£3,500
Balance payable to Customs & Excise		£5,250

The effect of the credit mechanism is that although VAT is charged on each business in the chain of import, production and distribution, each business in the chain gets a credit for the tax on its inputs, so that the whole tax is passed on to the consumer on the final sale to him. This is best shown by an example which uses the original 10 per cent rate for simplicity:

	Price (ex-VAT)	*VAT*	
Manufacturer imports raw materials	£10	£1	
Manufacturer accounts to C & E on import			£1

Manufacturer sells product to wholesaler	£100	£10	
Manufacturer accounts to C & E for VAT			£9 (10–1)
Wholesaler sells product to retailer	£150	£15	
Wholesaler accounts to C & E for VAT			£5 (15–10)
Retailer sells to consumer	£200	£20	
Retailer accounts to C & E for VAT			£5 (20–15)
Consumer bears VAT of		£20	
Customs & Excise collect			£20

This example, however, only shows how VAT is collected and borne over a series of transactions; it is not necessary to trace each item in this way, as the return at the end of each accounting period will cover all the inputs and outputs of the period. Credit for the VAT on unsold stock will have been given on its purchase and it will therefore be held tax free until sale.

Because of the credit mechanism outlined above a business does not normally bear much tax; it mainly acts as a collection agency. The ultimate consumer bears all the tax, which is why VAT is described as a sales tax. The difficulty of having a retail sales tax lies in determining when the final retail sale takes place. With VAT it does not matter; if the purchaser is a VAT registered business, he will generally get credit for the tax as input tax, and if he is not he will bear it. Another advantage of the credit mechanism is that the effect is neutral between supplies which go through a number of stages and those where the supplier is vertically integrated. In both cases the tax is on the amount of the final price to the consumer.

A turnover tax charges tax on tax and therefore encourages vertical integration which is not usually in the public interest.

As will be seen later (23.3), businesses which make some 'exempt' supplies do not normally get credit for the VAT on their inputs relating to these supplies.

23.2 VAT in practice

All businesses (23.4), except for the very small, are normally required to be registered with Customs & Excise and they have to make returns every three months. Some businesses which are likely to have repayments of tax, however, because they make zero-rated supplies, are allowed a one-month period. The return has to be completed and the tax paid by the end of the following month. Any amounts due to you will be paid but payments made to you in error may be recovered by assessment.

If Customs & Excise unreasonably delay any repayment to you, a repayment supplement of the greater of 5 per cent of the tax and £50 (previously £30) will be due. Also, you have the statutory right to claim interest on your overpayment of VAT due to the error of Customs & Excise. In future, interest rates will correspond more exactly with the Inland Revenue rates (16.8.2).

As from 18 July 1996, the powers of Customs & Excise to assess for undeclared VAT is limited to three years, except in cases of fraud and certain other cases, like 'do it yourself' housebuilders. Furthermore, the right to claim back overpaid VAT is restricted to a maximum of three years. Interest payable by the authorities is similarly limited (FA 1997, Ss44–49).

Businesses with annual turnovers under £300,000 which have been registered for at least one year are able to elect for annual VAT accounting. (Between 1 July 1988 and 9 April 1991, this figure was £250,000.) They make nine equal payments on account by direct debit and a tenth balancing amount with their annual return. Another arrangement open to businesses with outstanding VAT of not more than £5,000 and turnovers under £350,000 (before 1 April 1993, £300,000) is accounting for VAT on a cash rather than an invoice basis. Prior to 1 April 1993, written notice was required in advance.

From 1 April 1996 the voluntary annual accounting scheme is improved for businesses with turnovers below £100,000. Such a business is to make quarterly interim payments of 20 per cent of its VAT liability for the previous year. However, if this total is below £2,000, no interim payments need be made.

From 1 October 1992, very large taxpayers make monthly VAT payments. This applies to those with VAT of at least £2 million for their four quarters up to 31 March 1991 and they make VAT payments on account of the first two months each quarter. Other businesses join the scheme once it can be seen that their VAT liability will exceed the threshold. As from 1 June 1996, monthly payments are one-twenty-fourth of the annual liability, with an option to pay the true VAT monthly. However, all payments must be made by electronic means and cleared by the month-end.

23.2.1 Penalties

There are penalties which may be imposed by the Courts for overdue VAT returns and payments. Naturally, far heavier penalties apply in cases involving dishonesty.

The 1985 Finance Act contained stern provisions to counter VAT evasion and speed up tax payment. For example, failure to pay tax on time or submit returns could have involved a 'default surcharge' of up to 30 per cent of the VAT involved. This operated from 1 October 1986. From 1 April 1992, the maximum penalty was 20 per cent with 15 per cent applying from 1 April 1993. However, from 1 October 1993, a new minimum rate of 2 per cent applies for the first default after a surcharge liability notice.

From 16 March 1988, the penalties on late registration for VAT were varied to 10 per cent, 20 per cent and 30 per cent of the tax. These rates apply where registration is late by no more than nine months, 18 months and more than 18 months respectively. The rates of penalty are reduced from 1 January 1995 to 5, 10 and 15 per cent.

As from April 1990, a 'serious misdeclaration penalty' operated at 30 per cent of the tax. However, from 20 March 1991, the rate was reduced to 20 per cent, with 15 per cent applying from 11 March 1992. There is a 'period of grace' extending to the due date for the next return. Also, the penalty will not now normally apply where misdeclarations are compensated for in the next return, nor where the undeclared tax is less than the lower of £1,000,000 and 30 per cent of the 'gross tax'. 'Gross tax' means your VAT on both inputs and outputs.

Furthermore, FA 1988 S16 introduced a 15 per cent penalty on 'persistent misdeclaration resulting in understatements or overclaims'. This penalty will now only be used where a person has under-declared or over-claimed tax three times within twelve accounting periods and a written warning has been issued. Also, the misdeclaration in each period must be at least 10 per cent of the 'gross tax' or £500,000 if less. (Where a penalty is imposed for 'serious misdeclaration', it will also be included in the reckoning for 'persistent misdeclaration' penalty.)

Giving incorrect certificates of entitlement to zero-rating regarding supplies of fuel and power, new buildings or construction services is liable to a civil penalty. However, this is now subject to mitigation.

23.2.2 Allocation of outputs and inputs to periods

There are rules determining into which period a supply falls. For goods it is normally the date when the goods are removed or made available, and for services it is the date of performance. (There are special rules where VAT rates change.) There are two exceptions. If an invoice (which must contain specified information) is issued within 14 days after that time, the date of the invoice is taken. In practice this will usually apply and the advantage is that the VAT return can be made up from the copy invoices.

The other exception is for payments in advance when it is the date of invoice or payment which counts. This is the only time payment is relevant; normally it is the invoice which matters (see below under 'Special Cases' for the position of bad debts). An arrangement can also be made with Customs & Excise to use the last day of the calendar month or of a VAT accounting period as the time of supply.

The same rules apply for determining into which period the inputs fall. Consequently, relief for input tax will normally be available before the invoice has been paid. The invoices will need to be kept as proof. The VAT return will be a summary of invoices issued and invoices received. If tax is due to Customs & Excise, it will be paid with the return. Inputs of goods and services incurred prior to registration may subsequently be recovered in certain circumstances.

Strictly speaking, tax on *imports* by a business is due at the date of import. However, in practice the VAT is payable by the 15th of the month following importation. (Payment must be by direct debit and covered by bank guarantee.) No tax is due so long as the goods are in a bonded warehouse. Taxable persons pay no VAT on temporary imports for repair, modification etc, provided ownership does not change. Where the reverse happens, VAT on the re-import only applies to the repairs, etc plus freight and insurance. Imports from EC countries are subject to special rules from 1 January 1993 (23.17).

23.3 Zero-rating and exemption

So far we have assumed that all the inputs and outputs of a business are taxable at a positive rate. Certain types of supply are treated specially either because they are 'zero-rated' or because they are 'exempt'. Details of these types are set out in Schedules 8 and 9 to the Value Added Tax Act 1994 and summaries of these Schedules are given later in this chapter.

If a supply is *zero-rated* this means that no tax is charged on the supply but credit is given to the supplier for all tax on his inputs relating to that supply. *Exports* of goods, for instance, are often zero-rated so that these leave the country free of VAT in the UK, although they may be liable to VAT in the country into which they are imported if that country imposes a VAT. However, exports to non-VAT registered customers in other EC member states may be taxable in the UK.

A business which exports most of its products will probably find that its returns for an accounting period show more tax on its inputs than on its outputs (the majority being zero-rated). In that event, the business can claim back the difference from Customs & Excise. Zero rating also applies to goods shipped for use as stores on a voyage or flight to a destination outside the UK, or for retail sale in transit. However, this does not apply to private voyages and flights.

The EC requires its members to have a VAT with a similar structure although different rates are allowed. One of the reasons is that the similar treatment of imports and exports ensures equality between home-produced and imported goods. Exports to EC countries are subject to special rules from 1 January 1993 (23.17).

In addition to exports, food and many other items sold within the UK (23.14) are also zero-rated.

Exemption of a supply of goods or services is not so favourable as zero-rating, for whilst this means that there is no VAT on the supply (as with zero-rating), there is no credit allowed for the corresponding tax on the inputs of the business. Thus life assurance is one of the exempt items (23.16) so that there is no tax on a premium on a life policy but the life assurance company can get no credit for the tax on those inputs which it uses for its life assurance business. This introduces a hidden tax cost to its business.

A business which supplies both taxable (including zero-rated) and exempt goods and services is a 'partly exempt' business and will have an accounting problem. When claiming credit for the tax on the inputs from Customs & Excise, it is entitled to credit for the tax on those inputs which it uses for its taxable supplies but it is not entitled to credit for the tax on those inputs which it uses for its exempt supplies.

Normally, a proportion of the business's input tax corresponding to its taxable supplies is allowed. However, if exempt input tax is less than £7,500 per year credit for input tax is not restricted. A new requirement from 1 December 1994 is that the exempt input tax is no more than 50 per cent of total input tax. VAT is only recoverable if attributable to:

(1) business taxable supplies;
(2) supplies outside the UK which would have been VATable or zero-rated if made here;
(3) business supplies of certain warehoused goods disregarded for VAT;
(4) overheads supporting the above.

23.4 Business

Central to the working of VAT is the definition of 'business' because the credit mechanism is applied only to a business. It is defined to include any trade, profession or vocation. It also includes clubs and associations, such as sports clubs and members' clubs. The charging of admission fees, for example by the National Trust, is also taxable as a business. VAT is not charged on subscriptions to political parties, trade unions or professional bodies.

23.5 Small traders

From 27 November 1996 a person whose taxable (including zero-rated) supplies are not more than £48,000 (previously £47,000) per annum is not liable to be registered, although he can apply to be registered voluntarily. A business is required to register if the value of taxable supplies in the past 12 months exceeded £48,000. Alternatively, registration is required if there are reasonable grounds for believing that the value of taxable supplies will exceed £48,000 in the next 30 days.

A small trader who is not registered is in the same position as a business making only exempt supplies. He does not charge tax to his customers and has to bear any input tax.

From 27 November 1996 *deregistration* is in general allowed if Customs & Excise are satisfied that the taxable supplies for the ensuing year will not exceed £46,000 (previously £45,000).

23.6 Zero-rated supplies

A person whose supplies are all zero-rated can apply to be exempted from registration. He will not then be able to claim a refund of his input tax but he will not have to make VAT returns.

23.7 Groups and divisions of companies

A group of companies may be registered as a single business and supplies between members of the group will be ignored. The requirement that the companies should be UK resident has now been widened to include overseas companies with an established UK place of business. One company in the group is responsible for making returns for all the members of the group. Alternatively, a company which is organised in divisions can register each division separately.

Rules introduced in 1986 allow the Commissioners of Customs & Excise to direct that separately registered entities are treated as one for VAT purposes. This applies for companies and other traders. The object is to combat artificially splitting a single business to avoid registration. Certain avoidance schemes involving the movement of a company or the transfer of assets in or out of a group from 29 November 1995 are also countered. Further anti-avoidance measures take effect from 27 November 1996 regarding groups.

From 1 April 1990, capital items, such as computers, land and buildings over specified value limits are excluded from the VAT self-supply charge (23.11.3), which otherwise arises when assets are transferred to a partly exempt VAT group as part of the transfer of a going concern.

23.8 Local authorities

Local authorities are in the position of being both in business and also carrying on non-business activities, such as welfare services. Their business activities are treated in the normal way but the input tax on any non-business activities is refunded. In this way there is no hidden tax burden in the rates.

23.9 Charities

Sales in charity shops, fêtes, coffee mornings, etc of donated goods are zero-rated. Apart from this, business supplies of a charity are treated in the normal way; there is no exemption for charities. Non-business supplies such as distribution of free goods are outside the tax unless they are exported when they are zero-rated. Where a branch of a charity makes business supplies, for example sales at a fête, it may be treated as a separate entity from the charity and be entitled to the £48,000 limit before it is taxable. See zero-rating (23.14) for certain reliefs applicable to charities. The list of zero-rated items related to charities is being increased over the years. Further details may be found in VAT leaflet 701/1/92.

23.10 Retailers

Because retailers often cannot record each sale separately there are special schemes for calculating the amount of the tax which they pay. The schemes also deal with the difficulty of retailers which sell both zero-rated goods (eg, food) and standard-rated goods (eg, kitchen equipment). Details of the schemes are contained in Customs & Excise Notice No 727 and supplements describing each scheme.

23.11 Special cases

23.11.1 Motor cars

No deduction of input tax on motor cars is allowed on cars acquired for use in the business. This also applied to the acquisition of hire cars and taxis, except London-type taxis. However, from 1 August 1992, VAT is recoverable for vehicles used in their businesses by private taxi and self-drive firms and driving schools. From 1 August 1995, businesses may recover input tax on cars used for a demonstrably wholly business purpose, primarily leasing, but must charge VAT on any cars sold.

The VAT on the hire charge is available for credit as input tax. However, this is restricted by 50 per cent where from 1 August 1995, the car is leased from a business which has recovered the VAT and the car is partly used for private motoring. A car dealer is not affected and can claim a credit for input tax in the normal way, but if he takes a car out of stock and uses it in his own business, tax must be paid and it is not available for credit (see 'Self-supply', below). The definition of 'motor car' for this purpose excludes commercial vehicles, vans without rear side windows and vehicles accommodating only one or more than 11 persons.

Petrol supplied at below cost by companies and partnerships etc for private journeys is not allowable for VAT purposes so far as the input tax is concerned. This creates problems in computing the disallowance and a quarterly scale corresponding to the income tax figures (10.6.5) is used for each person concerned. (There is also a monthly scale.) The company, etc is charged VAT on the scale figures which effectively cancels the appropriate input tax. The basic scale figures are as follows:

Cylinder capacity	*Quarterly Scale* Accounting periods beginning on or after 6.4.96		6.4.97	
	Petrol £	*Diesel* £	*Petrol* £	*Diesel* £
Up to 1400 cc	177	160	200	185
1401–2000 cc	222	160	252	185
over 2000 cc	330	205	372	235

If a car is wholly used for business purposes, the scale charge does not apply; nor does it apply where a car is used entirely for private purposes, in which case input tax is not deductible.

23.11.2 Business entertainment

Input tax on business entertainment is not deductible. Entertainment includes meals, accommodation, theatres and sporting facilities. This does not, however, prevent deduction of input tax on subsistence expenses refunded to employees.

23.11.3 Self-supply

It is advantageous for a business which makes exempt supplies to produce its own goods since no input tax will be charged for which it will be unable to obtain a credit. To prevent distortion, an order charging printed stationery to tax even though supplied to oneself has been made. Thus a bank, which is exempt, printing its own stationery would be charged tax on the value of the stationery and it could not obtain relief for the tax. An order also applies to cars to prevent avoidance of the non-deduction of input tax mentioned above.

Regulations may be made to restrict the recovery of input tax on self-supplies by partly exempt businesses. Recovery will only be allowed to the extent governed by the business's partial exemption method.

Developers of certain non-residential *buildings* may be treated as making self-supplies in various circumstances. This applies where, for example, a lease is granted which is an exempt supply; also, when the developer is not a fully taxable person and occupies the building.

In such cases VAT is chargeable based on the land and taxable construction costs, subject to certain exclusions. These include where the value is less than £100,000 and where the construction was completed before

1 August 1989; also, if the freehold had already passed and the non-residential building is new.

23.11.4 Second-hand goods

Second-hand goods are chargeable to tax in the normal way, except that there are special provisions relating to cars, motorcycles, caravans, boats and outboard motors, original works of art, antiques over 100 years old, collectors' pieces, electronic organs and aircraft, which provide that VAT is payable only on the dealer's mark-up. Except in the case of cars these provisions apply only when no tax was charged on the dealer's acquisition or when tax was charged on another dealer's mark-up. Where goods are taken in part-exchange, full VAT is still payable on the new goods supplied.

From 1 January 1995, the dealer's mark-up is chargeable to VAT for all second hand goods, works of art, antiques and collectors items apart from precious metals and gems. VAT is computed on a global basis and other changes have since been made.

23.11.5 Sales on credit

A separately disclosed credit charge is exempt from VAT.

23.11.6 Gifts

Business gifts of goods are taxable on the cost price but items costing in aggregate under £15 (£10 before 29 November 1995) can be ignored. This applies to samples in general unless more than one indentical item is supplied to one person, in which case relief is limited to one item. Gifts of services are not taxable.

23.11.7 Personal use

If a person acquires goods in the course of business and uses them for his own personal use, eg, a shopkeeper who takes goods off the shelf, tax is payable on the cost price of the goods.

23.11.8 Accommodation for directors

VAT on repairs, refurbishments and other expenses relating to domestic accommodation provided for directors and their families does not rank as deductible input tax. This applies where the accommodation is provided by a business for domestic purposes but not to any rooms used specifically for business where a proportion of the total VAT would be deductible.

23.11.9 Bad debts

A limited relief for bad debts exists where the debtor goes bankrupt or goes into liquidation. The amount excluding VAT is claimed from the liquidator, etc and the VAT from Customs & Excise. Retailers in effect obtain bad debt relief as the special schemes are based on payments. (Relief extends beyond cases of formal insolvency.)

From 1 April 1991, the relief is more comprehensive. Automatic bad debt relief is now available on debts which are more than six months old (from payable date), and have been written off in the accounts. (This relief is only available to supplies after 31 March 1989.) If you have reclaimed VAT on inputs for which you do not pay, you must repay this if your supplier has claimed bad debt relief (FA 1997 S39).

23.11.10 Tour operators

Previously, the services of tour operators regarding overseas package holidays were not liable to VAT in the UK. However, FA 1987 S16 introduced a special VAT margin scheme. UK based tour operators buying in services pay VAT on the margin between their buying and selling prices. This applies if the services are used in the EC, including the UK. Furthermore they are not able to recover any VAT charged by suppliers for those services.

23.11.11 Fuel and power

Fuel and power were originally zero-rated but commercial use was standard rated from 1 April 1989 (23.15). FA 1993 has now provided that domestic fuel and power are to remain zero-rated until 31 March 1994, then being taxable at 8 per cent for the year to 31 March 1995. After that, the standard rate of VAT (17.5 per cent) was to have applied but Finance Act 1995 has kept the rate at 8 per cent.

23.11.12 Registration of racehorse owners

Subject to the Jockey Club changing the Rules of Racing to allow owners to seek sponsorship and appearance money, racehorse owners will be able to register for VAT purposes. This has retrospective effect to 16 March 1993.

23.12 Documentation

The legislation contained in FA 1972 and nearly all the subsequent Finance Acts was consolidated into the Value Added Tax Act 1983. In turn this together with further legislation in Finance Acts has been consolidated into the Value Added Tax Act 1994. Also a large number of statutory instruments have been made under powers contained in the Acts, all of which are available from HMSO.

Detailed information is contained in the following Notices issued by Customs & Excise which are available free from any Customs & Excise VAT office:

Number	
41	Trade classification
101	Deferring duty, VAT and other charges
197V	VAT on goods delivered from wet warehouses
200	Temporary importations into the European Community
201	Temporary imports from the European Community
480	Special import entry procedures: period entry
700	The VAT guide
702	Imports and warehoused goods
703	Exports
704	Retail exports
705	Personal exports of new motor vehicles (outside EC)
706	Partial exemption
708	Buildings and construction
711	Second-hand cars
712	Second-hand works of art, antiques and scientific collections
713	Second-hand motor-cycles
714	Young children's clothing and footwear
717	Second-hand caravans and motor caravans
719	Refund of VAT to 'do-it-yourself' builders
720	Second-hand boats and outboard motors
721	Second-hand aircraft
722	Second-hand electronic organs
723	Refunds of VAT in the European Community and other countries
724	Second-hand firearms
725	The single market
726	Second-hand horses and ponies
727	Special schemes for retailers
728	Motor vehicles, boats, aircraft: intra EC movements by private persons
730	Investigations-Statement of Practice
731	Cash accounting
732	Annual accounting
741	International services
742A	Property ownership

742B Property development
742C Land and property: law
744 Passenger transport, international freight, ships and aircraft
748 Extra-statutory concessions
749 Local authorities and similar bodies

It should be emphasised that these Notices are guides, and, with the exception of No 727 and the parts of the Notices relating to second-hand goods which deal with keeping records, they do not have any legal force. Several of the Notices are supported by numerous leaflets on specific topics.

23.13 Appeals

Independent VAT tribunals deal with appeals about the matters listed below. (From a date to be appointed, these are to be known as VAT and duties tribunals, with wider coverage.) There are tribunals in London, Edinburgh, Belfast and Manchester. The tribunal consists of a chairman who can sit alone or with one or two other members. The procedure is explained in a leaflet printed by the President of VAT Tribunals which is available from Customs & Excise VAT offices. The 1985 Finance Act (S27 & Sch 8) contains certain rules about VAT Tribunals. For example chairmen must be barristers or solicitors (advocates in Scotland) of seven years' standing.

The matters over which the tribunals have jurisdiction are as follows:

(1) Registration.
(2) Registration of groups of companies.
(3) Assessment of VAT by Customs & Excise.
(4) The amount of VAT chargeable.
(5) The amount of the deduction of input tax.
(6) Apportionment of input tax by a partly exempt person.
(7) Special schemes for retailers.
(8) The value of certain supplies.
(9) The provision of security.
(10) Repayment of VAT on certain imports.
(11) Refunds to do-it-yourself builders.
(12) Bad debt relief.
(13) Voluntary registration of a person whose turnover is below the limit.
(14) Appeals against certain Commissioners' decisions which in turn depend upon prior unappealable decisions which they made.

There is an appeal from the tribunal on a point of law (there is no appeal on a question of fact) to the High Court and from there to the Court of Appeal. There is a final appeal to the House of Lords if leave to appeal is obtained. In Scotland appeals go to the Court of Session and thence to the House of Lords.

23.14 Zero-rating

(VATA Sch 8)

The following is a list of the important items. Full details are contained in the General Guide (VAT Notice No 700) available from Customs & Excise. The group numbers have been changed in some instances by VATA 1994.

Group 1: Food All food except pet foods, alcoholic drinks and certain food products (such as ice cream, chocolate, confectionery including cereal bars, soft drinks and potato crisps). Meals out are, however, taxable and this includes hot take-away food and drink.
Group 2: Sewerage services and water Water except for distilled water and bottled water; emptying cesspools. (Standard rated from 1 July 1990 if for industrial use — 23.15.)
Group 3: Books, etc Books, newspapers, magazines, music, maps. But diaries and stationery are taxable.
Group 4: Talking books and tape recorders for the blind and handicapped and wireless sets for the blind, including (from 1.4.92) their repair and maintenance.
Group 5: Construction of dwellings, etc Sale of the freehold or grant of a lease for more than 21 years of a building by a builder; construction, and demolition of buildings but not repairs (now basically dwellings for your own, charity and community use — 23.15). Sales by a builder's merchant, and architects' and surveyors' fees are, however, taxable. A person building his own house can reclaim tax paid on items purchased. (Conversions, reconstructions, alterations and enlargements for industrial and commercial use are normally standard rated and sales of reconstructed buildings are exempt.)
Group 6: Protected buildings This includes alterations and reconstructions of listed buildings, ancient monuments and listed churches.
Group 7: International services Exports of services, such as professional advice to non-residents (except those resident in the EC) and overseas insurance. Also carrying out work on goods from abroad subsequently exported outside the EC.
Group 8: Transport Passenger transport (inland and international) including travel agents (except in relation to hotels in the UK or package

tours), and international freight transport. Taxis and hire cars are, however, taxable, as are pleasure boats and aircraft. From 1 May 1990, lifeboats and slipways, etc are all included; from 1 April 1992, spare parts, etc for lifeboats; and from 1 April 1993, for zero-rated ships and aircraft.

Group 9: Caravans and houseboats Caravans which are too large to be used as trailers on the roads (22.9 feet in length or 7.5 feet in breadth). But smaller caravans are taxable.

Group 10: Gold Transactions on the London Gold market.

Group 11: Bank notes

Group 12: Drugs, medicines, medical and surgical appliances Drugs dispensed by a registered pharmacist on a doctor's prescription. Other drugs purchased without a prescription are taxable. Medical and surgical appliances for the disabled. Donated computer equipment is zero-rated, as are lifts and distress systems for the handicapped and necessary work on bathrooms, etc in private homes and in bathrooms for the handicapped in charity residential homes. From 1 May 1990, more general relief is available for medical equipment, ambulances, etc purchased out of charitable funds or donated. This extends to the sale of donated goods and printed media advertising costs.

Group 13: Imports, exports, etc. This group has limited application.

Group 14: Tax-free shops Relating to travellers to other EC countries making purchases on planes, ships, at airports and ports within the limits (1 litre of spirits, 2 litres of wine, 60 ml of perfume, 200 cigarettes etc and £71 of other goods to be carried in personal luggage).

Group 15: Charities (23.9). This includes non-classified advertising, medical video or refrigeration equipment and motor vehicles with from seven to fifty seats. Also, drugs and chemicals used in medical (and veterinary) research by a charity are zero-rated, also welfare vehicles for the terminally ill and certain rescue equipment. The sale of donated goods is generally included, as is fund-raising and educational advertising on television, radio and cinema. Also covered are toilet facilities in charity-run buildings and boats adapted for the handicapped.

Group 16: Clothing and footwear Clothing for young children, industrial protective clothing (provided meeting UK or EC safety standards and bearing mark) and motor-cyclists' crash helmets. (Protective boots and helmets are standard-rated if supplied to employers for their employees — 23.15.)

Export of goods This does not include exports to Northern Ireland, which is part of the UK, or to the Isle of Man.

Note: Zero-rating has priority over exemption if a supply falls into both categories.

23.15 Changes to zero-ratings

On 21 June 1988, the European Court of Justice ruled that certain zero-ratings did not comply with European Community Law. As a result, the following items are *standard-rated* (*17.5 per cent*), details being in the 1989 Finance Act and VATA 1994 has reflected the resultant changes in the Group numbering (23.14):

(1) construction of buildings for industrial and commercial use;
(2) supplies after 31 March 1989 of fuel and power other than to final consumers for domestic use (domestic use taxable from 1 April 1994 — 23.11.11);
(3) sewerage services and water supplies to industry after 30 June 1990;
(4) supplies after 31 March 1989 of news services insofar as they are not provided to final consumers;
(5) protective boots and helmets supplied to employers after 31 March 1989 for use by their employees.

All contracts entered into before 21 June 1988 continue to be zero-rated. Owners of non-domestic property have the option to elect to charge VAT on rents, and on sales of certain used buildings, from 1 August 1989. If you elected before 1 November 1989, it could go back to 1 August 1989. Otherwise the election can take effect no earlier than the date when made. Owners can obtain no input tax relief before the election has effect, subject to transitional relief. Certain transactions in non-residential buildings may be treated as self-supplies giving rise to VAT.

Where the rent was payable by someone who was in occupation immediately before 1 August 1989, only half of the rent for the year to 31 July 1990 carried VAT. However, for charities, there was greater relief, starting at 80 per cent and tapering over five years.

23.16 Exemptions
(VATA Sch 9)

The following is a list of the more important items. Full details are contained in the General Guide (VAT Notice 700) available from Customs & Excise:
Group 1: Land Sales, leases and hiring out of land and buildings (unless within zero-rating Group 8 or taxable). Examples of taxable items are hotels (excluding conference facilities), holiday accommodation, camping, parking, timber, mooring, exhibition stands, sporting

rights and the sale and construction of new non-residential buildings and civil engineering works (23.15).

Group 2: Insurance All types of insurance and insurance brokers and agents. Both premiums and the payment of claims are exempt.

Group 3: Postal services Post, except telegrams. But telephones and telex are taxable.

Group 4: Betting, gaming and lotteries Bookmakers, charges for playing bingo. But admission or session charges, club subscriptions and takings from gaming machines are taxable.

Group 5: Finance Banking, buying and selling stocks and shares and charges from credit card companies to retailers etc. accepting the cards. But stockbrokers' commissions and unit trust management fees are taxable.

Group 6: Education Schools, universities, non-profit-making institutions teaching pupils of any age, or providing job training; private tuition by an independent teacher; government funded training programmes (including from 1 April 1993 where provided for profit).

Group 7: Health Doctors, dentists, dental workers, nurses, midwives, registered health visitors, registered opticians (including spectacles supplied in the course of treatment), chiropodists, dieticians, medical laboratory technicians, occupational therapists, orthoptists, physiotherapists, radiographers and remedial gymnasts, hearing aid dispensers, registered pharmaceutical chemists, medical and surgical treatment (except health farms, etc).

Group 8: Burial and cremation Undertakers, crematoria.

Group 9: Trade unions and professional bodies

Group 10: Sports competitions

Group 11: Certain works of art, etc.

Group 12: Fund-raising events Supplies of goods and services by charities and other qualifying bodies (including certain subsidiaries) in connection with fund-raising events.

Note: Zero-rating has priority over exemption if a supply falls into both categories.

23.17 Trading within the EC

F2A 1992 Sch 3 made detailed provisions related to the introduction of the Single Market from 1 January 1993. From that date, import procedures are abolished for movements of goods within the EC. Instead there is a concept of 'acquisition'. Supplies of goods between persons registered for VAT in EC countries continue to be zero-rated. However, the acquirer must account for local VAT in the member state to which the goods are sent.

If you supply goods to persons registered for VAT in other EC countries, you will need to submit quarterly EC Sales Lists. (Supplies between the UK and non-EC countries remain largely as before.)

Private individuals normally effectively bear VAT at the appropriate rate in the member state of the supplier. However, VAT in the member state of the purchaser (and not the supplier) applies to mail order purchases, new motor vehicles, motor cycles, boats and aircraft; also supplies to non-VAT registered businesses and non-taxable institutions.

If you supply goods from another EC member state to non-VAT registered customers in the UK and are responsible for delivery, this is known as 'distance selling'. Should your annual turnover from distance selling reach £70,000, you must register for UK VAT.

Different rules apply to the supply of services from one EC country to another. In some cases these can require local VAT to be paid in the country of receipt or performance.

Fiscal warehousing operates from 1 June 1996. New provisions allow VAT-free trading within fiscal warehousing regimes for qualifying commodities, such as specified foodstuffs, metals and chemicals. When these are removed from the regime, VAT becomes payable.

23.18 Optional rate for farmers
(VATA S54)

From 1 January 1993, farmers can choose whether to register for VAT or opt to become flat rate farmers. If your taxable supplies are below the registration level (£48,000) you will still have the option of not registering for VAT, nor will you have to become a flat rate farmer.

As a flat rate farmer, you will be outside the VAT system and so obtain no relief for purchases. However, to compensate you, a fixed rate is to be added to your sales and retained by you. The actual rate is 4 per cent. However, you will not be eligible if you would stand to gain £3,000 or more in a year by participating in the scheme.

24 Stamp duty

24.1 Introduction

Stamp duty is perhaps the most modest of capital taxes. However, even though the rates are very low, stamp duty is likely to arise on some of your major capital transactions and could involve significant sums. Therefore a brief outline is given below. This concentrates on the *ad valorem* duties, which are charged according to the value of a transaction, rather than the less important *fixed duties*.

The stamp duty rules are contained in the Stamp Act 1891, Stamp Duties Management Act 1891 and subsequent Finance Acts. The 1984 Finance Act (S105) halved the rates of some of the main *ad valorem* duties to 1 per cent from 20 March 1984 (12 March 1984 for most Stock Exchange transactions). The 1985 Finance Act removed certain fixed duties (S79) and abolished contract note duty. Also, *gifts* ceased to be liable to *ad valorem* duty; along with deeds of family arrangement (22.29.6) and divorce transfers. The duty on share transfers was further reduced to 0.5 per cent by the 1986 Finance Act (S58). Also, a new stamp duty reserve tax was introduced (24.5).

Stamp duty is essentially a charge on documents (instruments). (These must be delivered as well as signed.) It is not charged on the transactions and so if you carry out a transaction without documenting it, no duty should be chargeable. Furthermore if you later make a separate written record of an oral contract, this should not involve stamp duty. However, the Inland Revenue are re-appraising their attitude towards stamp duty avoidance and certain rules regarding shares are being changed. For example bearer letters of allotment are no longer exempted. In addition from 8 December 1993 surrenders of leases are dutiable whether or not they are documented.

The payment of stamp duty is confirmed by a stamp being impressed on the document. The stamp office may need to adjudicate the value of a transaction for duty purposes and you could need to supply balance sheets and other details. If documents are not stamped, you will not always be open to action by the Revenue but the instruments will not be admitted in evidence in court. Also, you may be liable for fines if you present the instrument late for filing—in practice after 30 days from when the instruments are first executed (or brought into the UK).

FA 1994 contains various anti-avoidance provisions generally taking effect from 8 December 1993. For example, exchanges of land interests are now treated as sales. Also, land interests must be valued if the price payable on transfer cannot then be ascertained.

24.2 Exemptions

The following table lists some of the more important exemptions from stamp duty:

24.2.1 Table: Exemptions from stamp duty

Transfers of Government Stocks ('Gilts')
Transfers of units in certain authorised unit trusts invested in UK government securities, etc
Transfers of short term loans (no more than five years)
Transfers of certain fixed rate non-convertible loan stocks
Transfers of bearer loan capital
Transfers of certain non-sterling loans raised by foreign governments or companies
Conveyances, transfers or leases to approved charities (FA 1982 S129)*
Conveyances, transfers or leases to the National Heritage Memorial Fund*
Transactions effected by the actual operation of law
Documents regarding transfers of ships (or interests in them)
Transfers brought about by will (testaments and testamentary instruments)
Articles of apprenticeship and of clerkship
Customs bonds, etc
Certain legal aid documents
Contracts of employment
Certain National Savings documents
Deeds of Covenant and bonds
Policies of insurance and related documents (excluding life assurance up to 31 December 1989)
One life assurance policy which is substituted for another according to the rules (FA 1982 S130)
Transfers (and issue) of certain EC Loan Stocks
Transfers of Treasury guaranteed stock
Property put into unit trusts (0.25% prior to 16 March 1988) (FA 1988 S140)

Agreement pursuant to Highway Acts
Appointment, procuration, revocation
Letter or power of attorney
Deeds not liable to other duties no longer liable to 50p duty
In Scotland, resignation, writ, etc
Warrants to purchase Government stock, etc (FA 1987 S50)
Transfers to a Minister of the Crown or the Treasury Solicitor (FA 1987 S55)
Transfers of insurance business under a demutualisation scheme (FA 1997 S96)
Conversions and mergers of open-ended investment companies and authorised unit trusts up to 30 June 1999
Certain on-exchange transactions by intermediaries

*Not treated as duly stamped unless they have a stamp denoting not chargeable to duty

24.3 Relief for take-overs and within groups

Prior to 16 March 1988, capital duty applied on the 'chargeable transactions' of certain 'capital companies'. Relief from capital duty applied where an existing 'capital company' or one being formed, acquired share capital of another 'capital company' so that it owned 75 per cent of it. Relief also applied if the whole or part of one 'capital company's' undertaking was acquired by another.

Similar relief applied from *ad valorem* stamp duty (FA 1985 S78) up to 24 March 1986. The exemption applied where a company issued shares, etc in exchange for those of another company, in the course of obtaining control, or if it already had control. *Relief normally remains*, however, where there is a company reconstruction with no real change in ownership. Also, relief applies for transfers between associated companies (broadly 90 per cent common control). FA 1995 Ss132–134 extends the relief to leases granted by one associated company to another and generally reduces the requisite control to 75 per cent.

24.4 *Ad valorem* duties

The most important stamp duties with which you may be involved are those which increase according to the consideration involved. These are known as *ad valorem* duties. Normally, *ad valorem* duties are charged at a fixed percentage but this is sometimes expressed in bands, so that the 0.5 per cent on share transfers, etc is 50p for every £100 or part thereof. Also, for some duties, sliding scales apply for small transactions.

In general, the rate for land and buildings is 1 per cent, but there is normally a £60,000 threshold, at or below which no duty is payable. Before 16 March 1993, the threshold was £30,000. However, for documents executed from 20 December 1991 to 19 August 1992 the threshold was £250,000, prior to which it was £30,000. (Once the threshold is passed, the entire value is charged to duty.)

The following table gives the basic percentage rates of various *ad valorem* duties:

24.4.1 Table: *Ad valorem* stamp duties

	Rate
Capital duty (1% before 16 March 1988)	Nil
Conveyance or transfer on sale other than share transfers*	1%
Share transfers (generally including unit trusts)	½%
Certain non-exempt loan transfers	½%
Exchanges or partitions of freehold land	1%
Inland bearer instruments‡	1½%
Overseas bearer instruments‡	1½%
Conversion of UK shares into depositary receipts (24.5)	1½%
Lease premiums	1%

Leases: *Ad valorem* duty on rents

Term	*Annual rent*	*Duty for every £50 or part thereof*
Not exceeding 7 years or indefinite	Not exceeding £500	Nil
	exceeding £500	50p
7–35 years	—	£1
35–100 years	—	£6
over 100 years	—	£12

(Where the rent does not exceed £500 a sliding scale applies.)

Life assurance policies—up to 31 December 1989	Amount assured: Up to £50	Nil
	£50–£1,000	5p per £100 or part
	Over £1,000	50p per £1,000 or part
After 31 December 1989		Nil
Superannuation annuity contract or grant	—	5p per £10 annuity or part
After 31 December 1989		Nil

*Includes land, etc. For most categories including houses, no duty is payable if the value is certified at no more than £60,000 (24.4).
‡Bearer loan capital exempt.

24.5 Stamp duty reserve tax
(FA 1986 Ss86–99 & FA 1996 Ss186 & 189)

A charge called stamp duty reserve tax applies at 0.5 per cent on certain transactions in securities otherwise not liable to stamp duty. The charge broadly operates from 27 October 1986 but does not apply to securities exempt from sale duty (eg, gifts) or traded options, etc. Examples of when the tax applies are renounceable letters of allotment and sometimes where there is no transfer document (eg, closing transactions within Stock Exchange accounts). A special rate of 1.5 per cent applies to the conversion of UK shares into depositary receipts after 18 March 1986.

From 1 July 1996, transfers of shares into electronic transfer systems are exempted from stamp duty. However, if the transfers are made for consideration in money or money's worth, the underlying agreement will be liable to stamp duty reserve tax.

24.6 Abolition of stamp duty on shares, etc
(FA 1990 Ss107–111 & FA 1991 Ss110–117)

It is intended that stamp duties on shares will be abolished from a date to be announced. This was to coincide as far as possible with the introduction of paperless dealing under the new Stock Exchange share transfer system. At the same time, stamp duty charges on property other than land and buildings would go, including on patents, goodwill and debt. However, the proposed 'Taurus' scheme having been abandoned, stamp duty on share transfers (except gifts) remained.

From 1 July 1996, transfers of securities into an electronic transfer system are exempt from stamp duty. However, stamp duty reserve tax (24.5) may apply, according to the rules.

The duties to be abolished include the 0.5 per cent stamp duty on individual share transfers, 1.5 per cent where UK shares are transferred into clearance services or converted into depositary receipts, stamp duty reserve tax (24.5), stamp duties on bearer shares and unit trust unit transfers.

A number of documents are still to be liable to a fixed amount of stamp duty amounting to 50p per document. All of these are to be relieved from stamp duty at the same time as the *ad valorem* duty on shares is abolished. After that, stamp duty will apply only to land transactions.

25 Social security

25.1 Introduction

The main social security legislation is now comprised in the Social Security Acts of 1975, 1985 and 1986. The subject is a wide one and only an outline is given below.

Arguably, social security contributions are not a tax but their effect is very similar. Although ultimate benefits such as retirement pensions are secured, when you pay the contributions, you must normally do so out of your after-tax income. Social security contributions payments do not reduce your taxable income any more than do income tax payments.

25.2 National Insurance contributions

Contributions are payable under four categories known as 'Class 1' (employees), 'Class 2' (self-employed), 'Class 3' (voluntary) and 'Class 4' (self-employed earnings related). Classes 2 and 3 are flat rate contributions and Class 4 is dealt with subsequently (25.5). The following points should be noted regarding Class 1:

(1) Contributions are graduated according to earnings up to a certain level and are collected together with income tax under the PAYE system (10.14). They are not allowable for income tax purposes.

(2) Your employer supplements your contributions. Your employers' contributions are deductible for tax purposes.

(3) No contributions are payable if the weekly earnings are less than £62 but once this level is reached, your entire wages (up to £465) carry percentage contributions.

(4) From 6 October 1985 there is no upper earnings limit for employers. They pay contributions on the total earnings of employees.

(5) If your employers operate an approved pension scheme which is contracted out of the state scheme, lower contributions will be

due. If you contract out via a Personal Pension Plan, you still pay full National Insurance contributions. The rebate is paid direct to the pension plan.

(6) You will not have to pay contributions if you have retired and passed normal retirement age (60 for a woman and 65 for a man). If you are still working beyond age 65 you will not be liable for contributions. Your employer remains liable, however.

(7) If you have a company car and earn no less than £8,500 annually, your employer will pay Class 1A National Insurance contributions at 10 per cent from 1997–98 on your taxable benefits. These comprise both your car scale benefit and fuel benefit, where applicable. This is an annual charge, payable for 1991–92 and subsequent tax years normally by the following 19 June.

The following tables give details concerning the rates of contribution.

25.2.1 Table: National Insurance contributions

	Tax year			
	1996–97		*1997–98*	
	Employee	*Employer*	*Employee*	*Employer*
'Class 1' — employees aged 16 & over:				
Lower earnings limit (LEL) pw	£61·00		£62·00	
Upper earnings limit (UEL) pw	£455·00		£465·00	
(*a*) earnings less than LEL:	Nil	Nil	Nil	Nil
(*b*) earnings LEL or more and contracted out:				
up to LEL				
on balance up to UEL	See Table 25.2.2			
(*c*) earnings at least LEL and contracted in:				
on earnings up to UEL				
'Class 2' — self-employed pw	£6·05*		£6·15*	
'Class 3' — voluntary pw	£5·95		£6·05	
'Class 4' — self-employed earnings related	6% on annual earnings between £6,860 & £23,660		6% on annual earnings between £7,010 & £24,180	
*Lower earnings limit	£3,430		£3,480	

25.2.2 Table: Class 1 National Insurance contributions

1997–98	*Not contracted-out*	*Contracted-out*	*1996–97*	*Not contracted-out*	*Contracted-out*
Employee			*Employee*		
Weekly earnings below £62	Nil	Nil	Weekly earnings below £61	Nil	Nil
Earnings above £62			Earnings above £61		
0–£61.99	2%	2%	0–£60.99	2%	2%
£62–£465	10%	8.4%	£61–£455	10%	8.2%
£465 or more	No further liability		over £455	No further liability	

1997–98 Employer Weekly earnings	*Not contracted-out %*	*Contracted-out % First £62*	*Excess over £62*
Under £62.00	Nil	Nil	Nil
£62.00–109.99	3	3	Nil
110.00–154.99	5	5	2
155.00–209.99	7	7	4
210.00–465.00	10	10	7
over £465.00	10	10	{ 7 on £403 10 on excess

1996–97 Employer Weekly earnings	*Not contracted-out %*	*Contracted-out % First £61*	*Excess over £61*
Under £61.00	Nil	Nil	Nil
£61.00–109.99	3	3	Nil
110.00–154.99	5	5	2
155.00–209.99	7	7	4
210.00–455.00	10.2	10.2	7.2
over £455.00	10.2	10.2	{ 7.2 on £394 10.2 on excess

25.3 Social security benefits

A wide range of benefits is payable. Some of these are summarised in the following tables and split between those which are taxable and those which are not.

25.3.1 Table: Taxable social security benefits

	From 10.4.97	*From 10.4.96 to 9.4.97*
	£	£
Retirement pension		
— Single	62.45	61.15
— Wife (or other adult dependant)	37.35	36.60
Old person's pension (non-contributory) (extra 25p payable if over 80)	37.35	36.60
Invalid care allowance		
— Single	37.35	36.60
— Wife (or other adult dependant)	22.35	21.90
Invalidity allowance (only taxable if paid with retirement pension)		
— Higher rate	13.15	12.90
— Middle rate	8.30	8.10
— Lower rate	4.15	4.05
Widow's benefit		
— Pension — basic (variable below 55)	62.45	61.15
— Widowed mother's allowance	62.45	61.15
Unemployment benefits — Standard rate under pension age		
— Single	—	48.25
— Wife (or other adult dependant)	—	29.75
Jobseekers allowance		
— Single person under 18	29.60	—
— Single person 18–24	38.90	—
— Single person 25 or over	49.15	—
Incapacity benefit		
— Short term	55.70	54.55
— Long term	62.45	61.15

25.3.2 Table: Non-taxable social security benefits

	From 10.4.97	*From 10.4.96 to 9.4.97*
	£	£
Maternity allowance	48.35	47.35
Severe disablement allowance		
— Single	37.75	36.95
— Wife (or other adult dependant)	22.40	21.95
Attendance allowance		
— Higher rate	49.50	48.50
— Lower rate	33.10	32.40
Child benefit		
First child	11.05	10.80
Each other child	9.00	8.80
One parent benefit — addition for first child	6.05	6.30
Increases for children — child's special allowances and guardian's allowances — each child	11.20	11.15
Disability living allowance (replaces mobility allowance)		
— mobility component — higher	34.60	33.90
lower	13.15	12.90
Industrial disablement pension (maximum)	101.10	99.00
— unemployability supplement	62.45	61.15
— constant attendance allowance (normal maximum)	40.50	39.70
— exceptionally severe disablement allowance (addition)	40.50	39.70
Widow's payment — lump sum	1,000.00	1,000.00
Housing benefits — various		
War pension — death benefit, disablement, widow's pension, widower's pension—various		

Note: In addition, earnings related unemployment benefit supplement is exempt from income tax.

25.4 Statutory sick pay (SSP)

Employers generally pay up to 28 weeks SSP for each employee in any tax year. (The employee does not need to have paid National Insurance contributions.) Only after that is any sickness benefit paid direct by the State. Employers can deduct their SSP payments in any month from the total National Insurance contributions payable to the authorities, subject to the rules.

SSP is paid at the following weekly rates (daily rates are calculated proportionally):

Normal weekly earnings	*1996–97*	*Normal weekly earnings*	*1997–98*
Less than £61.00	Nil	Less than £62.00	Nil
£61.00 or more	£54.55	£62.00 or more	£55.70

25.5 Class 4 National Insurance contributions

Self-employed persons and others liable to Schedule D income tax under Cases I and II may be charged, in addition to their normal flat-rate Class 2 contributions, an earnings related amount under Class 4. The following should be noted.

(1) The contribution rate for 1997–98 is 6 per cent which applies to your Cases I and II income between £7,010 and £24,180. The maximum is thus 6 per cent × £17,170 = £1,030.20.

(2) The rates, etc for recent years were as follows:

Year	*% rate*	*From* £	*To* £	*Maximum payable*
1988–89	6.3	4,750	15,860	699.93
1989–90	6.3	5,050	16,900	746.55
1990–91	6.3	5,450	18,200	803.25
1991–92	6.3	5,900	20,280	905.94
1992–93	6.3	6,120	21,060	941.22
1993–94	6.3	6,340	21,840	976.50
1994–95	7.3	6,490	22,360	1,158.51
1995–96	7.3	6,640	22,880	1,185.52
1996–97	6.0	6,860	23,660	1,008.00

(3) Prior to 6 April 1975, the charge did not apply.

(4) Class 4 is payable on your Schedule D assessments under Cases I and II for the tax year; after capital allowances, but with no deduction of personal allowances, pension contributions, etc. Your share of partnership income is thus included.
(5) If your wife has self-employed earnings, these are separately charged to Class 4.
(6) Class 4 does not apply to men over 65 at the end of the previous year of assessment and women then over 60.
(7) Your contributions for each year of assessment are normally collected through your income tax assessment on your self-employed earnings. Thus it is normally payable in two instalments (16.3.2).
(8) It is possible to defer your Class 4 payments in certain cases, such as where you also pay Class 1 contributions.
(9) If you are not resident in the UK (17.3) Class 4 will not apply.
(10) From 6 April 1985 to 5 April 1996, but not subsequently, half of your Class 4 contributions were deductible in computing your taxable profits (11.29).

26 Tax tables

26.1 Income tax table for 1997–98

Income	*Single person*	*Married man*
£4,000	—	—
5,000	191	—
6,000	391	117
7,000	591	317
8,000	791	517
9,000	1,017	743
10,000	1,247	973
12,000	1,707	1,433
14,000	2,167	1,893
16,000	2,627	2,353
18,000	3,087	2,813
20,000	3,547	3,273
25,000	4,697	4,423
30,000	5,847	5,573
40,000	9,822	9,548
50,000	13,822	13,548
70,000	21,822	21,548

Notes:

(1) Single personal and married couple's relief have been taken into account.

(2) Other reliefs have been ignored.

(3) The tax for a married man has been calculated on the assumption that he obtains the married couple's allowance (at 15 per cent).

26.2 Tax rates and allowances for 1985–86 to 1996–97

	85–86	86–87	87–88	88–89	89–90	90–91	91–92	92–93, 93–94 & 94–95	95–96	96–97
Income tax basic rate	30%	29%	27%	25%	25%	25%	25%	25%	25%	24%
Single personal allowance	2,205	2,335	2,425	2,605	2,785	3,005ø	3,295ø	3,445ø	3,525ø	3,765ø
Married personal allowance	3,455	3,655	3,795	4,095	4,375	Nil	Nil	Nil	Nil	Nil
Married couple's allowance	Nil	Nil	Nil	Nil	Nil	1,720	1,720	1,720§	1,720§	1,790§
Wife's earned income allowance (maximum)	2,205	2,335	2,425	2,605	2,785	Nil	Nil	Nil	Nil	Nil
Widow's bereavement	1,250	1,320	1,370	1,490	1,590	1,720	1,720	1,720	1,720	1,790
Dependent relative relief										
female claimant	145	145	145	Nil	Nil	Nil	Nil	Nil	Nil	Nil
other	100	100	100	Nil	Nil	Nil	Nil	Nil	Nil	Nil
Life assurance relief — normal percentage of premiums (deducted from premiums)	15%*	15%*	15%*	15%*	12½%*	12½%*	12½%*	12½%*	12½%*	12½%*

§Limited to 20 per cent for 1994–95 and 15 per cent from 1995–96.
øAvailable separately for husband and wife from 1990–91.
*Only on pre-14 March 1984 policies.
Note: Allowances for 1997–98 are detailed in Chapter 3 (3.0.1); income tax rates for 1997–98 are given in Chapter 5 (5.0.1).

26.3 Income tax rates: for 1982–83 and subsequent years

Slice of income	Rate	Total income (after allowances)	Total tax
for 1982–83			
£12,800 (£0–12,800)	30%	£12,800	£3,840
2,300 (12,800–15,100)	40%	15,100	4,760
4,000 (15,100–19,100)	45%	19,100	6,560
6,200 (19,100–25,300)	50%	25,300	9,660
6,200 (25,300–31,500)	55%	31,500	13,070
Remainder	60%		
for 1983–84			
£14,600 (£0–14,600)	30%	£14,600	£4,380
2,600 (14,600–17,200)	40%	17,200	5,420
4,600 (17,200–21,800)	45%	21,800	7,490
7,100 (21,800–28,900)	50%	28,900	11,040
7,100 (28,900–36,000)	55%	36,000	14,945
Remainder	60%		
for 1984–85			
£15,400 (£0–15,400)	30%	£15,400	£4,620
2,800 (15,400–18,200)	40%	18,200	5,740
4,900 (18,200–23,100)	45%	23,100	7,945
7,500 (23,100–30,600)	50%	30,600	11,695
7,500 (30,600–38,100)	55%	38,100	15,820
Remainder	60%		
for 1985–86			
£16,200 (£0–16,200)	30%	£16,200	£4,860
3,000 (16,200–19,200)	40%	19,200	6,060
5,200 (19,200–24,400)	45%	24,400	8,400
7,900 (24,400–32,300)	50%	32,300	12,350
7,900 (32,300–40,200)	55%	40,200	16,695
Remainder	60%		
for 1986–87			
£17,200 (£0–17,200)	29%	£17,200	£4,988
3,000 (17,200–20,200)	40%	20,200	6,188
5,200 (20,200–25,400)	45%	25,400	8,528
7,900 (25,400–33,300)	50%	33,300	12,478
7,900 (33,300–41,200)	55%	41,200	16,823
Remainder	60%		

for 1987–88			
£17,900 (£0–17,900)	27%	£17,900	£4,833
2,500 (17,900–20,400)	40%	20,400	5,833
5,000 (20,400–25,400)	45%	25,400	8,083
7,900 (25,400–33,300)	50%	33,300	12,033
7,900 (33,300–41,200)	55%	41,200	16,378
Remainder	60%		
for 1988–89			
£19,300 (£0–19,300)	25%	£19,300	£4,825
Remainder	40%		
for 1989–90 and 1990–91			
£20,700 (£0–20,700)	25%	£20,700	£5,175
Remainder	40%		
for 1991–92			
£23,700 (£0–23,700)	25%	£23,700	£5,925
Remainder	40%		
for 1992–93			
2,000 (£0–2,000)	20%	£2,000	£400
21,700 (2,000–23,700)	25%	23,700	5,825
Remainder	40%		
for 1993–94			
2,500 (£0–2,500)	20%	2,500	500
21,200 (£2,500–23,700)	25%	23,700	5,800
Remainder	40%		
for 1994–95			
3,000 (£0–3,000)	20%	3,000	600
20,700 (£3,000–23,700)	25%	23,700	5,775
Remainder	40%		
for 1995–96			
3,200 (£0–3,200)	20%	3,200	640
21,100 (£3,200–24,300)	25%	24,300	5,915
Remainder	40%		
for 1996–97			
3,900 (£0–3,900)	20%	3,900	780
21,600 (£3,900–25,500)	24%	25,500	5,964
Remainder	40%		

26.4 Inheritance tax rates: from 18 March 1986 onwards

Slice of cumulative chargeable transfers	*Cumulative total*	*% on slice*	*Cumulative total tax*
from 18 March 1986 to 16 March 1987			
The first			
£71,000	£71,000	Nil	£Nil
The next			
24,000	95,000	30	7,200
34,000	129,000	35	19,100
35,000	164,000	40	33,100
42,000	206,000	45	52,000
51,000	257,000	50	77,500
60,000	317,000	55	110,500
Remainder		60	
from 17 March 1987 to 14 March 1988			
The first			
£90,000	£90,000	Nil	£Nil
The next			
50,000	140,000	30	15,000
80,000	220,000	40	47,000
110,000	330,000	50	102,000
Remainder		60	
from 15 March 1988 to 5 April 1989			
The first			
£110,000	£110,000	Nil	£Nil
Remainder		40	
from 6 April 1989 to 5 April 1990			
The first			
£118,000	£118,000	Nil	£Nil
Remainder		40	
from 6 April 1990 to 5 April 1991			
The first			
£128,000	£128,000	Nil	£Nil
Remainder		40	
from 6 April 1991 to 9 March 1992			
The first			
£140,000	£140,000	Nil	£Nil
Remainder		40	

From 9 March 1992 to 5 April 1995			
The first £150,000	£150,000	Nil	£Nil
Remainder		40	
after 5 April 1995			
The first £154,000	£154,000	Nil	£Nil
Remainder		40	
after 5 April 1996			
The first £200,000	£200,000	Nil	£Nil
Remainder		40	
after 5 April 1997			
The first £215,000	£215,000	Nil	£Nil
Remainder		40	

Glossary

The following are a selection of terms which are explained in more detail where indicated.

Ad valorem duties	Duties which are charged as a percentage of the subject matter—particularly stamp duty (24.5)
Advance corporation tax	Tax payable by companies on dividend payments, etc, which is offset against the full (mainstream) corporation tax liability (13.6)
Back duty	Under-assessed tax for previous years, normally due to evasion (16.9)
Basic rate tax	Income tax at 23 per cent (2.2)
Business Expansion Scheme (BES)	Government scheme for encouraging investment in smaller companies by giving tax relief on money subscribed (11.25)
Claw-back	The loss of relief previously obtained, eg, life assurance relief (9.4)
Close companies	Companies closely controlled by generally no more than five shareholders and their associates (13.17)
Close Investment Holding Company (CIC)	A close company which is neither a trading company nor a property investment company, nor a member of a trading group (13.18)
Current use value	The value of property on the basis that its use is limited to existing planning consents
Current year basis	The uniform basis for assessing income tax liabilities from 1997–98 and sometimes earlier (11.7.4)
Domicile	The country which you regard as your natural home (17.2)

Earned income	Income derived from an individual's personal, mental or physical labour and some pensions (3.1)
Enterprise investment scheme (EIS)	Government scheme which took over from the Business Expansion Scheme providing revised tax incentives (11.26)
General Commissioners	Lay people appointed to hear tax appeals (16.5)
Higher rate tax	Income tax at the higher rates, currently 40 per cent (5.1)
Indexation allowance	Capital gains tax relief for inflation (20.12)
Interest in possession	Entitlement to receive the income of a settlement (22.30)
Lower rate tax	Income tax at the lowest rate, at present 20 per cent (5.1)
Mainstream corporation tax	A company's main corporation tax liability based on its accounts (13.6.5)
Partnership	The relationship existing between two or more persons in business together with the object of making profits (12.1)
Personal allowance	Certain deductions from your total income for tax purposes (3.2)
Personal equity plan (PEP)	Share purchase scheme under which up to £9,000 can be invested each year with income tax and capital gains tax advantages (8.10)
Potentially exempt transfers (PETs)	Gifts between individuals or to certain trusts which are only considered for inheritance tax if the donor dies within seven years (22.3)
Profit related pay (PRP)	Incentive payments to employees which attract limited income tax relief, subject to the rules (10.15)
Relevant base value	Main deduction in computing realised development value on which development land tax was chargeable
Residence	Where you are treated as living for tax purposes (17.3)
Self-assessment	A new system operating from 1996–97 under which taxpayers will play a larger part in working out their tax liabilities (16.1)
Special Commissioners	Full-time professionally qualified civil servants appointed to hear tax appeals (16.5)

Tax avoidance	Legally arranging your affairs to reduce your tax liability (15.10)
Tax evasion	Illegal tax saving (15.10)
Tax exempt special savings account (TESSA)	Savings account with bank or building society offering tax-free interest (8.11)
Trust	Otherwise known as a settlement—assets held by one or more trustees for the benefit of others (21.1)
Unearned income	Income from investments as opposed to earned income such as salaries and pensions (3.1)
Venture Capital Trusts (VCTs)	Quoted investment vehicles concentrating on smaller non-quoted companies and offering good tax benefits to shareholders investing for at least five years (8.12)
Year of assessment	Year ending 5 April, for which tax is payable (2.8)

Index